The Chronicles
of an
Old Campaigner
1692-1717

Louis xiv., members of his family, and Madame de Maintenon

The Chronicles
of an
Old Campaigner
1692-1717

The Recollections of a French Dragoon Officer
During the War of Spanish Succession

M. De La Colonie

Translated by Walter C. Horsley

LEONAUR

The Chronicles of an Old Campaigner 1692-1717
The Recollections of a French Dragoon Officer During the War of Spanish Succession
by M. De La Colonie
Translated by Walter C. Horsley

First published under the title
The Chronicles of an Old Campaigner 1692-1717

Leonaur is an imprint of Oakpast Ltd

Copyright in this form © 2012 Oakpast Ltd

ISBN: 978-0-85706-960-3 (hardcover)
ISBN: 978-0-85706-961-0 (softcover)

http://www.leonaur.com

Publisher's Notes

Contents

Preface   9

Family History—Cadet Experiences—Siege of Namur   11

Battle of Landen—Siege of Charleroi   30

The Countess—Arras and Bordeaux—The Lawsuit   51

The Cause of the War Between France and Spain
Against the Allies   64

Defeat of Generals Schlick and Stirum   83

Defeat of Imperial Hussars   115

The Campaign of 1704   133

Return of Boismorel   162

Quarrel With Boismorel   199

The Campaigns of 1705 and 1706   222

The Campaigns of 1707-09   248

The Allies Increase Their Efforts   270

Return to Munich   293

The Campaign of 1717 Against the Turks   308

Return to Belgrade and End of War   333

To
My Comrades
in
"The Artists"

Preface

It is reasonable to suppose that this work has been overlooked, at all events in this country; the translator now offers it in the hope that it may be found worthy to be included as an addition to the material bearing upon the war of the Spanish Succession. The memoirs were originally published in 1737, and more than one edition appeared at Brussels and Utrecht between that year and 1748, and there are probably now many general readers, besides expert soldiers, who will appreciate an old soldier's account of his personal experiences in the campaigns of France against those distinguished brothers-in-arms, Marlborough and Eugene, and in Prince Eugene's defeat of the last Turkish effort to invade Europe proper at Belgrade.

M. de la Colonie, a French dragoon officer, was seconded for service with the Bavarian army to organise the regiment formed from roving French soldiers and deserters of the same nation from the Imperial service. He throws a picturesque light, not only upon the details of military life and the conditions of war of two hundred years ago, (as at time of first publication), but on the social and political condition of the countries to which his varied service led him, and his southern origin seems to exhibit itself in his narrative and the energy with which he carried out his duty. The soldier will find many an incident recalling his own work of today, while the first-hand descriptions of the old-time sieges give us real pictures of a departed phase in the science of war,

I hope that the interest which the perusal of these old records afforded me may serve as my excuse for introducing the work to the notice of the public. I have omitted certain passages describing events in which M. de la Colonie took no personal part, and of which he was not an eyewitness. Most of these events have passed into history in a form more accurate than the rumours of the day which M. de la

Colonie records.

I desire to acknowledge my indebtedness to my friend, W. F. Felkin, who has very ably assisted me in elucidating the occasional doubtful diction of M. de la Colonie, and in curtailing the inherent prolixity of his story.

Walter C. Horsley

CHAPTER 1

Family History—Cadet Experiences—Siege of Namur

I should never have undertaken to publish these memoirs had not some persons of rank requested me to have them translated into German. I felt that I should be wanting in the necessary style to give them distinction, and had it not been for their prayers, which were to me absolute orders, I should never have made a beginning.

Besides, they asked for nothing more than the truth regarding facts, giving me to understand that the translator would supply that which would otherwise be lacking, and this softened the repugnance that I naturally felt to set myself up as a man of letters.

I was, however, encouraged to relate the story of my life from the commencement of my service, because of the singularity of my adventures and the perils to which I had been so often exposed in public affairs as well as private. I have obeyed, without daring to enlarge upon certain circumstances in which I might appear to play too important a part.

Notwithstanding precautions, I shall perhaps not be exempt from suspicion. But there are so many witnesses living of all that I have written about and of everything that has happened to me, that even if I were capable of trifling with the truth, that fact alone would check me.

Here, then, we have the memoirs put together without art or study, and without special consultation of authors and histories. It will not be surprising that a man who has passed all his life as a soldier should be found wanting in a style likely to embellish his work.

By the time I had reached the age of ten years I had learned to read and write in a market town in Périgord, my native country. I was the sixth child in a family by no means well endowed with this world's goods. The ancestors of my father and mother were well known by their services to the public and by the important posts that they had held, but certain reverses of fortune had so reduced their descendants that they could no longer maintain the position held by the family during a period of many centuries.

The House of Guînes, from which my mother was descended, is one of the most ancient in Picardy. A cadet of that house quitted the service in the reign of Francis II. in order to marry in Périgord. In this establishment affection played a greater part than opulence, and the beggarly inheritance that he left to his descendants so depressed the family that now it is only the elders of some of its branches who live as befits the nobility.

My paternal great-grandfather, the last of those who were able to sustain the lustre of their race by the excess of his courage, placed his descendants not only in the sad position of being unable to imitate him, but also in one that obliged them to live a middle-class life on the small patrimony that he left them. His fidelity and bravery under the rule of Henry III. caused the loss of all his property, and only left to his children the renown of the doughtiest and most intrepid man of his time.

He commanded a body of troops in Périgord under the orders of M. de Montluc, Governor of Guienne, in opposition to the Huguenot forces, who, under the protection of the Prince of Condé, committed the most fearful atrocities. He gained many advantages over their troops; among others he defeated a considerable detachment that Admiral de Coligny sent from Saintes to Quercy. This detachment passed through Périgord. He attacked it near a village called Bitarelle, and the action was so well and vigorously conducted that none of the enemy escaped. It was considered so fine and bold an affair that he was called to the day of his death "La Bitarelle."

But M. de Montluc having died, my great-grandfather lost his support and became the victim of the implacable hatred of the Huguenots. The Vicomte de Turenne[1] vowed his ruin, and was successful as regards his property; but my great-grandfather knew so well how to safeguard his person by ruse and stratagem that the *vicomte* was never able to capture him.

King Henry III., under whose rule my great-grandfather had rendered important services, was a king who, towards the end of his reign, gave himself up entirely to pleasure, and who neither punished nor recompensed, and my great-grandfather for the rest of his life dared not fix upon a permanent abode for fear of being surprised by the people that the *vicomte* employed to pursue him.

One night, having by chance taken refuge in a house near Périgueux simply in order to sleep, he found himself surprised by his pursuers, who, to prevent his escape, had surrounded the house on all sides and were proceeding to smash in the door. There was apparently no chance of escape, but it occurred to him to loosen the bolts himself, and then when his pursuers crowded in he took advantage of the obscurity, mingled with the mob, got out of the house unperceived, and gained the open country, partisan in hand.

When well out of danger he felt a veritable sorrow at having left the scene without having revenged himself on one or another of his persecutors. This feeling was so strong within him that he at once set to work to make good the deficiency. He began to shout as though he was one of the pursuers, "La Bitarelle is off!"

The first who heard him ran up at the sound of his voice, crying, "Where is he?"

"He is here," answered he, waiting for them unmoved. As fast as they arrived he cut them down with blows from his partisan, but he was obliged to retreat when he found that his opponents were closing upon him.

"La Bitarelle is off!" became a catchword in the country, and was still quoted in the days of my childhood. One might almost think that there was some resemblance between my grandfather and myself; our people said that I took after him in every way, and they gave me his nickname, to which I became so accustomed that I answered to it readily.

★★★★★★

I was about seventeen years old when the victories of Louis XIV. caused such a sensation in the kingdom. The Battle of Fleurus, the taking of Mons, and the supposed death of the Prince of Orange in Ireland caused such joy that even in the smallest villages bonfires were lighted and extravagant rejoicings everywhere manifested. The only talk was of war, and such was the spirit of emulation among the youth of the country that they crowded to join the new levies which were made almost daily.

My own enthusiasm was unbounded, but I wished to begin my career as an officer. This was not possible for anyone who had not served

---

1. This is probably a misprint in the original memoirs for "de Tavannes."

in one of the cadet companies[2] which the king had established in nine frontier towns of the kingdom. The aristocracy were there instructed in all matters necessary to render them capable officers. To enter these companies it was obligatory to be of noble birth or standing—a fact to which the governors of the provinces had to certify. I solicited aid from my friends as well as from my father to obtain the necessary funds for my journey, and M. de Bezons, Governor of Bordeaux, gave me a letter to the late M. de Barbesieux at Versailles, on the strength of which I was sent to join the company at Charlemont in Flanders.

The Marquis de Refuge, major-general in the army of the king, was the governor, and he was also captain of the cadet company in the place of M. de Reveillon, who had been "broken" for not having quelled a mutiny which had taken place here some years previously.

There were masters in these companies whose duty it was to superintend the training of a young man of quality. Besides military drill, to which the very greatest attention was given, fencing, dancing, riding, geography, fortification, and the principles of mathematics were taught; but these studies were not of so severe a nature as the manual and musketry exercises, for they were optional. It was sufficient to be present in the classrooms; and as young men do not care for what troubles them, hardly anyone profited by these classes. I regarded that opportunity for self-instruction in a very different manner to my comrades. I believed that if I could work up fortification, I should find thereby the means to meet the expenditure necessary for my advancement, as my family was hardly in a position to help me. This it was that inspired me to apply myself to drawing and other studies which would best enable me to qualify at once for a post in the Royal Works Department I also made a special study of fencing and gymnastics, these being my favourite exercises.

The mathematical masters, who from the first establishment of these companies had hardly ever found a student who really worked seriously at their science, were so charmed with my application that they assisted in every way my efforts to get on. In order to encourage me they singled me out before my comrades for their special praise, which drew upon me the envy and malice of several senior cadets;

2. Nine companies for the instruction of gentle-born cadets were formed in 1682, one each at the following towns:—Tournay, Cambray, Valenciennes, Charlemont, Longwy, Metz, Strasbourg, Brisac, and Besançon. Recruiting was stopped in 1692, and two years later these companies were abolished.—*Histoire de la Milice Française*, Daniel, 1724.

especially of one, who by his skill held the top place in the fencing school, and who, having been successful in several affairs of honour, had acquired a reputation for bravery. This, besides making him respected by the other cadets, rendered him at the same time presumptuous and insolent

He availed himself of every chance to affront me; nay, he did not even wait for an opportunity.

I was walking one day on the Esplanade in company with some other cadets when he purposely joined us. Addressing me personally in a scornful manner, he said a hundred unpleasant things, treating my work and occupation with derision. Then gesticulating ridiculously he asked me if I was able to draw a tierce or *quarte* with the sword's point as well as I could a diagonal or perpendicular line. These ill-bred gibes aroused my anger, hot words ensued, and feeling annoyed with his bragging self-assertion, I without further hesitation drew my sword.

Never was man more surprised than he. He imagined that his reputation would suffice to intimidate me, and certainly never thought I would dare to fight him. Nevertheless, he promptly took up the challenge, and the other cadets took care that we should not be interrupted in our duel. We each of us did our best, and in the end I was lucky enough, in this my first attempt, to defeat this redoubtable bully. I got home two hits, one of which, having pierced the tendons below the wrist, caused him such acute pain that he was quite disabled and was compelled to cry for mercy.

This affair robbed the boaster of all the reputation he had acquired, and caused the mathematical masters to increase their care for my instruction; for these gentlemen regarded the sneers of this cadet as insults to themselves, and the fact of my avenging them caused them to devote their energy more than ever to qualify me for employment in the Royal Office of Works, When they judged I had made almost sufficient progress they themselves approached the Marquis de Refuge and the engineer-in-chief, and owing to their very strong recommendations he gave me employment without my having to leave the company.

I was thus able to save from the pay which I drew from the works sufficient to provide for my proper outfit when appointed a regimental officer, without troubling my parents on the point. I was never given to dissipation, and I knew perfectly well that it would need very careful behaviour on my part to succeed by my own unaided efforts, as I had little or nothing to look forward to in the way of patrimony.

But my satisfaction was clouded by an unexpected occurrence, which was the more serious, being my first experience of the kind, and which might have entirely ruined my prospects. There was even reason to fear a yet more serious result, and without the protection that the late M. de Louvois[3] afforded to the cadet companies, which he regarded as his own particular institution, I should not perhaps have got off as well as I did. This affair did not concern the cadets only, for a young officer who held the rank of *aide*-or *garçon*-major[4] in a battalion of the regiment of Navarre, which formed part of the garrison of Charlemont, was also involved in it. This young man was a well -made fellow, with a budding moustache, after the royal fashion of that period, which gave him a haughty and warlike air, and no one had a better opinion of himself than he had.

On the day of the *Fête Dieu,* when the battalion was under arms for the procession of the Holy Sacrament, I, with three other cadets, happened to pass the colours of the *aide*-major's regiment. This officer inadvertently spat upon my coat, causing me to stop abruptly. His attention being thus drawn to the occurrence, he looked for his handkerchief to repair the accident, and thinking this was only his duty under the circumstances I did nothing to save him taking this trouble. The *aide*-major, who was a very conceited fellow, was annoyed at this, and believing that it involved a degradation to a man of his importance he turned on his heels without finishing his work and abused me roundly. I should have much liked to answer him; but seeing that he took the opportunity of raising his voice I passed on, telling him that I should have the honour of a meeting later on, and went into the church to attend the Mass.

The cadets who were with me left me at the door of the church. Their one idea was to inform everyone of what had happened, and the officers of this battalion and those of our company were soon acquainted with the facts. These gentlemen, who were well aware of the serious results that were likely to ensue from this affair, joined in endeavouring to find some way of stopping it. The accident which

---

3. M. de Louvois was Secretary of War. He died suddenly in July, 1697, and was succeeded by M. de Barbesieux, who also died suddenly in 1701.—*Hist. Memoirs Marquis de Feuquieres,* 1735.

4. *Garçon*-major. An officer in the old French service. He was selected from among the lieutenants of a regiment to assist the *aide*-majors with the general detail of duty.—James, *Mily. Dicty.*

had happened to M. de Reveillon had afforded evidence that this company, composed of seven or eight hundred harebrained fellows, would act without the slightest reflection.

After my affair with the cadet they felt sure that I would not let this occurrence pass without a word, and fearing that the company would find itself in serious conflict with their battalion they left no stone unturned whilst I was attending Mass to bind over their brother officer to apologise to me when I left the church.

Consequently I found, together with the *garçon*-major, a number of officers waiting for me at the door. The *commandant* of the battalion ordered the latter to apologise to me for what had happened. "I do so," said he, "because you order me to do so, and for no other reason, and he can take this apology for what it seems worth to him." I thanked them for their good intentions, and continuing my way, heard these gentlemen speaking severely to the *garçon*-major. This was not enough and did not satisfy me; besides, what had just passed angered me nearly as much as the original cause of dispute. My desire for revenge only increased, and fearing that the means to this end would be taken from me, I dined as soon as possible and went down to the town, not meaning to return until I saw that the gates were going to shut.

I then slipped into a little street near the ramparts, waiting till the password was given out on parade, for I knew that my opponent must of necessity be present, in order to receive it from the staff officer and communicate it to the sergeants of his battalion. When I saw that the parade was over, I betook myself to the road by which he must return to barracks, and placed myself in a doorway so that he would not be able to see me until he was close up to me. He did not leave until all the sergeants had been dismissed, and then came along with an easy, swaggering air, indicating that he was much pleased with himself. I saw him coming in this manner for a long way without showing myself, but when he was close to me I appeared before him, sword in hand, and called upon him to defend himself.

My sudden appearance so flustered and astonished him that he stepped back without thinking of drawing his sword, so that I had to challenge him a second time, adding that if he declined I would cut him down like the cur that he was. He then placed himself on guard, uttering inarticulate words, but in a loud tone of voice so that anyone near might hear. The fear of this happening increased my anger, and I pressed him so closely that we instantly got to very close quarters, but terror had so overcome the poltroon that at the first onset I threw him to the ground, and presented the point of my sword to his stomach to make him surrender. He was so frightened that he began to shout, "Rescue, rescue, *Messieurs de Navarre!*"

At his cries the soldiers rushed from the barracks, but some officers present, seeing nearly all our cadets ranged in line and waiting for the outcome of the affair, drove the men back to their quarters, fearing that their presence would rouse these excitable youths, who, on the least excuse, would have thrown themselves on them without in the slightest degree considering the consequences.

In the meantime I had disarmed my man, and being master of his sword I returned it to him, and betook myself to my quarters without a cadet coming near me. On the contrary, when they saw that the matter had come off to their satisfaction they disappeared instantly by different streets, and thus gave rise to the belief that they had only by chance found themselves on the scene.

I was certainly surprised to see our company present in such a manner, for I had told no one of my intentions, but I learnt that our cadets had been so sure that I would not let the affair pass without following it up that they agreed to wait about the whole afternoon out of their quarters, and not return before "Tattoo," so as to be ready to make a stand against the battalion if it should be disposed to take up the quarrel between its *aide*-major and myself.

I had not been long back in my quarters before I had a message from my superiors. One of our officers, a Norman by birth, who called himself Gerbonville, did me the honour to call upon me in company with the sergeant of our section, and sternly ordered me to hand over my sword and follow him. He conducted me to the door of a horrible cell, lighted only by a small hole three inches in diameter chiselled through the thick rock in which the cell had been excavated.

I asked my superior how it was that I merited such a gloomy tenement. "What, sir!" said he, "you ask me of what you are guilty? And this after exposing us all to a danger greater even than what we went through at the time of the mutiny under M. de Reveillon. What if the Battalion of Navarre had come to the rescue of its *aide*-major? Where should we have been had it not been for their officers? Were not the cadets at hand and ready to fall upon them? Was not the whole garrison within an inch of ruin by your imprudence? And yet you regard it as strange that you are not treated with more moderation. Do you expect to be congratulated on your performance and to be let off the consequences?"

I tried to assure him that no one of the cadets had any knowledge of my plan, that it was the cries of the *aide*-major which had attracted them all, and that if the latter had been a man of honour he wished to be considered, the affair would have been quietly settled between us. But the inexorable Gerbonville said that however sound my reasons might be events had taken a different turn, and that he must do his duty without discussion, and finally he drove me pitilessly into this horrible cell.

It was by common agreement among the officers of our company that I was treated with so much severity. They had run the risk of being "broken" ever since the mutiny under M. de Reveillon, and in fact were so frightened at my case that they met together at the house of M. de Refuge to demonstrate to him the danger to which I had exposed not only the garrison but himself also; the urgent need of keeping me close lest he should find himself in a similar predicament; and they advised him to report the matter at once to the Court at Paris.

Happily the day following was not a regular post-day, and my friends, the mathematical masters, had thus time to beg M. de Refuge to mitigate the severity of his language in writing about me. Besides, the officers of the Navarre Battalion feared that their *garçon*-major might find himself involved in the case. M. de Refuge took all this into consideration, but meanwhile I was safe and sound in the cell, orders being given to my jailor that I should speak to no one. I was well looked after in all conscience, and this honest man executed his orders so scrupulously that he would not speak to me himself. I questioned him whenever he brought me my food, but never a word could I extract from him; he placed my ration on the guard -room bed, the mouldy planks of which served as a table, the only furniture of my apartment, and instantly retired, closing and locking the doors after him.

I passed ten whole days in this cruel predicament, a prey to my own reflections, without counsel or consolation from anyone. Fearful ideas filled my brain, everything appeared to me gloomy and of bad augury.

The ten days were to me as ten centuries, and I endured in that time all the suffering possible to human nature. When my jailor on the eleventh day brought me my food as usual, he appeared to me to have a gentler air, and spoke to me in a mild tone of voice. He began on the subject of my troubles, saying that he had always taken my part, but that the orders he had received had not allowed him to show it. Also that I must not be anxious; everything was going well, and that he had just received orders to allow anyone I wished to come and see me.

Shortly after numbers of the cadets visited me one after the other, and on the next day Gerbonville delighted me by announcing my liberation in person, wishing by this good news to make up for the evils he had been instrumental in bringing upon me. He told me to leave my cell and report myself to the Marquis de Refuge to thank him for his kind offices. I carried out this order with the greatest pleasure, and I gathered from the long lecture I received that my actions had not proved so egregious in the end as they had been supposed to be at the first. All the same, M. de Refuge had written to M. de Louvois and reported to him the whole occurrence; but the minister, who did not wish to give His Majesty the opportunity of reprimanding the cadet companies, sent the Battalion of Navarre to another garrison, merely treating the matter, when reported to him, as an affair of small importance between young men, and forwarded the order for my release.

I had not been out of prison a week when my section sergeant brought me an order from M. de Jaillis, my immediate company commander under M. de Refuge, to come and speak to him. This order was given to me in such a way that I was under the impression that there was still some punishment in store for me. I racked my brains on my way to him to see if I could recall any other misdemeanour of which I had been guilty; but was agreeably reassured on hearing from M. de Jaillis that M. de Refuge had promoted me *sous*-brigadier, or lance-corporal, and that I was to go and thank him.

Overcome with delight I ran to headquarters, feeling, in the happy surprise of this my first promotion, a more lively joy than I had ever before experienced. I regarded it as quite an important affair, although, as a matter of fact, it merely raised me one step above the rank of an ordinary cadet. This did not interfere with my usual studies, for M. de Refuge struck me off all company duties so that I might retain my appointment in the Royal Office of Works. I was so delighted at this that I longed for the opportunity to be employed in such a manner that I could show in some way my love for and devotion to the service; and this came to me shortly after in the famous attack that the King made upon Namur in 1692.

This siege was one of the greatest undertakings of the kind that had happened in Europe for many centuries. The town was called "Namur la Pucelle," as it had never fallen into the hands of an invader. Even Caesar, in spite of all his efforts during a long and troublesome siege, was obliged to give up the attempt. Consequently the attention of all Europe was drawn to Namur when Louis XIV. appeared in person to direct the attack.

The king, who wished to conduct so important an operation himself, left Versailles on May 10th, 1692, followed by *Monseigneur* and all the court, and placed himself at the head of his army. He fixed his own quarters within the actual lines of circumvallation which were made around the stronghold, and Madame de Maintenon with the principal ladies of the Court who had followed him were lodged in the little town of Dinan, three leagues off, on the river Meuse.

Besides the army of the king, which formed the besieging force, there was another under the Maréchal de Luxembourg which acted as a covering body against any attempt on the part of the enemy to succour the town.

Namur is only seven leagues from Charlemont; consequently all the siege train and apparatus passed before our eyes, and nearly all our engineers were detailed for duty. I was sorely disappointed to find that I was not included in their number, and said as much to my friends the mathematical professors. To satisfy me they asked M. de Cladech (commanding our own engineers, and who was to command a brigade during the siege) to obtain permission from M. de Refuge for me to go as a volunteer engineer. He expressed his pleasure at my request and granted it. I thus had the honour of serving with one of the most important corps connected with this enterprise.

This fortress, without being at all regular in its designs, is by reason of the situation of its citadel one of the strongest of all on the frontiers of Flanders. The irregular design of its fortifications, and the number of works which cover it and each other, form a complication of difficulties nearly insurmountable to the besieger. These difficulties were greater then than now, because, as the place had never been taken, no one knew its weak points, and much had to be left to chance. This ignorance was a serious disadvantage to us, and if Fortune had not come to our aid after the reduction of the town, it would have been necessary either to break a treaty which we had made, or to raise the siege altogether, simply for want of knowledge as to the vulnerable points.

The treaty in question was made between the besieged and ourselves on the capture of the town, and expressly provided that on the one hand the garrison should not fire upon it, and that the king's troops and the citizens should be as safe in the streets as they had been before the siege; and on the other that the king should not attack the fortress directly or indirectly from the town side. It was through ignorance of the true state of the fortifications that these articles were agreed to, as it is only from the town side that the fortress could be taken, the rest being almost impregnable.

We began by laying siege to the town before undertaking the greater matter of the fortress, and opened our trenches on May 29th. We constructed several of the best manned and equipped batteries that were ever seen; the presence of the king excited such emulation that all ranks sought to surpass themselves in their duties. During the first few days of this attack the enemy appeared on their ramparts in good fettle, as though they had but little anxiety as to the result of our efforts, and later on made a small sortie from the Iron Gate side to reinforce a half- moon battery which covered the main town. This sortie met with so little success that they never repeated the attempt. It is true the garrison was not a strong one, as the enemy never imagined the king would begin the campaign with so important an undertaking. Most of their battalions were Spanish, weak and in a very poor condition; the better part of the garrison was composed of several Brandenburg and Landgrave regiments, but even they were not strong in numbers.

So it happened that we were not kept waiting long in front of the town, for it surrendered June 5th, and the garrison retired into the fortress according to the above-mentioned treaty.

Reducing a place of so much importance within so short a time encouraged us to hope that we should make short work of its citadel. The garrison had offered but a feeble resistance, and, moreover, had not now the same opportunities for making sorties as had occurred in the defence of the town, so that we hardly expected anything very serious from them. But we were not then aware that on the side that we were obliged to attack we should meet with numberless fortifications of extraordinary strength, besides the difficulties brought about by the most detestable weather. For three weeks it rained heavily and continuously; the camp roads became impassable to such a degree that it was nearly impossible to transport the necessary ammunition and supplies from the river up to the batteries.

The citadel is most favourably situated high above the town in the angle formed by the junction of the rivers Meuse and Sambre. The town lies just outside the point of the angle, separated from the fortress by the little stream of the Sambre, the two being connected by a fine stone bridge. The weakest sides of the fortifications—of the fortress—are along this stream, and are commanded by the town ramparts, whence they can be breached with the greatest ease. Again, there are garden plots adjacent to the ramparts which also command the fortifications in which many batteries could be placed; in fact, this section is the most advantageous in every way for the besiegers, but our hands were tied by the articles signed at the surrender of the town.

The section of the fortress overlooking the river Meuse is on a rocky height, scarped, inaccessible, and impossible to attack. The only part against which we might range our batteries was the section on the opposite side to the town facing the open country, and although this is situated on high ground, the approach to it was fairly level and open but for certain woods and ravines.

It was fortified, beginning first with the centre, by a keep with many earthworks covered by two good demi-bastions connected with a curtain and its ditch. This keep had another ditch in rear. In front of all this was a large and important horn-work furnished with an excellent and very deep dry ditch, counterscarp, and covered-way, well palisaded; the curtain was again covered by a fourth work, which, by reason of its shape, was called the Priest's Cap. It also had counterscarp and covered-way, but was not of great importance. Beyond this fourth work came a large and very deep ravine, and then a new fort, complete with its ditch, covered-way, and glacis, called Fort William, named after William of Orange, afterwards King of England, who constructed it. It was at this point, then, that we were obliged to begin the siege of the citadel.

The rains had begun when we attacked this fort, but the roads being still practicable, we had little difficulty in breaching it, and we carried it by assault on the 12th of the month. It served as a position in which to place our battery for the attack on the Priest's Cap, and also on one of the faces of the half-bastions of the horn-work. The rest of our batteries were in the open also opposed to the horn-work, but our artillery here was of small account owing to the difficulty of transporting the ammunition. The fields had become so sodden with the rain as to render cartage impossible, and all that could be done was to carry a few bombs and cannon balls on the backs of the bât-horses and mules. Even these animals had the greatest labour in extricating themselves from the bad places, and had constantly to make fresh tracks.

Owing to these difficulties our batteries were perforce silent, and everything took a leisurely turn. The cavalry, too, lacked forage; the

SIEGE OF NAMUR, 1692

country, chiefly woodland, was unable to provide supplies for any length of time, and so much was this the case that the men were obliged to feed their horses on leaves and branches, with the result that a great number perished. Such was our condition towards the end of the month of June. The king became very uneasy, and the first engineers of the kingdom who had the conduct of the siege had come to the end of their resources. The ill-success of our efforts, owing to the combination of elaborate defences and the increasingly bad weather, could not have been foreseen. Things being in this parlous state, M. de Vauban ran the risk of applying to the king for his permission to disregard the treaty and to attack from the town side. He represented to His Majesty that it would be less disgraceful to do this than to raise the siege—a contingency that would inevitably occur if the attack was continued in the present direction. On the other hand, if he was permitted to operate from the town ramparts and adjoining gardens, he could assure His Majesty of the capture of the fortress—firstly, because the weakest point in the defence lay there; secondly, because the ammunition supply could be properly maintained, the boats being able to land it at the very gates of the town.

He therefore very humbly prayed of His Majesty to consider all these points and to grant his petition.

The king was moved by the prayers of M. de Vauban and the general state of our affairs, but would do nothing rashly; and with extraordinary prudence sanctioned only the digging of trenches on the town ramparts along the river Sambre in preparation for the batteries and the construction of *epaulements* across such streets in the town as were enfiladed from the fortress to ensure safety and cover. He gave an order that the guns should not be moved there until he himself gave the directions to this effect.

I was detailed for duty on these works, which were singular in their nature, in that their construction was entirely free from interruption on the part of the besieged, who did not dare to open fire upon us, fearing to give us an excuse for ignoring the treaty. They could not understand what our intentions really were when they saw us setting hastily to work in a manner contrary to the articles of the treaty granted by the king himself. So far as we were concerned, we were so pleased by the permission granted by the king to M. de Vauban that we worked with the greatest diligence, assuming that the guns would be placed in position, and the breaching of the works overlooking the Sambre taken in hand at once.

But the Almighty decreed that the king should not perjure himself, and instead brought about one of the most unexpected and lucky chances, by means of which we became masters of the place, and that without the further construction of any more large works or the loss of any great number of men. Our works on the ramparts were completed, and as the king had nothing to fear from that side, he made up his mind to attempt the assault of the Priest's Cap. This work had been breached, but it was almost inaccessible on account of its excessive steepness; our last parallel, too, was yet some distance from the covered-way. The order was, however, given, and on the 29th of the month the assault was successfully delivered without much opposition; the defenders abandoned the work after their first volley and retired into the horn-work.

The breadth of the ditch only prevented the completion of the breach in the horn-work, but the transport of cannon and ammunition was still impossible. All this time we lived in the captured work in order to make what preparations we could, and so as not to remain idle until the weather would permit us to resume operations. We made a quantity of fascines intended for the ditch at the foot of the breach, which had an extremely steep ascent. These fascines were intended to check the fall of earth caused by the bombardment, and thus to produce quickly a ramped approach to the breach practicable for the assault. The next night, which was luckily a very dark one, the fascines were thrown into the ditch, the besieged making no sign of their existence.

This only excited us to make the most of the occasion, and a number of workmen were sent into the ditch itself to arrange the fascines at the foot of the breach, and to work the earth so as to form a suitable ramp. They worked in silence, fearing to draw the fire of the enemy, who might easily have sent bombs and grenades amongst our men. Nothing of the sort, however, took place. This extraordinary quiescence on the part of the enemy excited the curiosity of a grenadier belonging to the party covering the workmen in the ditch, and he clambered cautiously to the top of the breach in order to see if anything was going on. He had no easy task in getting there at all, but at last after many efforts he found himself on the top and lay down to listen.

When he had rested a little he raised his head, looked well about him, and then set to work to creep further along on his hands and knees. He stopped now and then to reconnoitre, until he saw a solitary soldier seated on the ground and half asleep. The discovery of this man incited him to closer examination, and he pursued his way still further in without finding a trace of anyone else. He then silently returned to report to his officer. As a matter of fact, we afterwards found that there were not above ten men all told, under a sergeant, in this great work, and that they were in the habit of retiring into a kind of underground passage for shelter from the rain and bombs, keeping only one man as sentry over the breach, the man whom our grenadier had seen.

This want of precaution on the part of the besieged was no doubt owing to their belief that the breach was not sufficiently advanced to cause them to expect anything in the nature of a surprise attack. Besides, the garrison was so worn out by the bad weather, and the numerous posts that they had to occupy during the day, that they were obliged to withdraw at night-time every man they possibly could to get rest and repose.

Such was the case when the grenadier made his discovery. This was duly reported to his officers, who at first could hardly believe it; however, the matter was considered to be so important that no time was lost in putting it to the test. There was certainly the fear that it might be a ruse on the part of the besieged to draw our troops within the work, and then to blow them into the air by means of mines laid beneath it. It would be hard to say, however, what would be gained by this, some certainly would have been blown to pieces, but the remainder would have been able to hold their own and effect a lodgement in the work.

After consultation, a lieutenant, a sergeant, and twenty grenadiers were detailed to follow the soldier, who would act as their guide, with orders to seize the enemy's sentry noiselessly and to make him tell what he knew of the situation. This little detachment began the climb, and it was not without some considerable difficulty that it attained the summit of the breach. Once there it crept on its way well within the work in order to cut off the retreat of the sentry; this done the sergeant and four men advanced to seize him. The former pointed his sword at his throat and threatened him with instant death if he attempted to cry out, but promised him his life if he answered the questions put to him.

The coward to save his life allowed himself to be taken without saying a word, and conducted the party to the underground passage, where the guard were found and at once slain in their sleep. He then led them to the two mouthpieces of the mines intended to blow us up,

when we should have entered the work on assaulting it. Our grenadiers took care to remove the quick matches, which they brought
back with them on their return as a proof of their discovery, and then
by the aid of this guide explored the whole work without seeing anything or anyone to prevent our taking immediate possession of it. The
officer ordered the party to remain in observation under the sergeant,
and taking four men as escort to the prisoner, reported full details to
the general officer on duty in the trenches.

All the troops at hand, together with the working parties, were
immediately pushed forward, and helping one another, clambered up
the breach; they then set to work to such purpose that before break
of day our works and lodgements were in a fit state to prevent any
efforts on the part of the enemy to dislodge us. But they were not in
a condition to attempt this; on the contrary, as soon as day broke, we
found that they had retired from the ramparts of the keep, and seeing
our new lodgements with our standards flying on the reverse side of
their works, they ran up the white flag and sounded their trumpets
for a parley. The king was at once awakened without much ceremony,
but he was more than content, as he never expected to hear such
good news. The articles of the capitulation were signed the very same
day, and the garrison marched out of the fortress at ten o'clock next
morning by way of the breach. It numbered thirteen battalions, and it
was remarked that the weakest and the worst conditioned were those
from Spain.

In this way, then, we mastered this important stronghold, a fact
which was much noised abroad and which occasioned so much rejoicing in the kingdom. No history, as far as I am aware, has gone so
fully into the details of this siege as I have. The difficulties which we
had to surmount, and the number of works with their variety and
complications, were for me full of information. I applied myself zeal-
ously to making notes thereon to serve me later on in case of need,
and I could not possibly have studied under better masters than Messieurs de Vauban and de Marigny, the most famous engineers in the
kingdom, who conducted the operations. Their salutary lessons have
stood me in good stead on many occasions since. But what a perilous
profession it is that I had now entered! There were sixty of us engineer
officers at the siege of Namur. Twenty-two came out alive. The rest
died in the trenches.

After the surrender I rejoined the company, and thanked M. de
Refuge for the leave he had granted. He carefully questioned me on

all that had happened, and appeared pleased with my conduct. He assured me at the same time that he would soon give me a commission in a good regiment; and in fact, in less than three months, the colonel of the Vexin Infantry Regiment having applied to him for a second lieutenant, I was appointed, and the papers forwarded me.

Most young men who have lived away from home for a length of time are anxious to return there at the first opportunity; but immediately I got my commission my one idea was to join my regiment, for I looked upon such a cross-country journey as merely an opportunity for spending more money than I could well afford. The pay that I had received as a cadet and during my appointment on the Royal Works enabled me to set myself up with my little equipment, and I felt as much satisfaction at being able to spare my father the inconvenience of contributing to my advancement as another would have had in squeezing a large sum out of the family purse.

When I joined the Regiment of Vexin, which lay only four leagues from Charlemont, I was most graciously received by the colonel, to whom M. de Refuge had kindly written a letter of introduction. Owing to this good, and even exaggerated, recommendation, he gave me plenty of work and took me under his protection. True, "the Service" was my first consideration; I never waited for duty to call me, but endeavoured to forestall it whenever possible, so as to merit my colonel's kindnesses. I felt, moreover, that my actions alone could win these for me, and I naturally felt as strong a wish to do what I could to deserve his praise as I had a repugnance to do anything that would lower me in his estimation.

CHAPTER 2

Battle of Landen—Siege of Charleroi

It was in the year 1693, in Flanders, that I entered upon my first campaign in the capacity of officer. This campaign was a glorious one for France. The king's forces captured the town of Furnes during the extreme cold of the month of January. The Maréchal de Luxembourg, who was in command, attacked Huy in July, and I found myself placed on the roster of engineer officers volunteering for the siege; but I was on duty for one night only, as the town surrendered three days after the trenches were opened.

The enemy remained strictly on the defensive, and the town was taken under their very eyes without the slightest movement on their part. They were very well entrenched between the villages of Sainte Croix and Neerwinden, their left flank resting on a large stream, and they appeared to think that they had little or nothing to fear regarding their position; at any rate, the precautions they had taken with their entrenchments gave them good reason to believe that our army would infallibly perish in the attempt to force their lines. M. de Luxembourg, however, was not to be denied, and, with the King's permission, resolved to lay siege to Charleroi, which town was covered by the enemy's camp at Neerwinden. It thus became necessary to drive the enemy out of their entrenchments or abandon this project.

The general, no stranger to peril, loved to risk all rather than give up one of his designs, and was the most adventurous and withal fortunate of men of his day. He appeared with his force before the lines on the 29th of July, brought up two heavy batteries, and effected a breach in the entrenchment with astonishing celerity. At the same time his infantry in battle formation advanced to the attack at a steady pace. The leading ranks carried fascines for the purpose of filling up the ditches, and scarcely had our men, accustomed as they were to war, found themselves within gunshot than they charged with inconceivable dash. Ignoring the enemy's heavy fire they forced their way into the entrenchments, but the cruel reception awaiting them obliged them to retire. They again returned to the charge, and effected an entrance as at the first attempt, but were once more repulsed.

Victory hung in the balance, for during the attacks and re-forming of the infantry our cavalry had suffered severely from the enemy's artillery, particularly the regiment of the Royal Household, the Maison du Roi. So stout a resistance would have disheartened anyone else but M. de Luxembourg, but this undaunted general would not give in; he again brought his infantry into the fray, and this third assault gave the finishing touch to the affair. Such was its fury that the enemy were driven clean out of their entrenchments and fled in complete disorder. The stream which had been of such use to their left flank, from a defensive point of view, became an obstacle in their line of retreat, and many were drowned in their hurried flight.

Their loss was reckoned to be at least fourteen or fifteen thousand men and twenty-eight pieces of cannon. Our own loss was so considerable that it was never exactly shown in the returns. The glory of victory was ours, but we paid dearly for it. We lost eighteen to twenty thousand men, including a great number of officers of distinction; a Prince of Lorraine de Lillebonne, the Duke d'Uzès, and many of the king's household were slain, and the Duke of Berwick taken prisoner. The enemy called this action the Battle of the Fascines, on account of those that our men carried and the immense number of our killed, who, as they declared, were used as fascines to fill in the ditches.[1]

Our army was too much exhausted after the battle to undertake the siege of Charleroi without reinforcements; these were drawn from various garrisons and a standing camp which the king had at this time at a place called Pontorson, near Mount St. Michael, in Brittany, under the command of *Monsieur*, his late brother. These troops, sent there originally to oppose a threatened invasion on the part of the English, were ordered to join the army of Flanders for the siege of Charleroi, *Monsieur* rejoining the court.

On the arrival of these reinforcements the lines of circumvallation were begun, and the trenches opened on September 7th. Officers of the army who wished to volunteer their services as engineers were allowed to place their names on a list kept for the purpose; an excellent method for the improvement of those who had a bent for engineering

---

1. Known in English history as the Battle of Landen.

and for giving the infantry officers a chance of attaining experience.

This custom, notwithstanding its advantageous nature, was given up in the following campaigns, and the officers who entered the service in later years did not attempt to revive it. Perhaps also the suppression of the cadet companies had something to do with this, as they had certainly tended to encourage the study of mathematics among their students. However this might be, there is no question but that in the last war there was neither the emulation nor the knowledge amongst the officers that had formerly existed; the authorities found themselves obliged to appoint many without any special qualification, and had to trust to luck for the result. Most of them really seemed to think a foppish bearing sufficed to prove them masters of the art of war. They even turned the older officers, who kept to themselves and their duty, to ridicule, calling them "Old school warriors," as if fashion in fighting changed with the cut of clothes, and many of the younger colonels even supported their regimental officers in this conduct.

I have no wish to set myself up as a censor, but I must say that since I have had to do with foreign troops I have found many of their regulations to be most excellent. For instance, the regiments are given to old lieutenant-colonels full of experience, by which means discipline and subordination are kept up without the least relaxation. Officers and men, being kept up to this habit, see nothing extraordinary in the varying brilliancy of one colonel over another, and so long as the latter possesses capacity and bravery they respect and obey him minutely, and all runs smoothly on the path of duty. I have also noticed that this sense of discipline which reigns amongst all ranks of foreigners, habituates them to such a degree of obedience that in many cases of disorder they are enabled to rally their troops and keep them well in hand. This is a point of the greatest importance, but which has been by no means well observed amongst us in the later campaigns.

However, I am wandering away from the siege of Charleroi. I need not say that I was not one of the last to add my name to the list of engineer volunteers, and my colonel was delighted with my professional ardour. He signified his approval by saying that he only wished all his subalterns were equally energetic, that I should make my way, and that I had only to continue on the same path, and he on his side would not forget me when occasion should arise. I did not fail to keep him posted day by day with all the details of the siege, which gave him a lively satisfaction, for he made use of these in writing to his friends. By this I succeeded in gaining his friendship and protection—not perhaps much to my profit, as he died the following winter in Paris.

The trenches were begun before Charleroi during the night of September 8th, 1693, and I was ordered as engineer to mark out the angles and distances for the attack on an advanced half-moon battery, which it was decided should be taken in hand at once. This is always an extremely risky piece of work, although conducted at night, for the noise made by the picks and tools is certain to draw the fire of the enemy. Unless, therefore, the trench is begun at a considerable distance from the enemy's works the besiegers lose a number of men to start with, and so it was with us.

The half-moon work was detached and well in advance of the general line of the fortifications, and we, being thus obliged to begin our work closer to it than usual, were, owing to the noise of the picks, soon discovered by the enemy, who showered upon us a hail of fire-pots in the same way as bombs would be thrown. A fire-pot is a kind of globe or large ball filled with old rope well tarred, which burns with a very bright light. This globe—set light to before being thrown—will burn for a considerable time, and lights up a wide area upon which cannon may be directed as effectively as if by the light of day. To prevent an attempt to extinguish it (in itself not an easy task, owing to the tar and composition therein) small pistol barrels are screwed into its surface, loaded with ball, which discharge themselves successively as the fire approaches them. Such were the lanterns sent us by the besieged to light up our work during the night, accompanied with volleys of grape and case, which rendered our position most uncomfortable, and killed two of our engineer officers engaged in marking out the trenches.

Before daylight, however, we got cover from this by means of the work completed during the night. The following nights we continued our approaches in front of the half-moon, finishing them during the days; and having effected a breach in one of the faces, the assault was ordered on the 16th. I found myself attached to the grenadiers, with orders to superintend the construction of a lodgement as soon as the place was taken, consisting of a covered-way from our trench to the breach and an *epaulement* across the gorge of the half-moon—the one to cover our men during the assault, the other to protect those detailed to occupy the work.

Ten companies of grenadiers were told off for the assault, supported by three battalions of fusiliers, who were formed up an hour after midday in the most advanced parallels. No time or hour as to their advance was given, but they were ordered to do so on the following signal being made, *viz.* twelve small mortars would be fired together three times into the half-moon battery, the third time the shells would be loaded with sand only, with long fuses, so as to keep the besieged lying flat as long as possible in expectation of the explosions.

We were then to profit by this, and leaving our trenches pass along the glacis of the two faces of the work and enter by the gorge. The enemy being thus surprised, would not then have time to spring their mines should they have prepared them.

From the wording of this order it was assumed that the signal might be given at any moment, and as there seemed to be no time to lose, each one of us set to work to examine his conscience in a most contrite manner, for it was accepted by all concerned in this assault that nothing short of a miracle could prevent our total destruction. It was necessary, in the first place, to defile the full length of the glacis to get at the gorge, at the mercy of the fire of the enemy occupying the covered-way, who would not be lying in fear of our shells; and, secondly, there were the works of the main fortification supporting the half-moon, which would certainly bring a terrific fire to bear upon us. These difficulties surmounted, there would yet be the garrison itself to be reckoned with, besides mines to send us skywards if we ever got inside. Nature suffers cruelly under such a strain—no one cares to talk, each being occupied with his own reflections and the thought of the death he is courting.

We remained in this painful state till three o'clock in the after-noon, without signal or even information of any sort. A little later the grenades were served out to the grenadiers, who were ordered to light their quick matches. We then had no doubt at all that the time for the signal was near at hand, and this state of tension brought on a renewed access of mental agony, or at all events it appeared so, judging by the faces of all concerned.

After all the signal did not come, and I took it into my head to examine the bearing of those in my immediate vicinity, wishing to see if I could discern their inmost thoughts, and the different degrees of anxiety as shown in their physiognomies. I looked them over most carefully, and the more I examined them the more it seemed to me that they were no longer the same persons I had known previously. Their features had become changed in a most extraordinary manner; there were long drawn-out faces, others quite twisted, others again, were haggard, with flesh of a livid hue, whilst some had a wander-

SEBASTIEN LE PRETRE
Seig.r de Vauban Commissaire General
des Fortifications et Marechal de France
mort a Paris le 30. Mars 1707. Agé de 74 ans.

Se vend à Paris chez E. Desrochers rue du Foin pres la rue S.t Jacques

Contre une Armée et ses menaces
Vauban fortifiant les Places
Servit la france utilement ;
Et ce qu'on a peine a comprendre,
C'est qu'il sçavoit egalement
Les attaquer et les defendre.

Cocon

M. DE VAUBAN

ing look about the eyes; in fact, I saw but a melancholy set of sinners apparently under sentence of death. I, too, imagined myself as much altered as the others; however, the pains I was always in the habit of taking to acquire a reputation did much to allay my own fear, and perhaps helped me somewhat to maintain an even countenance.

Waiting thus for the signal, not one of us wished for anything better than to see it given, if it were only to be delivered from our mental torment, but it did not appear, and our feelings still had us in their grip.

Six o'clock came, and hatchets were brought and distributed to the grenadiers to use in case of need upon barricades and the like that might lie in our path. M. de Vauban passed about this time, and assured us with a confident air that we should make short work of the half-moon battery, that it was defended only by a rabble, and that he was not at all sure it was mined, and that even if it were so we should so surprise the enemy, that they would never have time to put light to the trains. He cautioned us, however, to make a rapid inspection of the work on entering to prove this point, and told us that M. de Lux-embourg had promised a reward to anyone bringing him a port-fire or quick match, and that he would answer for this as well. After all, he gave us no information as to when to expect the signal, and thus we lingered till nine o'clock with little or no appetite for our supper.

The fact was that we were kept waiting all this time because it had been discovered to be too dangerous an affair to attempt the assault by daylight, and that the darkness of night would be of great advantage for the surprise of the defenders, tending to minimise the heavy musketry fire from the main ramparts; this reason was good enough, but our troops should not have been ordered out so early in that case. True, suspense made us long the more for the moment of action, which came at last at nine o'clock exactly. At the first volley from the twelve mortars, our troops made a hurried attempt to advance, and while waiting for the third, murmurs could be heard marking the impatience of the grenadiers.

While the shells of the final volley were still flying through the air, our men broke out from their post like madmen, but they were hardly out of the trench and preparing to pass along the glacis when the enemy occupying the covered-way brought a terrible fire to bear upon them. We broke into a run, and so crowded were our ranks that I was carried for some distance clean off the ground, and I thought that I should have been stifled in the press of our own men.

36

We certainly surprised the defenders of the interior of the half-moon, as had been projected; they never expected the assault at such an hour, and still less to see us enter the work by the gorge, which was their sole line of retreat. In the meantime, under cover of the darkness they became mixed up with us, and made for the main ramparts through the covered-way. They did not, however, gain much by this, for the noise of our assault had drawn the fire of the enemy from all sides, and these unfortunate creatures, thinking to have found a safe retreat, were shot down by their own comrades.

Four good-sized mines were found, sufficient to have blown up the entire work if there had been time to set light to them; but in hope of the promised reward, the leading grenadiers ran in all directions to discover them, and having come upon the miners who were actually preparing to set light to the trains, were enabled to seize them, and thus by their prompt action saved us all from the misfortune of finding ourselves buried in the ruins of the work.

We had scarcely gained the interior of the half-moon before I got to work upon an *epaulement* across the gorge, to cover our people from the musketry fire. With all our efforts, this took some time to construct. The grenadiers, therefore, were ordered to lie flat upon the ground, with the butts of their muskets in front of them as shelter; but notwithstanding all our precautions many were killed. At last by daybreak our work was finished, and we enjoyed, comparatively speaking, some rest and quiet. The capture of this work was of the greatest use to us, as it enabled us to construct a large battery opposite an entire polygon of the main fortification, where we subsequently made our final attack. We had a very hard time of it the while, I in particular having had so much to do and look after at night-time. An overpowering hunger now began to overcome me, so I left the work for the trenches, in search of the wherewithal to appease it.

On my way I was lucky enough to find a grenadier captain who had just had his canteen and rations brought to him, and who, to my great joy, stopped and invited me to join him in his meal. We established ourselves in an angle of the trench with our backs to the town for the sake of cover. A grenadier of his company came up whilst we were breakfasting, carrying the clothes and accoutrements of one of his comrades killed during the night. This grenadier was one of those jocular creatures typical of the Royal Guard, and he at once, pipe in mouth, began to tell us how his comrade had died.

"We were," said he, "lying flat on our faces side by side, like two good comrades, when away he rushes to the other world without giving me any warning. I didn't think this quite our form, as we never think of parting without a stirrup-cup, so I just stripped him to teach him proper manners." The poor devil amused himself with this yarn, thinking we were equally diverted, when a small cannon-shot passed from the town above our two heads, struck him through the arm holding his pipe, pierced his chest, and laid him at our feet.

The garrison of Charleroi made a better defence than that of Namur, being more numerous and composed of better troops. The Prince of Orange, seeing the town threatened after the Battle of Neerwinden, had taken care to reinforce it, and thus enabled it to make several sorties at the beginning of the siege, which retarded the progress of many of our works. It took us more than a month from the opening of the trenches to push our sap up to the palisades of the covered-way, and M. de Luxembourg, who had now become impatient and would not wait for any further development, carried them by an assault which cost us six hundred men.

We were then enabled to bring a battery of twelve heavy guns to bear, thanks to two *epaulements* and a turning-sap made under the direction of two engineers and myself. The breadth of the ditch only separated us from the breach already begun in the polygon, and the besieged, seeing no help for it, hung out the white flag and assented to a capitulation on October 12th, the second day after our battery had opened fire.

The taking of Charleroi was the last feat of the Duke of Luxembourg, one of the bravest and most intrepid generals of the day. The officers who had volunteered for this siege as engineers received through M. de Vauban a small gratuity of fifty *pistoles* each—not a very great burden on the government, as very few of us were left to enjoy it.

The English, to avenge losses of their allies, sent a fleet into the Channel, which anchored opposite St. Malo on November 22nd with the intention of destroying the town with an infinite number of shells and carcases filled with grenades, bullets, and large masses of metal covered with cloth soaked in tar, and other inflammable things. These were to be discharged in volleys from an engine called an infernal machine.

The fire-ship carrying this machine ran ashore close to the place where it was designed to anchor her; but the engineer in charge had time to blow her up, which caused such a terrific explosion that many of the houses were unroofed. Thus ended this attempt on the part of the English.

Towards the end of the year and the beginning of 1694 the population of France suffered intensely from scarcity of corn and the bad quality of such as existed. A certain acid formed in the bread, which quickened digestion to such an extent that shortly after eating it hunger made itself felt more than ever, and this with the unhappiest results. Necessity obliged the people to eat bran soaked in boiling water, and many, in want of even this, ate the grass in the fields. Finally death followed the steps of famine, so much so that three-quarters of the population of certain provinces perished by hunger alone, without any possibility of averting it. In fact, this was the severest famine known for many centuries.

Our regiment after the siege of Charleroi took up its winter quarters in what was left of the town after the bombardment. The Count of Montignac d'Autefort, our colonel, left for Paris, where he died the same winter. I felt his death very much. He was a gentleman of merit, and would have done much for my advancement if he had lived. This loss, and the fear of being under a colonel who would not have the same consideration for me, had not a little to do with my leaving the regiment so as to be with one of my friends in the dragoons. He was a sub lieutenant, and a particularly good fellow. We had been chums at the Military School, and we were as one in all our interests. He had a near relation at Versailles in the War Office, under M. de Barbesieux, and as he was tired of the infantry, he took it into his head to exchange into the dragoons, who were at that time very smart and much the fashion. He had long tried to persuade me to follow his example, assuring me that his relation, to whom he had written a thousand kind things about me, would be only too delighted to advance us in the service; but my attachment to my colonel, and the fear of displeasing him, had caused me hitherto to refuse his propositions.

However, after the death of Count de Montignac d'Autefort I gave in, and we arranged to travel together to Versailles. My friend's relation was so prepossessed in my favour that I received every kindness at his hands. He sent us each the commission of cornet in the regiment of dragoons belonging to the Marquis de Gramont-Fallon, of Franche-Comté, and promised us that when the opportunity of promotion occurred in the regiment we should not be forgotten. He also had the goodness to present us to the Marquis de Gramont, who was then at the court and in the ministry; he enlarged upon my efficiency in an exaggerated manner, just as if he had himself personally witnessed my career, and his recommendation was not without its use to me.

My new colonel believed all the good that was said of me, and shortly after I had reported myself, gave the detail of the regiment into my hands under the *aide*-major. The little addition to my pay brought me by this post suited me very well.

We made the campaign of 1694 with the army of Flanders, but it was not as brilliant or as glorious as those preceding it. Our army attempted but little, and saw the enemy lay siege to Huy 22nd September and take it on the 30th of the same month without opposition. This little success raised their spirits; they saw that we allowed the campaign to pass without any special effort on our part, were convinced they could make a greater advance in the next, and redoubled their exertions to organise and prepare for a descent upon the frontier as soon as the season would permit. The Maréchal de Luxembourg was ill, and France unfortunately lost him towards the end of the year.

The hostile forces organised a descent upon our coast- line on June 18th, at a place called Camaret, near Brest; but they were only able to disembark about a thousand men, who were almost all drowned or cut to pieces. After this failure, their fleet made for the town of Dieppe, in Normandy, and bombarded it three days running with such fury that the town was practically reduced to ashes. The fleet then appeared off Le Havre-de-Grace, where the same thing would have happened had the ships been able to approach sufficiently near the port. They left after burning a few houses.

The campaign of 1695 was not favourable to France. The enemy opened the campaign on the Flanders frontier with a very large army; and it would seem they wished to profit by the death of the Duke of Luxembourg in daring to lay siege to the town and fortress of Namur. It was a bold stroke, and more brilliantly conducted than in our case. It is true that we were at a disadvantage, as we were ignorant as to the best point of attack, but then it had an inferior garrison. They, on the other hand, had to contend with excellent fortifications and a complete little army of fine troops commanded by a marshal of France.[2] In this case the advantages on our side were such as to inspire an enemy with the fear of having ignominiously to raise the siege, and, in fact, we looked upon this result with perfect confidence.

But what a terrible scourge is war! Human life counts for nothing when such an enterprise is determined upon. Given a wish to go right through with a certain design, ten thousand men more or less are not counted in the cost of the affair; and this is just what happened in this case. The more the Allies grasped the fact of our having reinforced Namur, the more they increased their forces at this point; and the great precautions we had taken regarding the defence of this place only brought about the loss of a greater number of brave men, and in the end the place was captured.

Our dragoon regiment was one of those sent to assist in the defence, and all of us had plenty of opportunities to distinguish ourselves during this long and tedious siege. Maréchal de Boufflers, who had plenty of troops to spare, made numerous sorties upon the besiegers, especially when their attack was developing upon the town itself. Its vast extent, with its many gates, lent itself to the purpose, and we succeeded for some time in keeping the works of the enemy at a distance; all the same, we often had to retire with loss and even precipitation. When I was in command of one of these sorties, our detachment having pushed well to the front and destroyed several lengths of the trenches, a strong force of the enemy advanced to cut us off, whereupon we were obliged to retire promptly. Just then I had the misfortune to have my horse killed under me, and if I had not learnt to vault or had been less active, I should undoubtedly have been killed or, at all events, taken prisoner, but whilst running at full speed, I vaulted up behind a dragoon and just saved myself.

The town held out for fourteen days, when it became necessary to come to some arrangement. Maréchal de Boufflers did his best to bind the Allies to the same articles that had been signed when we took the place, *i.e.* not to attack the fortress from the town side; but this they would not listen to, and preferred to run the risk of any loss we might cause them to that of having to raise the siege. They were, therefore, at liberty to make their attack from whatever quarter it pleased them, and they knew well enough how to profit by this. What was really strange was the antipathy displayed by the inhabitants towards our nation. To oblige the enemy to abstain from attacking us through the town was in their interest and tended to the preservation of their houses, effects, and even lives; but they were quite determined to meet any peril they might be exposed to rather than associate themselves with a treaty by means of which the capture of the fortress would certainly be retarded, and the chance of their remaining under French rule promoted.

They had always been treated with every consideration, and it

2. Maréchal de Boufflers.

would seem to have been more to their advantage to have a French garrison than a Dutch one. The former represented a large consumption of food and merchandise, whilst the Dutch imported all theirs, and spent no money. Again, the latter had little or no politeness or society among themselves, but doubtless this did not render them less agreeable to the citizens of Namur, who are themselves gross and brutal in their habits.

They preferred the drowsy air of the Dutchman to the wide-awake Frenchman, who, they said, turned their brains with his flighty movements and eternal chatter, and who found everything bad that was not to his own way of thinking. They added that we thought too much of ourselves, despised the rest of the world, and considered it beneath us to conform to the customs of the country in which we had to live.

The enemy being in possession of the town, made their principal attack on the fortress on this side. They ranged three large batteries, two in the gardens above the Church of St Aubyn and in the ramparts near the Brussels Gate, the third between St. Jean and St Aubyn. Thence they battered a breach between a ravelin "*en Bec de Moineau*" and a work "*à Pâté*," which abutted on the river Sambre, and razed the "cordons "of other works which might trouble them, besides dismounting the cannon on the parapets.

We found ourselves entirely restricted to the fortress, and the nature of the ground no longer enabled us to make sorties as we had done when occupying the town. The last chance to hold out and give time for Maréchal de Villeroi to send us assistance was to defend each work foot by foot; we did our best to this end, and each night worked hard to repair the breaches made during the day, but the enemy's batteries were so numerous and well served that they soon laid them open again.

The work "*à Pâté*" and the "*Bec de Moineau*," both now breached, were chosen by the enemy for their first assault. M. de Boufflers took every precaution to strengthen them. We dug good entrenchments in rear of the breaches connected with *epaulements*, from point to point, to give cover to our troops during their retirement should they be driven out of the works. The enemy chose the evening for their assault, which was delivered and received with equal vigour, but after a very heavy loss on their part, our opponents were forced to retire. They returned to the attack next morning with considerable reinforcements, and such energy that, after a long resistance, our people were driven out by superior weight and numbers. The besiegers thus

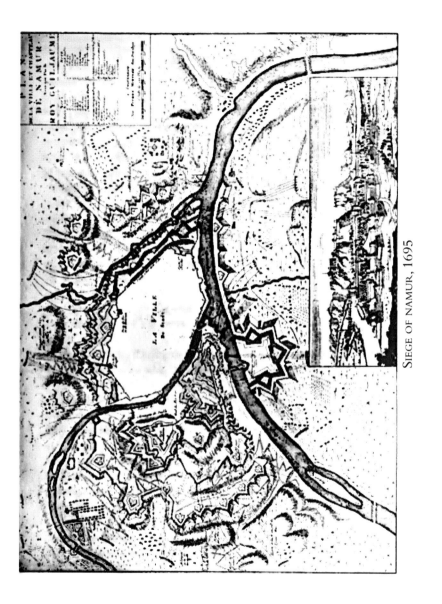

SIEGE OF NAMUR, 1695

effected their lodgements, under cover of which they brought up their guns to batter in one of the sides of the large horn-work; as this was hardly more out-flanked than any of the other works on this side, we merely cut a new entrenchment to strengthen it in case of assault, and for the purpose of communication.

The enemy also took Fort William after two separate assaults, one on the covered-way, the other on the main work; it was stoutly defended, and they lost many men. They also attacked the "Priest's Cap," but the principal attack of all which forced us to capitulate on August 4th was that on the face of the horn-work opposite the work "*à Pâté*." I was lucky enough to be present at two different assaults delivered by the enemy, and did not receive a scratch; on the other hand, my friend was unfortunately carried off by a cannon-ball, to my greatest possible grief.

The Elector of Bavaria and the King of England commanded the Allies, who lost more than twelve thousand men at this siege.

Maréchal de Villeroi could give us no assistance, as the enemy had taken up a position so favourably situated that they were enabled to hold our army of succour in check, and at the same time entirely cover their besieging force. The general being therefore unable to act in our direction, bombarded the city of Brussels and burned an entire quarter. The inhabitants have since rebuilt it in modern style, so that now it is quite an ornament to the town. Our loss in the defence of Namur was very severe, but the king seemed well satisfied with the resistance we had maintained, and rewarded many of our officers. Our colonel was made major-general, selling the regiment to the Marquis Descorailles. I also got a step, being made full lieutenant.

I will here relate a joke concerning one of our captains in the dragoons, who always caused us endless amusement, although usually the besieged have no excessive desire for mirth. He was the Sieur de Vigouroux, a native of Rodez, the capital town of Rouergue, and known throughout the army by his eccentric habits. Vigouroux during his career had never experienced any serious danger, and the sensation of finding himself ordered to take command of one of the sorties had such an extraordinary effect upon him that he brought back miraculous reports of feats of valour, giving himself the credit of being the principal performer.

He wearied everyone by interminable recitals of his deeds in this sortie, pure inventions which after so much repetition he ended in believing himself. He took every opportunity of publishing these noble actions and bored even M. de Boufflers himself with them. One day he asked him with some emphasis if he could not put him in the way of giving a fresh proof of his valour. The *maréchal*, tired of his discourses, replied as follows before all the company present:

Well, M. de Vigouroux, you shall have your wish. A most convenient opportunity presents itself at this moment—the breach is now practicable in Fort William; the enemy, as far as we can see, will not be long before they make their assault I therefore make you its governor. Go now and take over the fort, and if this rabble show themselves, kick them out in proper style, and let them feel the weight of your arm; as a matter of fact, I doubt whether our opponents will be willing to run the risk if it comes to their ears that you will be there. Run and gather the laurels and spite the envious. I give you the preference in this as every other consideration should give place to your well-known bravery.

Poor Vigouroux, whose intention was but to be credited as valiant, and who had no wish to be taken too literally, was aghast at M. de Boufflers answer. He was struck dumb, his Gascon repartees deserted him, and all present roared with laughter. After thinking a while, he thought he had found a way out of the difficulty, and said to M. de Boufflers:

That, *Monseigneur*, is hardly the post for Vigouroux. I cannot stand being boxed up between four walls, for the intense desire I feel to dash right and left amongst these scoundrels would rebel in so confined a space, I should stifle with rage; but let me give vent to my valour in the open country, and you will soon see what Vigouroux can do.

At these words, "give vent to my valour," etc., the entire company burst into shouts of laughter, which quite nonplussed Vigouroux; he left the room without uttering another word. This bit of boasting was not lost on us, but was instantly noised abroad throughout the whole garrison, and Vigouroux soon had the annoyance of hearing the soldiers chaffing each other and quoting, "give vent to my valour in the open."

The same man, when quartered the following winter in the little town of Thuin, in Flanders, had made certain purchases at a shop kept by a widow, who became uneasy as to the payment due to her.

She learnt one day that Vigouroux was preparing to leave for Aix-la-Chapelle, to be treated for some malady he had acquired, so she ran to me, bill in hand, to get me to guarantee its liquidation. I told her that Vigouroux had just drawn money in advance of his pay, and besides, that the bill must be passed and signed by him as correct before I could pay it out of money that might become due to him later on.

Without this I could do nothing. This woman then besought me to accompany her, and get him to pass her account. For charity's sake I went with her, and we found him in the act of getting into his post-chaise. He was much annoyed at our appearance, for he had hardly time to run through the bill, and meanwhile the shop-woman pressed him hard to endorse it.

Vigouroux, exhausted by her persistence, called for writing materials, and wrote at the bottom:

If I die, I pass this account; if I live, to be looked into.

Signed,   De Vigouroux.

Then handing it to the woman, he shouted to the postillion to whip up the horses, and vanished in a moment. When I read this endorsement it struck me as so comic that I could not help reporting it to the officers of the garrison, who did not fail to add this new joke to the "give vent to my valour," and these became so well known to all the army that, during the next campaign, everyone tried to make Vigouroux's acquaintance.

The campaign of 1696 closed without any event of importance to either side; negotiations for peace were begun, and M. de Catinat arranged a truce for a month, from the beginning of July, with the Duke of Savoy. Whilst this lasted the marriage was arranged between the Duke of Burgundy and the Princess of Savoy. This was followed by peace being declared between France and Savoy on September 7th. In October the princess left Turin for Versailles. The English and Dutch were not pleased with the Duke of Savoy deserting them in this way, for they now found themselves hardly in a position to attempt much in Flanders, in consequence of our reinforcing our army there with the troops we had hitherto been obliged to keep in Piedmont. They, however, still raided our coastline with their fleet, doing some damage to Calais, Rochelle, and other places.

France in a way avenged herself for these injuries by the enterprise of the Chevalier Bart. This officer having been informed at the beginning of June that the Dutch were sending a fleet of ninety merchant ships to the Baltic, escorted by five men-of-war, put to sea with a squadron of ten good ships and sighted them near Stralsund. He at once attacked, boarded, and captured the escort without much trouble, and then made chase for the merchant vessels. He took half their number, burning some after emptying them of their contents, and brought the remainder into the port of Dunkerque on June 8th. The above comprises the most important events during this campaign.

Our regiment was quartered in Alsace, broken up into detachments, I myself being at Pfalzburg, where we had four companies. The duties were not heavy, and when peace was made with the Duke of Savoy, the probability of a general one became all the talk, which did not at all please us. However, we now had a little war of our own to wage, occasioned by some squadrons of the Imperial cavalry, who had made their appearance in the little plain beyond the marsh at the foot of the town ramparts. We could only reach this plain by means of a causeway, defended by two machicolated towers or redoubts and a palisaded covered-way.

M. Desbordes, major-general and governor of the place, noted their arrival, and not wishing it to be said that anyone could approach us thus with impunity, posted in the covered-ways, unknown to the enemy, a detachment of infantry, and then at the head of our four companies of dragoons proceeded to make a reconnaissance of the plain. Beyond the plain was a large wood whence the enemy had debouched, and which served to conceal their movements. The affair began with merely an exchange of shots, but warmed up by degrees until it became altogether another matter, when, finding we were not strong enough to hold our own and were becoming too seriously engaged, we retired helter-skelter upon our redoubts.

The enemy gave chase, and their zeal and excitement carried them so far as to bring them within range of our infantry, who opened fire upon them in the most opportune manner possible. Many were laid low, and the rest took to their heels. We then returned to the charge, and pursued them nearly as far as the wood, where we took several prisoners, and finally retired unmolested.

The enemy, mortified at this check, waited for a chance to make up for it; but some time passed before they saw fit to reappear. They doubtless thought that if they showed themselves as before they would find us upon them as on the first occasion, and did not wish to precipitate matters so as to endanger the failure of an ambush which they had prepared.

At last they returned, advancing close up to our lines to induce us to make a sortie; and they had not long to wait for it. As soon as M. Desbordes knew of their approach he ordered out our dragoon companies, disposed his infantry as on the first occasion, and away we went. The enemy, to draw us on, only showed two small squadrons, but they had other troops hidden in the recesses of the wood into which they wished to lead us. These two squadrons made but a show of fighting, and after exchanging a few blows gave ground and took to flight, relying upon our following them in our excitement and the confusion; but happily we did not join them in their circus-like movements, not wishing to get too far from our infantry.

After several skirmishes of this sort, the enemy, seeing we were not going to let ourselves fall into their trap, finally retired, or at all events made a show of so doing. We, on our part, waited a little on the field of battle, but as nothing more was to be seen of them, M. de Desbordes ordered us to retire, he occupying himself meanwhile by reconnoitring the neighbourhood for another occasion. Whilst the dragoons and infantry were defiling along the causeway, curiosity had drawn him a little too near the wood, when out dashed at full gallop a handful of hussars, sword in hand. Fortunately they were noticed in time for him to attain the shelter of our redoubts, thanks to the speed, however, of his horse.

As it was, a hussar officer, still better mounted than he was, would have made short work of him had not a large Danish hound, his constant companion, come to his rescue. She flew between the legs of the officer's horse, barking and biting in such a way that it was impossible to make him gallop, thus undoubtedly saving M. Desbordes' life. An unfortunate groom who had followed him was not so lucky, being cut down and killed. M. Desbordes joined us on the causeway, and took more care in future.

I superintended the office work of the dragoon companies stationed at Pfalzburg, and this duty brought me into unpleasant contact with one of our quartermasters, who always made out that he was of gentle birth, but who really was a very coarse and uneducated individual.

One day when I had given out a certain order, which he either did not quite understand or wanted to argue about, he took what I said in a bad sense, and answered me very impertinently. When I asked him if he knew exactly what he had said, he replied, seizing the hilt of his sword, that he was as much a gentleman as any officer, could measure his sword against mine any day, and that I could take the matter as I liked.

This demonstration and the words accompanying it so excited me that I at once drew my sword, he doing likewise, and although the three other quarter-masters were present, we in an instant thrust at each other, with the result that he received a sword cut in his right side. This affair made such a sensation in the regiment from a disciplinary point of view, that many of the officers asserted that the consequences would be disastrous if the quartermaster were not court-martialled; but the colonel, after consideration, merely saw fit to give him his discharge when cured of his wound.

The campaign of 1697 was the last in this war. The peace just signed with the Duke of Savoy produced the greatest relief throughout the whole kingdom. The maintenance of the army in Italy, the enormous expense of the transport of munitions and provisions, together with the losses among the troops from sickness year after year, had been the source of much difficulty and a heavy charge upon the State. France was now, free of this, in an excellent condition to carry on the war on her other frontiers, and across them into the enemy's country. Therefore the Allies opened negotiations for a general peace. The king appointed Messieurs du Harlai and de Creci as his plenipotentiaries. They left Versailles in February, going to Delft, and then on to Ryswick, where the conference was held.

The two forces, however, kept the field as usual. Ours in Flanders was very numerous, and that of the Allies, although considerable, was not in a state to oppose us, who were prepared to cross the frontier in case they were not willing to agree to the articles of peace. The enemy were always raising new difficulties on this score, and France, believing it to be the best way to cut the matter short, set her troops in motion. To this end, M. de Catinat, commanding the army of Flanders, received orders to lay siege to Ath, and the Duke of Vendôme to Barcelona.

The trenches were opened before Ath on May 20th with but little loss to us. The besieged made no resistance, and being unsupported, surrendered June 5th. Barcelona made a better defence, which gave time for the Viceroy of Catalonia to march with a Spanish army to its assistance; but M. de Vendôme left his siege works for the nonce, and entirely defeated him. The town then, seeing relief impossible, capitulated on July 10th, 1697.

The result of this last action was such that all obstacles were cleared away, and England, Holland, and Spain signed the Treaty of Peace on

September 20th.[3] The emperor, who took exception to a few details, demanded a delay of six weeks, in order to secure his own rights and those of the Empire; these were agreed to and ratified on October 30th, and the war terminated to the great relief of the nations concerned. But the officers of our army were much troubled when they learnt of the reduction of his army, to which the king had pledged himself by this treaty.

Many who had exhausted their means to keep themselves in the service and in the advancement of their promotion, now found themselves penniless, inasmuch as all chance of another war seemed to have disappeared. The succession to the Crown of Spain was the only subject which could bring discord anew between France and the other European powers, and the articles of this treaty were arranged to meet this. The Prince Elector of Bavaria, the only son of the Elector by his first wife the archduchess, herself the only daughter of the Emperor Leopold by his first wife the Infanta Margaret, sister of Charles II., King of Spain, was recognised as the successor of the latter, who was a valetudenarian, whilst the Prince of Bavaria was in the best of health.

All this disquieted me, and I saw my career arrested, and all my care, and the risk I had run to gain a reputation, thrown away. We had great hopes, however, that our regiment would not be entirely disbanded, and imagined the worst that could occur would be a reduction of our strength. There were then forty-seven regiments of dragoons, and as this branch of the service had distinguished itself on numberless occasions, mounted or dismounted, we had great hopes of the State paying due respect to this point; at any rate, we believed half at least of the regiments would be maintained, and that ours, being the twenty-second, would not be reduced; but high politics and the Treaty of Ryswick decided otherwise. The king kept only fourteen of the oldest regiments, and although our turn to be broken up and incorporated amongst others did not come at once, we did not escape this fate, for our establishment was reduced and the residue handed over to the *Mestre du Camp Générale*.

---

3. The Peace of Ryswick, by which Louis XIV, agreed to give up all he had taken or conquered since the Treaty of Nimeguen in 1678, to place the chief fortresses in the hands of the Dutch garrisons, to recognise William III. as King of England and Anne as his successor, and received, moreover, an effectual check to his growing power and ambition. A month later a second treaty was made between Louis and the emperor. Louis restored all towns taken since 1678, with the important exception of Strasbourg. Louis' willingness to make peace and yield so much was due to his desire to have his hands free on the death of Charles II, of Spain.

CHAPTER 3

The Countess—Arras and Bordeaux—The Lawsuit

I always kept as much as possible in touch with the War Office official, and the loss of my friend (his relation) in no wise diminished his friendliness towards me; I took all care to let him know everything that went on wherever I might be, giving him the most detailed accounts I could on every point. I now besought him to use his influence with M. de Barbesieux to give me some return for my devotion to duty and service rendered, and that as I saw no chance of gaining further promotion, I only asked for the step of captain on the retired list, with no increase of pay.

I had almost lost hope, when I received a letter from him apologising for the delay which had occurred in answering my application, owing to the press of work in the office, on account of the changes taking place in the army. At the same time, he said that he had already got my demand in hand, and that though he could not tell me anything positively, he would suggest my reporting myself at Versailles, and he would do all he could to help me.

I set out for Versailles the instant I received this letter, but when I got there, my friend told me that he had taken rather too favourable a view of things, M. de Barbesieux was overwhelmed with work, and so put about by the favours constantly being asked of him that he rarely, if ever, granted them. However, he added that if I left it to him I should be satisfied, as he would do his best, and was sure that I should soon be able to bear witness as to his efforts and goodwill. I begged him to leave no stone unturned, reminding him that it was well within the power of the king and ministers to grant such harmless petitions, in which they would be answerable only to the Almighty, and if he would but further my cause, I should have every reason to hope for the best.

He arranged matters so well that one day I found myself in a room reserved for privileged persons only, through which M. de Barbesieux would be sure to pass alone. The minister was kind enough to stop, and after having heard my tale, took my petition, saying he would look into it, and then passed on. This answer disconcerted me a good deal, and I came to the conclusion that I had nothing left to hope for. I then called upon my friend, who asked me if M. de Barbesieux had heard my story quietly. "Certainly," said I; "but he did not seem to be quite pleased with my request, for he simply said he would look into the case." He told me not to worry about it, as it might turn out better than I expected.

And he was right, for in less than eight days I got my captain's commission, which made up for all previous disappointments. So far there was nothing further to wish for. I therefore determined to stop in Paris for a time to compensate myself for all the anxiety I had passed through, and put up at a well-known hostelry in the Rue Traversine, much affected by people of quality, where I had no trouble in finding congenial companions. I met with a hearty reception, but found there was not a man amongst them who was not a gambler, and notwithstanding my fear of bad luck, I had to join in with them or find myself out in the cold. This I did, however, with as much discrimination as possible. I was fortunate enough to be successful at the start, and my winnings went to balance the ultimate bad luck that befell me, as is usual with every inexperienced gambler.

A rich and childless widow lived in this quarter of the town, named the Countess de ——. This lady was very clever, and lived in very good style, but owing to her dislike to card-playing, had not a very extensive acquaintance. Although no longer in her first youth, her beauty of features and figure rendered her none the less attractive; the charm of her manners and conversation delighted all who knew her, and finally, her establishment and surroundings were delightfully comfortable and easy-going.

I was introduced to her by a lady of rank and of the highest respectability, who vouched for my being a sensible young man with a natural dislike for gambling—giving me, in fact, all the characteristics the Countess liked best to see in her acquaintances. I was most warmly received, and such a gracious welcome encouraged me gradually to detach myself from the selfish group, who pressed me to gamble as much for the monetary profit brought by cards, as to satisfy their own longing for the excitement of the game.

This lady made so lively an impression upon me that I limited my companionship entirely to hers, and found immense pleasure in so doing, I added the study of music and instrumental playing to my pastimes, and was perfectly content in the enjoyment of this gentle occupation. By the assiduity of my attentions the countess and I became so intimate that I formed quite one of the family, as it were, and as she always had covers laid at table for any chance caller, I dined oftener at her house than at my hotel. I said to her one day, in joke, that my hostess being so hospitable in every way, all I could possibly wish for more would be a room in the house itself.

"There is nothing to prevent it," said she, with graceful courtesy. "I have an empty one now, and it would give me the greatest pleasure in the world if you would occupy it."

"If I took you at your word, madam," I replied, "I might perhaps give you cause to regret the kind offer you make."

"No," said she, "I am not joking, but say what I mean, and you could not show your regard for me better than to avail yourself of my offer."

I replied that I accepted with all pleasure, but feared lest my inclinations might take further flights.

"Don't be afraid," said she, smiling. "You have always behaved discreetly so far; continue to act up to my desires, and nothing shall interfere with any of your prospects."

This equivocal answer put ideas into my head that I had not ventured to entertain so far, and I flattered myself, in the manner of youth, that she had more than an ordinary friendship for me. However, such was my respect for the charming manners of this lady that I dared not give her any idea of this, and taking possession of the apartment obeyed her injunctions in every way.

I found my new circumstances perfectly delightful, and the kindness of the countess was such that she interested herself in carefully putting me through quite a new course of discipline.

One gets plenty of this sort of thing in the army, particularly in an old regiment, but there always remains a taint of coarseness and withal a touch of sharpness, which is not in good taste. No one was in a better position to correct me on this point than this lady; her superior mind, her gentle ways and birth and polished manners—in fact, everything about her—placed her above ordinary women. She divined with ease the different natures of those about her, and knew how to adapt herself to their characters and thoughts. She was kind enough to make me aware of anything that might offend good manners, and taught me how to avoid those dangerous and seductive characters who cause us to swerve from the perfect way. She did not stop here, but strove to inspire in me that polite bearing which, avoiding all self-consciousness, obstinacy, and gossip, teaches us to make use of our wits in a manner pleasing to all around us. Finally, so elegant was her conversation and so tactful was her method of instruction, that I derived infinite pleasure and delight in listening to her.

I had not long enjoyed this tranquil existence with my charming hostess when an unexpected trouble befell her.

Among the several ladies who formed the circle of our society was a young Marquise, whose husband was very old and cross-grained, but who, on the other hand, had made over to her the whole of his fortune. Rather ungratefully she found means to keep away from him the best part of the year. Her house was near that of the countess, and this neighbourhood resulting in intimate friendship, she often came in to spend the evening. It was my habit to see her home when she left, and leave her at her door without any particular ceremony.

One evening, accompanying her as usual, it struck me that she might perhaps think it wrong of me not to offer to conduct her to her apartment, and made the suggestion on arrival at her door. She put on a surprised air, and asked me whether I had any further design hidden under the guise of the compliment, "for up to now," said she, "you have never expressed such a wish, and therefore you must have some further purpose. However," she continued, "I will allow you to do so, provided you are prudent, because my maids are discreet and will not come into the room as long as you are there, and if I cannot count upon your discretion too, I will not permit you to come up."

I did not need an interpreter to understand her discourse, and as nothing flatters a young man like an adventure of this sort, I forgot in a moment all I owed to my true friend, and without thinking of the consequences of carrying on two intrigues at the same time, I gave myself up to the delightful thought that I had inspired the mind of this lady with tender feelings towards me. When we found ourselves in her apartment, I did all I could to prove to her that she was not mistaken in her choice; but being not inexperienced in the game, she knew how to damp my ardour after having brought me to the point she wished. In fact, she had the address to raise within me a passion sufficient to induce me to make all the vows and protestations she could wish; I may say I even went further than altogether pleased her. She then thought that matters might go too far, and took the precaution to call my attention, with an anxious air, to the fact that her servants were in the ante-room, whence they could hear all and might come in at any moment.

Finally, she declared it only needed the least imprudence on my part to ruin her entirely, that if I had any consideration whatever for her, I ought not to expose her to such a danger, and even should she forget her duty so far as to listen to my vows, that this was neither the proper place nor time. She also said we had gone too far already, prayed me to calm myself, and withdraw for fear that her people should get suspicious, and then she pulled at the bell rope to summon them. I was thus obliged to retire in the midst of my declarations, and left my new mistress consumed with the fire she had kindled within me.

When my feelings had calmed down I was struck, without knowing why, with a premonition of some coming disaster. I was grieved at my faithlessness towards the countess, who so little deserved such treatment, and instantly made the firmest resolutions to be true to her; but then immediately afterwards the charm of my new conquest touched me, I forgot her and myself entirely, and became incapable of reasoning. In proportion as my pride was flattered by this double intrigue, so everything seemed easy to me regarding it, and I dreamed only of the pleasure in store for me; but when I returned to my senses I saw nothing but obstacles and insurmountable difficulty; thus I argued the matter over and over to myself without ceasing, and without being able to come to any fixed purpose on the point.

The young *marquise*, who was a thoughtless creature, was of the age that thinks a woman of thirty-five has but the most straight-laced feelings towards a man, and placed the countess in this category, never doubting for a moment but that she and I were on this footing together.

Her giddy nature was too ready to gossip about anything that had amused her, and so pleased was she with her love passage that the very next morning she went to the countess and, with the greatest eagerness, told her in strict confidence all that had occurred between us, exaggerating the terms and phrases which I had used in expressing my feelings.

The countess, who had never imagined the possibility of such a thing, was extremely shocked, but she knew how to control herself, managed the conversation so as to draw from the *marquise* all she wished to know, soon made herself intimately acquainted with every detail of the matter, and pretended to be quite amused with it all. Nevertheless, she suffered the greatest mental agitation, for it seemed to her impossible that I could hide such perfidious feelings under a modest and honest exterior. She was a prey to these reflections when I returned from the opera; but I found no change in her manner, and she behaved as if she was quite ignorant of my conduct.

The *marquise* came in after supper to pass the evening with her as usual, and I admit that the expectation of seeing her gave me pleasure, and still more the prospect of escorting her home, for I hoped that then she would give me a fair hearing and accede to my prayers. I at least thought that this lady would have been so far careful as to do nothing in the presence of others which would lead them to imagine the feelings which existed between us; but here I was mistaken. This flighty creature, wishing to show the countess the truth of all she had told her, now talked and behaved for all the world as if we were a couple of lovers.

This conduct—so contrary to what I had expected—quite took me by surprise, and I could see no escape from the embarrassing position I found myself in. The countess on her part, notwithstanding all her prudence, could hardly preserve an even countenance, and insensibly allowed herself to bear witness of her inmost thoughts. The *marquise* noticing this, then began to suspect us; words failed her, and we all three became silent and subdued. The time had come to go. The *marquise* rose, and I advanced to offer my hand, whilst the countess herself, with a troubled air, carried the candles to light us out without calling the lackeys in the ante-chamber. This act rendered us dumb; but when we found ourselves in the street the *marquise* began to cry, saying how sorry she was that she had not known sooner what she had only then just become conscious of, and then and there told me all she had confided to the countess and the hopeless despair she suffered in consequence.

Troubled as I was, I tried to disabuse her of this, to make her believe that she was really mistaken in what she had seen, and that the countess had never had a thought on my account in the way she imagined. But my discourse was uttered in such a hesitating style that it alone would have been sufficient to proclaim the truth, and she remained none the less perplexed with the part that was left her to play.

I parted from her at her door quite overwhelmed, without offering to conduct her to her apartment, for I knew well enough that if I had suggested such an idea she would never have permitted it.

This sad adventure entirely quenched our ardour, and for my own part I thought of nothing but how I could justify my conduct on rejoining the countess, for I still had sufficient self-respect to condemn my conduct as unworthy of an honest man.

As it turned out, no opportunity was offered to me, for I learnt on my return that she had retired to her apartment with strict orders that she was not to be disturbed; in fact, after this occurrence I never once found myself alone with her. These precautions drove me to despair. I would have given my life to have made my peace with her, but all means to this end were denied me.

Experience taught the countess not to allow herself to be drawn into explanations, which could only recall to her an occurrence in which her prudence had overstepped itself. She maintained towards me her most proper manner, tinged, perhaps, with a slight indifference, and behaved, in fact, as she would to any other member of her acquaintance. She neither reproached me nor made advances, and kept up this attitude until she was quite sure of my contrition and the lack of desire on my part to again meet the *marquise*, who had never since visited her neighbour.

When at last she saw that all my actions and attentions had for their object a return to her good graces, she began to treat me with less severity, and little by little admitted me to the same favour as I had previously enjoyed, and this without any questioning or reproaches concerning the *marquise*. So noble and so unusual did this punishment and pardon appear to me that I became more than ever attached to this lady, and took the greatest care on all occasions to avoid doing anything that could in the least degree cause her uneasiness respecting my conduct. In this happy state I passed two years.

The only occasion on which I ever quitted the side of my dear countess was my regimental inspection, and then I returned as soon as possible. But my happiness came to an end too soon, for I grieve to say I had the misfortune to lose her during my absence on this very occasion. She was not well at the time of my enforced departure, and the fever having increased later, she died on the ninth day of her illness. Her loss plunged me into the very depths of misery and grief

During my stay in Paris I made, through the countess, many very influential friends; among others, the Marquis de Ricous, with whom I became intimately acquainted. Besides being a man of integrity, full of genius and merit, he was closely connected with, and had the support of, the court, and was now waiting his chance to be appointed ambassador or envoy to some foreign state. He managed his affairs so well that the king took him into his confidence and sent him to Munich to negotiate the alliance between the Elector of Bavaria and France, which he carried through according to His Majesty's desires. It was this that gave him the opportunity of bringing me to that country, as I shall explain later on.

After the loss of my beloved countess, my only thought was how to while away the time during my enforced retirement, and my regiment being then quartered at Arras, I made up my mind to pass my days there. This town in every way suited my purpose, gaiety and society were unknown there, and excepting in the case of one or two of the middle-class houses, the garrison were nowhere received.

I saw in this town a ceremony which had doubtless some remote connection with the idolatrous worship of the ancient Romans; the cult or worship of an immense wax candle, enshrined in a silver sheath, which the populace annually made the object of their adoration for the space of eight days. The bishop and clergy were powerless to prevent this, for they feared a riot if they attempted to do so; thus their efforts in this direction were not very serious. This solemnity takes place during the *octave* of the *Fête Dieu*, especially on the Sunday, when the holy candle is carried in state. Here is the legend of its origin as related in the country.

Two violin players who had married sisters were at enmity with each other to such a degree, owing to family matters, that no one was able to pacify them. The Holy Virgin, interesting herself in the quarrel between these illustrious personages, appeared one day in the cathedral church, where they both happened to be at their devotions, on the altar of a chapel dedicated to her, bearing in her hand an immense candle. She besought them to become reconciled and then disappeared, leaving the candle upon the altar. The two brothers-in-law instantly embraced each other, and took the candle to the mayor of the town, to whom they recounted the whole affair.

By a divine inspiration the people gathered together, shouting, "A miracle! a miracle!" and from that moment looked upon the holy candle as the protecting genius of their town. They built a chapel for it near the principal square, and enclosed it within a silver sheath, and ever since it has been shown annually to the populace, who come as far as ten or twelve leagues distance for the purpose. They pray to it with great fervour, constantly repeating the words, "Our Good Lady Saint Candle pray for us."

There is also a Brotherhood of the Holy Candle, under a director, who is elected annually. He who holds the post sets so much store by it, that he will spend upon it as much as fifteen hundred *livres*, which is a great sum among the brotherhood, seeing that the richest among them is at the most but a small tradesman. On the Sunday of the *octave* of the *Fête Dieu* a procession is formed, with the same detail and reverence as that of the Holy Sacrament; the streets are draped, holy water is sprinkled, temporary altars are erected to represent the twelve stations of the Cross, and the holy candle itself is borne under a magnificent canopy, escorted by all the brotherhood bearing long white wands in their hands.

It might be imagined that the Church assists in this ceremony, but the contrary is the case; she discountenances it, and owing to the origin of the miracle, the violin players are the leaders. Four of this profession support the canopy, under which another reverently carries the candle in his arms, the crowd following with intense devotion. They stop at each "station" as in the ceremony of the Holy Sacrament, and proceed thus to the cathedral, where the brethren have the right of entry. Here the worthy carrier has need of his skill. He is permitted to elevate the holy candle, but not so as to let it actually touch the high altar, for if it did so, he would not be allowed to take it up again, and it would then become the property of the chapter, who would certainly abolish the ceremony altogether. To avoid such a contingency he is careful to hold it in such a way that only his hands touch the altar itself.

On leaving the church the procession is continued to the chapel, where a halt is made at the door, till all the people are assembled; then a brother, after a genuflection, lights the candle with a wax taper, when the candle-bearer raises it on high, gives the Benediction, and immediately after extinguishes it. During the Benediction the devout crowd bow reverently, repeating their "*Mea culpa*" and "Our Good Lady Saint Candle, pray for us" in mournful tones, and finally humbly kiss the pavement. Such is the ceremony as I witnessed it, but I do not know whether it is still kept up. On mentioning the holy candle to the people of Arras, they were careful to give me detailed accounts of its miraculous healing powers among the sick and crippled, all due to the faith they held in it.

In addition, they declared that it had lasted over five hundred years, and in that period, moreover, had produced more than a thousand candles without having diminished its substance by a single ounce. It is not difficult to understand this, as when the holy candle is lighted, the wax which falls freely from the taper furnishes more material than it is able to consume during the very short time that it remains burning, and as to the candles it is said to produce, they are provide by pieces of wax touched by it, and which, according to the people, become part and parcel with the wax of the holy candle itself.

A friend of mine, an officer of the garrison, did his best to persuade me to make a trip to the country with him. He was fond of his home because he had property there—quite the reverse of my own case. I had lost my mother the year that I joined the cadet company, and I knew that since her death my family affairs were not in the best possible state, besides which I had not enjoyed such a happy time in my early life there as to make me anxious to return. However, his solicitations and the want of distraction in Arras were too much for me; I determined to accompany him, and thus found myself back again at home. Here I found that my existence was scarcely likely to be more exciting than in the garrison life I had just quitted. I would not have stayed there very long had it not been for a disastrous and unexpected event; I found myself entangled in a tissue of embarrassments which, owing to my want of experience, I was unable to avoid.

This was a lawsuit at the Parliament of Bordeaux, which, according to the advice of many people, I found myself obliged to engage in. I foresaw neither its length nor its consequences; withal, one result was my marriage from this town, wherein I never should have found myself had it not been for this matter. This was its origin. The father of a young man of my acquaintance had a rich and pushing neighbour, who had bought up a debt incumbent on him, and who vexed him with an action-at-law on the subject The young man, who had honourable feelings and but little patience with the tactics of the opposing side, which sought to rob him of his patrimony, threatened the prosecutor and his two sons, the one an advocate, the other a doctor. These two families were constantly on the lookout for each other, and never left their own houses unarmed.

One day the young man was returning from Périgueux, where the case was being heard, when he met the creditor, accompanied by his doctor son, in a narrow part of the road. As soon as they saw each other the two parties drew their pistols, and the father and son, wishing to profit by their superiority of numbers, separated so as to attack the young man on the flank as well as in front. He did not, however, give them time to carry out this manoeuvre, but made promptly for the doctor, fired, and stretched him dead on the field of battle. This so intimidated the father that he made off as quickly as his legs would carry him. One can imagine the sequel of an affair like this: the young man was obliged to seek a refuge from the hue-and- cry raised against him; and coming to me in his distress, I gave him secretly certain letters of introduction, after which he disappeared.

Notwithstanding my precautions, his adversaries got wind of this, and looking upon me as one of their opponents, resolved to avenge themselves on me whenever the occasion might arise. They were rich folk and belonged to an important set, which increased their arrogance and enterprise. For my part, I had no idea of all this, and consequently took no special precautions, and as often as not left my sword at home when taking my solitary walks in the district we all lived in. Sometime after the death of the doctor I met the father, his lawyer son, and a nephew, who alone had his sword with him. As they approached me I stopped to allow them room to pass, and noticed that the son made a movement as though to attack me, which I avoided. Then he had recourse to abusive language, and I saw at once that our parting would not be an amiable one.

I determined to anticipate them by seizing the nephew's sword, which I snatched from its scabbard, but was not able to secure it, as he grasped the blade with both hands so tightly that I dragged him along the ground without being able to make him let go. As soon as I got hold of his sword, his two comrades took to flight and regained their house nearby; but the son, plucking up courage, retraced his steps armed with a gun. I saw this, although fully occupied in trying to shake off my opponent, who shouted at the top of his voice for help, and I then began to realise the danger in store for me.

Flight, no doubt, would have been justifiable, but I would have rather run the risk of perishing than to have had resort to such a measure, so I made up my mind to raise my opponent from the ground, where I then had him, and use him as a shield of defence. I managed this so well that I was always able to hold him between my body and the advocate, and by this means prevented the latter from taking proper aim at me.

It is quite possible that in the end I should have fallen a victim, but luckily a number of people now appeared on the scene. The gun went off harmlessly in the air, and the sword in dispute between us was seized, and finally deposited in the *Greffe de la Jurisdiction*. My adversaries then proceeded to barricade themselves in their house, for they feared lest I should lead on those who had come to my rescue to a further attack upon them. But they were far from advising such a violent measure; on the contrary, the most important of my friends escorted me to my house, and helped me so well that I lodged a complaint before the *Juge des Lieux*, thereby forestalling my assailants. They persuaded me that I was in a position to exact most honourable satisfaction, the only course to take under the circumstances, and that they themselves would do all they could to assist me in this.

I endorsed my complaint in due form—the first occasion on which I had placed my name to a stamped document. The witnesses were heard the same day, the warrant for the arrest of my three assailants issued, and a party of archers told off to carry this out forthwith.

Never was a case better supported than mine. This beginning confirmed my highest ideas of justice; but the very next day the defendants obtained their liberty under bail, appealed to the Parliament of Bordeaux, and got the *Juge des Lieux* to take their part.

Here was I, an ignoramus on such subjects, engaged in a lawsuit; but happily I found at Bordeaux some charitable people, who, in return for my apprentice fees, gave me certain instruction in the matter. I had the best case in the world, and the legal gentlemen of the Tournelle were so convinced of this that they adjudicated in my favour, and cast my adversaries in costs, including interest. It is true that the total did not amount to a third of what I had disbursed, but my suit was over, as I thought, and I promised myself that it should be my last.

Whilst waiting for the payment of the damages awarded me, my adversaries, better at sharp practices than I, laid an embargo on the money and prevented its delivery to me, giving as a pretext that some of the expenses were not liquidated. By this departure I found myself as embarrassed as ever. I had recourse to my counsel, who still persuaded me that my case was an excellent one, that I could make my opponents seriously repent of their action; he recommended that the archers should be sent to arrest them, or, failing this, to distrain upon their goods, even if I had to break into their house to effect this.

As this expedition savoured of my beloved war, I was charmed that my adversaries should have given me such an opportunity of practising it upon them, and without foreseeing the consequences of the violent nature of the advice given me, I at once despatched a troop of archers, who, finding the doors close barred against them, immediately broke into the house and carried off all the furniture worth taking.

But far from getting quit of the affair in this way, I found myself engaged in a new lawsuit, and I was obliged to go back to Bordeaux to defend myself against an action brought by my opponents regarding my seizure of their goods. Then it was that I began to regret very sincerely that I had ever quitted Mars to follow St. Yves, but it was too late. My lawyers still continued by fine reasoning to argue that my case held good, and that I should soon see the end of it, although to tell the truth my interests were no further advanced now than on the first day, notwithstanding all my tactics and the expense I had been put to.

Lawsuits are tempting affairs; everything seems plain sailing at the outset, whether in the eyes of the litigants or their advisers, but the results are often disappointing. The original object becomes so obscured by the intricacies raised, that the best case, after much expenditure of money and anxiety, is as likely to be lost as would be the worst.

The sequel of this affair would have kept me still longer at Bordeaux had not war broken out afresh. The king made an alliance with the Elector of Bavaria, in order to induce that Prince to take up arms in favour of the Duke of Anjou, who had been called to the Spanish throne by the will of the childless Charles II.

The Marquis de Ricous had been sent to Munich to negotiate this alliance, and the services he rendered me in connection with it obliged me to abandon my lawsuit, which I left to those on my side without taking any special precaution as to the outcome. I then quitted Bordeaux for Munich, as I shall explain later, after having described the motives and reasons of the war.

CHAPTER 4

The Cause of the War Between France and Spain Against the Allies

This war, which has cost so much blood among the Christian States, had its origin in the death of the Electoral Prince of Bavaria, which took place on February 6th, 1699, twenty-one months before that of Charles II., King of Spain. At the Peace of Ryswick the prince had been declared successor to the Crown of Spain.

The powers who, for the sake of peace, had resolved[1] to maintain his rights, seeing their precautions upset by his death, took new measures to avert war by arranging a Treaty of Partition, [2] by which France ceded to the emperor, as representing the archduke, the greater portion of the Spanish kingdom. This was the only possible means of maintaining peace in Europe, which would have been ensured for a long time had His Imperial Majesty agreed to this treaty. But this prince, regarding himself as head of the House of Austria, to which, according to him, the kingdom of Spain had fallen after the death of

1. The First Partition Treaty was agreed to secretly by William III. and Louis XIV., and signed October, 1698. The young Electoral Prince was given Spain, the Spanish Netherlands and the Indies; France was to have the kingdom of Naples and Sicily and Guipuscoa, and Austria the Duchy of Milan. In 1699, however, the Electoral Prince died, hence the necessity for the second treaty in the following year.

2. The Second Partition Treaty was signed in 1700. Spain, the Spanish Netherlands, Sardinia, and the Colonies were given to the Archduke Charles, the second son of the Emperor Leopold, and the Dauphin was to receive Naples and Sicily, Guipuscoa, Elba, and the Duchy of Milan, which was to be given to the Archduke Charles in exchange for Lorraine. Thus the French dominions were rounded off in the northeast, France would become supreme in the west basin of the Mediterranean, and the supremacy of the Hapsburgs in Italy was transferred to the Bourbons. The Spaniards were furious at the very idea of partition, and Charles II. made a will, giving the whole succession to the second son of the Dauphin, Philip Duke of Anjou.

the Electoral Prince, preferred vague ambition to the glory of contributing to the establishment of peace.

He maintained that as Louis XIV. had renounced his claim to the succession to the throne of Spain when he married Maria Theresa, sister of Charles II., his descendants had no claim thereto, and that it ought to return to the Austrian branch in case the King of Spain died childless; upon these grounds he refused to sign the treaty. Charles II., on the other hand, maintained that his will and testament was law in itself, and that it only should be observed to settle this matter. His death took place on November 1st, 1700, and the Crown of Spain was placed on the head of the Duke of Anjou, who arrived in Madrid amid the rejoicings of the Spanish nation. The different peoples who formed this kingdom submitted themselves to Philip V., who found no difficulty in getting himself recognised as king in the vast states of which it is composed.

The foreign States followed the example of Spain; they almost all declared for the king, and England and Holland, after having deliberated for some time, came to the same determination.

Since the Peace of Ryswick the Elector of Bavaria had been Governor of the Spanish Low Countries, which, under Charles V., were included in the Empire under the denomination of the Circle of Burgundy.

In that capacity he obeyed the orders of the new King of Spain, to whom the Low Countries belonged, and introduced French troops into all the fortresses under his command in place of the Dutch garrisons, which had occupied them hitherto.

Everything combined in favour of Philip V., and the will of the late king was popularly regarded as a divine injunction.

The latter prince had not only determined himself that this arrangement should be carried out, but had been confirmed in his resolution by Pope Innocent XII., whom he had consulted on the point many months before his death. However, the emperor did not regard it as a divine decree to which he ought to bow, and was not afraid of the consequences—the inevitable intrigues, or the Christian blood which was about to be shed over the dispute. He refused to recognise Philip, and determined to dethrone him; and as he was not strong enough to accomplish this single-handed, he employed all the means he could think of to persuade the other Powers to take his part. Here we have the whole basis of the war.

The King of England, William III., had received from the emperor material services when he was only Prince of Orange, and in some measure owed to him his throne, and was not ungrateful withal.

He it was upon whom the emperor most depended to assist him to attain his object.

He was the very man to devise the surest means of placing the archduke upon the Spanish throne. His prestige in his own States and in Holland, and the close relations which he had always kept up with the Protestant princes of Germany left no room for doubt that he would in the end bring the remaining Powers to the side of the emperor; in fact, the treaty concluded on September 7th, 1701,[3] to the effect that they should use their utmost efforts to dethrone Philip V., would never have been brought about without the help of this prince.[4]

On the other hand, he had recognised Philip V. as king, and had caused the States General to do likewise; but as it was a question of rendering a service to the Emperor and of revenging himself upon the House of France, which had crossed his path in his designs upon England, he made light of going back on his word, and induced the Dutch to do the same.[5]

Motives Which Caused the Elector of Bavaria to Ally Himself With France and Spain

The powers leagued together against France used promises and threats to oblige the whole body of the German States to take the Emperor's part. I wish to point out that besides the Electors, they made every effort to bring in the Sovereign Princes and the various Circles which formed the German Empire. How be it, the war proposed to them was entirely contrary to the interests of that Empire, which should have been glad to see the Crown of Spain fall to the lot of a prince of France instead of a prince of the House of Austria, for in the latter case they would have reason to fear the power of the emperor, who, with a king of Spain to back him, could make the whole German body tremble.

It was hardly prudent for them to enter upon a war which only

---

3. The Triple Alliance of England, Holland, and the emperor.

4. The real reasons which determined the action of England were the recovery of the Low Countries, which Louis XIV. had seized, the protests of Holland generally, and the question of the balance of power. William III., personally, would have preferred to hold by the Treaty of Partition if the Emperor had been willing, and the Powers were all on the side of the will of Charles II.

5. This seems to be unfair to William.

Et trahit, et terret, servat, frænatque, domatque.
Cives, Odryßos, propria, regna, Batavos.
Relligione, manu, studiis, victricibus armis.
Patris, Avi, Proavum, Cæsaris, atque Suis.

THE ELECTOR OF BAVARIA

had for its object the aggrandisement of the House of Austria itself. The Elector of Bavaria was then in Brussels, the seat of Government of the Circle of Burgundy. He foresaw the danger with which Germany was threatened, but it was within neither his power nor his duty to attempt to thwart the principals concerned in this matter. He knew the spirit of unrest of some and the weakness of others, and he rightly feared the consequences.

Every day the highest dignitaries of the Empire besought him to return to his own territory, as he was regarded as a prince capable of leading those who were opposed to the violent policy with which Germany was threatened by the Court of Vienna, backed by England and Holland.

In the end he listened to them, and returned to Munich, his capital town. Scarcely had he got back to his own State, when the Swabian and Franconian Circles proposed that he should join in a treaty that they had already made among themselves, prohibiting the signatories from joining in any foreign war. They pressed him to take up arms with them, in order to resist any power that might wish to force them to join the alliance against France.

Their troops would then give confidence to such of the princes who were in favour of tranquillity within the Empire, and the Elector daily received assurances of fidelity to the proposed treaty from the principal groups. The Elector of Mayence, chief of the Circles of the Lower Rhine and Franconia, had already signed one at Heilbronn, under which the Elector of Bavaria would be bound to spare neither care nor expense, in order to have a body of troops ready to move to the succour of whichever ally was in danger of attack, and sufficient to ensure his own country from invasion.

During these negotiations the army of the emperor invaded Italy, which decided England and Holland to take the field against France and Spain.[6]

Prince Eugene surprised a detachment of French troops 1,500 strong, which he entirely defeated on July 9th, 1701,[7] when the Marquis de Cambout, brigadier-general of the king's army, and the Chevalier d' Albert, the son of the Duke de Chevreuse, were killed. After this a revolution broke out in Naples in favour of the archduke, but it was put down by the Viceroy. There could no longer be any doubt but that the emperor was determined to take violent measures against those who would not espouse his cause, for his Allies—the English

6. War was not declared by England till the 4th May, 1702.

and Dutch—now seized by his orders several fortresses belonging to the Elector of Cologne and the Dukes of Brunswick and Wolfenbüttel, although none of these had done more than take the necessary measures to remain neutral.

During this time certain other princes supported a less stringent policy, and sold their troops to the emperor and the Dutch; the Circles of Swabia and Franconia, which hitherto had seemed so resolute, now began to waver, and the Court of Vienna, evidently desirous of their co-operation, spared neither pains nor money to secure their help, and ultimately succeeded. In consequence of this, the Diet of Ratisbon decided for the emperor, and the verdict of the Three Colleges [8] of the Empire was to declare conjointly with His Imperial Majesty and his Allies war against France, in order to dethrone the King of Spain. It was then that the destiny of the Elector of Bavaria, who had no intention of taking part in this war, was determined.

He was surrounded by powerful enemies, and his timorous friends abandoned him day by day. His policy had been discussed at the Ratisbon Conference, but the emperor took care to insist that he should join his forces to those of the Empire. This order of the emperor obliged him to take a definite course. The choice only remained to him, either to be the ally of the emperor and make war against the Duke of Anjou, son of his dearly loved sister, or to join the King of France, and support his nephew on the Spanish throne, which had fallen legitimately to him. Things were in this state when M. de Ricous, whom the king had sent to the Elector of Bavaria, was enabled to bring the Prince to a decision on this point.

He declared himself in favour of France, and promised to employ his forces to support Philip V. These, then, were the causes which led to the war, and the reasons which induced the Elector to ally himself with the king by a secret treaty of which I now give the substance:—

(1) That the Elector, in taking the part of France and Spain, should not bear the onus of declaring war against the emperor, or make overt act of hostility against his troops or fortresses; but that under the pretext of maintaining the neutrality which he

---

7. At Carpi, on the Adige.

8. The Imperial Diet was divided into three colleges—the first consisted of the seven Electors with the emperor as their president, the second of the hereditary Princes and Prince-Bishops of the Empire, and the third of the representatives of the Free Cities.

had engaged himself to keep with the Swabian and Franconian Circles, he should seize the principal strongholds of Swabia and give out that his only intention was to ensure the defence of the country against the invasion threatened by the Conference of Ratisbon.

(2) That he should complain of the conduct of these Circles, inasmuch as they had abandoned the neutrality agreed upon with him, and thus laid him open to the wrath of the Court of Vienna.

(3) That nevertheless he should still propose an agreement with them, if they would revoke their treaty with the emperor, and keep to that made with him in the first instance.

(4) That he should show them that the only means of enjoying peace in their provinces was to ally themselves closely with him, and for his part he would promise to use his troops and power for their mutual defence.

(5) That if the Circles would not accept these propositions, he would seize their fortresses, so as to secure the communications with Alsace, and establish magazines for the sustenance of the French army.

(6) That the principal town seized should be Ulm, as being the most suitable place of defence in the province of Swabia. The possession of this Hanseatic town would render it easy to seize the rest of the province as far as the Black Mountains, which separate Alsace from the Empire; the magazines and munitions therein would be useful to facilitate the junction of the army of France with that of the Elector of Bavaria.

(7) That this place being one of the strongest in the Empire, the result of a siege would be an uncertain quantity, considering the favourable chances of its relief. Under these circumstances, the first opportunity should be taken to seize it by stratagem.

(8) That after the capture of this town, it should not be a difficult matter for the Elector to overpower the rest before the emperor could collect his troops to prevent it, and being once master of Swabia, he should advance as far as the Black Mountains to cover the arrival of the reinforcements that the king would in the meantime do all he could to send him.

(9) That if by some mischance the French force was not able

to push so far forward when the Elector appeared, or that he should find himself obliged to postpone the expedition and take another course, that the prince should effect his conquest of the Circles without oppressing the population, always under the pretext of preserving neutrality and guarding his States from invasion.

(10) That in case the emperor began operations by open hostility against Bavaria, the Elector, who would be in possession of numerous fortresses outside his own State, should defend himself and immediately attack without ceremony any of the Austrian fiefs and territories of the Empire; that he should exact winter quarters for his men, and subsidies from the conquered countries, and, independently of what he might be able to raise thereby, France would always advance the sums necessary for the maintenance of the considerable army corps that he had mobilised.

(11) That in order to prevent the emperor from destroying the Elector with an overpowering force before the junction of the French Army, the king would take care to make a diversion on the German frontier with his principal force, over and above that employed for the reinforcement of the Elector.

(12) Finally, that they would work together to their common interest when making conquests in the Empire, and that these should be shared and divided conveniently to both the king and the Elector. But if, when all these precautions had been taken and acted upon, God saw fit to dispose otherwise, and the Imperial forces gained possession of the Bavarian States, France and Spain bound themselves to recompense the Elector with full sovereignty over the Burgundian States or over the Spanish Low Countries, on the same footing as he possessed the States of Bavaria.

This treaty was ratified by the king, and nothing remained but to carry it out as secretly as possible.

This became the duty of the Marquis de Ricous. He managed the matter with so much capacity and tact in all its varied phases, that he was beloved and protected by Bavaria equally with France. The Elector pressed upon him the commission of a lieutenant-general in his army, and always had the greatest confidence in his counsel. France had never before found herself in such a favourable position for making war upon her enemies; not only could she count upon being able to keep Philip V. upon his Spanish throne, but it seemed as if the stubbornness of the House of Austria would furnish her with the best of opportunities for fresh conquests. For what could one not expect after the war just concluded by the Peace of Ryswick? The whole universe had borne witness to the power of France.

This monarchy had fought singlehanded with almost the whole of Europe leagued against her, and had been victorious. I say this, as the whole Germanic body—England, Holland, Spain, Portugal, and Savoy—had combined forces against Louis XIV., and this prince had invariably defeated them. France now thus found herself in a very favourable position, for she had just added to her forces those of Spain, Portugal, Savoy, Bavaria, and of Cologne, which had made a private treaty in her favour.

What hopes for Philip V. and for the aggrandisement of our king!

M. de Ricous told me, after our return to France, that the article in the treaty giving the Elector the Spanish Low Countries, in the event of his own country being taken from him, was inserted more as a matter of form than in any real fear of such a calamity; and truly, judging by appearances, one quite expected to see Bavaria in a very short time become a powerful State.

The Elector soon got his troops into a condition to carry out the treaty just concluded, and M. de Ricous, anxious to increase their number, took the opportunity to raise a regiment of Frenchmen in the centre of Bavaria. After the Peace of Ryswick the king had made so great a reduction of his army that numbers of discharged soldiers left France for other kingdoms where wars still lingered. Some betook themselves to the Elector of Brandenburg, others joined the forces of the Emperor then attacked by the Turk; but these unfortunates, driven from their country by necessity, no sooner learnt that there was an ambassador from their king in Bavaria who gave passports back to France by way of Switzerland, than desire to see their country again and renew their service in its ranks brought them in numbers to Munich.

M. de Ricous, fearing for the fate of these men on the journey that they had laid out for themselves, looked for means to keep them in Bavaria. He proposed to the Elector that a regiment for the king should be raised, with a high rate of pay, so as to induce these wanderers to join as soon as possible, and (as it was hardly yet time to throw off the mask) that this corps should be called the Prince's Foreign

Guard, in the same way that the Swiss form the Foreign Guard of the King of France. To save appearances, it was to consist of the same establishment as the Bavarian Guard, three battalions, of which the first were grenadiers; no company should consist of less than one hundred men, and it should do duty as belonging to the Elector until the occasion presented itself for handing it over to the king. This project met with the Elector's entire approbation, as tending to the common interest of the two countries. He wrote at once to the court, and the king's sanction was obtained.

It was then that M. de Ricous bethought himself of me. The king gave him a free hand in the selection of officers for this regiment; he was also to commission them by the Elector's authority, it being understood that they were duly presented to the prince for his approbation.

Having this authority, the idea struck him of reserving this regiment for himself and calling it after his own name. He kept this part of the plan quite quiet, as he wished to wait until the establishment was complete, in order to avoid giving rise to any suspicions of working for his own ends rather than those of the prince. He contented himself with proposing me to the Elector as lieutenant-colonel and commanding officer until the three battalions had completed their establishment. "Then," said he, "would be the time to look about for someone to appoint as colonel," as it did not appear to be so certain that the 2,000 men necessary for this scheme would be forthcoming. He added that this kind of regiment was not always a success, owing to the difficulty of keeping the men in hand, and that he had seen a similar regiment raised in France for M. de Tessé give such endless trouble to those in command, owing to the murders, robberies, brigandage, and absence of discipline, that it had to be disbanded shortly after its formation.

As the same thing might occur in this case, he suggested that it would be prudent to save the expense of a complete staff until it should be seen how the corps comported itself. In the meantime it was absolutely necessary it should have a chief who would be able to control it, and he assured the Elector that he knew of no one better fitted for the post than I was. In order that the matter should not appear premeditated, he begged His Highness to give me the command of a company of dragoons in his own army, which I could take over on my arrival and command until there were enough recruits to form a battalion.

73

The Marquis de Ricous, having obtained the Elector's assent to my appointment, informed me that the friendship he had always preserved for me since he had known me encouraged him to profit by an opportunity which had presented itself to do me a service; that I must accept this information in good faith, without demanding details of the matter he was interesting himself in, as it was impossible to put them on paper; it was simply a question of joining him at once at Munich. If I agreed to come without further consideration, I should have no reason to regret the step, and he himself counselled me to do so. In this case I should have to take the Soleure road to Switzerland, where I should find the Marquis de Puisieux, the ambassador of the king, who would hand me a passport to facilitate my entrance into Germany.

This letter filled me with an infinite joy, although there was something about it which seemed to weigh upon my mind. The idea of leaving the kingdom was distasteful to me, and this led me to say in my answer to M. de Ricous that although I had every confidence in his friendship, he would do me a real pleasure if he could possibly let me know more of the service he had been kind enough to forward for me in Bavaria. However, should this not be in his power, I was ready to carry out his wishes, and in the meantime was arranging my affairs so as not to lose a moment in setting out on the receipt of his answer. As a matter of fact, I received a second letter from him, which, though equally pressing in its nature, did not give me more details than the first; so I started with my horses and one servant, who knew a little of the German tongue, as there are no posting arrangements or carriages to be found on the road to Soleure.

THE CAMPAIGN OF 1702

I set out from Bordeaux in the beginning of July in the year 1702, throwing lawsuits and procedure to the winds, without a thought for the consequences, as matters not worth consideration. My adversaries did not fail to add to their scribblings that my departure was a flight from the kingdom, and they worked at this point to such purpose that they actually obtained considerable damages against me. Although I was only condemned by default, after the interval prescribed by law they issued a warrant against me which brought me very serious trouble on my return to Bordeaux from Bavaria, as I shall relate afterwards in its proper place.

The road from Bordeaux to Soleure is a very unfrequented one; it is a mere chance if the traveller meets with a companion to share its solitude. As it turned out, I was quite alone for a distance of one hundred and forty leagues. The first person I met was the military police officer of Franche-Comté, with whom I supped in a little town called Bellegarde, situated on the river Saône. We talked over my journey and the best route to take. He told me that the shortest and best was by Salins, at the further end of Franche-Comte, and that I ought to avoid Bâle, where I had already arranged to go. I resolved to follow his advice, and next morning, after we had ridden three leagues together, he put me upon my road wishing me good luck. I had no suspicions of so obliging an individual; but as a matter of fact, imagining he had discovered in me a religionist flying to Switzerland, he hurried on to Salins by a different road. He there warned the deputy-governor of the citadel to arrest me, assuring him that in his conversation with me he had extracted sufficient evidence to prove that I was escaping from the kingdom on account of my religious principles.

Thus they did me the honour to await my arrival in the town in all impatience, and next morning, just as I had finished my dinner, an emissary arrived at my inn, and entered into conversation with me in order to assure himself more positively of my intentions. This gentleman approached me politely with the story that he had just had the good luck to hear that I was going to Soleure, and he begged me to be good enough to allow my servant to take charge of a small parcel that he wished to send to his brother, who was secretary to the Embassy in that town.

Owing to the compliments in which he wrapped up his request, I pledged myself to deliver the parcel myself, and thus we drifted into a general conversation. As I gave somewhat reserved answers to certain questions that he put me, and being moreover prejudiced, he had no doubt as to the opinion that the provost-lieutenant had formed of me, and on leaving me, he went direct to him and told him that there was only just time to arrest me, as I was about to start on my journey again. Shortly afterwards ten or twelve officers entered my room—as I thought, about more commissions for Soleure; but the most important amongst them, with an air of severity, asked me who I was, and why I was leaving the kingdom, whilst the rest surrounded me to listen to my answer.

I began to smile, and without betraying any emotion replied that I hardly knew enough of him to justify me in confiding to him the object of my journey. He was not much pleased with my answer, and putting on a still fiercer air, asked me to have the goodness to answer him with a good grace, or I should probably have reason to repent my conduct.

"Since when, sir," replied I, "has France declared war on the Swiss, and decreed that I should give you a reason why I betake myself to that country? What does it matter to you what I do, seeing that I have no designs upon your citadel? Forsooth, don't let your nerves be upset by my little stay in your town, as I am this moment about to continue my journey."

"Softly," said he. "You are not setting off just yet, so it please you. From your appearance, I am rather of the opinion that your stay here will be longer than you think. We know who you are and why you are trying to escape from the kingdom, and if you persist in hiding your intentions, give up all hope of mercy. In order to convince you, I will have you searched, and we shall then see if the laugh is all on your side."

This threat made me smile more mischievously than before. I then told him that even if I had anything to repent of and to ask indulgence for, I could not bring myself to believe that he was a man of sufficient importance to be able to grant it. My determined manner ought to have shown him his mistake; but so infatuated was he that he then and there ordered my portmanteau to be brought in; his men emptied it, rummaged out the last article therein, and then finding nothing to satisfy them, came towards me with the intention of treating me likewise.

"It is a pity, gentlemen," said I to them, "that you do not happen to be custom-house clerks, for you seem to know their business to perfection."

"You would do better, sir, if you were not always joking," said the chief of the troop to me. "We are now going to see if you will not change your tune, so set to and search this gentleman."

"Gently," I answered, with a serious air. "What right have you to search me? I only recognise the king's order."

"Very well, I order it to be done in the king's name, and according to his ordinances."

At this they sprang upon my pockets and drew therefrom various letters, amongst others, one from M. de Ricous, which happened to be the first one they opened; and the whole troop closed round with impatient murmurs to hear it read. According to them, the proofs of their suspicion were at hand, but they were far from being satisfied after all.

The address of the letter astonished them, but when they had read it right through, and saw the complimentary terms in which an ambassador of the king addressed on my behalf another ambassador at Soleure, with whom they were well acquainted, they entirely changed countenance; and passing from one extreme to another, they made such exaggerated apologies that they inspired me with feelings of the greatest contempt, accusing the provost-lieutenant and his emissary of having taken them in. For my part, I only thought of mounting my horse, whilst they wished me a happy journey and the best of futures.

I continued my journey to Soleure without any further incident, and at once called upon the Marquis de Puisieux, who would not hear of my lodging elsewhere but at his own house. He, owing to M. de Ricous' instructions, had in readiness for me my passport as a captain of dragoons in the Elector's service, signed with that Prince's own hand, with which I ought to have been able to pass the German frontier. M. de Ricous begged the *marquis* to examine it, and should it not be sufficient in itself, to add anything that would ensure my safe passage. The emperor had begun to take umbrage at the neutrality of the Elector, and if by chance I had been arrested, my detention would probably have lasted some considerable time, which M. de Ricous, with his particular consideration for me, wished to avoid.

Such a recommendation from him weighed so much with the Marquis de Puisieux that he gave great attention to all his demands; but his anxiety to take every precaution under these circumstances so confused him that it caused him to think of expedients that turned out to be just as bad as his intentions were good. Moreover, as M. de Ricous in sending the passport had directed that further precautions should be taken, this made us both suspicious of its validity. Hence in our uncertainty, we consulted together day after day what should be done, and the more we talked the greater appeared the obstacles to our designs. I was nearly a fortnight at Soleure, and then my business was no further advanced than on the day of my arrival. Had I only known German, things would have been much easier for me. I could then have found some disguise, and so got through, but I did not know a word; and my valet's knowledge of that tongue was not enough for me to risk such a metamorphosis, which would have rendered my case a criminal one had I been caught.

I could think of nothing, when Madame de Tibergeaut, sister of the Marquis de Puisieux, got us out of the fix. She was a lady of standing and of much sense, and was staying with her family in Soleure, in order to keep her brother company, owing to his advanced age.

As the emperor also had an ambassador in Switzerland residing at Baden, where I should have to pass, we arranged that I should tell him that I was a gentleman of the suite of the Prince of Auvergne (who three months before had left France owing to some disagreement), who had sent me to his estates in Périgord to collect from his agents certain sums due to him, which I was to hand to him in Venice; then, having ordered me to join him at once, he had sent me a passport from the Elector of Bavaria, which had been obtained for me at the request of his aunt, the Princess Maxse; but fearing that this passport might not be sufficient, he directed me to ask the ambassador to oblige the prince by endorsing it, or to give me one of his own.

If the ambassador refused to do this, as was quite possible, owing to the existing antipathy to the French nation, I was to ask him point-blank for permission to have one sent him for me direct from the emperor, and to say that I intended to stay in Baden for it. It was hoped that by this second demand he would rest assured that I did not mean to continue my journey at once, and would abandon any idea that he might have of having me arrested on the frontier, but that nevertheless I should secretly start off and get into Germany before he had warning of my departure.

This arrangement being settled upon, I left Soleure as much regretted by the entire family of the Marquis de Puisieux as if I had really belonged to it. Three days later I arrived at Baden at ten o'clock in the morning, put up at the first inn that I came across, and after dining, directed my valet to take my horses outside the town, and to wait for me on the road I proposed to take. I then hastened to present myself to the Baron de Troschmandorf, and laid before him most respectfully the story and scheme we had agreed upon, but only got rudeness offered me in return. He curtly told me in a brutal manner that he was not in the habit of putting his signature on other people's passports, still less on those of a foreign country. I then begged him to arrange for one to be sent me to his care from His Imperial Majesty, and told him that I should stay in Baden until it arrived; he made no answer to this, and left me to let myself out of his house in a most humiliating way.

I did not lose a moment, but made off at once to join my horses, determined not to spare them in my flight, even if they died of exertion. I marched without a halt all the rest of that day, and was surprised by night in so deserted a part of the country that I could see but one solitary house with a miserable-looking barn alongside of it.

I inquired of an old woman, who, attracted by the noise of the horses, had appeared at a window, whether there was any chance of arriving soon at some town or village where I could put up. She declared that it was more than two leagues to the next village, and offered to give us shelter if we liked. Night was coming on, my horses were done up, so I was forced to sleep in this miserable place, which had far more the air of a robber's retreat than of an hostelry.

Next morning I pulled myself together to make up for lost time on the road, with such effect that two days later I arrived at a large village called Rochart, situated on the shore of Lake Constance. This lake is about fifteen leagues in length, by six in breadth, and separates Switzerland from Germany. The source of the Rhine is above, on the southern side in the Grison Mountains, and it flows through the middle of the lake without mingling its waters. This river as far as the lake is so shallow that it can be forded on horseback in any season or weather. Rochart is near the upper part of the lake, and is not on the ordinary road; but chance had caused me to take this route instead of that of Constance at the lower end, which is the usual one and shorter withal.

This mistake of mine was a happy one for me, as the road is less frequented, and they were not so particular in examining travellers who entered Germany from this side as they were on the high road. Mine host where I put up was a Genevese, who, to my joy, spoke French, so I was enabled to go into the question myself as to the best means of passing the frontier. I had called myself a Lorrainer since quitting my ambassador at Baden. This was according to the advice of Madame de Tibergeaut, who told me that people from that province were always welcomed in Germany, and my host, who believed me, appeared to have conceived quite an affection for me.

He told me that I had the choice of two roads to enter the Empire, and that the one leading to the lake (to cross which he could let me have a good boat) would be the easiest for the horses, and would bring me to the town of Lindau, opposite Rochart. He did not, however, advise me to take this, as since the declaration of war against France the Governor had become distrustful of all entering his town, and though I was a Lorrainer some difficulty would certainly crop up owing to my ignorance of the language.

To be on the safe side I ought to take the other road alongside of the lake for about three leagues beyond Rochart, till I came to the Rhine. "You can pass the river at a ford," said he, "without the least danger, and rest yourself at a village called Reineck, about five leagues from here, belonging to the Swiss. Thence you will not have to go more than two leagues to reach the town of Bregenz, which is the first town you come to belonging to the Empire. I have not heard whether there is a garrison there yet, nor whether any difficulty is made as to passage of travellers, as it is a cross-road which does not lead to any district of importance. As soon as you have passed this town," continued he, "you will find yourself in the flat country of Swabia, where no one will question you. You will certainly lengthen your journey by four or five leagues, but you will be freed from anxiety."

I gave my host my very best thanks and followed his advice, which, though not devoid of drawbacks, was not the less safe.

I took the road by Bregenz, and by three o'clock in the afternoon had passed through the town without meeting a soul, either in the streets or at the gates, and was delighted to find myself in the open country without any trouble.

The fears which had haunted me ever since leaving Soleure now vanished, and I went on my way rejoicing. After a time the high road gradually led right down to the shore of the lake among a number of rocks, which appeared to have been quarried, so that it might pass between the shore and the mountains; but less than half a league further on it became so narrow that I began to have misgivings. These increased when I saw a large arch, like a carriage entrance, with a gate and a sentry, barring the road from the cliff to the lake. At this sight my joy entirely gave place to sinister presentiments, and I presented myself at the gate with an air of depression rather than dignity. The sentry challenged me with a loud "*Verado*" (*wer da?*), signed to me to halt, and called up his lieutenant, who was in command of a guard posted by the side of the gate. This officer set to work to question me in German, but not understanding a word he said, I told my valet to answer for me; when hearing me speak French, and understanding my difficulty, he ordered the corporal of the guard to act as interpreter.

I told him I was from Lorraine, and that I had a passport as captain of dragoons written in Latin, which I showed him.

At the mention of Lorraine the corporal became quite effusive, saying that he also came from that part, and I also expressed the joy I felt in meeting a countryman, and started questioning him on my own account.

The lieutenant, who was told by the corporal that I was one of his neighbours at home, seeing our mutual recognition and friendship, believed that we were comrades of long standing; he went off to the guard-room without taking any further trouble regarding my personality, and simply ordered the corporal to take me before the commandant. I asked where it was necessary to go for this. "To the town you came from," said my Lorrainer, "and you must retrace your steps. So few strangers arrive by the way you entered it that a guard there is found unnecessary; had there been one, you would not have had the trouble of going twice over the same road, for you would have been brought before the *commandant.*" I proposed that we should do without this ceremony, but he said that this was quite impossible, as his officer would be punished if he granted me such a favour; on the other hand, he would gladly accompany me and interpret for me.

"In return for that, my fellow-countryman," said I, "I should like to stand you a drink before we part," and as we set off I pressed a crown in his hand and assured him that there was another for him where that came from on our return.

This mark of my appreciation caused him to interest himself strongly in my affair, and I saw that he was disposed to do all he could to oblige me. On the way I inquired how it was that a guard was posted at this place and for how long this had been the case. Said he:

"A very short time, the declaration of war against France is the reason of it. Information has been received that a number of French soldiers are deserting from the Imperial army, and under cover of passports from their ambassador at Munich, are taking this road, which was unguarded, in order to escape into the Grison Mountains and thence to France. Three or four companies of infantry, who occupy three or four passes, have been posted to cut them off, with orders to refuse quarter to any that may be captured; for this deceitful nation is so hated by all, especially by Germany, that if unhappily you chanced to be a Frenchman instead of from Lorraine you would be arrested, notwithstanding your passport, and run the risk of wasting away for a very long time in the dungeons of Bregenz. Who would then be able to find you out in a town so far from the main roads and merchants' routes? But being a Lorrainer, it is just the same as if you were a German; you will be sent on without troubling you to get off your horse."

"I fear," said I to him, "lest some difficulty may arise owing to my passport being in Latin."

"Don't be afraid," replied my corporal. "I am sure he won't understand it, but I shall just say that you are one of my friends, and that will settle it."

As a matter of fact, having arrived at the *commandant's* door, the corporal took my passport, and the next moment I saw him reappear with a smiling countenance. Said he: "Here we are, countryman, you can go as soon as you like to the uttermost parts of Germany." This last remark completely restored tranquillity to my mind; for notwithstanding all the assurances he had given me, I felt that my fate hung in the balance until my passport had been accepted. I returned with my companion to his guardhouse, where we mutually reiterated protestations of warm friendship, and most welcome to him was the doubloon I presented him with, according to my promise. Finally, he pointed out to me all the places I should pass on my road to Munich, and shook me heartily by the hand when we parted.

CHAPTER 5

Defeat of Generals Schlick and Stirum

I arrived at Munich on August 15th, and was there received by the Marquis de Ricous in the most friendly manner possible. He wished, before presenting me to the Elector, to inform me of his purpose in bringing me to this country. In making me acquainted with the matter in all its detail, he showed me his confidential information, not excepting that of the Embassy and its negotiations, all of which he had the goodness to tell me without the slightest hesitation. I thus learnt the special articles in the treaty between the king and the Elector. He then pointed out to me the difficulties I might have in maintaining discipline in the regiment he proposed to raise, such as had been found in M. de Tessé's case, adding that he was sure that I would bring to bear every means to this end; finally, I was not to become impatient because the affair had got no further in its development, as, until the emperor declared war upon the Elector, it was impossible to advertise in the Imperial army for French recruits.

He was certain that the formation of this corps would precipitate matters, whatever precautions we took not to arouse suspicions by any act on the part of the Elector. The Court of Vienna, accustomed to act with vigour, would not hesitate to pour its army into Bavaria immediately that of the Elector showed itself in the Swabian Circle, which would then be the time to distribute notices to invite the French in the Imperial service to enlist in the new regiment, point being made of the additional pay given therein. The study of all these conditions was absolutely necessary to the success of our projects, because since the emperor had caused the passes into Switzerland and the Grisons to be watched, the deserters did not dare to leave the Empire, not knowing which road to take. Above all it was necessary to maintain absolute secrecy, to which end I was appointed to a company of dragoons which bore my name, and which I was to take over just as if I had no other object.

After M. de Ricous had given me full instructions on all he thought most important, he presented me to the Elector in such a favourable light that the prince received me with all the grace of manner which to him was so natural. The latter had the kindness to converse for a long time with me, and appeared pleased with the frank nature of my answers. I lost no opportunity of attending his court during my stay in Munich, though this was but a short one, as I was obliged to join my regiment to make the acquaintance of my company and make ready to start on the famous raid on the town of Ulm. This was one of the boldest and best arranged affairs ever seen, and was absolutely vital to the proper execution of the treaty.

To lay siege to a fortified town of this description was a doubtful business, the best means, therefore, to attain our end was to surprise it by some stratagem, for though the Elector's army was strong, it was not strong enough to invest the town and at the same time provide against the relieving force that the Empire would certainly send. An immense siege train—necessary in an affair of such importance—would have had to have been prepared far from its objective, and, under the circumstances, would have demanded much thought and work. Moreover, it was impossible for the Elector to make such preparations so secretly that the Viennese Court, which watched all his movements, should not discover his purpose and take measures to prevent it. On the other hand, should the attempt fail, a formal siege could be undertaken as a last resource, so it was decided to be less dangerous to attempt a surprise.

The plan was designed by the Sieur de Beckmant, lieutenant-colonel of the Elector's Guards, a most intelligent as well as brave man, who was placed in command. All those connected with the expedition preserved an inviolable secrecy, and preferred the glory of such an enterprise, however dangerous, to the rewards with which the Empire would have recompensed those who might have betrayed it.

The Elector of Bavaria was admirably served, but the enterprise cost poor Beckmant his life. A townsman having attacked him, one of our people in trying to rescue him wounded him accidentally. From the effects of this he died some time after.

The town of Ulm was garrisoned by its inhabitants with as much care and precision as if they were regular troops. All the guard-houses in the fortifications and outworks were properly provided with fusiliers, organised in regiments and companies, and the same order and attention was paid to all duties as would be observed by the most efficient garrison. Ulm is a Hanseatic town and independent; hence its defence was in its own hands.

Beckmant had selected a hundred officers of approved fidelity to second him.

They dressed themselves up as sheep or cattle dealers, corn and beer merchants, and sellers of salt and tin ware; others, again, as Savoyards, and each was accompanied by attendants and boys.

They entered the town by different gates, and lodged in prearranged quarters, only armed with small pistols and daggers. They agreed not to recognise one another should they meet in the streets, and held themselves prepared to act on September 8th, the day of Our Lady, this being the date fixed by the Elector for the execution of the enterprise.

By early morning, according to the Elector's plan, all were to converge by different roads upon the bridges and march up to the outermost barrier on the glacis of the gate whose capture had been determined upon. As soon as this barrier had been opened and the keys brought to the main guard, they were to seize the arms of the guard and cut the throats of all who attempted any resistance.

It was arranged that at this juncture fifty other officers, disguised as peasants carrying chickens, eggs, hay, and other things, should enter and join their comrades. Whilst these hundred and fifty officers thus secured the interior gate, the bridges, and outside barricades, three regiments of dragoons, concealed during the night as near as possible to this point, were to leave their horses at the instant the signal was given, enter the town, and occupy the two bastions flanking the gate itself. They were to entrench themselves securely until the arrival of the infantry, and thus effect the surrender of the burghers and the keys of the town to the Elector.

I therefore left Munich to join my regiment, which was detailed for this expedition and then quartered on the frontier of Swabia, twenty-five French leagues from Ulm, the two other regiments being not much less distant. The distance had to be covered in a single night, in order to find ourselves close to the gate before daybreak.

The commanding officers only knew the object and the roads to be taken, as there was always the fear of some deserter carrying the news. The regimental orders for September 7th were simply to saddle the horses at six p.m. to be ready to march fully armed, carrying only a few oats. Half an hour later the start was made. We took different roads, to avoid checks in the defiles, and rode at a fast trot all night. A grenadier had been ordered to ride behind each dragoon, but it ultimately became impossible to carry them as far as the rendezvous.

We were lucky enough to arrive close to Ulm well before daybreak. We reconnoitred the ground, and posted ourselves noiselessly in a convenient spot by the river Danube, which runs near the walls of the place, where some rising ground afforded us a capital shelter.

Notwithstanding all our precautions, the sentries on the ramparts would have seen us when day broke had we not been favoured with a thick fog, which rose from the river and increased with the daylight. The *burghers* would not open the last of the glacis gates until it was light enough to distinguish objects in the country beyond, and our three regiments of dragoons occupied two much space to be altogether covered from the view of the rampart sentries. In fact, all our designs would have been upset had it not been for the fog, which is an ordinary occurrence on the Danube at this season; not only on account of the sentries, but also because we should have been discovered by the peasants on their way to the market which took place that day, notwithstanding it being a holiday. These people are Lutherans, and make no distinction between one day and another.

Daylight appeared, and the burghers opened the outermost gate, and perceiving nothing to raise their suspicions, returned their arms to the guardhouse and handed in the keys. Then our people lost no time; some threw themselves upon the *burghers*, and despatched with *poignard* and pistol those who offered resistance, while others held the bridges and gates to facilitate the entrance of our dragoons, to whom the pistol-shots had served as signals.

We at once abandoned our horses and made a dash for the bridges and gates, though it was by the merest chance that the whole business did not miscarry just at the moment when everything seemed in our favour. Two of our disguised officers luckily overheard a *burgher* tell another to run quickly and let down the portcullis of the principal gate, but they followed and killed him. Otherwise all our efforts might have been in vain, and we should have been obliged to retire rather more quickly than we should have liked, for this passage once closed, the *burghers* would have been under arms in an instant, and the artillery on the ramparts would have opened fire upon us.

Our people were still struggling with the *burghers*, whose numbers were increasing, when our dragoons entered. They succeeded in clearing out the guardhouse and its neighbourhood, gave chase to those who were inclined to oppose them, and they soon manned the two bastions right and left of the gate.

We cut a trench in no time across the street abutting thereon, and entrenched ourselves without delay to resist any efforts made by the *burghers* to turn us out and retake the gate we had just captured; in fact, so quickly was this completed, that we were entrenched before the inhabitants were enabled to rally and reassemble.

They were astounded at what had happened, and ran about in utter confusion, without knowing what to do or where to stop. However, they closed the other gates, and after they had pulled themselves together and saw the works we had just constructed, came to the conclusion that we were not of sufficient force to render ourselves complete masters of the town. They wished to make the most of their position to turn us out; they stretched chains as barricades across all the streets which led to our entrenchments, placed in position there a number of pieces of cannon, and when they had completed these preparations, and so secured the safety of the inner part of their town, they occupied the attics and roofs of the houses which commanded us, and opened fire from loopholes made among the tiles.

Immediately this began we lost quite a number of our men, including several in my own company, and it was a mere chance that I was not amongst them myself, for a ball passed through the brim of my hat and killed a dragoon standing behind me. So bad was our case that we were obliged to set about the construction of *epaulements* to provide cover as quickly as possible, and my previous experience in fortification here proved of the greatest use to me. Notwithstanding our efforts, however, the position we were in became so critical that I really do not know how matters would have turned out had not our commanding officer, Count de Feldz (a lieutenant-general and colonel of one of the dragoon regiments), bethought him of warning the *burghers* that if they did not cease their fire upon us he would instantly set light to the town at every point of the compass, and that the Elector, whose arrival he momentarily expected, would put them all to the sword, not excepting even the women and children.

These threats (and that of the fire was no mere threat) completely terrorised them, so much so that they laid down their arms and begged for mercy. Nay, they even sent us provisions, of which we stood in great need, and assured us that when His Highness did arrive they would surrender, present him with the keys, and in every way behave as if they were his own subjects.

Thus we reduced the principal fortress in Swabia, a most important factor in the designs of the king and Elector, which finally sealed the treaty drawn up between these two powers.

Three days passed before the Elector with his army appeared before Ulm. The town delegates met him with the keys, and took the oath of fidelity. They were grieved to see their territory handed over to the horrors and chances of war, but they were no longer in a position to make terms, and could only yield to force. In the town was a fine arsenal, provided with all sorts of munitions of war, which proved very useful to the Elector in carrying on his subjection of the province, and facilitating the junction of his army with that of France. It was found necessary to disarm the burghers, and after a good garrison and magazines of provisions had been established in the town to ensure its possession, the Elector continued his march with his army.

To complete our line of communication it became necessary to lay siege to several towns lying between the Black Forest and Ulm, such as Lauingen, Illingen, Munderkingen, Riedhausen, and Biberach, the last of which only offered any resistance. It made a show of sustaining a siege, but a few volleys of cannon shot caused it to see things in the Elector's light.

In these little affairs the Elector found himself embarrassed by the want of engineers, a want which had not been foreseen. His Highness had not felt their want in the previous war when allied with the Emperor, for both the Dutch and the King of England had a sufficient number present with them; besides, his ministers were so ignorant of the science of engineering that they did not foresee the necessity of making provision on this point. There certainly were two or three officers with us who acted as engineers, but they were good for nothing that required originality. M. de Ricous, who saw how little could be expected from these gentlemen, and the pressing need that existed for engineers, brought me to the notice of the Elector as a person capable and experienced in the art. The necessity in which the prince was placed caused him to accept the proposition of my services with the greatest eagerness, and I was then and there ordered to supervise all such duties. This post brought me into much personal contact with His Highness, whereby I received many kindnesses from him, which were continued towards me as long as he lived.

The taking of Biberach opened my eyes to the incapacity of the engineers who served under me. I could do but little to remedy this, but as the sieges we undertook were not of great importance in detail or development, it did not weigh upon me very much.

The operations before this place brought us quite close to the Black Forest, and the Elector despatched six officers of rank, by different routes, some to inform the King of France of our conquests and progress; others to the King of Spain, who was at the head of the army in Italy, and to warn M. de Villars, who commanded that in Alsace, of the route the Elector was taking in order to effect the junction, if the means were offered him to do so. These officers were perfectly well acquainted with the country they had to pass through, its customs and dialects, but they had many difficulties to surmount before they could reach their destination.

When the Elector had seized the town of Ulm, the emperor ordered strict measures to be taken to prevent the passage of travellers unless their passports were specially endorsed; the letters even, which came from the army of the Elector of Bavaria, were stopped and opened. It was extremely important that France should be informed of our dispositions, but impossible to trust such a secret to the medium of paper.

The six officers then set out and did their best to conceal their aim and status; four were lucky enough to get through without accident, but the two others were arrested, namely, the Count Maxe Taufkirken, the Elector's chamberlain, and the Sieur de Locatelli, an Italian by birth, and lieutenant-colonel of *cuirassiers*.

The count was arrested at Bregenz by the same *commandant* who had allowed me to pass so easily, thanks to his corporal, and was placed under such close confinement that he ran the risk of losing his life. If I had only been consulted as to the route they proposed taking, I could have given them some useful information. Locatelli was caught on the frontier of the Canton of Bile, and came off no better than the Bavarian Count'

An important town in Swabia still remained to be besieged by the Elector; this was Memmingen, the inhabitants of which had put it in a state of defence the moment they heard of the surprise of Ulm.

Being a Hanseatic town it was garrisoned by its inhabitants, who were at least as good as regular soldiers. They kept guard at the gates with all precision, worked at repairing the fortifications, and added others in the places thought to be weakest or most exposed to attack.

The Elector, who did not deem it advisable to await the return of his messengers, left Marshal d'Arcko before Biberach with a detachment to hold that position, and moved with the remainder of his army to lay siege to Memmingen. I served with him as engineer-in-chief.

As this town demanded more attention than those we had just taken, I felt it would be necessary to inform myself thoroughly of its situation and the details of its fortifications, but the Elector somewhat impatiently wished to make short work of our attack. He did me the honour to explain to me that he was unwilling to make a long business of this affair lest the Emperor should determine to send a relieving force which might cause the siege to be raised—a possibility which demanded that special care to do nothing which would in the least degree retard the capture of the town.

In any case information and knowledge of the outworks was at least imperative, and no one with us could afford me this, but His Highness thought out a plan of reconnaissance.

Although the inhabitants of Memmingen had taken every precaution against surprise, and were resolved to defend themselves in case of actual attack, the Elector well knew that they would only open fire when they saw their town actually invested in regular form, as they feared to give any pretext for an onslaught or an accusation of having been the first to begin hostilities; this would have given their opponents a free hand in making requisitions upon their country, an eventuality they were much desirous of avoiding.

I should, therefore, run no great risk in entering the town disguised, ostensibly to buy provisions. According to report, I should not be allowed to enter the town itself, as the inhabitants refused entry to all who were not actual citizens, but I might make a circuit of the place, going from gate to gate to attempt this, and thus become acquainted with the strength and weaknesses, if any, of the outworks. Thus proposed the Elector.

"Your Highness," said I to him, "your idea is most excellent. I certainly do not know the language, but this fact shall not prevent your orders being carried out. Give me someone who understands German and French, he will inquire as to the provisions, and I will attend him as his valet."

"You are right," said the Elector, who immediately summoned the Baron de Manteufel, lieutenant in his bodyguard, to whom he gave full instructions. We at once got ourselves up for our parts. I took the dress of a servant with a wallet on the pommel of my saddle and followed Manteufel, who started off to present himself at the first gate of the town we might come to. On our approach we saw numerous burghers on the ramparts, who demanded the reason of our arrival. Manteufel begged them to allow us to enter in order to purchase meat and other provisions; they declared we could not do so at that gate, but might pass round to the other side of the town, where we should find a barrier specially arranged for the ingress and egress of the townspeople, and that there only could we get what we required. They incidentally remarked that since the Elector of Bavaria had encamped in the neighbourhood they were on their guard lest they should give him the same opportunity of treating their town as he had that of Ulm.

We immediately took the road to this barrier, which necessitated our making a circuit of the glacis, and gave me the opportunity of thoroughly examining it.

It was useless to go further, but Manteufel, seeing the docility of the burghers, wished to satisfy his curiosity by making their closer acquaintance, and perhaps pick up some more information as to their intentions. He led the way right up to the barrier, behind which a burgher guard was posted, who at once repeated that we could not enter the town, and when Manteufel told them of his need for provisions, they took his money and sent someone to carry out his commission.

While we waited the return of the messenger, Manteufel started a conversation, and I remained respectfully in the background. These burghers began in their turn to question him, trying to discover somewhat of the Elector's designs. He answered that he did not belong to the army they spoke of, but to a detachment at Biberach, which was short of victuals, and that the Elector would soon withdraw his troops, as he did not wish for war, but was solely anxious to induce them to preserve the neutrality to which they had agreed.

"Oh, that is all very well," cried they, "but they tell us that the Elector means to bring his dogs of Frenchmen to this country. They will not get any quarter from us if they are caught on our frontier, and quite right too, because that accursed nation should be exterminated to the last man."

During the conversation a young man, gun in hand, was examining me attentively, and thinking he recognised in me one of the aforesaid "dogs of Frenchman," cried out in a frenzy of suspicion to Manteufel, "Have you not got one with you now? I am sure that is one. It shan't be said that I haven't killed one, at any rate," and at the same moment he deliberately took aim at me.

"What are you doing? "said Manteufel. "He is only an excellent Italian, who is waiting until I have an opportunity of sending him to Vienna, where he has an uncle in the Emperor's service. As for me, you understand, if I did not think the Elector was friendly to this country I should soon enough leave him to join the Imperial troops and my relations, who are longing to see me. Besides, no one hates the French better than I do, so you can judge if I would have one in my service, and the young man here is of the same way of thinking. Just speak French to him, I am sure he would run away at once."

Thus Manteufel saved my life, risked to satisfy his curiosity, but the young man was so anxious to "tumble me off" my horse, as he called it, that it needed all this explanation to prevent him. At last the provisions arrived and put an end to a conversation which would have caused me considerable perturbation of spirit had I understood German.

We completed the circuit of the town as we left the place, and I had time to make all the notes I required, while Manteufel told me all that had passed, which made me appreciate to the full my obligation.

There was no other building outside the town except a mill situated on a large stream, which I judged would be of the greatest use to us in beginning our principal attack. I rendered a minute report to the Elector, in which I assured him I had found such favourable lines of approach that he might hope to be master of the place in a few days time; and he was so much pleased with my report and entered so thoroughly into all its details, that he made up his mind to see the ground himself.

I took the liberty of pointing out to him that he should not risk exposing himself to a handful of armed *burghers* on the walls, for though they might not deliberately open fire, there was always the fear that they might lose their heads when they saw a troop of armed and mounted men approach the town. "Very well," said His Highness, "I shall only take a page and Ryberck (now Minister of War). At five o'clock this afternoon be at the little gate of my quarters, when we will get away without my suite, or anyone else, being a bit the wiser."

We thus set out as four ordinary civilians, and partly as a necessary precaution, and partly because the high wind pained his eyes, the Elector wore a half-mask, with glasses which enabled him to recognise the various places as I pointed them out to him. So great was his curiosity that he was always in advance of our party, and before we noticed it we were within half a gunshot of the ramparts. Our proceedings soon attracted a number of the *burghers*, one of whom, becoming impatient at seeing our examination of the place, began to abuse us, and eventually so lost his self-control that he took aim at the Elector, declaring that he would smash his "Shrove Tuesday Mask" for him.

Happily a worthy lawyer was of their number, who knocked aside the gun and advised the man to be careful what he was doing, saying that the Bavarians wished for nothing better than to have such a pretext for ravaging their town and lands. But the brute was obstinate and aimed a second time at the Elector, exclaiming that the mask annoyed him, and that he did not care for consequences of any sort. The lawyer, who kept a sharp eye on him, once again prevented him from firing, and thus saved the life of the Elector. It made one tremble to learn from the *burghers*, after the surrender of the town, the risk His Highness had run. Had not the lawyer prevented this single shot the Bavarian War would have come to an end.

Next night we opened our trenches, and employed a great number of workmen to push forward the work as quickly as possible. I had need of the assistance of our engineers; the working parties occupied so great an extent of ground that it was impossible for me to superintend the operations single-handed. I had, nevertheless, personally pegged out all the angles necessary to guide them, but such was their ignorance that they missed them at one point, with the result that in two places the trench was enfiladed by a bastion. The besieged opened fire at these points with two guns, which at their first discharge killed a captain and ten men.

The sensation caused in the trench by this accident attracted me to the spot, and just when I arrived there seven more men were killed. I was in despair at the ignorance of the engineers, which had caused the death of these unlucky men, and I determined to give them my mind on the subject if I caught them, particularly as one of them knew quite enough French to act as interpreter.

In the meantime I busied myself in directing the retirement of those in the enfiladed trench, and ordered *epaulements* to be constructed as rapidly as possible to provide cover.

But the more I hustled them the less was done, and no one understood what I said.

At last an infantry ensign named Kol, who understood French, came up, and saw to the carrying out of my orders most energetically.

His ardour brought him the company commanded hitherto by an officer named Royere, who had just been killed, as I took the liberty of suggesting his promotion to the Elector, who granted him his step.

I dared put no more faith in the engineers after this, and was obliged to superintend every detail of the works myself up to the end of the siege. This brought me plenty of trouble, risk, and fatigue; but the desire to render myself useful made up for all the care and danger.

The town surrendered on the sixth day after the trenches were opened. The delegates who came to arrange the capitulation and hand the keys to His Highness made careful inquiries after the masked individual who had reconnoitred the place the evening before the siege was begun, and recounted to the Elector the risks run by this personage at the hands of a rough member of their community, and the prudence of the lawyer. One could see these delegates shake in their shoes when they learned that it was the Elector himself who had gone through this danger.

The *burghers* were disarmed, and after leaving a good garrison in the place, the Elector retraced his steps to Biberach, in order to await the news from France, and moved his army nearer the frontier, so as to facilitate the return of the officers he had sent as messengers.

The season was somewhat advanced before two of these gentlemen found an opportunity to rejoin our army.

They reported to the Elector that M. de Villars was quite unable to force a passage through, or even attack, the enemy's lines, owing to the precautions they had taken since the capture of Ulm. He was not, therefore, to count upon the junction of the two armies until circumstances altered, but that France would make every effort at the beginning of the next campaign to give the Elector the aid he expected.

The campaign soon after closed, the Elector retired to Munich, and each regiment marched to its winter quarters.

The rapid sequence of conquests that the Elector had just achieved, quite at the end of the campaign, made considerable stir in Germany and the rest of Europe. The whole Germanic body was excited by the Elector's prompt and vigorous action, and although His Highness made several attempts to persuade them that his sole motive was the preservation of neutrality, the Allies, none the less, had their suspicions as to his real intentions.

The Emperor henceforth devoted himself to thinking out the best means of revenge, and reckoned that, without weakening his force on the Alsace frontier, he would be able to collect a considerable army to invade Bavaria and ravage the country. The Allies were the more piqued at the Elector's success, as it detracted from the satisfaction derived from their success at the beginning of the war.

They had taken the towns of Kaiserwert, Landau, Ruremonde, and the citadel of Liege, but their rejoicings over these conquests were rudely interrupted by M. de Villars, then only a lieutenant-general, who won a brilliant victory over the Prince of Baden in the month of October at Friedlingen. The Imperial army was changing position when he attacked; it lost nearly three thousand men, and he pursued the remainder for more than a league from the field of battle.

The campaign at an end, and winter quarters being apportioned, each regiment sought them independently. I then found myself, a solitary Frenchman, in a regiment where it was customary for the officers to hate all of our nation. They were in despair at the campaign the Elector had just made in their own country, and would have much preferred that His Highness should take up arms against France, which they regarded in every way in a hostile light: they had served against her all their lives, and had thus contracted an irreconcilable hatred against her. Many amongst them found it impossible to support any longer a policy so opposed to their sentiments, and Lieutenant-Generals Count Felds, La Tour, and others of mark, left the service of the Elector after the taking of Ulm, and went over to the emperor.

Some officers in our regiment, shaken by these examples, were doubtful as to which side they would take, and I was a subject of execration with them, though there was nothing against me but the original sin of my birth. They went out of their way during our march to afford me every annoyance in their power. A major in a regiment in the Elector's army has more authority than one in the French service, because, whilst he has the control of his own company, he is the third in rank in the corps; and ours, for this reason, had the best of opportunities to pick a quarrel with me.

He was a small man and churlish, eaten up with conceit; and such was his hatred for our nation that a single word of French pronounced in his hearing was sufficient reason to make him leave the best company in the world. He was always looking for a chance to provoke me, but my ignorance of German made it impossible for me to say anything he could take hold of, and consequently he sought for other means less direct.

The only man in my company who understood a little French was the quartermaster, whom I was obliged to employ as my interpreter since the death of my valet from a contagious fever just before leaving Munich. He it was against whom the major directed his attack, finding me so far impervious. To this end, he made it a practice to send for my host whenever we left our billets, in order to ascertain how I and my quartermaster had conducted ourselves; not because it was against the rule in this country to get what you could out of your host (the major, by-the-by, being a past-master in this art), but because he could find no other means of picking a quarrel with me.

At last his opportunity came. One of my hosts admitted under cross-examination that he had supplied several pints of beer to my quarter-master for which he had not asked payment, as he had done it out of pure good nature. This, however, was enough for the major, who had made up his mind that my poor quartermaster was a defaulter, and going up to him at the moment we were making our start, gave him twenty strokes with his stick in my presence, and without a word of explanation to me.

I hardly knew what to think of this outbreak of passion. I knew too little of the customs obtaining amongst these troops to make up my mind on the spot, and it was out of my power to enter into an argument with the major, who immediately after this exhibition of temper had turned on his heel and made off. I asked the quarter-master, whose head was bleeding, what crime he had committed that he should earn so rude a chastisement.

"It is on your account, sir," said he, "that I am guilty, simply because I study to do my duty towards you."

He then proceeded to tell me of the spite these gentlemen entertained towards him since he had acted as my interpreter, and the evil designs they had formed against me. He said that not finding an opportunity of putting into a practical form their antipathy to me, they had turned upon him to make him leave me, and he foresaw to the full all the misery in store for him.

As he spoke it so affected me that I felt I could no longer restrain myself, so I went off on the spot to find the major, and challenged him then and there to fight.

He was astonished at the compliment I paid him, and had not counted upon my coming to so prompt a determination. He made out that his rank gave him the right to beat my quartermaster without giving me any reasons, and I for my part gave him to understand that I was not ignorant of the motive of his bad temper, and that I knew the way to curb it.

He knew quite enough French to understand my remark, for the Elector's troops had served for a long time in the Low Countries, and there was hardly an officer who did not know a little of our language; but as it was not quite to his liking, he made as though he did not hear me, and said something I did not exactly know in German, thinking to embarrass me.

I told him that it was no good pretending not to hear, and that if he did not give me satisfaction I should return to him with my stick the same strokes that he had given my quartermaster; he had the choice between sword or pistol, and a beating.

My determined air made it clear to him that he would have to fight or be dishonoured, so, seeing no help for it, he told me that he would mount his horse for a pistol combat, and that he would join me in the fields outside the village. I lost no time in getting ready to meet him, though he kept me waiting long enough. In fact, I began to have doubts lest his courage had failed him, when I saw him, apparently much upset, draw his pistol while yet some distance away from me, and wheel his horse about evidently uncertain whether he would ride at me or keep on the defensive.

The exhibition he thus made of himself increased my anger ten-fold, so as soon as I saw him carry out this manoeuvre I went straight for him, stood the fire of his first pistol, and then fired mine in my turn; the ball entered his right breast, and damaged some of his ribs. He fell over upon the neck of his horse, more by reason of fear than anything else, and from the grimaces he made I really thought that he was dead.

I then left him to find someone to look after him, and rejoined my company as if nothing had occurred. As for my adversary he had himself taken off to the nearest town to get his wound cured, which turned out to be an easier matter than the soothing of his mortified feelings.

In the meantime, as we were on the march, the senior captain took the major's duty until his wound was cured—a necessary step, as there are no *aide*-majors in these regiments as we have in France. There is certainly an adjutant, but his status does not permit of his giving an order on his own responsibility, and he is there only to see that those of his superiors are carried out. The officer who acted for the major had just as great an aversion for our nation as the major himself, but the accident that had befallen his comrade kept him at least respectful, and he dared not attempt to quarrel with me openly, though, with more regard to nationality than good feeling, he embraced the first opportunity which presented itself of embarrassing me.

It happened that I had a young lackey who had always pleased me, particularly as he understood my ways, and afforded me an opportunity of learning German. A remark I made to this captain that I had an idea of training the boy as a servant after my own notions was sufficient for him to set about seducing him from me. He inspired him with such an aversion for me and my nation that he got him to promise to leave me when the different companies separated to go to their respective winter quarters. The project was well enough conceived, but owing to the impatience of one or the other it came to my knowledge, whereby I had time to avenge myself before it was carried out.

When the time came for the companies to diverge, my lackey did not wait till I was mounted, but went straight off to his new master, under the belief that I should not notice his absence. But as usual with these sort of people who have not the sense to keep their plans to themselves, he had dropped a word here and there before my other servants, with the result that they were quite aware of his intentions; consequently, when I came to mount my horse, it struck me that there was something going on that I did not quite understand. I asked what had become of the little lackey, and the mysterious reply I got roused my suspicion as to his disappearance; but my quarter-master, who never left me, made a show of answering by compulsion, and unfolded the whole plot.

He told me that he had kept his eye upon the boy without being observed, and that he was just about to go off with the captain-major. I made my way at once to the latter's quarters, and found him ready to mount with my lackey by his side. I then seized the youth by the collar, and gave him some good cuts with my whip and whipped him back to my lodgings, telling the captain that I should be back again directly to teach him to entice my servants from me.

I lost no time in mounting, and set off to meet my man, who, I found, had already started; but it did not take me long to catch him up. As soon as he saw me coming he made for the open ground, pistol in hand, although he maintained no bolder a bearing than did his predecessor. As soon as he saw I was within range he hurriedly fired his first shot, and was ready with his second, when I fired in my turn and shot him right through the arm. His pistol dropped to the ground, and he showed the white feather to such an extent that I had half a mind to finish him altogether, had he not cried out to me in the best of French to spare his life. This I accorded him together with a stiff reprimand, and forthwith set off to rejoin my men.

In the distribution of winter quarters the greatest care was shown in assigning the worst to my company, a small village surrounded by a dismal wood in a lonely country was my lot. Five or six miserable peasants inhabited the place—more objects of charity than anything else. To add to the inconvenience, I had to go more than half a league to hear Mass. Moreover, I was at the most distant point of the frontier from Munich—exactly where there was most danger in case of war with the emperor, for the entrance to the kingdom of Bohemia from where I was posted was not more than four leagues distant. I was thus deprived of any opportunity of going to attend the court at Munich, and I found myself obliged to spend the winter in this miserable solitude without any chance of amusement.

The only companion I had was my quartermaster, and making a virtue of necessity, I determined that with his help, and that of a German-French Grammar, I would profit by my imprisonment to learn German. I was not aware at the time that a league away was a little Lutheran town, which belonged to a count of the Holy Empire. These counts had the same sovereign rights in their districts as were possessed by the Electors themselves; hence the town enjoyed exemption from the billeting of troops other than those of its own over-lord. In common with most of these princelets, whose honour was greater than their riches, his whole territory consisted of this little town and a few neighbouring villages, the place of residence being a castle outside the town itself.

The count had died the year before, and left a young and beautiful widow with an only son eight years of age, who had been sent to Vienna for his education. This lady, who saw my company of eighty dragoons established near her property, feared with some reason lest her subjects might suffer from their presence in the neighbourhood, and knowing that on such occasions it was best to secure the captain's influence, collected information regarding me in various indirect ways. Inquiries were made of my quartermaster, who drew a lively portrait of me and exaggerated my good breeding, manners, and power at the Elector's Court. The countess thereupon sent me an envoy in the shape of a gentleman, who brought me a magnificent present of game accompanied with as many compliments as if I also had been a reigning prince. I thanked the gentleman, through him made myself acquainted with the places inhabited by the subjects of the countess, and begged him to present my respectful assurance that I should observe all her wishes in the matter.

My quartermaster, who acted as interpreter between us, added on his own responsibility everything that he could think of to prejudice this gentleman in my favour, and drew his attention to the difference between my manners and those of their own officers, who are not, as a rule, welcomed in winter quarters, for they are too much in the habit of getting the most they can out of the inhabitants. The envoy was so pleased with the result of his embassy that when he made his report to his mistress he enlarged upon all that my quartermaster had said as to my good qualities, with the result that a few days later he returned, bearing an invitation from the countess for me to dine with her.

I told this gentleman that it was a matter of extreme regret to me that owing to my ignorance of the language I dared not avail myself of the honour the countess had done me, but that I hoped soon, with the care I was taking to educate myself on this point, to be in a position to visit and offer my very humble respects to *Madame la Comtesse*. The envoy replied that I already had an interpreter, whom I could bring with me, and assured me that the lady would consider this a favour on my part.

After such a pressing invitation I felt that it would be impossible to refuse altogether, though I would not accept the dinner, as I wished to avoid the embarrassment of the interpretation, which would have bored me to death, but I assured him that I should do myself the honour of presenting myself that afternoon.

The countess was delighted at the opportunity of receiving a foreigner with all the state due to her sovereignty; and the result was that when I appeared I was introduced with nearly as much ceremony as if I had been an ambassador at his first audience.

A number of gentlemen, ladies of honour, valets, and extra footmen were ranged in order, and a Master of Ceremonies conducted me round—through halls and ante-chambers—before ushering me into the presence of Her Excellency. She was seated in an immense armchair of black velvet, set upon a dais covered with the same material, with a magnificent canopy over her head. The Master of Ceremonies respectfully introduced me, and thought proper to make a long and tiresome speech, of which I did not understand a single word. My interpreter was much put to it with this oration, for the compliments it contained were so elaborate that he found their translation quite beyond him. However, it came to an end at last, and I was directed to seat myself in a chair beside the dais, whilst the rest of the company remained standing. The ladies of honour were posted right and left of Her Excellency, the gentlemen at the sides of the platform, and the remainder were arranged as a sort of guard in double rank.

During this imposing ceremony I noticed that this beauteous sovereign lady possessed a most expressive pair of eyes, which she well knew how to employ to the best advantage, whether from a ceremonial point of view or the reverse, and I had a great desire to make their further acquaintance. I did my very best to meet her glances whenever the chance of so doing was afforded me, but further advances on my part came to a full stop, owing to my inability to enter into conversation.

This first visit put everything upon a proper footing, and etiquette being satisfied, I was made to promise to return in a day or two in order to enjoy the hospitality of her board.

I did not fail to carry out this promise, and shortly after my arrival we sat down to the table, for I had arranged the hour so that there should be as little waiting about beforehand as possible.

The places of the guests at table were all assigned them according to their rank and status, just as at the Imperial Diet.

Most of our company were gentlemen of portly habit and few words, but I had the honour of being seated at the right hand of the sovereign. Opposite to us on the table was a space where an equerry carved the various meats which were served in due order plate by plate. The countess was helped first, the servitor making a profound bow, then I, and then all the guests, each according to their rank, thus following the custom observed by the *dames de robes* in certain provinces in France on the occasions when they dine together.

The procession of dishes was unending, and it seemed to me as they appeared one after the other for the space of three hours, as if the supply must have been quite inexhaustible. So much for the viands: let us now come to the wine. Their manner of drinking was no less tiring to me than that of their eating. It was the duty of the countess to propose the toasts with all formality, making in the first instance a low bow in honour of the favoured personage, followed by another still lower after the act of drinking. The health of all those at table having been drank in due form, a large crystal glass like a chalice was brought in full of wine and covered with a crown of like material, which fitted the top.

On the arrival of this treasured glass the countess rose up with a solemn air, in which act she was followed by all present at table, and took it in her hands. She then turned towards me with the same grave manner, when my interpreter cautioned me to remove and take charge of the cover. This done, she pronounced in a solemn voice her intention of drinking to the health of the Sacred Person of the emperor, when the whole company made profound obeisance, only to be repeated when she had drunk or made an appearance of so doing, after which all resumed their places. A little later on I was presented with this great cup full of wine, and was directed to rise, replace the crown which I still held, and then face the left-hand neighbour of the countess, who took the cover as I had done previously, and this toast went round, too. After the health of the emperor came that of the King of France, which, without exaggeration, His Majesty owed to me, as saving my presence, it would certainly have been omitted.

The health of the king was followed by that of the Elector, and the crowned heads of nearly the whole of Europe, so that half our repast seemed to be taken up with a continual bowing and scraping.

I noticed that in drinking all these toasts, the countess merely placed the glass to her lips and passed it on almost untouched to her neighbour, so I thought it advisable to do the same. As for our German nobles, they would have deemed themselves wanting in respect to the crowned heads whose healths they drunk had they failed to drain the chalice to the last drop—with consequences which were a source of much amusement to me; for this was the first occasion on which I had ever seen so many people solemnly intoxicate themselves from a ceremonial point of view.

In the course of this carousal I noticed that the eyes of the beautiful countess were often upon me, and I received more than one gracious smile from her, which I reciprocated to the best of my ability, though in despair at being obliged to express my feelings in such a limited fashion; it even seemed to me that she would not have been sorry had it been otherwise, but there was no way out of the difficulty.

I was by her side as she left the table, when my quartermaster took the opportunity to ask my leave to go to his own dinner.

"Let be so, sir, let be so," said the countess, who had not dared hitherto to risk the few words of broken French she apparently knew, but which the excitement following the banquet now brought forth.

"How is it, *madame*," I exclaimed, "when you can talk French, you leave me to offer you my very humble respects at the hands and mercy of an interpreter? There would seem to be a grain of mischief within you, and that you wished to punish me because I happened to be a Frenchman; but if you will only permit me the liberty to prove to you the high esteem in which ladies of your merit are held by my nation, I shall hope to compensate myself for all I have suffered in the absence of converse between us."

"I can only speak a little, sir," said she, "and do not wish to punish you."

"You know quite sufficient, *madame*," I continued; "and I feel immensely relieved that there is no longer any need for an interpreter in any conversation that I may have the pleasure of holding with you."

"My speech will not content you much, for I speak so that you understand nothing that I tell you."

"Well, *madame*, you will teach me German and I will teach you French."

"I wish it with my whole heart, sir. If you teach me to speak French well, it will be both a pleasure and a privilege."

Whilst this conversation was passing between us, the German nobles who heard us conversing in a foreign tongue held respectfully aloof. I continued to chat with her ladyship, and after some talk we arranged that in future I should visit her whenever I felt inclined and waive further ceremony; and by thus adopting the French mode of life, which she appeared to be anxious to do, we should banish all those formal customs which prove such a hindrance in society.

So well did this scheme succeed that it was not long before I became master of the situation, and was expected to give my decision upon all sorts of matters. It was quite enough for me to say that such and such was the custom in France to secure this lady's approval, such was her liking for everything done in French fashion.

The husbands in this country would not have been so easy to deal with, but their wives willingly accept the kindnesses and attentions bestowed upon them, because they so seldom have the chance of receiving them; the men know next to nothing of the charms of Venus, but give themselves up to those of Bacchus, to whom they devote almost all their worship.

So it came about that it was quite sufficient for me only to suggest some rule or another for this amiable lady to carry it out to the letter, as I prescribed. It must be confessed that, while my intention was to give her a high conception of our manners and customs, I was also careful to introduce nothing that would interfere with the object I had in view—the solution of the problem how to metamorphose a weary period of winter quarters into a delight. The countess was so pleased with the fashion of our amusements that she could no longer bear with the coarseness and drunkenness of her countrymen. We passed the winter in a variety of ways; I got the young people to contribute to their sovereign's pleasure by giving balls and masquerades; and her subjects began to look upon me as a man to whom she had delegated a portion of her authority. They crowded in numbers to the hunting parties, rendering them easier to organise, and therefore more interesting. All was joy within the town.

Our happiness would have been perfect if the emperor's troops had not arrived on the scene, as I shall proceed to explain.

The emperor, who had not had at the time a body of troops at hand to oppose the victorious Elector, had waited for an opportunity to avenge himself and to render him and his politics odious in the eyes of the rest of the German States. He caused a *Diet* to be assembled at Ratisbon, when all the measures and conduct of this prince were published and discussed in a circumstantially aggravating manner, calculated to alienate as many from his party as possible. This led to a fresh resolution on the part of the Three Colleges, recommending, without any regard to the views of the Elector of Bavaria, that he should immediately without delay withdraw his troops from Ulm, Memmingen, and other places which he had seized outside his own frontier; and, moreover, that he should throw in his lot with the Empire against France and Spain, in order to dethrone the Duke of Anjou. Failing this, he would be considered a rebel against the Imperial Decrees, and war would be declared against him as an enemy to their common country.

The Court of Vienna kept secret its attack on the Elector, but he was not ignorant of what was going on.

He had private information of all the preparations made against him; he knew even the names of the generals who were to take command, and the towns and country through which it was decided to invade his territory; in fact, he was in a position to checkmate their designs if he chose to take the offensive at once; but he preferred that the emperor should be responsible for this. Nevertheless, so as not to expose his subjects to the burdens of heavy requisitions without taking some steps to defend them, he moved his troops into Lower Bavaria, near a little town called Scharting, where he knew a considerable force of the Imperialists was concentrating. We therefore left our quarters towards the end of February, 1703.

I happened to be with the countess when my quartermaster brought me the order for this written in German, and he acquainted me with its purport without her comprehending a syllable; nevertheless, his rather mysterious air aroused her suspicions. She insisted on being informed of its contents, and showed so much determination to see them with her own eyes that I was obliged to hand her the document itself.

This charming lady was so moved at the sight of the order for our separation that she dropped the paper from her hand and became motionless. I likewise fell a victim to profound grief, although I used my best endeavours to console her. I pointed out to her that the troops could not possibly enter upon a campaign at a season of the year when the cold was yet so extreme, our movement being more likely to be a mere change of position than anything else, to be followed soon by a return to our old quarters; moreover, even if we were to remain billeted in Scharting in readiness for the warmer season, it would always be in my power to visit and pay my respects to her, so that it was entirely unnecessary to be frightened at the prospect. But still she had too true a presentiment of the future; fear caused her to foresee our complete separation, and filled with such ideas, she was reduced to tears and lamentations. She had given her heart to her darling Frenchman, and could not help repeating this every moment that I was with her. A thousand protestations on both sides were mingled with sighs and sobs from the countess, and at last, not finding words to express our sorrows, we parted.

Climéne et moi nous regardâmes;
Nous ne dîmes rien, que n'avions nous pas dit;
Mais d'un air doux languissant, interdit,
Nous nous prîmes la main et nous nous séperâmes.

THE CAMPAIGN OF 1703

The Court of Vienna, wishing to surprise and ravage the Elector's territory whilst his troops were still dispersed in their winter quarters, sent an army of twenty thousand men under the command of General Schlick, who at the end of February entered Lower Bavaria, which marches with Austria, and inflicted the severest exactions upon the people.

The Elector now felt that the conduct of the Imperial troops was so cruel that it behoved him to take serious measures to drive them back. To this end he advanced by different roads a considerable body of troops, surprised General Schlick at a moment when he least expected it, and utterly defeated him.

This action took place on March 3rd near a village called Heyzempirne, when the snow was still very thick upon the ground. Schlick had encamped his army in the plain near this village, and for greater security had occupied another village, a league to his front on the road into Bavaria, with a strong detachment of infantry and cavalry. With this advanced guard it seemed impossible to surprise him, as it would have been necessary to attack and capture the post in order to get at his main body. To do this without information reaching him appeared to be out of the question; but the fates decided otherwise.

Before setting out to attack Schlick, the Elector thought wise to withdraw the garrison of one of the forts forming part of the defences of Passau on the Danube. This fort was threatened by the Imperial army, which occupied two other strongholds near the town, which was under the rule of the two sovereign powers, one part belonging to the emperor, the other to the Elector. In order to facilitate the retirement, three companies of dragoons, one being mine, were advanced in support.

Herein lay an opportunity for our officers to exhibit their dislike for me; without informing me of the exact tenor of the order we had received, they began by posting me and my company in the midst of a fir wood full of snow, three days before the garrison was to leave Passau. Despatched in this way in such bitter weather, without rations or forage, it was natural to suppose that we were not intended to remain any length of time at our post. But as the hours rolled on and no further orders arrived our hunger increased, and I despatched some dragoons to find out if it were not possible to obtain a provision of some sort for man and beast in the neighbourhood. After a tedious search they returned, bringing but a small quantity of mouldy black bread, and only enough forage to make a daily ration of five or six pounds for each horse. As to the two other companies, they remained at their ease in villages in the rear, and did not advance on Passau till the actual day for the retirement of our garrison. After all, it simply came to this, that the whole of my company, which, as a matter of fact, belonged to the chief of our regiment, and not to me, was the victim of their ill-natured spite. I had been over three days in this wood when the garrison began its retirement from Passau.

The Imperialists only realised what was taking place after our force had started on its road from the town; they then advanced to the attack, but our dragoons appeared on the scene and obliged them to retire after the exchange of a few shots, which resulted in trifling loss. We covered the retirement of the garrison for about three leagues, and then moved on Scharting, where we rejoined the regiment.

The whole army was paraded the next day on the plain outside this town in expectation of an immediate advance on the enemy, who were but four leagues distant. This fourth night was no pleasanter for me than the three preceding ones. New reasons were found for putting me on duty, so that I had to remain nearly all night under arms without the luxury of a fire, and my only means of keeping at all warm was by stamping my feet and swinging my arms.

Next morning, at break of day, the army was formed into column of march, and the order to advance given so as to take the enemy unawares. Twelve squadrons of dragoons formed the advanced guard; after them came the mass of the infantry, supported by forty squadrons of cavalry, which also covered the rear. When we approached the village forming the enemy's advanced post, the sky became overcast and down came the snow, so thickly, in fact, that their sentries could only distinguish the leading files of our column of dragoons. This they took for a reconnoitring party, and as their commanding officer determined to cut it off, he concealed a part of his infantry in a cemetery, the walls of which bordered on the single street which ran the length of the village, and the rest in the houses opposite, so as to bring us under a crossfire.

He also caused his cavalry to mount at once and take up a position outside the village, opposite the mouth of the street, so as to cut off any dragoons who might push on in order to make their escape; and waited patiently, until fate and our impatience to get on before General Schlick could receive information of our advance should draw us into his trap. We had no particular reason to mistrust this open village where there was no sign of advanced picquet or sentry; our dragoons entered and filed up the street without taking any precaution, and the enemy seeing this, made up their minds that they had them in the hollow of their hands.

They withheld their fire until all our men had advanced towards their cavalry, but happily they waited until too late to take good aim; nevertheless, a great number of our people were killed, and the rest thrown into confusion. As it was, we hurried to gain the end of the village, where we found their cavalry, which added to our surprise, but we pulled ourselves together, dismounted our dragoons, and threw ourselves into the houses right and left at the end of the street, where we soon found ourselves under cover and in a state of defence. My company with the rest had fallen into the ambuscade, but we were lucky enough to get off with a loss of twelve killed. Duchâtel, who commanded our advanced guard, was killed, and much blamed after his death for having entered the village without previous reconnaissance.

So far the enemy's commandant had reason to be satisfied with the success of his manoeuvre, but his elation was not destined to last long, for on the news of the surprise our main body was speedily brought up, and invested the village on all sides, the enemy's cavalry being thus completely surrounded. A strong body of our infantry then entered and cut down these unhappy creatures to the last man.

This prelude to the general engagement which followed shortly afterwards excited our Bavarians to such a pitch of fury that they begged to be led at once to the attack. Schlick, however, had news by this time of what had taken place, and without knowing the actual number that we could bring into action, got his men, a little hurriedly perhaps, into line of battle.

We found he had posted himself in front of the village of Heyzempirne, and as the country was extremely open, it was not difficult to see the strength of his force and its position. The Elector was soon ready, and both armies opened a desultory cannonade whilst deploying. Our force scarcely had time to get into battle array before the Elector set us moving at a steady pace and with well-closed ranks, due regard being given to the maintenance of an equal pace throughout. When we had moved thus a sufficient distance, our two wings, consisting of cavalry, advanced at a rapid trot, whilst the infantry quickened their pace, in order to dash upon the enemy without firing, reserving this until they were in close contact. The first shock was a very sharp one, and gave one the impression that animosity between people of the same nation was more obstinate than if they had been strangers to one another.

Victory hung for a long time in the balance between the opposing cavalry, so stubborn was the fight, for the Emperor's *cuirassiers* are really among his very best troops. Our infantry did not experience the same resistance: they stood the first effect of the enemy's fire, charged home with bayonets fixed, and crushed all resistance. Soon afterwards the enemy's cavalry gave way and their rout became universal. Schlick escaped with the *débris* of his army, leaving more than five thousand dead on the field. He abandoned all his artillery and train, a number of copper pontoons, anchors and cordage, of which he had made provision against the crossing of the Bavarian rivers, counting upon being able to invade and devastate the country, and thereby give the Elector reason to repent of his disobedience to the mandate of the Court of Vienna. I put to the test at this battle a small frame of well-tempered iron, which the cavalry officers, not in the cuirassiers, were in the habit of placing in the crown of their hats. It certainly saved me from the effects of two heavy sabre cuts which I received in the *mêlée*, to the extent that I got off with merely a few bruises.

I had for my share in this day's work the honour of going through two important engagements, the one as perilous as the other, and to crown all I was again, the fifth night in succession, ordered on duty to protect the artillery and baggage left on the field by the enemy, which for the want of teams could not be removed before the evening of the following day. Nevertheless, although the snow lay very thick, I did not suffer so much from cold as on the four preceding nights, because the enemy had in their flight set fire to the village, so that we had plenty of opportunity of warming ourselves. The artillery was moved rather late in the following day, when I was directed to take up my quarters in a little village eight long leagues from the battlefield; and thus my sixth night was passed in a long and toilsome march. I got at last to this wretched village, and the comfort in finding there a cover to my head in so distant a land was all I had to console me for the impossibility of again seeing my sovereign lady.

After this expedition it suited the Elector's plans to make himself master of the bridge and town of Ratisbon. This Hanseatic town is almost surrounded by his territories; its suburb called Beyricheoffen actually belonged to him. I had been but a few days in my village when I received an order to march and join that portion of our army which was on its way to invest Ratisbon, in order to prevent the Emperor from seizing it. I had the direction of the siege of this place, the defence of which lay in the hands of its inhabitants, but I was much hampered in my work owing to the regard which the Elector manifested for the delegates of the *Diet* then sitting there.

However, after the suburbs had fallen into our hands, I constructed a battery intended to destroy a traverse on the bridge. As this traverse was of stone, it was feared that the ricochet of the cannon shot would cause alarm to some of the delegates, and damage their houses, consequently I had to place my battery at such an angle that my attack would have been useless. I constructed a second with the same caution on the other side of the Danube, and the burghers, who were not aware of the care and consideration we had for the *Diet*, were so alarmed at the prospect of seeing their town bombarded by an investing army that they surrendered, handed its keys to the Elector, and admitted a Bavarian garrison. The Elector enforced such good discipline meanwhile that nothing was allowed to disturb the freedom of the deliberations. He even did his best to persuade the Court of Vienna to agree to a treaty by which this town should be declared neutral, in which case he was prepared to withdraw his troops; but the proposal was not accepted.

My company was detailed to form part of the garrison of Ratisbon. I found much to interest me in this town, for the number of delegates from all parts of Europe, most of whom had their families with them, such as M. de Charmois, who represented France, with his wife, the Elector's representative with all his family, and many others, formed a most agreeable social circle, quite apart from the interest connected with the war itself. But I was not destined to enjoy this for long, as I was obliged to be on the march again, and to practise my profession as an engineer in connection with various fresh enterprises that the Elector had determined upon before the formal opening of the campaign.

We began by investing Neuburg on the Danube, which owned the Elector Palatine as its suzerain. This town was necessary to the Elector; first, because it lies between Donauwört and Ingolstadt, which belongs to him; and, secondly, by reason of its bridge being the means of communication with the flat country of the interior of Bavaria. The conquests of the Elector within the Swabian Circle no longer sufficed, as since the declaration of war with the Emperor, it became necessary for the security and protection of his own country to secure the points by which the enemy might seek to invade it

Neuburg was one of the most important points of this character, and hence the Elector's anxiety to secure it. The enemy, who had no doubt that the town would be attacked after the Battle of Heyzempirne, added new works to the old walled *enceinte*, with which the place was provided; but they were not of much use, for we took possession of it five days after the trenches were opened. I found, however, several difficulties to contend with at the suburb situated on a low hill abutting on the Danube; here we lost a few men, and after the capitulation, installed a small garrison on account of its situation.

The town of Augsburg offered considerable opportunity for either the defence or invasion of Bavaria, because it lies within its borders. We had no difficulty in taking it. The defence of this Hanseatic town was in the hands of its own *burghers*, who immediately after the taking of Ulm had the astuteness to ask of the Elector recognition of neutrality, which he accorded them. Notwithstanding this, intelligence was brought to the Elector which proved to be only too true—that the inhabitants were in league with the Imperialists, and he certainly ought to have seized the place after the capture of Neuburg; but notwithstanding the ease with which this could have been done, he preferred to take the risk of leaving things as they were, in order to give proof to the Empire of his moderation and the rectitude of his policy.

The enemy, less scrupulous, profited by this, and gained admittance to the town, the loss of which could not be repaired until after the first Battle of Hochstett, and then only after a tedious siege. M. de Ricous accompanied the Elector during his campaign, and we had many opportunities of discussing the means of raising the proposed regiment of French deserters. Notices had been distributed in the principal towns and among the troops of the Empire. So far we had got together a certain number of soldiers, who were meanwhile billeted in a Bavarian town, in the hope of more arriving, and were under the command of some subaltern officers, who, like their men, had left foreign service to come to Bavaria.

About this time two good-looking young gentlemen presented themselves with the story that owing to some trouble connected with a duel in Italy they had been obliged to leave the French army and seek refuge in a foreign land, and that hearing of the war in Bavaria, they had come there to implore the king's ambassador to help them to find some employment suitable to their rank and condition. M. de Ricous, undecided as to his reply, sent them to me to see if they would suit our new regiment. These gentry, who had taken good care to inform themselves of the part of the country I came from, appeared to be enchanted at having found in me a neighbour, and told me that they both belonged to the same family in Périgord, on the confines of the Agenois, one being the Count de la Bastide, the other the Chevalier de la Bastide.

I inquired of them why they had left the French service, and was told the story of an imaginary duel, the details of which were so pathetic and well studied that I was quite carried away by the tale of woe; in fact, my two neighbours made such an impression upon me that I felt I could do no less than to recommend them for the command of the two first companies of our future regiment. On my report their commissions were sent them at the time we were engaged in the siege of Neuburg, and they were duly sent off to the depot to organise their companies.

As a matter of fact, these adventurers were not in the least what they made themselves out to be, and far from having served in the army, were merely two young men from Villeneuve, in the Agenois, married and without relations, who had both begun life as small shopkeepers in order to supplement the slender patrimony left them by their parents. Want of business experience, together with a mania for gambling, so wrecked their affairs that they found themselves forced to abandon their wives and children in order to evade the pursuit of their creditors. After having worked their way through Italy, they found themselves in Bavaria, where they had the good fortune to fall on their feet. They really belonged to the best burgher families of their town, though I did not become acquainted with all the above details until my return from Bavaria, as I shall explain later on.

After the taking of Neuburg our army was broken up into detachments, our regiment being with that under Major-General M. de Wolframsdorf. He set out for the upper part of the Bavarian Palatinate to operate against a corps of Imperialists who were ravaging this part of the frontier.

Our last day's march found us camped near a large village, Schmidmidel, where, according to the reports we received, the enemy often put in an appearance, and were now in greater force than we had been led to expect. Our *commandant* sent out parties to obtain details as to their strength, and having learned that it was not so very superior to our own, set out with our force at night, with the intention of surprising them at a point four leagues distant. It was daylight, however, before we had discovered their advanced posts, the vedettes of which managed to report our advance. Thus the enemy had plenty of time to get into position to receive us, and we found them drawn in readiness. When our detachment had formed in like order, neither force dared attack the other, but each watched to see what their opponents would do.

During this lull curiosity impelled me to ride out on the flank of our squadrons, to get a better view of the strength and position of the enemy, when a young Imperialist officer caught sight of me, and left his place in the ranks with the intention of exchanging pistol-shots with me. My first feeling was to rejoin my own troop as if I had not seen him, for experience had by this time convinced me that these single combats were quite useless, and that it was the duty of an officer, in the interest of the service, to reserve himself for the leading of his men, to fight only in company with them.

But the reflection of what our Germans would say of me under these circumstances flashed across me, and I immediately turned about to face my hot-headed adversary, who cantered towards me firing his pistol. He then took to his heels, to return again and repeat the operation, after the fashion of the hussars. This circus business, which he enacted to the amusement of both sides, ended unhappily for him, as, thanks to the over-employment of his spurs, his horse took the bit in his teeth and bolted right into our squadrons, where he and his master both met their end.

This occurrence, trivial as it seemed, sufficed to bring on the action: the officer who had just been killed happened to be the nephew of the Imperial commander, who was so incensed to see him thus perish before his eyes that he determined at once to give battle and avenge his death. At the first indication of movement on the part of the enemy we advanced to meet them, so as not to lose the advantage of being on the move when the shock should occur. The fury of both sides was so great that the collision was violent in the extreme, and we remained locked together in the confusion of the *mêlée* for some considerable time.

The cavalry on both sides, after having driven its way through the opposing forces, whilst their infantry were still engaged, retired, reformed, and actually met once again in the charge; but after a long and hard fight each side retired for a second time to their own part of the field, both losing a great number of men.

We encamped near the village of Schmidmidel in order to remain in observation of the enemy, who, in fear of a slight reinforcement which had joined us, decided to beat a retreat. I lost the horse I rode during the fight; he died that day from sabre cuts in the head—steel is more murderous than fire in these cavalry fights, though the iron framework in my hat saved me once again from many hard blows.

Whilst our detachment was on the frontier we learnt that Maréchal de Villars had captured the fort of Kiel, opposite Strasbourg, on May 9th, after a ten days' siege, and having seized the passes in the Black Forest, had effected a junction with the Elector's forces in the Swabian district. Needless to say, this important news filled us with inexpressible joy. We now flattered ourselves we should achieve a thousand conquests, and we no longer felt disposed to show any mercy to the German confederation.

This junction, however, in no way frightened Count Stirum, who commanded the Imperial forces, for he appeared with about twenty thousand men in the plains near Hochstett after having partially pillaged that frontier of Bavaria.

The Elector wished to oppose him in person, and marched to meet him with all the troops he had at hand, including a French detachment under M. Dusson. He made nearly the same dispositions in dealing with Stirum as he did when he surprised Schlick; he found him in a position in the plain of Hochstett ready for the fight, and in possession of all the advantages that the locality afforded. The encounter was a very stubborn one, and although at first, perhaps, the issue was doubtful, the enemy at last gave way; their cavalry, closely pressed by ours, began to retire, and deserted their infantry altogether, who, finding their flanks unprotected, broke and sought safety in retreat. The better to effect this, the whole of their troops were formed into a single square, which gradually retired, fighting the while, until the woods in their rear were reached and their safety secured. The enemy's losses amounted to more than three thousand men, besides prisoners and some artillery.

This affair was followed by the siege of Kempten, and later on that of Augsburg, when my services as engineer-in-chief to the Bavarian forces were dispensed with because there was a sufficiency of officers of this branch of the service present with the French Army.

CHAPTER 6

Defeat of Imperial Hussars

It now became necessary to the army of France, which had just penetrated without any great opposition as far as the centre of Germany, to see that the passes between Swabia and Alsace were kept open, for it would have been hardly prudent to advance further into the Empire as long as any army of the enemy had it in its power to cut the line of communication by seizing certain fortified towns. It was therefore most advisable to act without precipitation and to watch the action taken by the Allies.

It was doubtless quite possible to advance beyond the Swabian district if thought proper, but in the belief that a blow struck at the heart of the Empire itself would be the most efficacious means to its destruction, it was decided that whilst the army of France continued and consolidated the conquests in Swabia, the Elector with a portion of his own army and a French detachment should force a passage through the Tyrolese Mountains, to enable the army of the Duke de Vendôme of effect a junction with that of M. de Villars, and to postpone all other enterprises until this had been brought about, or had been frustrated.

There were, however, great difficulties to be surmounted in the execution of this plan, chiefly on account of the mountainous nature of the country to be traversed; on the other hand, the passage once secured, the army of Italy, together with that of Bavaria, would have it in their power to put the Empire into a terrible plight. The presence of the Elector was deemed necessary in this famous expedition, and he conducted it with so much skill and forethought, that if similar ability had been manifested on the Italian side, everything would have come about as had been arranged.

As a beginning, His Highness caused four principal points, which covered the approach to the mountains from Bavaria, to be attacked, namely, Rosenheim, Kufstein, Hochstein, and Scharnitz, towns situated on the sides of the mountains, or on almost inaccessible cliffs; these he seized in spite of all difficulties, either by assault or by making terms. After the capture of these points, by which he assured himself a safe line of retreat, he advanced with his army by a single road cut in the sides of the mountains as far as Innsbruck, a Hanseatic town and the capital of the Tyrol. The magistracy, having no garrison to protect them, and considering it inadvisable to attempt a defence of the town, came out to meet the Elector, to whom they presented the keys and took the oath of allegiance. So far it would have been impossible to wish for a happier outcome to our projects; the capital appeared to be held in great respect by the rest of the province, and above all would make a most convenient base of supply for the army of Italy whenever the junction took place.

We had overcome the principal obstacles, and it only remained to send a detachment to seize the more difficult passes between Innsbruck and the approach from Italy, and to inform the Duke de Vendôme of the favourable state of affairs, so that he might set his army in motion with all the speed possible.

In the meantime the Elector and his staff remained at Innsbruck, the better to control the inhabitants and to arrange for the prospective junction.

The force detached from the Elector's army was duly detailed, and successfully passed the most difficult defiles as far as one called the Brenner, which was the most important of all; the Marquis de Novion, son of the Premier President of Paris, and de Caretti, a Piedmontese, both captains in the Elector's Guards who knew the country and patois, were also sent by the road over the Grisons, in order to communicate promptly with the Duke de Vendôme. These arrangements being settled, the Elector took up his residence in Innsbruck, and enjoyed the relaxation and amusements which the inhabitants provided for his pleasure in a manner which would have done credit to the devoted subjects of any sovereign.

But while fortune thus smiled upon us and the people appeared so submissive and quiet, a movement of quite a different character was beginning to make itself felt in the country itself. The Courts of Vienna and Savoy were weaving a plot against us, in which the Tyrolese joined only too successfully, and which ultimately had the effect of upsetting all our projects.

This unfortunate reverse was brought about by a sudden change of policy on the part of the Duke of Savoy, who abandoned the interests of France and Spain and secretly joined the Imperial party. This prince not only forgot his obligations to a solemn treaty, upon which the seal had been set by the marriage of the princess, his daughter, to the King of Spain, and his promise of armed support to his son-in-law, but went over to his enemies in order to do his best to dethrone him. In fact, he had been preparing for some time to cut these ties, which should have been most dear to him, in order to side with the emperor and his Allies.

The King of France believed he had secured the duke by bringing about the alliance between his daughter and the King of Spain, and that the bond of relationship would be sufficient to ensure the support of his son-in-law and the maintenance of peace in Italy, which was threatened by the emperor's action. But whether it was that he had a national aversion to France, or had been induced by some other motive, he made a secret arrangement with the emperor just at the time when His Majesty imagined him most attached to his interests. He was, moreover, accused of supplying the Imperialist generals with information of the most confidential nature regarding the intentions of France at the very moment that he appeared most devoted to her.

The emperor offered him Montferrat, and promised that England should furnish him with considerable subsidies if he would break his treaty with the two crowned heads and enter into alliance with him. He pointed out to him the duty he owed to his *suzerain*, and promised to allow him to return into his good graces provided he made no delay in declaring himself. Won over by these, he promised the emperor to furnish only a moiety of the forces which he had agreed to contribute to the king's army, and to keep his best troops within his own territories to be employed as occasion offered.

Although this was a secret treaty, there were too many persons engaged in it to admit of its being concealed from the king. His Majesty, however, did not wish to take immediate cognisance of it, as he hoped that his superior force in Italy would be able to control the Duke of Savoy until the junction was effected with the Elector of Bavaria in the Tyrol; then the emperor would be obliged to withdraw his troops for the defence of his own dominions, and the duke, left to his own resources, would have been forced to refuse the alliance.

But news came that there was no time to spare for this; the convention with the Viennese Court had just been signed, and the duke was using all his efforts to seduce several of the Swiss Cantons, especially the Grisons. To defer matters longer was to risk everything; all thought of a junction in the Tyrol was abandoned; it became necessary to look to the safety of Italy, because General Staremburg, who commanded the Imperial army there, had just sent considerable reinforcements to the Duke to place him in a position to resist the French army, and raise a revolt among the religionists of the valleys of Pragelas, Barcelonette, and others on the borders of Piedmont.

Besides which the fanatics hidden in the Cevennes only wanted encouragement to rise and wage war in the Dauphiné, which would add embarrassment to the kingdom and create a diversion whilst the Germans effected an entrance by Alessandria. In such a pressing condition of affairs, His Majesty saw fit to put such of the Savoy troops as were found in the ranks of his army under arrest, lest they should turn their arms against him in the first action that might take place, an eventuality that the Allies would not fail to attempt to bring about. As a reprisal the Duke of Savoy caused a detachment of the king's troops passing near Turin to be stopped and disarmed, and then, his intentions being clear after such an act of hostility, he threw caution to the winds, and formally declared war against France and Spain.

All this happened at the time the Elector was endeavouring to bring about the junction with the army of Italy. We now found ourselves forced to make a precipitate retreat, for a delay of twenty-four hours would have exposed us to the risk of massacre by the Tyrolese, who rose in revolt at the mandate of the emperor, upon the new treaty with Savoy. Had the Elector given them time, they would doubtless have closed the defiles behind us, for they had every means at their disposal for effecting this, owing to the nature of the country.

The Court of Vienna, having thus assured itself of the Duke of Savoy, desired to take advantage of the mountains and the character of the inhabitants of the Tyrol to destroy the Elector and his army during their forced retreat. Confidential agents were sent to persuade the mountaineers to take up arms and oppose our passage, and in order to rouse their emulation, some grenadiers were also sent to reinforce the local huntsmen. The chase is a special calling in these mountains. Those who engage in it are dispersed among the Cantons, and are regarded as leaders by the peasants.

On the arrival of the first information of all this, he drew in his advanced detachments by forced marches, but notwithstanding his precautions, they were not allowed to leave their posts unmolested;

if their losses were not great, this was simply because the people had not completed their arrangements for rising. It would not have been possible to have got out of this tangle if they had had the time to seize the various points of passage as ordered by the Viennese Court, for the nature of the country is so favourable to the defence that in some of these defiles an entire army corps could easily be brought to a halt.

No human power could conquer the difficulties to be met there; the only means of passage is a single road, the result of enormous labour on the part of the inhabitants, cut in the side of the mountain, and so precipitous that on the one side is a frightful chasm, while on the other rise beetling cliffs inaccessible to all but the natives.

By means of crampons fixed to their knees and their hands, they climb places only known to themselves; there they have the lives of passers-by at their mercy, as they can destroy them with impunity by raining down rocks and stones from the mountain-tops. They were thus in a position to annihilate a column of troops finding itself on such a road, with the further alternative of cutting the road itself at various places in its course, by no means a difficult operation, and could so shut in the Elector that it would be out of his power to save a single man of his army.

As a matter of fact, the inhabitants were not yet ready for action, but rumours of the rising had attracted many to the difficult places that we had to pass through, and they showered down rocks, putting us in such danger that the grenadiers had to climb wherever possible to drive them off. No one of us was in greater jeopardy than the Elector himself, for a hunter posted himself behind a rock with the special purpose of picking him off at the time when he was passing along one of these terrible roads; His Highness escaped death at the hands of this assassin simply because he was not recognised.

Count d'Arcko, husband of the countess who died several years ago in Paris, was taken for the Elector, and died in his place as follows. The fates ordained that on this day the Elector should dress himself in simple attire with the Order of the Golden Fleece hidden beneath his coat, and a thousand paces before arriving opposite the ambuscade, the wish to converse with one of his suite had caused him to drop somewhat to the rear, whilst the Count Arcko, left alone, found himself at the head of the party. Two young Italian scouts, who usually followed the Elector, accompanied the count, who that day wore a magnificent uniform. The glitter of the gold lace, and the two scouts in attendance, imposed upon this wretch. As soon as he saw that he was within range, he fired upon him with his carbine, which was loaded with a silver ball, and mortally wounded him.

No sooner had the assassin fired his shot than he climbed away by paths that could not even be seen, and published far and wide in the Tyrol that he had killed the Elector of Bavaria; he gave such circumstantial evidence in support of his assertion that the inhabitants, who desired nothing better, easily persuaded themselves of the truth of his story, and looked upon this ruffian as the saviour of their country and a hero worthy of their admiration.

After all, there was nothing strange in this conduct on the part of the Tyrolese, who are utterly uncivilised, and derive satisfaction from a detestable deed because it is in accordance with their savage habits. But similar action on the part of a civilised people merits eternal condemnation; I speak of the Court of Vienna, who, believing that the Elector was really dead, not only signified its approval of the murder, but went further and rewarded the murderer. He was given a golden chain, which he slung over his shoulder like a belt, and was conducted in triumph through all the streets of the Imperial capital.

The news of the death of the Elector spread over the length and breadth of Germany, and it was a considerable time before the people discovered the mistake. The Tyrolese, who were now fully aroused, were so encouraged by it that they mustered in still greater numbers; they invested certain places on their frontier, and even found means to gain an entrance to Rosenheim, where they slaughtered more than a thousand Bavarians. Their cruelty did not stop there: they caught poor Count Veritas, a brigadier in command at this place, an intimate friend of mine and a particularly charming man, paraded him round the streets, and finally beat him to death with clubs.

Two other places were saved from their fury by means of garrisoned forts, which held out until the Elector sent forces to relieve them. I was with the troops sent to Kufstein, which the besiegers had shut in with a line of circumvallation formed of an abattis of wood, extremely strong and well designed, which they occupied and guarded with the exactitude observed by the best regular soldiers. The senior lieutenant-general of the Electorate, who commanded us, ordered me to force these lines. As soon as I had reconnoitred the position I made three attacks, two being feints, in order to draw away the besiegers, whilst the real one was carried out by my own grenadiers and dismounted dragoons, led by myself.

I arranged for these attacks to take place at the break of day, while in the meantime our General attended Mass in a village a quarter of a league away to implore divine support to our arms. The country we had to force a way through was covered with large forests consisting of tall and thick fir trees, and a number of the natives, thinking to save themselves from the fury of our troops, climbed the trees and hid themselves in the thick evergreen foliage. Unhappily for them, one of their number failed to conceal himself sufficiently, and our people at once set about searching tree after tree, and bringing down their occupants as if they were out squirrel shooting. Had not this scene been somewhat repugnant to one's feelings it might have been amusing, at all events, there was the merit of novelty in this method of gathering, by means of powder and ball, the large fruit which dangled at the tops of the fir trees.

More than eight hundred of these roosters lost their lives, and after having killed more still when cutting our way through the entrenchments, we relieved our garrison, which was on the point of starvation. The fourth town seized by the Tyrolese was Hochstein, which experienced more favourable treatment than Rosenheim. Baron de Heydan, the *commandant* who capitulated, was deluded by false appearances and dread of the masses of the enemy who had gathered to the investment. This officer, otherwise a brave man, paid too much attention to the reports of certain monks, who managed to convince him of the death of the Elector by means of most circumstantial evidence. They persuaded him that the unexpected death of the prince at the hands of a miserable huntsman was decreed by Providence as a means of restoring peace to the German Empire, which, owing to the cruel war that he had been responsible for introducing into the country, had been threatened with inevitable disasters. They added that the hand of the Almighty had made itself felt with the best results, as the French army had retired from the country, and that there was not a single invader left therein.

Neither did they fail to point out to him the danger that he and his garrison would run if he chose to oppose this decree of Providence, as now his master was gone, he could no longer hope for relief, and besides, being at the end of his provision supply, he would find himself at the mercy of the Tyrolese, who in their fury had actually determined to flay him alive should he hold out to the last. Finally, that he had before him the example of poor Count Veritas, who would have saved the lives of his garrison besides his own, had he been fortunate enough to find mediators; common prudence suggested that he should make honourable terms in good time. So gifted were these holy monks with the power of persuasion, that poor Heydan allowed himself to be won over by their seductive arguments, surrendered, and retired with his garrison into Bavaria. On leaving the town Heydan led his troops boldly into Bavaria, expecting to meet with nothing but desolation on account of the death of the Elector; he was much surprised to find on his arrival what a mistake he had committed. The ease with which he had been led astray by the discourses of the monks caused him the most cruel disappointment.

The Elector, who had been duly informed of his conduct, caused him to be put under arrest until he could explain the reason of his surrender. In the inquiry which followed there was entire want of evidence to show that he had had any sinister design against his master's interests, and his capitulation was proved to be due but to his credulity and a desire on his part to save the garrison from the dangers with which it was menaced. Thus, according to all appearance, the punishment of death would not have followed as a consequence of his misdeed; His Highness was noted for his clemency and appreciation of true intentions in such cases, but the luckless star of Baron de Heydan led him to the scaffold in an unusual manner.

One of the Counts d'Arcko in the Imperial service was in command at Brisac when the Duke of Burgundy laid siege to it in August, 1703. This prince, who began operations in the night of 24th-25th, quite expected that so important and well fortified a place would have offered a long resistance; however, it surrendered on September 7th. His Imperial Majesty, disgusted at the slight resistance made, to his mind, by Count d'Arcko, had him court-martialled and beheaded. Information of this had scarcely reached our army, before violent representations were made to the Elector that Heydan's case was just as criminal as that of Count d'Arcko, and that he should treat it as the emperor had done, both for the good of the State and as an example to the army. The Elector, who did not wish his Allies to think him lacking in energy in anything concerning their common interests, ordered a court-martial to be convened, which sentenced Heydan to be beheaded.

After our return from the Tyrol, the force under M. de Villars joined the army in Swabia at the siege of Augsburg. This was followed by an encounter with five thousand Imperialist cavalry under M. de Latour; the same who had left the Elector's service after the capture of Ulm. They were attacked by MM. Legasle and du Heron, near the little town of Munderkingen, and entirely defeated.

In Lower Bavaria, on the frontier of the Linz country which marches with Swabia, the Elector undertook in person the siege of Passau and its forts, although the season was somewhat advanced; notwithstanding this, and the resistance offered by the excellent Imperial garrison, he became master of the place in less than three months. This took place towards the end of November, when the prince advanced upon the lines constructed by the Imperialists on the frontier, forced them, and levied requisitions throughout the district.

I had had the honour, before the Elector laid siege to Passau, of being promoted lieutenant-colonel of the regiment of "deserter-refugees," which I have previously referred to. There were as yet but five companies which did duty at this siege under my command, and His Highness had every reason to be satisfied with their behaviour.

M. de Ricous, who had accompanied the Elector to the Tyrol, was attacked by an obstinate fever, which compelled him to return to Munich at this period. His absence gave rise to a misunderstanding, which caused him much annoyance, and from which he could certainly have saved himself had he been less secretive. He had only to signify to the Elector his desire to reserve this regiment for himself, and all would have been well; but the Prince knew nothing of his wish, and gave it to Boismorel, his own *aide-de-camp*. This person was in attendance when the town of Passau surrendered, and taking advantage of His Highness' elation at the submission of so important a place, he begged of him and obtained the regiment, as I shall explain, after having related how it came about that he found himself on the Elector's staff.

Boismorel, who when quite young was in the household of the late *Monsieur* the only brother of the king, was held to be one of the handsomest men of his time, and had a most charming presence. He knew how to make himself useful to this prince, who showered kindnesses upon him and favoured him in every way. He might have become a rich man had he but known how to profit by his good fortune, but whether he was too fond of amusement or relied too much upon his luck, it is certain that he no more made the most of his opportunities than he restrained the passionate temper of which he was the slave. His conduct was so violent that it was reported to the king, who apparently ignored it, in consideration for *Monsieur*, his brother. France had the misfortune to lose this latter prince at the beginning of June, 1701, and the position of Boismorel became precarious.

However, the Duke of Orleans, who took his part, seeing him in danger of arrest on a charge of killing a gentleman opposite the Palais Royal, sent him off to Bavaria, to join the army then entering Swabia, and gave him letters of introduction to the Elector. His Highness could not but take a favourable view of one in whom a prince of the House of Bourbon was interested, and made him his *aide-de-camp* with the rank of lieutenant-colonel. Boismorel appeared before the Elector on his best behaviour. He was by no means ignorant of the requirements of high society, and had all the appearance of a perfect courtier; in fact, he made court to the Elector to such purpose that His Highness, with the good nature that was his characteristic, admitted him to a free and intimate friendship.

He made the most of his opportunity when he found the prince overjoyed at the news of the capitulation of Passau, by asking him for the regiment of French grenadiers. The prince was hardly prepared for this, and hesitated before answering, but Boismorel, not wishing to give him time for reflection, threw himself upon his knees before him, and enlarged upon the great obligation under which His Highness would place the Duke of Orleans in acceding to his request. He even advanced as an argument how much he had counted upon his goodness; that, in fact, he had relied upon this favour being granted him ever since he had had the honour to be nominated as *aide-de-camp*, and, moreover, all his friends had offered their congratulations in advance, so that if His Highness declined to consent, he would be a dishonoured man.

The Elector, who believed that the Duke of Orleans was really interested in the demand of Boismorel, acceded to it, and gave him the regiment. I naturally took the greatest interest in all matters connected with M. de Ricous, so that this was sad news for me; besides, I felt that a colonel should be a real chief to his regiment and in every way be a man of complete experience, whereas Boismorel had no war service, and could neither lead these deserter recruits through the intricacies of a campaign nor control them with the rigid discipline necessary in such a case.

I had heard enough of Boismorel to give me the greatest uneasiness as to his fits of temper. My reflections on the matter caused me so much irritation that I ended by taking a thorough dislike to the man, so much so that I made up my mind to go to the Elector and ask him to dispense with my services in the regiment, and to transfer me to any other in his service that he might think fit and proper.

His Highness was not visible when I presented myself, so I called on Maréchal d'Arcko, who had always honoured me with his friendship. I told him of my trouble and intentions, and found him as sympathetic as ever in any matter regarding my welfare. Nevertheless, with his greater experience, he was able to convince me that sovereigns never made mistakes, that they are absolute masters in the distribution of such favours as they think right, and that it is one's duty to accept every situation that may arise from the exercise of their will. He told me further that I need not be alarmed at the favour shown to Boismorel, and exhorted me to continue my efforts to bring the regiment into a good state of discipline, adding, that as this officer was ignorant of his duty, it would follow that I would always be looked upon as its real chief, and that all orders and communications would be sent direct to me. I was much comforted by his advice, and determined to follow it, come what might.

After the expedition against the lines of Linz, the Elector returned to Munich, and the troops went into winter quarters. Our regiment was told off to the town of Straubing, on the banks of the Danube, to which I took it, whilst Boismorel accompanied His Highness to Munich.

Boismorel spent the winter at Munich without troubling himself about the regiment, whilst I did my best to get it into shape at Straubing, He had fallen in love with a woman whose wiles so fascinated him that he managed to miss a notable action in which his regiment took part in the next campaign. Such was his infatuation that he took no count of the humble station of the object of his affections, for she was a woman no longer in her first youth, who had obtained the place of cook in the Elector's household.

Whilst he fanned the flames of his adoration before his goddess, I set to work to organise his company, making the sixth in the regiment. They were all over a hundred strong, and formed a really fine battalion, which was placed on the establishment as grenadiers. We were obliged to wait for more recruits until we were in a position to form the two fusilier battalions in accordance with the organisation of the Elector's Guards; but the misfortunes which had taken place in Bavaria prevented this development.

I did my best to suppress the thieving ways and brigandage which obtained with these men and rendered them unbearable. The best of them deserved hanging ten times over, and it was almost impossible to put a stop to the bad habits they had contracted. The *burghers* of

Straubing never ceased to complain of them the whole winter long, and the quarrelling and fighting that went on between the grenadiers themselves took up nearly my entire attention. Finally, after exhausting all the ordinary means of maintaining discipline, I was compelled to ask for power to flog them at my own discretion, without convening a court-martial. This was granted me, and in order to get clear evidence as to the guilty parties, whom I found it perpetually necessary to chastise in this severe fashion, I organised a service of patrols, night and day, in all the streets of the town. These, relieved every six hours, were obliged to report to me all disorder and the names of the offenders. In this way I put a stop to a greater portion of the evil under which the citizens suffered, owing to the absence of proper barracks.

However, the military art was not my only occupation, for the exigencies of the war had brought a charming society into the town, rendering it one of the most agreeable places in the Empire, The proximity of Straubing to the frontier necessitated a large garrison, and besides the troops composing this, many families of good standing in the country took up their residence in the town to escape the raids constantly made by the enemy's hussars. A number of young ladies also, who, as is usual in this part of the country, were very good-looking, joined our circle. They had never seen such a gathering of fine people at one and the same time, and were delighted beyond measure at the attentions paid to them by the officers.

We gradually became the best of friends, which resulted in the organisation of entertainments, and we officers, in order to make the most of our opportunities, formed a club to bear expenses amongst ourselves; consequently balls and *fêtes* took place without ceasing during the whole of the carnival. I could not help noticing the refining effect of this association with the fair sex; hatred and malice became unknown in our society. Formalities as to rank and station were banished, and in this tranquil enjoyment our term of winter quarters slipped by with such speed that we found ourselves entering on a fresh campaign almost without noticing it. I was lucky enough to have as my particular friend the daughter of Baron de —— a charming young lady who spoke French perfectly—the mark of education in these parts. This gave us an advantage over the others, in that we were able to converse freely when in company with others on any subject which best pleased us, as she only among the ladies knew the language.

However, mingled with so much enjoyment, I had a certain feeling of regret at the deception I was now practising towards my sovereign lady of the past winter. The tender memories I had of all the kindnesses she had shown me arose so vividly in my recollection that I could hardly forgive myself for my present conduct.

The countess herself, meanwhile, had impatiently awaited my return to her feet ever since the end of the campaign, and no sooner did she learn the whereabouts of my winter quarters than she began to have presentiments of what might occur. She well knew the reputation for gaiety attaching to Straubing, and being in doubt whether I should reappear, owing to the distance and the danger of the journey by reason of the Imperial hussars who scoured the country, she sent me a letter by the hand of a special messenger. Moreover, to show how much she cherished everything relating to me, she took the trouble to write this letter in French, so far as her slender knowledge of the language would permit. I have kept it for the sake of its curious expressions. It ran as follows:—

> I have just learnt with great grief, my dear sir, that you are in garrison far distant from me. Oh, how much this is contrary to my wish! I have always hoped, that once the campaign over, you would come and see your dear countess, who has ever felt the same for you; but I trust that if you cannot come yet that you will come very soon. Ah! why has not this moment come to pass already, and then how great would have been my joy! If this cannot yet be, bear in mind how much I promise to love him who is always in my thoughts.
> I much fear, my dear sir, lest in that little town you may find ladies who would try to render you unfaithful to me; but no, my dear heart, you are too honest a man to ever forget the beautiful promises you so tenderly made to me. Ah! when I remember your words, 'My dear countess, I love you more than anybody in this world, and will never change for another, although that other should be as beautiful as the day.'
> What great joy had I because you gave me your promise to hold to your word!
> *Adieu*, my dear heart, and do not listen to the fair ladies of your garrison; but come at once to one who awaits you with a cruel impatience.

This letter touched me very keenly. I realised all the trouble that this lady had taken to write to me in French, merely to give me pleasure, and I read in it her sad feelings, which touched me beyond measure. Had it been in any way possible to avoid the dangers of travelling through the country, I should have set out there and then to try and see her; but as it was, I was obliged to content myself with sending her a reply couched in the most dutiful and consolatory language. All the charms of the countess returned to my imagination and materially disturbed the reality of the pleasure derived from our new society; but as time ran on fresh distractions offered themselves daily, which served but to fan my new flame.

During all this I had my grenadiers to look after, who time after time obliged me to inflict severe chastisement upon them, after exhausting all other means to counteract their cunning and rapine. But, notwithstanding all this rigour on my part, they did not dislike me, for I accompanied these punishments with remonstrances on their conduct, and did my best to get them out of their bad habits, so that I might not be put to the constant necessity of chastising them. Ferocious as they were, they were not altogether without feeling, and thoroughly understood the connection between their own duty and the power that lay in my hands, which they knew was not wielded under the influence of temper or caprice. They appeared quite satisfied in having me as their commandant. An action which occurred during the siege of Passau had prepossessed them in my favour, and a second, during our term of winter quarters, increased this good opinion. Experienced warriors, such as these soldiers, make light of peril and dangers, and are able to form a better opinion than most of the character and bravery of their officers.

This second action took place about the beginning of March, 1704. Whilst we were in the Tyrol, the Imperialists had seized two small towns in the Upper Bavarian Palatinate, about ten or twelve leagues from our garrison, on the other side of the Danube. These served as bases from which their hussars raided the country, almost up to the gates of Straubing, seizing the goods of the Bavarian peasants and lifting their cattle. The poor people for the most part moved into the town for shelter, but daily there were fresh lamentations and complaints from them, for which there was little or no remedy.

The hussars are, properly speaking, nothing but bandits on horseback, who carry on an irregular warfare; it is impossible to fight them formally, for although they may when attacking present a solid front, the next moment they scatter themselves at full gallop, and at the very time when they might be thought to be entirely routed and dispersed, they will reappear, formed up as before. They have no fixed point on the frontier assigned them, as they are constantly on the move; and whatever the tactics employed against them, regular warfare at least is of no avail to hunt them down, unless, indeed, some exceptional opportunity presents itself, as happened in the following case.

M. de Wolframsdorf, who commanded at Straubing, was much affected by the miserable state of the country people; he wished with all his heart to correct this state of affairs, but had no idea how to set about it. One day we were talking together on the subject, when he remarked that it appeared to him that the best troops to employ against them would be my grenadiers, as they were even more artful than the hussars, as well as being hardened warriors, and that if I cared to take the business in hand, he felt sure I should be able at least to prevent the enemy's constant inroads, and to force them to devote their attention to some other district altogether. He added that if I accepted this commission he would leave the conduct of it entirely in my own hands, and that I could take what force and arm I considered appropriate for such an expedition. I instantly felt an intense desire to hunt down these bandits, so did not hesitate a moment in accepting his proposal; and I only asked for two squadrons of cavalry to act with three hundred of my grenadiers.

From information furnished me, it seemed that a large body of hussars had appeared near a little town called Hochemburg, two long leagues from Straubing, so I forthwith crossed the Danube with my detachment, and made straight for this point. As the inhabitants were entirely at one with us in this expedition, I sent on a trustworthy person to notify my advance to the magistrates, and to request them to despatch someone to meet me capable of pointing out the exact locality in which were the hussars, and of answering any further questions on the subject.

One of the magistrates came in person to give the information I was in need of, and after giving me a full and doubtless much exaggerated list of the ravages committed around his town, told me that he did not personally know where I should meet with them, but that he would bring me a countryman, just arrived on horseback, who had slept the night before in a large village where five or six hundred of them had taken up their quarters, with many waggon loads of plunder. I knew that this village was not more than a league away from Kamp, one of the two towns seized by the Imperialists, under the cannon of which the hussars always sought safety with their plunder.

Having thus obtained the required information, I marched my detachment into Hochemburg with the avowed intention of halting there for rest and refreshment, and said not a word of my true design to anyone. I made an ostentatious show of taking things easily, and later on, observed that it was too late to think of returning to Straubing; I then ordered billets and stabling to be prepared, so that we might sleep in the town that night. I took these precautions to prevent any evil-minded person giving notice of my movements, and so ruining my design, and quietly extracted from the peasant the while details as to the village where he had left the hussars, what care they took at night to guard against surprise, and the distance and state of the road thereto, with the result that I found it was a good eight leagues off. This would have been a bit too far in the ordinary way for the infantry, although it was necessary to cover the ground in the night if I wanted to surprise the enemy. Fortune had evidently determined that I should have something at least to contend with, so I set to work to find the solution.

At nightfall I disclosed my plan for surprising the hussars to the captain in command of the two squadrons, and in a few words told him how I was going to set about it. In the first place I asked him to mount a man whom he could rely upon, who was to ride into the town as if he had come with an order from the officer commanding at Straubing, which order would be for me to rejoin the garrison with my detachment. The trooper carried this out quite to my satisfaction. In accordance with this imaginary order, the two cavalry squadrons saddled and mounted, and I marched off the whole detachment, with the countryman at my side as a guide.

But when we were well away from the town I left the Straubing road and made for the village where the hussars were. The moon, which was up most of the night, was a great help to us, and in order to render the march less exhausting to my infantry, I made a point of talking and conversing with them. I made much of the booty awaiting their arrival at the place I was leading them to, and convinced them that owing to the measures I had taken nothing possibly could escape from our hands; such was the charm of future profit that no one amongst them played the part of straggler.

A quarter of a league from the village my guide told me that a little mill lay a hundred paces off the road, inhabited by a miller who would certainly be able to give me the latest news of the hussars, so I sent him on to fetch him quietly. The miller told me that he had left the village at nine o'clock that evening, and that the hussars had made themselves quite comfortable there in strong force, without watch or guard of any sort, and that all the barns were full of their horses. On my questioning him further, he said that the country was flat and open on this side of the village, but that there was an almost inaccessible cliff on the other, impossible for troops to hold or even retire over if pursued. As concerned the village itself, it consisted of a single street, in the middle of which was a small square opposite the church, in the cemetery of which I could post a number of my men. The miller turned out to be a loyal Bavarian; he joined my guide in order to point out to me all these details, as well as the principal houses in the village.

When we got to the open ground outside the village I formed up my troops in battle formation as quietly as possible, and taking with me the officers of the grenadiers and my two guides, we noiselessly made a circuit of the place, noting all the points which should be occupied by infantry.

This done and each detail settled, I told off my grenadiers, posted them myself, and gave them their orders couched in the clearest possible terms.

Having thus made sure of the interior of the village with my infantry, I sent my cavalry at a foot's pace to occupy its two outlets, after having despatched some smaller parties to watch the flanks. This was carried out so promptly that my men were all in position before daybreak, and as there was not long to wait for this, they had no time to get wearied at their posts. As soon as it was possible to see at all, I took my two peasant guides, with a small escort, and went quietly to the house wherein was lodged the commanding officer of the hussars. I had his host called up by name, as if one of his neighbours had something to say to him. He came to the door, and under threat of being *poignarded*, was ordered to show us the officer's chamber. This done, I went to the occupant's bedside, requested him to get up, and took him to our post at the cemetery.

After thus securing him, we went to the quarters of four others, who were treated in a similar manner, when, day beginning to break, someone in the village must have caught sight of my grenadiers in their red uniform, for the alarm spread at once. The astonished hussars, in a state of nature but for their shirts, rushed about the town. Some ran to their officers' quarters; some made for the stables to escape on horseback; but as fast as these worthies showed themselves they were saluted by my grenadiers with volley after volley, and those who sought to save themselves by flight through the fields at the back of the houses fell into the hands of our cavalry, who received them with pistol shot and the sabre.

The result was that they lost more than four hundred killed, and the remainder, seeing the hopelessness of their case, hid themselves in sheds, lofts, and even under the beds. When everything was quiet I called the inhabitants together and ordered them to produce all the hussars hidden in their houses, threatening to burn the village over their heads if I found one left after their search; and it was not long before I had one hundred and forty prisoners. My victory was complete. I had not lost a single man, and had the satisfaction of keeping my word as to the plunder that I had led my people to hope for; it turned out to be very considerable indeed. I made no distinction as to my own share, but put the whole up by auction, and distributed the proceeds to each according to his rank.

We returned in triumph with waggons, horses, and prisoners in our train; the people of Straubing and the country round poured in to gaze at their defeated opponents and manifest their joy. But no one took a greater interest in this than the daughter of Baron de ——; she looked upon the compliments showered upon me as belonging in part to herself, and quite imagined she was the heroine of the hour. The other ladies congratulated her; never was woman more delighted than she, and her regard and affection for me was so much augmented that I dreaded the despair which would overcome her when the inevitable moment for our separation might arrive.

Thus, whilst our Bavarians and I made the dalliance of love our chief occupation in life, the officers of the French army had not, in their Swabian quarters, the same distractions to relieve their idleness; they spent their time in making requisitions upon their hosts and landlords, and took upon themselves, in the most painstaking way, the guardianship of the funds which the inhabitants had for some years past so painfully scraped together. It was reported that each lieutenant-general became a "trustee" in this fashion of more than fifty thousand crowns, and the other officers in proportion. Thus these gentry left their winter quarters loaded with specie, and the Bavarians loaded with kindnesses. They differed also in that the Bavarians in leaving were parted from the objects of their desire, whilst the French took the greatest care to carry theirs off with them; in fact, it was said that, not finding Germany the safest place in the world for their prizes, they longed for nothing more than a speedy return to France.

CHAPTER 7

The Campaign of 1704

The opening of the campaign of 1704 caused a truce to love-making, and as the field of action was in distant Swabia we were obliged to set out for the point of assembly of our own army more than three weeks earlier than the rest of our detachments. But as I could not bear to leave without seeing the daughter of Baron de —— again, I handed over the regiment to the care of the Messieurs de la Bastide, and set out to join her.

After having stayed the time I allowed to myself, which we employed in exchanging vows of eternal love, I tore myself away, and set out to rejoin my regiment.

During my absence our officers and grenadiers had made the most of their opportunity by imposing small requisitions on the inhabitants of almost every village where they had been quartered. I was informed of this on my arrival, and as these exactions had occurred in territory actually belonging to the Elector, I, after strict inquiry into the matter, had the plunder disgorged and returned to the rightful owners; dispensing, at the same time, punishment to some and severe reprimands to others.

We joined the army near Ulm, where it had been mobilised at an earlier season than is usual for entering upon a campaign. I was surprised to find that the Elector had taken this course so early; Boismorel was with him and took over the regiment. It appeared to me that His Highness must have had a design in hand to forestall some movement on the part of the enemy; but I found that it was because the regiments in the French army in Bavaria had not been able to receive their quota of recruits, on account of difficulties on the line of communication. For the above purpose the Court of France had called out the militia in various provinces of the kingdom to the number of fourteen thousand men, and added thereto young men of gentle birth to fill the posts of sub-lieutenants.

These had been collected on the frontier of Alsace, but they could not enter Bavaria except under the cover of our army, which was accordingly placed thus early upon a campaigning footing in order to receive them at the passes in the Black Forest, before the enemy were ready to interfere with this operation. Our march to the frontier, however, roused their suspicions, and they forthwith set themselves in movement.

Prince Louis of Baden, who commanded the Imperial troops, was able to follow us, and on the last day of our march took up a position close to us.

The recruits, indeed, had scarcely joined us when we noticed several of the enemy's squadrons on the high ground commanding the road we had to take and posted to reconnoitre our camp. We had every reason to fear that our return march would not be so easy a matter, for Prince Louis had taken care to secure the defiles that we should have to repass, and consequently, as the country itself is much cut up by woods and hilly ground, the Elector and Maréchal de Marsin, who had taken over the command since the departure of M. de Villars, found it difficult to decide upon their line of action.

We were scarcely in a position to attack the Imperialists, on account of the defiles that separated the two armies, nor could we stay where we were; the bread which was to be sent us from Ulm was wanting, and there was no other way of providing it; so that in our extremity there was nothing for it but to break up our camp and set off under cover of night with as little noise as possible. This was done, and we passed through the Canton of Bâle, in Switzerland, which was not far off on our left flank. On any other occasion we should not have ventured this, but necessity has no law. The enemy were ignorant of our route, and we made a forced march of it the whole night long, in order to secure a defile eight long leagues from our camping ground. The road, which passes between two high cliffs on the shoulder of a mountain, was such that at one place, eight hundred paces long, it was only possible to advance with a front of six men.

The Prince of Baden had not reckoned on the possibility of our daring to move an army through Swiss territory. Had he done so, and kept a watch upon our movements in this direction, it would have been perfectly easy for him to have blocked our passage and cut us off altogether. The Lake of Constance, which lay at our rear during this march, formed a serious obstacle, and would have destroyed any chance of our escape had we found the pass we made such efforts to reach closed against us.

The apprehension lest the enemy should become aware of our march gave our generals much uneasiness. This bad commencement seemed to be a presage of the evils that befell us later on, and, as a matter of fact, we were employed during the whole of the rest of the campaign in evading the attacks of the enemy.

We marched the whole night without stopping on this cross-country route, and found ourselves at nine o'clock next morning within sight of the mountain over which was the pass. Here some scouts that the Elector had left in observation of the Prince of Baden's movements came in and reported that this general had become aware of our movements shortly after our departure; that he had broken up his camp, and was advancing to bar our progress with all diligence, so that, notwithstanding the start that our army had gained over his, there was every necessity for us to push on to forestall him.

As a result of this information, our regiment was ordered to relinquish the duty of rearguard, which had been in its hands all the night (the most dangerous duty of all), and was marched to the head of the rest of the column, so that it might be in position to lead the first attempt to force a passage through the enemy if this defile had already been blocked. This sudden move from an extremely dangerous post to another still more so, with the proud privilege of marching in front of the senior regiments of France, gave me the impression that our regiment would often have to bear the brunt of the fight.

The general officer who brought the order added the most graceful compliments imaginable, to the effect that our removal to the head of the column was but a proof of the confidence which existed in our valour. I thanked him for the honour shown us, without letting him see that I was just as much aware as he was that we were selected rather more on account of the blows to come than to give us any special precedence.

Our grenadiers took this opportunity to ask for the bread which was travelling with our rearguard. This was already a scarce commodity, but the general thought the situation and need of their services to be so urgent that he ordered the contents of several waggons to be immediately shot down in front of them, when they were allowed to help themselves without any account being taken. The result was that they made a good thing out of it, for they sold the surplus dearly enough during the following days. I should never have thought it possible that they could carry the vast number of loaves they managed to cram into their haversacks and effect the rapid march that we made to reach the head of the column.

Over and above the clothes they stood in, their equipment was composed of gun, bayonet, heavy sword, grenade pouch, a pistol in their shoulder-belt, and a hatchet, which alone one would have thought sufficient, together with the night's work they had just gone through, to overwhelm them. Notwithstanding this load, it was not long before we found ourselves at the head of the infantry column. There was, indeed, something altogether extraordinary about this "refugee" regiment, for they never failed to behave magnificently on all occasions of risk and difficulty.

At last we reached the entrance of the defile, which was commanded by high rocks on either side; but we were still in doubt lest we should find some detachment of the enemy holding the exit at the other end against the arrival of their main body. In this state of incertitude, we marched with arms shouldered and fixed bayonets, and we were lucky enough to reach the exit of the defile without meeting a soul. As, however, the Imperialists might have easily arrived on the scene before we had a sufficiency of troops clear of the defile, we formed ourselves into battle order to hold the ground, to cover the passage of our troops, and to make head against any possible attack.

The length of time necessary for the passage of the army and its train was such that we were kept in position until the evening of the following day. At last we were quit of this difficulty, and few amongst us realised the great danger we had just passed through. Prince Louis of Baden duly appeared, but too late to attack us; finding himself checkmated, he encamped about half a league away, in a country so cut up by woods and ravines that his force had to be divided.

We, on our part, remained halted after the last of our army had passed through, in order to rest the troops and enable our generals to reconnoitre the enemy's position, which they found rather badly chosen.

Maréchal d'Arcko, who was most assiduous in this duty, advised our attacking them at once, and pointed out all the advantages we enjoyed with our superior force and the weak position they had selected. As a matter of fact, our opportunity was an excellent one, and everything lent itself to aid our troops in overwhelming their opponents. The general declared that we should not put off the attack for a single moment, as the Imperialists still lacked the reinforcements they were expecting from their allies; that it would be too late to think of doing so when the Duke of Marlborough had joined them with his force, as rumour said he was about to do, and that if we dare not take action now, still less should we be justified in doing so when they were reinforced. But his advice, sound as it was, was not listened to.

He was answered by the arguments that our army was in want of bread, the unarmed and unorganised recruits a burden to us rather than a source of strength, and that the reinforcements expected by the Imperialists were not in a position to join them; the army of France which had them in observation would give them plenty of employment in that quarter, so that they would never think of transporting themselves to a point so distant as ours. Moreover, our army being primarily destined for the important siege of Nuremburg, it would be wrong to hazard a battle which, if not favourable to us, might have the effect of upsetting all our plans, and it would therefore be more prudent to continue our retirement

The advice given by Maréchal d'Arcko was to the point and well conceived, and was only too well justified by future events; to have followed it would have been greatly to the advantage of the State.

More than one critic said that the real cause that prevented this battle taking place was the excellence of the winter quarters, wherein most of the generals had enriched themselves so much that they did not care to expose their lives or treasures to any possible risk. One could, however, except Maréchal de Marsin from this category, for, besides the fact that he had not been long enough in Swabia to accumulate riches, he was personally so little interested in such things, that he could hardly be said to have known the value of money. It was, therefore, decided that our army should take the road to Ulm, on which was yet a shorter defile to pass on the enemy's flank, the approach to which was not very difficult, or sufficient to cause us serious apprehension. Nevertheless, the Prince of Baden, not wishing to throw away this small opportunity, constructed a battery, which opened upon us during our passage, but the range was so great that we suffered but slight loss.

Having effected the passage of this last defile, we entered a plain of some considerable extent, where it was easy to effect a junction with the convoy from Ulm, which brought us the much-wished-for bread. Our regiment was the only one which had not suffered the pangs of hunger; on the contrary, it had made an extremely good thing out of the bread which had been so liberally served out to it, and this was not the only occasion on which it profited during this march.

These "refugee" soldiers, full of experience and dodges in the art of marauding, had scarcely left the Bavarian territory for that of Swabia when they set to work to put their knowledge to a practical use and elude my vigilance whenever possible. They had the best of opportunities for this, as the country people were not aware that they could procure passports for themselves as safeguards against pillage, and Maréchal de Marsin did not understand the principle of forcing such upon them, and making the usual profit from the fees. Moreover, the post of provost-marshal of the army was non-existent in this campaign, and consequently the marauders had a fine time of it. I thought I had done my best in taking measures to control them, but they found means of the most tricky nature to defeat my intentions. On their arrival at each camping-ground it was their custom to go and seek for wood and straw, and under this pretext they set out in organised parties, turn and turn about, to scout and pillage the country; but everything they brought in was handed over entire to the battalion and fairly divided.

The *bandolier* and pistol concealed under their coat facilitated their proceedings, and with such arms of offence they were enabled to undertake quite important expeditions and few were able to withstand their raids. They brought in four or five hundred sheep at a time, besides cows and oxen, from pasturages far away from the camp, where the inhabitants had believed themselves to be quite secure from robbery of this sort. The army butchers being in collusion with them, bought these herds, and the whole transaction was conducted with such skill and precaution that it would never have been discovered had they not met with a sharp reverse in one of their principal attempts.

A number of the peasants had taken refuge, together with their cattle and goods, in a strongly built country house, and our grenadiers, having found them out, set to work to force them to disgorge their property. The peasants, finding them attacking their outer gates with hatchets and levers, tried to mollify them by the offer of refreshments and hospitality. The robbers would listen to none of their overtures, consequently the peasants opened fire with the idea of frightening them, which only had the effect of causing them to redouble their efforts to break into the place. The defenders then saw that desperate measures were necessary to save themselves from the fury of these madmen; they minced matters no longer, and slew in no time twenty-four of them, and obliged the rest to take to their heels. The scandal of this business, together with the death of so many grenadiers, could not fail to reach my ears. I then learned the whole history of their brigandage, and immediately took fresh measures to control them during the remainder of the march.

The best that I could do was to avail myself of the permit I had obtained, and camp them apart by themselves; one half of the regiment mounted guard over the other, and I made the sergeants and corporals personally responsible for all absentees from the surprise roll-calls which I ordered at uncertain hours. When the question of fetching wood and straw arose, I caused each party to be properly organised, and accompanied by non-commissioned officers who were responsible for such as could not return to camp with the rest, and by such precautions, stamped out most of the misdeeds that these brigands were in the habit of committing.

The army having continued its way to Ulm, finally encamped near the town in a district called Langenau, to await the advance of Milord Marlborough, who purposed joining the army of Prince Louis of Baden. We had received information of this, but we relied upon the army of the king, which had him under observation, to prevent it. We expected that our army would soon be called upon to undertake the siege of Nuremberg, the apparatus for which was all ready at hand in the Arsenal of Ingolstadt. Lord Marlborough, however, was able to move his army without opposition, and we soon learnt that he had effected his junction with the Prince of Baden. This was a new shock for our generals, and I am convinced that the approach of the reinforced Imperialists caused them to regret not having followed the advice of Maréchal d'Arcko, but there was no help for it now.

Reconnaissances having been made, and the enemy being found stronger even than we had supposed, it became necessary to alter our projects; there was now no longer any thought of the siege of Nuremberg, and we were forced to remain on the defensive.

Our attention was therefore directed towards securing the various lines of advance by which the enemy might invade Bavaria, and the districts we had acquired.

Scouting parties were sent out all over the country to discover their movements, and on their report that an advance was being made, which threatened the safety of Augsburg and Donauwört, a Bavarian infantry corps, with several squadrons of dragoons, was detached under Maréchal d'Arcko to occupy the heights of Schelemberg, and several French regiments were sent to garrison Donauwört. This town is on the Danube, which flows under its walls on the Bavarian side, and on the other is the height of Schelemberg, a strong and citadel -like position.

As soon as this force had started, our army broke up its camp at Langenau and moved on to Lauingen and Dillingen, where, after having made some stay, it set out for the river Leek, and entrenched itself near Augsburg.

The force under Maréchal d'Arcko consisted of the regiments of Bèarn and Nectancourt, besides other French regiments destined for Donauwört, and ten Bavarian battalions; the latter were without any doubt excellent and strong, consisting of at least seven hundred men each, and were detailed to occupy the Schelemberg height.[1] There were three from the regiment of the Elector's Guards, of which the first were grenadiers; three from the regiment of the Prince Electoral, none of which were grenadiers; three from the regiment of Liselbourg, and our own battalion of French grenadiers, which made the ten. Besides these ten battalions, we had twelve French and Bavarian squadrons. On the heights we found the remains of an old entrenchment constructed in the past by Gustavus Adolphus, King of Sweden, as a defence against the Bavarians.

The Schelemberg height is oval in plan, with a gentle slope on the southern side, which affords very easy communication with Donauwört; whilst on the northern the country is covered with *very* thick woods and undergrowth, reaching close up to the old entrenchments.

The two *entremities* of the entrenchment were practically safe from assault, and the attack on this height could only be made on one of the two flanks; a choice had to be made between the two, owing to the lack of good communication. Both flanks had precipitous contours, leading to flat country of a considerable area. It would be hardly possible to take the town of Donauwört without first seizing the Schelemberg, for it commanded all the flat country of Bavaria; withal having occupied it, we did not believe that the enemy would dream of approaching from this direction; had it been otherwise we should certainly have worked with more diligence on the entrenchments we

---

1. The Duke of Marlborough designed and commanded the attack on the Schelemberg position, which covered the town of Donauwört, though the Dutch attributed the victory to Prince Louis of Baden and struck a medal to that effect. (*Marlborough's Wars*— volume 1-1702-07, and volume 2–1707-09 by Frank Taylor published by Leonaur.)

JOHANNES BARO DE CHURCHILL, DUX ET COMES DE MARLBOROUGH.
MAGNE BRITANÆ REGINÆ À CONSILIIS SECRETIORIBUS, ORDINIS PERISCE LIDIS EQUES.
REI TORMENTARIE ET COPIARUM BRITANNICARUM PREFECTUS GENERALIS, SACRI
ROMANI EMPERII PRINCEPS.

DUKE OF MARLBOROUGH

began on the old lines we found there. As it was, working parties were detailed two days after our arrival, that is on the eve of St. John, but these were not strong enough for the extensive operations necessary. They were told off to work on the east flank, and where the wood approached our alignment, whilst the entrenchment of the opposite side was postponed until this was completed.

Such was the state of the Schelemberg position when the enemy made their appearance to attack it. I shall now leave this subject in order to speak for a moment concerning Boismorel.

Boismorel, who was new to the profession of arms, had not learnt to distinguish between the seasons consecrated to Mars and to Venus. The latter divinity had made so complete a subjection of his senses that he found himself no longer able to support the absence of his darling cook; he considered our detachment to be a thing of secondary importance, and we had hardly left the main army before he had formed plans to go and rejoin her. As we were more than fifty leagues away from Munich, he found himself obliged to obtain leave of absence from Maréchal d'Arcko, but as he was afraid to do this in person, lest the general should go into details, he asked me to take the business in hand for him.

At first I thought he was joking, but when I saw that he was in earnest, I pointed out the probable consequences of such a trip; begging him to think of the situation we now found ourselves in, the danger we were exposed to, his duty, and the bad example he would be giving, besides the small grounds he had as a pretext for asking leave; but his infatuation was so great that all my remonstrances were vain. To get over the difficulty, he told me to say that he was sick.

"That might do," said I, "as a pretext, if you were able to prevent the discovery of your true reason; but with the knowledge that you are bound for a place as far off as Munich, the real reason for your indisposition will not be long in forthcoming, and if an engagement takes place during your absence, what regret you will suffer when reproached with not having been present, and all owing to your own fault."

"Well, well, don't say anything about the place I am going to," he replied; "but if anything happens, send me a courier to warn me."

"Very good," said I, "if Marlborough shows signs of attacking, I will just beg him to wait a bit, for otherwise you certainly can't hope to be one of our party."

All this, however, was powerless to recall him to a sense of duty, even to himself; and I took upon myself to ask for his leave. Maréchal d'Arcko smiled maliciously, and after thinking a little, told me that Boismorel could go if he thought right, and said curtly that his presence or his absence was a matter of indifference to him. I had no sooner told Boismorel that he could go, than in a transport of joy he took post, and left to us the care of the defence of the Schelemberg position.

Our entrenchments were in the state detailed above when a corporal belonging to the regiment of the Electoral prince deserted from us, and reported to the enemy our position, the number of our troops, and our preparations, about which he had taken care to obtain correct information. He was brought before Prince Louis of Baden, who, aware of the importance of the position, took good care to make the best use of such important news. The deserter not only swore to the correctness of his report, but offered himself as a guide to direct the enemy's forces along the best line of advance for their attack. Thus, through a single individual of no special importance, their generals surprised us on the flank on which no work had yet been bestowed, and his advice was tantamount to a death sentence on thousands of men.

The entire force of the enemy began its advance as night was closing in on July 1st. The combined armies marched in several columns, to facilitate their progress, and early next morning were clear of the woods and over a large stream called the Wörnitz. The march was long and the pace forced (in order to avoid information of their design reaching the Elector, who otherwise might have set out to our support), and was continued until they were in sight of our entrenchments, before which they appeared at midday on July 2nd. Some small detachments, however, which we had placed to cover our front, came in at nine in the morning to warn Maréchal d'Arcko of the enemy's advance. He at once sent off a courier to the Elector with a request for support, and set his infantry to work with picks and shovels to improve the defenceless flank upon which the enemy was advancing.

The time left to us was too short to complete this satisfactorily; we could only place fascines one on the other, sparsely covered with earth, so as to form something of the nature of a parapet, which, moreover, was neither high enough nor wide enough to be of much use. As to the ditch on the enemy's side, from which works of this sort derive their chief strength, the Imperial forces gave us no time even to begin it.

No attention had been paid hitherto to this flank because the town of Donauwört protected this side more than the other; its glacis so commanded the line of approach to it that a column would have to defile along the edge of the wood to avoid the fire of the fortifications, which thus ought to have formed one of our principal defences.

It was, however, at this point, by the corporal's advice, that the enemy appeared and made their attack—pernicious advice for our cause and for the many brave men who fell in the action.

As soon as I learned that the enemy were upon us, I did my best to let Boismorel know the state of the case; but as the posting office had no horses to spare, the general having requisitioned them all to keep up communications with the Elector, I could do nothing; and, after all, it would have been useless, as the enemy hardly even gave us the chance to get together.

The Imperialists, whose first object was to lose no time, formed up their army as fast as its units arrived at the point along the edge of the wood where they were sheltered from the fire of the fortress. Having planted a battery of ten guns, they began by cannonading us high and low, with the idea of smashing our feeble parapet, shaking the courage of our troops, and covering their deployment.

Maréchal d'Arcko, who had flattered himself when they first appeared that they would hardly be in a condition to attack us that very day, and that the army from Augsburg would have time to send us reinforcements, now realised from the prompt action of this battery that they had resolved to make short work of us before this could happen, and that it was upon the defenceless flank that the enemy were about to deliver their assault.

He also saw that the fire from the town must oblige them to keep so close to the wood that their front would be narrowed to the width of two battalions; he therefore massed his force opposite the side of the wood, and brought up eight pieces of cannon to reply to their battery. As soon as he had disposed the infantry along the parapet, he posted my grenadiers at a most dangerous point, fifty paces in rear, in order to have them ready at hand to despatch to the actual locality chosen by the enemy for their assault. My regiment thus found itself, owing to the slope of the ground, so much above the crest of the parapet that it was actually face to face with the muzzles of the Imperialist guns. Maréchal d'Arcko, when posting us, told me that his reason in so doing was the great confidence he had in us, and as he expected an attack from the direction of the wood, we were there so as to be in touch with either the flank or the extremity of our oval-formed position, and that he left it to my judgment to lead the regiment to whichever point I thought fit when the assault was made.

He added that he did not believe the wood itself to be practicable for troops, or that they would make a serious attack at this point, but that it would be a feint at most, which, however, might develop into a real attack should they find our resistance to be but slight. He thought that appearances were all in favour of their advancing close alongside the wood, and then throwing all their force directly upon the angle of the flank, as it was hardly possible that they would extend in the direction of the glacis.

"M, de ———, brigadier in the king's army," said he, "is in command in the town, and has without doubt taken every care in lining the glacis with his infantry, therefore I have decided to concentrate my force at this angle, and disregard the ground covered by the town; however, to be on the safe side, I ordered him to place a battalion in position there, and he has sent the regiment of Nectancourt, but it will be much spread out. I leave the supporting movement of your regiment," continued he, "entirely in your hands." He then left to give orders elsewhere.

I was still mounted when I received my orders from Maréchal d'Arcko, as I had had much ground to cover in carrying out his orders in connection with the works he had given me to superintend. As soon as he had left I dismounted, but did not discard my heavy boots, which, being soft, did not seem likely to incommode me; I then gave over my horse to a drummer, whom I ordered to get under cover as near as possible, in case I had need of him.

Maréchal d'Arcko's orders gave me serious cause for reflection, as I should have to decide hurriedly, in a moment of time, the fate of the regiment, and this moment would be one of the gravest importance; I knew further the difficulties that arise in disposing of a regiment to most advantage when pushing it into the turmoil of an attack, and therefore I made a point of impressing upon my men the necessity of attention to orders, and of prompt obedience in carrying out any manoeuvres during the action with courage and in good order. I assured them that herein lay our safety and, perhaps, victory.

I had scarcely finished speaking when the enemy's battery opened fire upon us, and raked us through and through. They concentrated their fire upon us, and with their first discharge carried off Count de la Bastide, the lieutenant of my own company with whom at the moment I was speaking, and twelve grenadiers, who fell side by side in the ranks, so that my coat was covered with brains and blood. So accurate was the fire that each discharge of the cannon stretched some of my men on the ground. I suffered agonies at seeing these brave fellows perish without a chance of defending themselves, but it was absolutely necessary that they should not move from their post.

This cannonade was but the prelude of the attack that the enemy were developing, and I looked upon the moment when they would fling themselves against one point or another in our entrenchments as so instant that I would allow no man even to bow his head before the storm, fearing that the regiment would find itself in disorder when the time came for us to make the rapid movement that would be demanded of us. At last the enemy's army began to move to the assault, and still it was necessary for me to suffer this sacrifice to avoid a still greater misfortune, though I had five officers and eighty grenadiers killed on the spot before we had fired a single shot.

So steep was the slope in front of us that as soon almost as the enemy's column began its advance it was lost to view, and it came into sight again only two hundred paces from our entrenchments. I noticed that it kept as far as possible from the glacis of the town and close alongside of the wood, but I could not make out whether a portion might not also be marching within the latter with the purpose of attacking that part of our entrenchments facing it, and the uncertainty caused me to delay any movement. There was nothing to lead me to suppose that the enemy had such an intimate knowledge of our defences as to guide them to one point in preference to another for their attack.

Had I been able to guess that the column was being led by that scoundrel of a corporal who had betrayed us, I should not have been in this dilemma, nor should I have thought it necessary to keep so many brave men exposed to the perils of the cannonade, but my doubts came to an end two hours after midday, for I caught sight of the tips of the Imperial standards, and no longer hesitated. I changed front as promptly as possible, in order to bring my grenadiers opposite the part of our position adjoining the wood, towards which I saw that the enemy was directing his advance.

The regiment now left a position awkward in the extreme on account of the cannon, but we soon found ourselves scarcely better off, for hardly had our men lined the little parapet when the enemy broke into the charge, and rushed at full speed, shouting at the top of their voices, to throw themselves into our entrenchments.

The rapidity of their movements, together with their loud yells, were truly alarming, and as soon as I heard them I ordered our drums to beat the "charge" so as to drown them with their noise, lest they should have a bad effect upon our people. By this means I animated my grenadiers, and prevented them hearing the shouts of the enemy, which before now have produced a heedless panic.

The English infantry[2] led this attack with the greatest intrepidity, right up to our parapet, but there they were opposed with a courage at least equal to their own. Rage, fury, and desperation were manifested by both sides, with the more obstinacy as the assailants and assailed were perhaps the bravest soldiers in the world. The little parapet which separated the two forces became the scene of the bloodiest struggle that could be conceived. Thirteen hundred grenadiers, of whom seven hundred belonged to the Elector's Guards, and six hundred who were left under my command, bore the brunt of the enemy's attack at the forefront of the Bavarian infantry.

It would be impossible to describe in words strong enough the details of the carnage that took place during this first attack, which lasted a good hour or more. We were all fighting hand to hand, hurling them back as they clutched at the parapet; men were slaying, or tearing at the muzzles of guns and the bayonets which pierced their entrails; crushing under their feet their own wounded comrades, and even gouging out their opponents' eyes with their nails, when the grip was so close that neither could make use of their weapons. I verily believe that it would have been quite impossible to find a more terrible representation of Hell itself than was shown in the savagery of both sides on this occasion.

At last the enemy, after losing more than eight thousand men in this first onslaught, were obliged to relax their hold, and they fell back for shelter to the dip of the slope, where we could not harm them. A sudden calm now reigned amongst us, our people were recovering their breath, and seemed more determined even than they were before the conflict. The ground around our parapet was covered with dead and dying, in heaps almost as high as our fascines, but our whole attention was fixed on the enemy and his movements; we noticed that the tops

---

2. Also dismounted dragoons. The 1st, 3rd, 5th, 6th, 7th Dragoon Guards, 2nd Dragoons and 5th Lancers (then 5th Dragoons) served in this and the succeeding campaigns under Lord Marlborough. The 2nd Dragoons (Scots Greys) were led at Schelemberg and Ramillies by Lord John Hay.

of his standards still showed at about the same place as that from which they had made their charge in the first instance, leaving little doubt but that they were reforming before returning to the assault.

As soon as possible we set vigorously to work to render their approach more difficult for them than before, and by means of an increasing fire swept their line of advance with a torrent of bullets, accompanied by numberless grenades, of which we had several waggon loads in rear of our position. These, owing to the slope of the ground, fell right amongst the enemy's ranks, causing them great annoyance and doubtless added not a little to their hesitation in advancing the second time to the attack. They were so disheartened by the first attempt that their generals had the greatest difficulty in bringing them forward again, and indeed would never have succeeded in this, though they tried every other means, had they not dismounted and set an example by placing themselves at the head of the column, and leading them on foot.

Their devotion cost them dear, for General Stirum and many other generals and officers were killed. They once more, then, advanced to the assault, but with nothing like the success of their first effort, for not only did they lack energy in their attack, but after being vigorously repulsed, were pursued by us at the point of the bayonet for more than eighty paces beyond our entrenchments, which we finally re-entered unmolested.

After this second attempt many efforts were made by their generals, but they were never able to bring their men to the assault a third time. They remained halted halfway in a state of uncertainty, seeking an opportunity of extricating themselves and improving their position. They had all along feared the effect of the fire from the covered-way of Donauwört, and this was why they had narrowed their attack along the edge of the wood; having failed, therefore, to penetrate our particular angle of the entrenchments, they sent off a lieutenant and twenty men in the direction of the town to reconnoitre it closely.

This officer, who fully believed he had received his sentence of death, was agreeably surprised to find the glacis deserted, and his party only received a few shots from the loopholes in the old walls of the town.

The town commandant, upon whom Maréchal d'Arcko had relied so much, instead of lining his covered-way with his best troops, had withdrawn them all into the main works; he seems to have considered that the best way of ensuring the safety of the place was to shut up his troops and lock the gates, and the result was our ruin. It is quite certain that if he had occupied the covered-way, as was naturally to be expected, the enemy would never have been able to get into our entrenchments, for they would have found it impossible to do so under the flank fire from the glacis, against which they could have in no wise protected themselves. I am of opinion even, that had they cared to run this risk we should have had notice of their line of advance from the resistance offered by the garrison, in time to have afforded support in that quarter by filing to our left along our entrenchments. As it was, we were not in a position to know anything of this, owing to the formation of the ground which hid their movements from us; and at the same time it seemed clear, owing to the resistance maintained against them at every point and the great loss they had suffered in their repulse, that their chance of success in a third assault was as hopeless as the two first.

Besides this, the day's failure apparently spelt ruin to them; reinforcements from Augsburg were on their way to join us, and certainly would have had time to arrive by nightfall, when the enemy would find themselves in a very awkward position owing to the demoralising effect of the woods and defiles to be repassed in the retreat. France would have then been able to carry out her original plan of campaign, particularly as the enemy had already lost nearly fourteen thousand men, as I learned from themselves later on, a number that would, as far as could be judged, be largely increased during a forced retreat. But as it happened, matters had a different ending.

When the enemy found themselves safe from attack on the town side, they hastened to make the most of the daylight left to them. It was nearly seven in the evening when they began their movement to turn this flank, which they did without making any change in their order of battle. They had merely to turn their column to the flank, and by reason of the fall of the ground, succeeded in changing their position to their right, near the glacis, without meeting any obstacle, or being seen by us. If we only could have been informed of this movement, we could have moved to any place at which they might have presented themselves, but we never believed it possible that they would approach from this direction; on the contrary, we had been absolutely assured of the safety of this point, and seeing no signs of a renewed assault, as the day waned, looked upon the victory as ours, and, in fact, never was joy greater than our own than at the very moment when we were in the greatest danger.

We pictured to ourselves all the advantages produced by our successful resistance, and the glory of the action itself, perhaps the most memorable in the history of the world; for after all, although the enemy might in the end, as I shall show later on, find themselves masters of our entrenchments, it could not diminish the glory due to our ten battalions, for having sustained, unbroken, two determined assaults of a formidable army, which after five hours' fighting no longer dared to make even an appearance.

If this action had been described in detail by a practised hand, it would be the subject of the admiration of the century, but however good my own intentions in making a vivid and touching description of it might be, I could not give effect to them, because my literary powers would not be equal to the task. I shall content myself, therefore, by remarking that our ten battalions, with hardly the pretence of an entrenchment, held their own at Donauwört against the violent and reiterated efforts of a whole and powerful army, which five weeks later defeated, on the plain of Hochstett, the combined forces of France and Bavaria, in which battle none of our battalions took part.

I leave the appreciation of the valour of our troops to those who read these memoirs, and those more curiously inclined who have studied the subject in other histories, to draw their own deductions. I should not know how to set about it, for I declare, before God and man, that I have never read any treatise on this war except one regarding the Belgrade affair, in a book entitled *The Campaigns of Prince Eugene*, which one of my friends brought my wife, as it contained a paragraph or so concerning me. I would go further by saying that owing to the dislike I have always had of speaking of war itself, I wrote these memoirs under a species of compulsion, and would never have done so had I had my own way in the matter.

The enemy then, having found means to change their position and their line of attack unobserved, formed up on a broader front than before, and advanced to attack part of the entrenchments guarded only by the regiment of Nectancourt. This regiment, which was strung out in single rank, was in no wise in a position to offer a serious resistance, and retired into the town on their approach without giving the slightest information of their movement to our ten battalions. Our dragoons, who saw all this going on, came into action, but a volley from the enemy killed so many of them that they were obliged to retire without any possibility of their approaching the angle we were holding. Maréchal d'Arcko and Major-General M. de Liselbourg, who were at this point when the enemy broke through, were also cut off from us, and never doubting but that our ten battalions had already retired, made their way to the town, which they had some difficulty in entering, owing to the hesitation of the commandant to open the gates.

We, however, remained steady at our post; our fire was as regular as ever, and kept our opponents thoroughly in check. But while we were thus devoting our attention to our own part of the field, the enemy had possessed themselves of all the entrenchments on our left, and shut us off completely from any communication with the town, which ought at least to have served us as a haven of retreat. I was the only commanding officer left among the ten battalions, and I had a far from pleasing prospect before me.

Maréchal d'Arcko and Major-General Liselbourg had vanished, and Count Emanuel d'Arcko, who had just been wounded, was drowned during the retreat. He was colonel of the Prince Electoral's regiment, and his lieutenant-colonel, M. de Mercy, had been sent to Italy; the latter's brother, the Chevalier de Mercy, lieutenant-colonel of the guards, was also wounded, as well as the officer commanding the Liselbourg regiment. Thus I was left alone at the head of a body of men full of pluck and confidence, but about to be deserted by Fortune.

Although the enemy were in possession of all the entrenchments on our left, they took, out of respect for us, every precaution when advancing to attack us. As fast as the infantry entered the position, their generals formed them up four lines in depth, and although we now were lining our parapet and had our left flank at their mercy, we had inspired them with such fear of our powers that they advanced upon us in slow time with shouldered arms, either as if to warn us it was time to retire, or because they still felt that our aspect was too dangerous a one to risk anything rash.

What made our position still more trying was that taking us thus in flank they caught us, as in a trap, between their main line of battle and the entrenchment which faced the wood on our right. However, to our great good fortune, they never thought of dividing their force when they had got into the entrenchments, and sending one portion to cut off our retreat, whilst the other pressed us on the flank.

They arrived within gunshot of our flank, about 7.30 in the evening, without our being at all aware of the possibility of such a thing, so occupied were we in the defence of our own particular post and the confidence we had as to the safety of the rest of our position.

But I noticed all at once an extraordinary movement on the part of our infantry, who were rising up and ceasing fire withal. I glanced around on all sides to see what had caused this behaviour, and then became aware of several lines of infantry in greyish white uniforms on our left flank. From lack of movement on their part, their dress and bearing, I verily believed that reinforcements had arrived for us, and anybody else would have believed the same. No information whatever had reached us of the enemy's success, or even that such a thing was the least likely, so in the error I laboured under I shouted to my men that they were Frenchman, and friends, and they at once resumed their former position behind the parapet.

Having, however, made a closer inspection, I discovered bunches of straw and leaves attached to their standards, badges the enemy are in the custom of wearing on the occasion of battle, and at that very moment was struck by a ball in the right lower jaw, which wounded and stupefied me to such an extent that I thought it was smashed. I probed my wound as quickly as possible with the tip of my finger, and finding the jaw itself entire, did not make much fuss about it; but the front of my jacket was so deluged with the blood which poured from it that several of our officers believed that I was dangerously hurt. I reassured them, however, and exhorted them to stand firmly with their men. I pointed out to them that so long as our infantry kept well together the danger was not so great, and that if they behaved in a resolute manner, the enemy, who were only keeping in touch with us without daring to attack us, would allow us to retire without so much as pursuing. In truth, to look at them it would seem that they hoped much more for our retreat than any chance of coming to blows with us.

I at once, therefore, shouted as loudly as I could that no one was to quit the ranks, and then formed my men in column along the entrenchments facing the wood, fronting towards the opposite flank, which was the direction in which we should have to retire. Thus, whenever I wished to make a stand, I had but to turn my men about, and at any moment could resume the retirement instantaneously, which we thus carried out in good order. I kept this up until we had crossed the entrenchments on the other flank, and then we found ourselves free from attack. This retreat was not made, however, without loss, for the enemy, although they would not close with us when they saw our column formed for the retirement, fired volleys at close range into us, which did much damage.

My men had no sooner got clear of the entrenchments than they found that the slope was in their favour, and they fairly broke their ranks and took to flight, in order to reach the plain that lay before them before the enemy's cavalry could get upon their track. As each ran his hardest, intending to reform on the further side, they disappeared like a flash of lightning without ever looking back, and I, who was with the rear guard ready to make a stand if necessary against our opponents, had scarcely clambered over the entrenchments when I found myself left entirely alone on the height, prevented from running by my heavy boots.

I looked about on all sides for my drummer, whom I had warned to keep at hand with my horse, but he had evidently thought fit to look after himself, with the result that I found myself left solitary to the mercy of the enemy and my own sad thoughts, without the slightest idea as to my future fate. I cudgelled my brains in vain for some way out of my difficulty, but could think of nothing the least certain; the plain was too wide for me to traverse in my big boots at the necessary speed, and to crown my misfortunes, was covered with cornfields. So far the enemy's cavalry had not appeared on the plain, but there was every reason to believe that they would not long delay their coming; it would have been utter folly on my part to give them the chance of discovering me embarrassed as I was, for as long as I was hampered with my boots, a trooper would always find it an easy affair to catch me.

I noticed, however, that the Danube was not so very far away, and determined to make my way towards it at all risk, with the hope of finding some beaten track or place where there would be some chance of saving my life, as I saw it was now hopeless to think of getting my men together. As a matter of fact, I found a convenient path along the bank of the river, but this was not of much avail to me, for, owing to my efforts and struggles to reach it through several fields of standing corn, I was quite blown and exhausted and could only just crawl along at the slowest possible pace.

On my way I met the wife of a Bavarian soldier, so distracted with weeping that she travelled no faster than I did. I made her drag off my boots, which fitted me so tightly about the legs that it was absolutely impossible for me to do this for myself. The poor woman took an immense time to effect this, and it seemed to me at least as if the operation would never come to an end. At last this was effected, and I turned over in my mind the best way to profit by my release, when, raising my head above the corn at the side of the road, I saw a number of the enemy's troopers scattered over the country, searching the fields for any of our people who might be hidden therein, with the intention, doubtless, of killing them for the sake of what plunder might be found upon them.

At this cruel prospect all my hopes vanished, and the exultation I felt at my release from the boots died at the moment of its birth. My position was now more perilous than ever; nevertheless, I examined under the cover afforded by the corn the manoeuvres of these cavaliers to see if I could not find some way out of the difficulty. A notion came into my head which, if it could have been carried out, might have had a curious ending. It was that if one trooper only should approach me, and his comrades remained sufficiently distant, I should keep hidden and wait until he got near enough for me to kill him with a shot from my pistol, for I had two on my belt; I would then take his uniform, mount his horse, and make my escape in this disguise, a plan which would be favoured by the approaching darkness. But not seeing any chance of being able to carry out this idea, I thought of another, namely, to get into the river up to my chin in the water under the bushes on the bank, wait for nightfall and the return of the troopers to their camp, and then to escape in the dark.

But there were more difficulties to contend with in risking this even than in the other case, and as a last resource it struck me I might save myself by crossing the river, for happily I knew how to swim, although the risk here was very great owing to the breadth and rapidity of the Danube. I hurriedly determined on this plan, as I now saw a number of troopers approaching ever nearer to my hiding-place, who were refusing to give quarter to the unhappy wounded they found hidden in the corn, whom they ruthlessly despatched the more easily to despoil them. There was no reason to suppose that they were likely to show any more mercy to me, particularly as I was worth more in the shape of plunder than a private soldier, nor was there time to lose in making up my mind, so I then and there determined to swim the river.

Before taking to the water I took the precaution of leaving on the bank my richly embroidered uniform, rather spoiled as it was by the events of the late action. I scattered in a similar manner my hat, wig, pistols, and sword, at one point and another, so that if the troopers came up before I had got well away, they would devote their attention to collecting these articles instead of looking in the water, and it turned out just as I thought. I kept on my stockings, vest, and breeches, simply buttoning the sleeves of the vest and tucking the pockets within my breeches for safety; this done, I threw myself upon the mercy of the stream. I had hardly got any distance when up came the troopers, who, as I had hoped, dismounted as quickly as they could to lay hands on the spoil lying before them; they even set to work to quarrel over it, for I distinctly heard them shouting and swearing in the most delightful manner.

Others apparently got no share, and they amused themselves by saluting me with several musket shots, but the current of the river which carried me on my way soon put me out of their range. Finally, after a very long and hard swim, I was lucky enough to reach the other bank, in spite of the strength of the stream.

When I had left the water and with it all anxiety regarding the safety of my life, I suddenly found myself completely overcome with exhaustion. This was not surprising, considering all the labour of my day's work, which only a robust constitution, such as mine was then, could possibly have supported. As it was, one piece of luck was followed by another, for I found to my relief on the river-bank a quartermaster and a dragoon of the regiment of Fonboisar, who, on their way back from some duty, had stopped there in order to satisfy their curiosity as to what was passing on the other side of the Danube. I landed exactly at their feet, and the quartermaster, who gathered by my waistcoat and linen that I was an officer, came forward most politely to ask who I was and what he could do for me.

As soon as he had learned that I was the lieutenant-colonel of the French grenadiers, he immediately dismounted and searched the dragoon's valise, producing a cap and a shirt, which he made me put on, together with a cloak over-all, and insisted that I should mount his horse, while he rode that of the dragoon, whom he took up behind him. He kindly escorted me thus to a little town called Rain, four leagues distant, which I had pointed out to him. There I discovered at the best inn of the place all the train of Maréchal d'Arcko, which had escaped from Donauwört.

The officers of the *maréchal's* staff received me with great attention and dressed my wound, which was of no great consequence; but while affording me this relief they also gave me grounds to fear the fate of my own baggage. They told me that it had been possible to save but a very little belonging to those who were encamped round the entrenchments, and that mine was not included in it. It seemed that all the baggage-waggons bolted off together at the beginning of the attack, and the drivers, in trying to secure their own safety first, had crowded down upon the bridge of boats, which had been constructed over the river close to the town. Here the over-weighted bridge had separated into several parts; numbers of waggons went to the bottom of the river, and those that remained had been plundered by the enemy.

Up to now I had not given a thought to my baggage, having been too much occupied with other things, but this report from the *maréchal's* people brought home to me the evil case I was in if it was really lost; and by the circumstantial account I had just received, there seemed to be no doubt at all about it.

I found it impossible to get a wink of sleep all that night. A confused picture of all the incidents of the battle passed before my brain, and notwithstanding all my efforts, I could not dismiss it from my thoughts. To add to my misery, the windows of my room looked out upon the town square, whence came a rumbling sound the whole night long, caused by the baggage-train waggons from Donauwört. Though daylight had already appeared, I was still in bed when I thought I heard the voice of my valet. I sprung in one jump from my bed to the window to see if I was not mistaken, and sure enough I saw him below me, fussing about to get some miserable carts out of the way in order to let my carriage by. I hurriedly waved my hand and shouted to him, but my man only looked at me aghast, and never moved an inch.

I redoubled my efforts of voice and gesture to get him to come to me, and at last, having approached my window and examined me well, he uttered a cry as if he thought I had returned from the other world. He then rushed up to my room, and when I asked him why he had not recognised me, he said he was so convinced by circumstantial reports that I was dead that he could not believe his ears when he heard me call. It finally appeared that my other servants had wished to divide between them such of my property as had been saved, and that he had only prevented this being done on the spot by saying this should take place as soon as it was got away to a safer quarter, hoping thus to put them off till some news of the regiment might turn up. The pleasure brought by the recovery of at least a part of my effects prevented me paying much attention to my valet's tale, and my only thought was how I could collect together such remains of my battalion that I might find in the town.

Maréchal d'Arcko, after leaving Donauwört, had gone to the army at Augsburg, where his staff, who joined him there, told him the story of my adventures, and that I was in the town of Rain, occupied in rallying my grenadiers.

This little town, which lies beyond Donauwört on the edge of the Bavarian Lowlands, was a much-exposed position, and there could be no doubt but that the enemy having captured Donauwört would presently seize it, in order to further their design of ravaging the country up to the gates of Munich. The town itself was by no means in a position to offer resistance, having only an old brick enceinte, very thick, with towers at intervals, and a dry ditch. The necessity of placing it in a state of defence had never been thought of till now, when it became indispensable to create a bulwark for almost all Swabia, and it needed an extraordinary combination of circumstances, such as had just occurred to us at Schelemberg, to cause Rain to be regarded as a fit position to cover the rest of the country; however, this had come about, and the safety of the inhabitants of the district depended on the town.

When Maréchal d'Arcko heard that I was there, he wrote to me detailing the Elector's intentions on this point. After having complimented me on the retreat from Schelemberg, he pointed out that His Highness hoped I should show no less zeal in the defence of Rain, which he now placed in my hands, and as the enemy would doubtless attack it, he had ordered a detachment of six hundred men, some cannon, and stores, to join me, which were already on their way. He was confident that, with the remains of the French grenadiers and the above, that I should be able to hold out for some days, though he was quite aware that the place itself was not defensible, but that he could not better show the great reliance he had in me than by placing the conduct of the operations in my hands and leaving me to act in the matter entirely as I might think best.

Orders had been given in the neighbouring districts for the constant supply of a great number of peasants to work under my direction at the construction of such defences as time would permit, and, with every faith placed in my efforts, I was requested to take the work in hand at once.

By this time I had about four hundred grenadiers, who had managed to save themselves and the colours, by way of Ingolstadt. These latter, although quite new at the opening of the campaign, were now torn to rags by the enemy's balls; they had not even respected the motto embroidered upon the white standard. This motto was in two words, "*Vae Spectanti*" ("Woe to him who looks upon me"). My grenadiers, and the detachment with six small pieces of cannon, gave a thousand men for the defence of the worst place in Europe for such a purpose, against two powerful armies; nevertheless, it was absolutely necessary to check the enemy's advance with this handful of men, the policy of the State demanded this, a thousand men were exposed to sacrifice in order to bring salvation to a much larger number.

I lost no time in the construction of works around the town, and the labourers soon cut a covered-way, which was strongly palisaded. I made as well two ravelins of earth and more palisades, which commanded ground outside the covered-way, over which the enemy would be likely to advance. I also took care to construct a number of gun platforms with embrasures on the flanks of the towers, so arranged that my cannon could be easily mounted and dismounted, and moved from one point to another, according to the exigencies of the case. All this being prepared, I waited resolutely for any lot that might befall me. I had not long to wait; in a short time an army arrived on the scene, and occupied the whole of the surrounding country, treating my little town with such disdain that no arrangements were made to invest it in a regular fashion.

The enemy's camps were pitched some distance away, and their general, without even opening fire upon us, merely sent a trumpeter to summon us to surrender, with a threat that if I offered any resistance no quarter would be shown to me or my garrison. I sent him back with the answer that I was extremely touched at the consideration shown for my life and my garrison, but as we had passed through many other similar experiences when such an honour had not been paid us as that now offered, I hoped that we should be considered worthy of obtaining an honourable capitulation by means of a real resistance, which owing to our numerous garrison we felt we were in a position to offer, rather than to surrender without any attempt to defend ourselves at all.

The enemy, however, did not seem to think much of our town, for, without opening a regular trench, they merely traced a small parallel in which they mounted a battery of ten pieces of cannon, for they believed that it would prove but a simple matter to level our old ramparts with the ground.

For three days they treated us to a leisurely cannonade without doing much damage, as the balls merely cut their way into the brickwork without wrecking it in any way whatever, so that as a result this was so much time gained for us. Whilst this was going on I amused myself with my six pieces of cannon, moving them from one emplacement to another to disconcert their gunners, who were never certain where to aim in order to dismount them, and who suffered much discomfort in their battery from our fire.

At last, finding their efforts were no nearer finality at the end of these three days, this fine army, to do us the honour of laying siege to us in a regular fashion, began the construction of trenches after nightfall, according to the usual custom.

I was waiting for this to occur in order to raise an alarm amongst their working parties to further delay their work, for in such a case the first intimation of a sortie is usually enough to cause them to cut and run. When the noise of the enemy's picks warned me of their designs, I ordered two hundred of my grenadiers, who were most accustomed to the stratagems of war, to move out in two parties, each under a captain and a lieutenant, one to the right and the other to the left flank of the works. They were ordered to march as quietly as possible, to avoid risk of discovery, in the direction in which they could hear the work going on, and as soon as they had neared the position, the lieutenants, in each case, were directed to take thirty picked men and place themselves at a distance from their captains still more on the enemy's flank, in order to make a greater show of strength.

This done, the whole were to lie down and wait until my six cannon had opened fire upon the working parties, when they, in their turn, would also bring a hot fire to bear upon them, accompanied with loud shouts, in order to spread alarm and give the impression that we were making a sortie in force. As soon as their volley had been delivered, they were immediately to lie down again to avoid the fire of the enemy. Also, should they notice the enemy preparing to advance against them, which was hardly likely, they were to retire without any further order.

On the other hand, if the enemy appeared contented with merely holding their position and not delivering any counter-attack, they were to remain concealed, in order to alarm the working parties a second time should they return to their work, and, in fact, prevent them doing anything, if possible, the whole night through. Finally, I ordered them not to wait for daylight to appear before retiring into the town.

My sortie came off just as I had hoped, and I thus gained another night of delay; but our besiegers took a multitude of precautions the following evening. They posted infantry everywhere to give warning and prevent their working parties being disturbed. This, however, did not prevent my giving them some more wholesome exercise and alarm by means of a number of small detachments which I sent out for the purpose that night, with the result that they once more got no work done. I got my grenadiers quite accustomed to this form of warfare, and they became so keen for it that they found means on their own account to disquiet the enemy, even during the day, and so to retard their work.

The siege had now lasted twelve days, and their army had invested me so closely that no opportunity was left to make terms. The fear that an unexpected assault would force my hand, determined me to hang out the flag, as a signal that I wished to enter into negotiations to capitulate. The enemy had no intention of according me terms, and called upon me to surrender at discretion; but when I spoke as if I was yet in a position to defend myself and cause them further loss, they relaxed so far as to propose holding me a prisoner of war only till the end of this campaign.

I refused absolutely to consent to this, and demanded a capitulation with all the honours of war, without which, I assured them, I would sustain any assault that they might make, which, however successful, would cost them at least as much as us. Then they tried cajoling, then threats, to induce me to accept their proposals, but finally, seeing that I refused the bait, granted what I asked. I here had proof how essential it is in all military matters to maintain a firm attitude. We left this wretched place next morning for Munich, and the enemy, who were persuaded we had a numerous garrison, arranged for us to pass through two ranks of their best troops, as is usual when an important place is taken.

It was singular how many of their officers, seeing the small party of men I had with me, seemed to be under the belief that I formed but the advanced guard of the garrison, and, either from impatience or curiosity, asked me, one after the other, whether the rest were coming on soon, I assured them that they would not be kept waiting long, as the remainder coming after me were not likely to be a burden to them, and after attaining a considerable distance on our route, I was amused to see, on looking back, that the double rank of troops were still at their post, waiting patiently until the "rest "of the garrison had left the place.

As soon as my capitulation had been signed, I sent off a courier to

Maréchal d'Arcko to report all that had passed, together with the line of my retirement, and received an answer full of compliments. I was also told that I should find recruits at Munich to reinforce the regiment, and that I was to wait there for further orders from His Highness. I had already sent on an officer to report my advent, the day of my arrival, and to look out for billets, as there are no barracks in Munich. Boismorel, who was still engrossed in his amours, having learned from this officer when I might be expected to arrive, and that we should enter the town by the gate adjoining the palace, thus marching past the windows of the Electress, made up his mind to shine at the head of the regiment on its entry into the town, counting on the Princess giving us the honour of her presence on the occasion. Never was man, in fact, better turned out than Boismorel, but his brilliancy only served as a more striking contrast to our war-stained, dishevelled appearance, and the Electress, who was by no means ignorant of Boismorel's proceedings, could hardly control herself at the sight.

CHAPTER 8

Return of Boismorel

As soon as the regiment had entered the town I had the honour of being received by Her Highness. I described to her the vigorous defence her troops had maintained at Schelemberg, the unexpected turn of events which had given the enemy this position, our retreat, and the defence of the town of Rain, every detail of which appeared to affect the princess most acutely, and wrung from her an expression of her fears for poor Bavaria. I took the liberty of pointing out to her that the enemy's successes were not yet sufficient to decide everything in their favour; that as we had every reason to hope for that help which we ought at any moment to receive from the hands of France, we should therefore arrange matters so as to delay the enemy's advance; for, after all, they had only taken from us two of the worst places in Bavaria, which could by no means be regarded as the equivalent to those that the Elector had acquired in Swabia.

The Electress, who no doubt saw that I was endeavouring to console her, made as though she agreed with all I said, but to the best of my belief it was otherwise with her innermost thoughts. Fear is a natural outcome of danger, and causes presentiments of evil which are often realised. The princess was in that state of mind which anticipates misfortunes, and a few days later on she had the sorrow of seeing their advent. From the windows of the palace she could distinguish the light of the conflagrations caused by the enemy in the country round, and the terrified inhabitants who poured into Munich for refuge spread reports of additional horrors, which had their birth merely in their imagination.

Everything was in a frightful state of confusion according to the talk of the populace, and I will go so far as to say that things were at such a pass as to somewhat justify a belief in the truth of these calamities. However, notwithstanding the current reports in Europe regarding this conflagration, the idea that all the countryside of Bavaria had been reduced to ashes, owed its origin simply to fear and panic. I do not deny that some houses were burnt, but the enemy's generals had no part in this; it was the work of marauders and camp followers who, disgusted in finding the peasants' houses abandoned, burnt some of them, and as is usually the case with a people wild with fear, they carried the panic with them. The crowds of peasants and refugees in Munich astounded the Electress and the Council of the State; public prayers and religious processions were ordered, Her Highness taking part in the latter barefooted and with exemplary devotion.

As there were no other troops left in Munich but the palace guards and my grenadiers, the Council of State proposed to me that I should set out with a detachment of our regiment to reconnoitre the ravaged districts, and quell as much as possible any existing disorder therein. I therefore set out, provided with a list of the most exposed villages, a guide thereto, and two hundred grenadiers only, to make the most of the concealment afforded by the woods which covered the country, and the greater ease derived from a small force in moving quickly from one point to another. Before leaving I had also come to the conclusion that the panic the Munich people were suffering from was of much the same character as that which had obtained at Straubing, which was a further reason why I decided not to take more than two hundred men with me.

I followed a route through several villages said to have been reduced to cinders, and although I certainly found a few burnt houses, still the damage done was as nothing compared with the reports current throughout the country. By means of the woods I was able to push on from village to village in the direction of the enemy's army, and found there even less evidence of damage; the villages seemed practically entire, and it was only on entering them that it was possible to see any trace of burning in a house here and there. We came across some marauders on our road, who were promptly shot to prevent their continuing their errand in the future, and after having passed through almost all the places mentioned on the list, I retired to Munich with information which brought some small calm on the subject of the present evils, but did not prevent the dread of those likely to come.

Notwithstanding that all Germany was resounding with the report of the burning of Bavaria, the Court of Vienna seemed to think this time of calamity an appropriate moment to suggest to the Elector sentiments of a peaceful nature; it counted on the compassion and love for his people to oblige him to listen to the propositions it made him, namely, to abandon the interests of France and to join with those of Austria, or, at all events, to lay down his arms.

Two envoys were sent to the camp at Augsburg, who represented to him the extremities to which his people were reduced, and the clemency the emperor would show him if he would voluntarily approach him and abandon a cause contrary to his own interests and those of all his nationality. They assured him that the Allies would not only recompense him for all that he had suffered, but also that he would find himself in the future in a superior position regarding them than had been the case during the preceding war when he was in possession of the Vicariat of the Circle of Burgundy. Moreover, he might well follow the recent example of the King of Portugal and the Duke of Savoy, who had recognised the justice of the Emperor's cause, and at the present juncture there was a special reason to think seriously of his own interests, as his territory was surrounded by the rest of the Empire and menaced by speedy disaster.

Also that he ought, for the sake of his people, his family, and himself, to take the course most advantageous to them; that if his delicacy of feeling led him to believe that owing to his engagements with France he would be leaving her army in the lurch in Swabia by thus abandoning her cause, he had the means of remedying this by allowing the French generals the choice of making a truce, to enable them to withdraw their army in safety within their own frontier, or of continuing the war where they were. He was also assured that these reasonable conditions would be approved of by all the Powers of Europe, and that it was time that His Highness thought of the preservation of his State from what appeared to be inevitable disaster.

Not only were all these propositions most artfully placed before the Elector, but the most touching and seductive solicitations were added to give them weight; to wit, those of the Electress, on whom the general misery and panic had been vividly impressed. This princess even went herself to Augsburg, and spared neither prayers nor tears to induce the Elector to free his State from the misfortunes threatened it, by accepting the propositions that had been made to him.

But this prince, who regarded the citation of the example of the Duke of Savoy as an insult to himself, answered that neither adversity nor gain would make him perjure himself and break the oath he had taken with the King of France, and that he would never give the world or his posterity the opportunity of reproaching him for allowing himself to be seduced into breaking any treaty for such frivolous reasons. As for the princes who were held up as models, they would never be such for him, and he would submit to the lot that it pleased the Almighty to award him without a murmur. In this manner His Highness firmly maintained that greatness of soul which is hereditary in his family.

Whilst these negotiations were going on at Augsburg, news was received that the enemy had detached a body of eight thousand men from their army in Italy, which having traversed the Tyrol, had invaded Bavaria, and seized several important positions, which were used as bases from which to harry the Elector's subjects. These evils were well attested, and His Highness, wishing to remedy them, ordered his three regiments of dragoons and six thousand infantry to march under the command of the Marquis de Massey, one of his major-generals, in order to bring on an action and retake the captured positions. Our regiment was attached to this flying column, and marched at once for the Tyrol, which is in the opposite direction to that of Augsburg. This further weakened our army, as several regiments had already been sent away to strengthen some threatened garrisons, and to occupy various posts in the interior of the country.

There were hardly any Bavarians left with the army at Augsburg except a few regiments of cavalry, the rest being dispersed in various directions. It had, in fact, been resolved to keep the army under cover of their entrenchments until the arrival of the expected help from France; it was there thought to be in a sufficiently safe position to send detachments to places deemed necessary for the safety of the country, the more so as it was easy to recall them in case of need.

Our regiment, which had been completely reorganised in Munich, was ordered to join the other troops, which were marching towards the Tyrolese frontier. Boismorel was with us, and placed himself at its head for this business. I learned on our way that Baron de—— had left Straubing, and that he was living with his family in a district through which our regiment would pass; consequently, the infatuation that possessed me for *mademoiselle* his daughter, compelled me to travel several days ahead of the regiment in order to visit her. I took strict account of the time at my disposal, lest, blinded by my devotion, I should lose sight of my duty.

I then set out, my mind full of airy imaginings and the most delightful thoughts of how I should surprise my fair one, as I felt assured that my arrival would afford her a pleasure equal with my own. I brought to mind the despair evinced by this charming creature on my departure from Straubing, and our reciprocal vows and protestations when we separated. All these thoughts filled my mind when I arrived at the Baron's *château* at the fall of night. Having knocked at the door, I told the lackey who let me in to say that a French grenadier was desirous of speaking to *mademoiselle*.

As I waited for an answer to this message I could feel my heart beating as I pictured to myself her hastily hurrying to ask for news concerning her dear Frenchman; but I was a long way out in my reckoning. I had chosen a bad moment. The young lady was enjoying the society of a noble bumpkin of the most uncouth appearance, who had taken care to console her in my absence. This wild animal, who knew somewhat of our Straubing relationships, could not control himself when the lackey gave the message. He broke out into reproaches at the idea of her receiving any person whatever of our nationality. Thus, after I had waited a considerable time at the door, a message came down to say that I could wait in the kitchen until *mademoiselle* found time to come and speak to me. I asked if she was ill, but received a blunt "No," and I swear that I never felt more foolish in my life than at that moment. All my fine ideas vanished, and I nearly choked with vexation. I forced my way into the room, feeling the greatest difficulty in moderating my anger.

Nevertheless, in order not to make a scene, I asked the young lady if she did not recognise me, when she, in fear of displeasing her lout if she spoke in language unknown to him, answered me in German, to the effect that she had forgotten how to speak French. This unexpected answer made me long to reproach her in German, so that her new lover might understand, and ask her if it was this great brute before me who had caused her to forget me, but at this moment, remembering the history of Joconde, and profiting by the good training that I had had in Paris, I made as though I had been mistaken in addressing her at all, and went off to find her father and mother, informing them I had merely come to see them when passing through their neighbourhood. I left next morning at break of day without inquiring further after the young lady, and resumed my way to rejoin my regiment.

A few days later we arrived at a little town called Rosenheim, where we found the Marquis de Massey with his command. This place is not very far from a village called Marquartstein, which lies at the foot of the Tyrolese Mountains, overlooking a river and a pretty plain, on which were encamped the enemy we were in search of. The neighbouring peasants kept us supplied with news, exaggerating as usual. According to their report, the whole plain of Marquartstein was covered with troops, and that a force of even twice our strength would not be sufficient to make head against them.

The Marquis de Massey, paying no attention to this, simply sent out an officer in disguise, who came from this part of the country; he being a very intelligent man, and having reconnoitred the enemy closely, brought in a reliable report of their numbers and positions, and then our general no longer had any hesitation in advancing to attack them, and, if possible, to surprise them. We had some obstacles to pass through in the shape of woods before attaining the plain on which they were encamped, but as we were in a friendly country, we found no lack of guides to show us the way. We marched the whole night, and were free of these defiles by daybreak. Nevertheless, it was ten o'clock in the morning before we were able to form up into battle formation, and the necessary orders for the attack were issued.

The Imperialists, who had seen our advance, struck their camp with all possible haste, and retired across the river by means of a wooden bridge, which they afterwards set light to. This river runs close along the foot of an inaccessible range of mountains, the level bank at that side being just wide enough for the purpose of a road, which ran along it. On this road lay the village of Marquartstein, which consisted of a single street, where the Imperialists took up their position with their line extending a short way to either flank. They thus left the river between them and us in the belief that by means of this rampart they would be altogether safe from attack.

Our peasant guides told the Marquis de Massey that it would be impossible for the enemy to retire over the mountains in their rear, as there were no gorges or passes whatever, and in such a case they would find themselves obliged to follow the river upstream for a good league, in order to arrive at a point at which they could hope to cross the range; moreover, before reaching this point, they would have to traverse a small plain, where it would be easy to head them off, as the river there was only about three feet deep. I was with our general and the colonels, Messieurs de Sauligny and de Mercy, reconnoitring the enemy's position when the peasants made this report, upon which we took counsel together there and then.

It was arranged that the three regiments of dragoons should be sent off to seize this point, and that when they had got beyond the enemy's flank we should cannonade the village across the river with eight small pieces of cannon that we had brought with us until they were driven out, so that when their troops began to retire and our infantry should take up the pursuit, they would then find themselves between two fires when they passed into the little plain, which was to be held by our dragoons; in short, the plan was so well thought out that the defeat of our opponents was certain if only our dragoons could seize the point ahead of them.

The order was then given to the dragoons to make their way along the further edge of the plain, so that the enemy should not discover the direction of their march; and the artillery officers were directed to bring up their cannon to where we were standing in order to bombard the Imperialists; but the sentries posted by the enemy on the top of a church belfry noted the movement of the dragoons and gave the alarm, whereupon the enemy immediately began to move in order to get a start. Boismorel, who had remained with the main body of our troops, as he was not on intimate terms with our generals, knew nothing of our plan of operations, and seeing the enemy begin their retirement, believed that we could catch them like mice in a trap, and that we were letting them go scot free either from fear or collusion on our part.

Besides this, want of knowledge of the art of war prevented him from weighing such matters in the least degree, consequently he worked himself into a passion, and we now saw him dashing up to our group at full gallop with his face distorted by astonishment. He accosted us like a madman, and addressing the Marquis de Massey, shouted out in a loud and threatening voice, "In the name of God, sir, what do you mean by letting the king's enemies escape in that manner, just at the time when we could have taken every man of them? You are a traitor, and unworthy of your rank, and I shall certainly report you and complain of your conduct."

We were dumb with amazement at this discourse, and could hardly believe our ears that anyone could have spoken thus to a general officer. The first thing the general did on hearing himself apostrophised in this manner was to carry his hand to his pistol, but he had scarcely done so before Boismorel whipped out his own, and had we not promptly laid hold of him, the general might have been killed at the very moment when he was devoting himself to the interests of the king and the Elector.

We had a world of trouble to calm the violence of Boismorel, and we should never have succeeded had we not forcibly disarmed him of his pistols. The Marquis de Massey acted most prudently on this occasion; no one could possibly have blamed him if he had ordered Boismorel to be shot, or killed him with his own hand on the spot. He contented himself with ordering him to be put under arrest; but this was never carried out, for no sooner did Boismorel find himself free of our grasp, than he galloped off to the regiment, shouting to it to follow him.

It had just arrived close up to where we were, in accordance with the general's orders, and several grenadiers made as though they were going to obey him, but were kept in their places by my orders. Three or four, however, of his own company followed him across the plain, and later he sent a man to fetch the pistols of a sub-lieutenant, after which he disappeared for the time being.

This incident so far over, we thought over our line of action with regard to the enemy. Our regiment of grenadiers had come up, but the rest of the infantry were still some distance away, because the affair with Boismorel had had the effect of checking the general movement Nevertheless, it was full time to begin our movement, if we wished to close with the Imperialist rear guard, and seeing our general getting impatient, I suggested crossing the river with my grenadiers, and engaging it until the rest of the infantry were at hand. My proposal was at once accepted, so with the guides' assurance that the stream was everywhere fordable, we plunged in file by file and crossed with ease.

This crossing, however, was not effected as quickly as I could have wished, and I feared, from the time it took, that the enemy might escape me; I therefore started in pursuit with the first half of the regiment that had passed over, and left an order for the rest to follow on. We were now in hard chase of the enemy's rearguard, and came up with it a good quarter of a league from the village, owing to their march having been hindered by the woods and my extreme diligence in pursuit. I first caught sight of them retiring over the brow of a wooded ridge, when I gave my grenadiers orders to fix bayonets and not to fire without permission from me.

We then hastened our pace, and the enemy seeing us on the point of falling upon them, halted, turned about, and opened fire upon us, with the result that a number of my men were killed on either side of my horse without, strange to say, even wounding him. This animal was so gun-shy that he became quite paralysed, and trembled so violently that, though I had no idea of dismounting, still I was obliged to do so, as there was no possibility of getting him to move on at all. After delivering this volley, the enemy continued their retirement with even more precipitation than before, and without reloading.

Here, then, was our turn in the game. We let ourselves go headlong upon them, and every one of our shots told. They quite thought that the whole of our army was at their heels, and were soon seized with panic; my grenadiers followed eagerly, slaying them with bayonet-thrust and gunshot, giving no quarter, so as not to delay the advance, and everywhere driving them before them. We met with hardly any resistance, for they sought safety only in flight, though this was by no means easy, as the hilly country had already put them out of breath; they had no possible reason to expect any succour from those in their van, as their one thought was to secure the open position before the arrival of our dragoons.

The rest of our infantry were unable to join us in time; indeed it was judged unnecessary to push them over the river, so that in this action of August 8th I and my grenadiers disposed of the entire regiment of Schvein, eighteen hundred strong. They fell victims to the fury of my men, excepting a very small number, who were made prisoners under singular circumstances which somewhat calmed the excitement of my people. This is how it happened.

A youth of good family, a cadet in the regiment of Schvein, seeing death staring him in the face, crouched behind a large tree, towards which I chanced to be making my way. This poor boy, who had kept his wits sufficiently to notice me, and thinking he might perhaps receive quarter at my hands, waited in this position until I had come right up to his tree, when, suddenly dashing out, he threw himself upon his knees right between my legs, crying for mercy. His action and handsome face so excited my compassion that, fearing that the grenadiers might run a bayonet into him, I held him in my arms and shouted loudly that no one was to harm him, as I wished to obtain intelligence through him regarding the enemy.

This excited the curiosity of my grenadiers, who crowded round to see what was going on, with the result that their fury calmed down, and they thought that I wished for more prisoners to be taken. Thus, instead of shooting down all that they met, they ran to make them prisoners, and in this way were saved the lives of the lieutenant-colonel, four captains, six lieutenants, and about two hundred and sixty soldiers of the regiment. We also took the six colours of the regiment, for in the Imperialist service each battalion has two of these, and the regiment of Schvein had three battalions.

After this was over, I rested my men in the midst of the wood, when I found myself overcome by severe pangs of hunger and thirst. I had ordered my grenadiers to leave their haversacks in the village of Marquartstein, in order to give them more freedom for the advance, which thereby removed all chance of ministering to our wants; but it struck us to search those of our opponents, wherein we found bread and small bottles of brandy, which much refreshed us. This halt over, I set off to rejoin the rest of our little army, which we found had already encamped M. de Massey, witnessing the dragoons return from their fruitless attempt, being forestalled by the enemy's advanced guard, and believing, moreover, that our grenadiers had failed to get into touch, and were merely amusing themselves in the woods with the chase of sundry laggards, determined to pitch his camp, and therefore sent us an order to retire.

Everything was over by the time his order arrived, so I descended the side of a mountain to re-enter the plain with my troops and prisoners, whom I placed in the centre of my grenadiers. Boismorel now joined us, puffed up with victories he had achieved on his own account. He was so taken up in recounting his deeds of valour that he had accompanied us for some time before he had noticed our prisoners and their colours, and I really believe that we should have arrived in camp without his seeing them at all, had I not interrupted his discourse to call attention to them. He informed us that he had pursued a runaway, who had attempted to escape behind a hedge, and despatched him with a pistol-shot; then, having caught sight of another who was creeping away, he ran as hard as he could towards him, and made him bite the dust likewise.

Whilst he was thus congratulating himself, I reflected on his case and how dangerous it was to put inexperienced people such as he in command of a body of troops. I saw in him, moreover, a true personification of that conceit which causes us to think everything of one's own deeds and nothing of those of others, and felt compassionately for the error under which he was labouring in actually lauding himself for being absent from his regiment at the very time when it was in action. When we arrived in camp I suggested to him that he should himself present the colours and prisoners to the Marquis de Massey; but he did not agree to this under the circumstances, and left the matter to me. This I did, and agreeably surprised the general, who had never expected so happy a result.

After complimenting me, he declared that had I not been in command of the regiment he would have sent an *aide-de-camp* much sooner to recall us, as he believed we could do no good in the wood, and, moreover, had a dread of the marauding habits of our grenadiers. He added that if he had known what was going on he would have sent reinforcements, but as the dragoons had missed their mark, he had concluded the affair was over, so that the joy he felt at so glorious a result was increased since it was entirely unexpected.

As I wished to profit by this opportunity to speak in Boismorel's favour, I did my best by pointing out Boismorel's share in the fight and attributing all the glory thereof to him, hoping thus to obtain his forgiveness; but the Marquis de Massey had been just as well informed of his conduct as I had, to the effect that after the action Boismorel had gone straight to the quarters of the regiment and retailed to each officer all that he just had told me. His story had been reported word for word to the general, who could hardly prevent himself from smiling at my endeavours, and told me that if I were in Boismorel's position I should not find in him the same ardour to serve my ends, and begged me to talk of something else.

A house in a village near the camp had been secured as quarters for Boismorel, and as soon as M. de Massey knew of his arrival there, he sent a lieutenant and twenty men as a guard, with orders to request him to hand over his sword. Boismorel was much surprised at this very natural attention: he had flattered himself that his victorious achievements would suffice to whitewash his previous conduct, and that his person was safe; he remonstrated loudly and vaunted his bravery for all it was worth, but his complaint was entirely unheeded.

The next morning deserters came in with the information that the enemy, owing to the losses they had sustained, no longer believed themselves able to hold their own on the frontier, and had, therefore, retired by the road to Italy, after having left three hundred men in a *château* about three leagues from our camp.

M. de Massey, thanks to the French grenadiers, having rid himself of his opponents, decided to lay siege to this *château*, and set out for this purpose the next morning. Before leaving, he took care to detail a lieutenant with twenty dragoons, with orders to escort Boismorel to the Tower of Munich, and report his conduct to the State Council. Our start took place at such an early hour that I found it impossible to see Boismorel myself before leaving, but I sent an officer of our regiment to bear him company till his departure, and receive any instruction he might wish to give. It was not long before this officer returned, for as soon as our troops were set in movement, Boismorel and his escort set out for Munich. When I asked him if he had brought any message, he replied, "M. Boismorel has certainly given me an order, but except by your leave I feel I can hardly carry it out."

When I inquired what caused this repugnance on his part, he said that he was ordered by Boismorel to make a speech to the regiment, so as to prevent any dangerous feelings arising in the minds of the grenadiers, in consequence of his arrest, which would doubtless bewilder them and depress their spirits; and to make them understand that they need not be disquieted on his behalf, as his reputation could quite hold its own against his enemies. He therefore hoped that the occurrence of this accident would in no wise lessen their valour, and he exhorted them to do their duty on every occasion during his absence, as if he were present with them, this being his only anxiety.

I told the officer that he ought to obey the orders of his colonel, to which he made reply that he would do so on any other occasion, but in the present case he felt himself quite incapable of making a speech in any way worthy of him who had given the order. "Very well," said I, "I will go and do it for you." I soon posted myself at the head of the regiment, and as it passed before me I gave out to the grenadiers their colonel's message; but these unfeeling scoundrels made light of his reputation, and I was obliged to order silence to put a stop to the outrageous language they used.

We invested, without any great preparation, the *château* which the enemy had taken possession of, for we did not consider the siege thereof to be of sufficient importance to necessitate regular trenches. We simply constructed a battery with our little cannon to breach a tower which supported the gate of the first outer court, and hoped thereby to damage the chateau as little as possible, for it belonged to the Grand Master of the Bavarian States. As soon as the garrison found a small breach had been effected, they asked to capitulate, but we only agreed to receive them as prisoners of war. We found in this *château* a great quantity of warlike stores which the enemy had collected there, intending to scour the country and levy contributions.

Our conquests augmented the enthusiasm of our little army, which was in a most joyful state of mind, and our general was preparing to seize another *château*, said to be occupied by the enemy, when a courier arrived bearing an order from the Electress, to the effect that the Marquis de Massey was to return with his troops at once to Munich, by forced marches, so as to ensure the safety of the Electoral family. This courier told us, with tears in his eyes, that all was lost; the army of France had been totally defeated on the plains of Hochstett,[1] the Elector had fled to the French frontier, the Electress was in the saddest possible condition, and the State Council knew not what steps to take for the protection of the princess and her family. For this reason the arrival of our troops was awaited with extreme impatience, for until our arrival there would be continual panic. It would, therefore, be necessary to march day and night to relieve this cruel situation.

It would be out of my power to find words strong enough to express the depression into which we were plunged at so unexpected a piece of news. It wiped out all the agreeable sensations produced by our little victories. What a dreadful turn of the wheel of fortune, affecting nation and individual alike! All our manoeuvres, plans, and conquests came to nothing in an instant; it was no longer possible to derive any advantage from our past efforts, and our thoughts were cruelly exercised regarding the future. I had hoped for some reward for all that had occurred since the affair of Schelemberg, flatterers had often suggested it, and one's own feelings, which often cause us to exaggerate the least of our own merits, made me cherish pleasant hopes. But the finest deeds of individuals disappear at a time of general adversity; even those who merely bring the news of great victories are rewarded, although they may have had no share in them.

We marched without a halt to Munich. Although the council had met many times, they had not been able to come to any definite resolve, but on the arrival of our troops the principal officers were admitted to the deliberations, and the following line of action was then decided upon. It was settled that the Electress and the princes should, under escort of three regiments of dragoons, take the road with all speed to join the Elector, and if it was possible, to escape with him. In order to avoid the enemy, she was to take the road by Memmingen, whilst the infantry covered her progress by moving between them and the escort, the better to ensure her safety.

As a matter of fact, the enemy thought only of following up their victory. They left but two flying columns in the country, one to undertake the siege of Ulm, under General Tungen, and the other that of Ingolstadt, under General d'Herberfeld, whilst their main army took up the pursuit of that of France.

The Electress and her suite arrived at Memmingen without mis-

---

1. Blenheim.

hap, but having learned at this town that it was quite impossible to join His Highness, she found herself obliged to retrace her steps to Munich, and there await the fate that the Almighty should decree.

The battle, disastrous alike to France and Bavaria, was fought on August 14th on the plains of Hochstett. Many persons have accused Maréchal de Tallard of undue contempt for his opponents and want of caution, thus giving them an opportunity to engage at the very time that he ought to have made every possible provision for the good of the State and the destruction of the Empire. It was also said that elated by his victory at Spires, after leaving the lines of Landau to fight the Prince of Hesse Cassel, he made an entire mistake in leaving those of Augsburg, from which he might have ravaged the very heart of the Empire.

But it is a common mistake to judge such matters after their event, without remembering that the outcome of a battle is often due to circumstances which human intelligence cannot foresee. If Maréchal de Tallard had been successful, no one would have found fault with him; at the same time, what astonished me, and what no one has been able to explain to me, was that on deciding to leave his entrenchments, he did not recall at least fifteen thousand men from the Bavarian army, including our own detachment. Such a considerable reinforcement might well have given us the victory, for the valour of these troops was beyond question. The total defeat of General Schlick at Heyzempirne, that of Stirum at the first Battle of Hochstett, and finally the affair at Schelemberg were proofs of their bravery too certain to justify the neglect of their recall, supposing this point ever to have been considered at all; at any rate, such are my reflections on the matter.

Not having been present at this battle, I cannot myself bear personal witness as to its details, but I have often heard of it from various persons of distinction, opponents as well as friends, among others, Prince Eugene himself, who many times accorded me this favour, so that I have drawn from most varied sources that which I am going to tell.

After the capitulation of Rain the enemy were willing neither to leave the Danube nor to advance too far into Bavaria, being afraid lest their lines of communication might be cut They followed the course of this river in order to seize Neuburg, where the garrison of four hundred men, being in no condition to offer resistance, were ordered to throw all the stores into the river and retire before the place was invested. They then seized Aichach and Scheremhausen, neither of which were fortified or garrisoned, and finally encamped in the plain of Ingolstadt, which town they threatened to besiege.

It was then that M. de Tallard, who was occupying the lines of Augsburg together with Maréchal de Marsin, who had lately joined him, decided to leave his entrenchments to give battle, overruling the counsel of M. de Marsin, being his senior officer. The enemy having by this time ascertained our intentions, now began a movement to take us by surprise.

Our army was a fine one, but not so numerous as that of the enemy, for although we had twelve more battalions, they had many more men than ours, and, moreover, they had about forty more squadrons than we, comprising the pick of their troops.

Maréchal de Tallard crossed the river Leek and directed his march straight for the little plain of Blenheim, near Hochstett, where he encamped with the intention of remaining a few days before proceeding further to a more advantageous camping-ground nearer Ingolstadt. By this movement he would have foiled the enemy's designs upon this place, but they did not give him time to carry it out.

As soon as they had learned the direction of his advance they left the plains of Ingolstadt in order to meet him, effecting their change of position in such a way as to conceal their movement, and it is quite surprising that so considerable an army should have been able to do this without any information reaching our generals. It was believed that they were still in their original position when they suddenly made their appearance at six o'clock on the morning of August 14th, in front of our outpost line, the driving in of which was the first intimation we received of the Allies and their intention. At this moment part of our army was scattered in foraging parties, which was an additional misfortune.

Signal guns were fired to bring back the foragers and their escorts; the "Alarm" and the "Assembly" were beaten hurriedly, and, without attempting to strike the tents, every effort was devoted to forming line of battle in front of the camp. The hurry and precipitation of all this brought confusion and fear in its train, whilst the foraging parties and their escorts, alarmed by the unexpected signals, returned one by one, rather a prey to misgivings than animated with any desire to fight. The difficulty of having to think of many things at once in the actual presence of the enemy reacted upon the nerves of those in command, and, above all, upon those who had their carriages packed with the valuables accumulated during their period of winter quarters; such a state of unreadiness is a serious disadvantage in the case of a battle of these dimensions, the preparation for which should have been made much earlier. Our generals set to work most energetically to draw up the army, but as they had made no previous plan, it became necessary to change the position of many brigades to support the flanks and reinforce exposed or weak points.

The enemy profited by these confused manoeuvres of ours to pass a large stream, which they probably could never have effected without suffering great loss had our troops been ready in position.

This large and rather marshy stream offered much difficulty to the passage of cavalry and artillery, but the enemy, having solidified the bottom with fascines and constructed bridges with pontoons, beams, planks, and trestles, at which they worked undisturbed and with extreme diligence, were able to effect a passage for their army in several columns, which formed to their front as fast as they crossed. They were only checked, and that for but a short time, on the right of their line of advance; for after crossing the stream a marsh was met with, which obliged this portion of their force to close to its left in order to take up its position in the line of battle.

During this operation our army was getting into its own position, brigades were sent to occupy the village of Oberhausen, which lay on its left, and if our generals had only had the time to push forward troops to dispute the passage of the stream, the enemy would have found much danger in this undertaking, instead of which, as soon as they had constructed their bridges, they immediately passed over without meeting with any opposition whatever.

As soon as the Allied army had crossed the stream their generals advanced to the attack, without waiting for their right, which was checked by the marsh on their front. Those on their right, which attacked our left, were repulsed by Maréchal de Marsin with the greatest possible vigour, but they rallied on a body of infantry advancing to their support, returned to the charge, and were repulsed a second time in the same vigorous manner. Prince Eugene once more reformed these troops, and made a third assault, yet again on our left, which had no better success than the two former, for they were driven back a long way beyond the village of Oberhausen; but now Milord Marlborough, who had arrived with a reinforcement of thirty squadrons, recommenced the attack with such vigour that our troops could not stand against it, and began to fall back.

The right of our army was in a much worse case, owing to the arrangements the enemy had made in forming for their attack. They were convinced that the senior regiments and picked troops would be found there, in accordance with the custom of the army, whether in camp or order of battle, and in order to make headway against these fine troops they took care to strengthen their left and concentrate their efforts to drive in that portion of our line, being sure that the defeat of our right would give them the battle.

They attacked, therefore, with such superior force and super-abundant energy that our very finest cavalry at the first shock distinctly gave way, although every effort was made to steady them, but the shock and confusion was so great, partly owing to the immensely superior force of the enemy and partly to our inferior disposition at the beginning of the affair, that there was no possible means of resisting it. The only movement our cavalry made was to retire, and then, seeing the enemy preparing for a fresh charge, they all at once broke into flight, so panic-stricken that, finding the Danube behind them, the most part threw themselves therein, regardless of the danger, and were drowned. Lieutenant-General M. de Clerambault was, unfortunately for himself, one of these, and it was on the banks of this river that Maréchal de Tallard gave himself up as a prisoner of war.

After the cavalry of our right wing had been routed there remained twelve squadrons of dragoons and twenty-seven battalions completely cut off, as the enemy had forced their way almost right through the centre of our line of battle, thus separating our right from our left and destroying all means of communication. An orderly and combined retreat became impossible. The left wing found the retirement easier than the right, the wood of Luthingen and the defiles of Hochstett affording some protection; but the right were not so fortunate, as they were obliged to throw themselves into the village of Blenheim on their extreme right, where they entrenched themselves in the hope of finding later on some means of escape. Unhappily their hopes were in vain, for they soon found themselves invested by the enemy on all sides, and seeing no chance of help and their line of retreat entirely cut off, they surrendered as prisoners of war at the fall of night.

This capture of so great a number of troops at one stroke was the most brilliant feature in the enemy's victory, and was their chief boast when they recounted the deeds of this day's work. I spoke of this incident to the principal officers of the Imperial army three months later, when I formed one of a deputation to Prince Eugene, and found that they attributed glory without end to it, and I must confess I could hardly justify the conduct of our soldiery.

In fact, if these twenty-seven battalions and twelve squadrons had consisted of really determined men, they might have cut their way, sword in hand, through the enemy's lines during the night, an undertaking the glory of which could only have been compared with the danger attending it. It was said that personages of rank and distinction took upon themselves to surrender the colours, so that the force should escape the fate of two other brigades which had also been surrounded in the centre of the first line. These, however, stood firm and maintained the fight for a very long time, in and about the camp and amongst the tents, with all possible valour; but overcome at last by numbers, their defeat became inevitable.

The Electress, after her return to Munich from Memmingen, found that the prince, her husband, had invested her with plenary powers on his retirement to France. This princess was therefore in a position to act, govern, and dispose of the State's welfare in any way that she might think fit and proper, and the prince consented, in advance, to all treaties or negotiations made by her, and notified his wish that all her decisions should be as fully respected and acted upon as though formulated by himself. With this power in her hands, the Electress convened the State Council together with the general officers of her army, in order to make arrangements for the safety of the country and her family.

Reliable information had been received that the allied armies had continued their march after the battle of Hochstett towards the frontier of Alsace, had crossed the Rhine, and were preparing to lay siege to Landau. A flying column only now remained in Bavaria, which was then engaged in besieging Ingolstadt, with the greater confidence, as it was believed that the country was quite devoid of Electoral troops. For this reason the enemy omitted to take precautions against any possible attempt to relieve this place, and had not even occupied the banks of the Danube, which runs beneath its walls and which is crossed by an excellent stone bridge. They contented themselves with pitching their camp on an extensive plain near the river, where they had opened their trenches of approach without any covering work whatever.

Being thus certain of the enemy's design, the Council of the Electress determined to profit by their carelessness and relieve Ingolstadt. To this end all detachments were recalled, formed into a *corps d'armée*, and put into movement with all speed for the purpose of raising the siege of this town, which is one of the most important in the Electoral

States.

It had already been decided that the best way of bringing about an honourable settlement with the emperor was to maintain as effective a resistance as possible, to prove that Bavaria was not yet reduced to that extremity she was believed to be in, and that she had sufficient troops and resources yet to hand to cause anxiety to the Allies. It was further decided to make a diversion to support the French Army, and in order to accelerate the advent of peace, all her forces should be brought at once to the front and war be prosecuted without any hesitation.

It was reckoned that the siege of Landau would occupy the enemy's army for the rest of the campaign, and thus leave us free to clear and reoccupy Bavaria; so even if the flying column under General Tungen, then laying siege to Ulm, should decide to retire into Bavaria after the fall of that town, we should be ready to withstand him, for our troops were accustomed to beat the Imperialists and did not fear them, even if they proved to be two to our one in strength.

Finally, if it should so happen that we had to lose everything, glory would accrue to the nation if it surrendered, sword in hand, instead of being driven by fear to submit to a yoke, the burden of which would be made all the harder to bear by the contempt of the conqueror.

It became necessary, therefore, to issue orders without delay for the concentration of the troops, and the march on Ingolstadt.

During these deliberations I took the opportunity of doing all I could on behalf of Boismorel. I got all my friends to work, and succeeded so well that I obtained from the Electress an order for his release from the prison in which he had hitherto been strictly confined, so that he was merely kept under arrest in his own room with a sentry at his door. This favour was an essential one to him, as it eased his mind from the fear of further penalties, and the chance of his escaping in case of need became a matter of certainty. Appearances against him were of so threatening a nature, that it was not without reason that he feared for his life, so I had at least the satisfaction of relieving him of this apprehension before leaving Munich.

On September 6th the concentration of our army, under the command of M. de Vequel, late lieutenant-general of the Electoral forces, being completed, the troops began their march, and by nightfall of the 9th were close up to the bridge of Ingolstadt. The enemy were encamped on the other side of the river, too far beyond the town to learn anything of our approach, with the result that we defiled over the bridge and passed through the town to the open country without being perceived.

As soon as we saw it was light enough to move against them, we drew up our army in four lines for the purpose of facilitating the advance, and so that when sufficiently forward the second and fourth lines should close upon the first and third, with the result that order of battle of two lines was formed instantaneously. The enemy's vedettes, however, caught sight of us when we were yet at sufficient distance to give them time to strike their camp and get themselves into battle array to receive us.

The Imperialists made at first sight a very fine show, though we saw that in the hurry of their formation they had placed the whole of their *cuirassiers* on the right flank of their infantry. This brought about a change on our part; several squadrons of dragoons were sent to our left to oppose their cavalry, followed by our regiment of grenadiers to support the dragoons. The enemy availed themselves of the time necessary for these movements to place their baggage column in a position of safety, and it was nearly nine o'clock before the battle actually began. The hatred that existed between the Bavarians and Imperialists was such that they rushed upon each other like madmen, and the collision was terrible. So much so, in fact, that the enemy did not think fit to stand a second charge; they gave way, and took to flight over the plain, the woods at the end of which afforded great protection to their infantry.

The dragoons and my grenadiers pursued them for more than two leagues; we took many prisoners, and the enemy's loss amounted to more than three thousand men, without reckoning prisoners and eight hundred horses, which we found very useful for remounting our dragoons. Some booty was taken during the pursuit, but my grenadiers did not approve of robbing dead men and prisoners. However, they found an opportunity during the pursuit to detach a party for the express purpose of scouring the country and plundering the neighbouring villages and pastures, whence they brought in at least four hundred head of cattle and cows, and so well did they conceal their booty that I knew nothing of the matter until there was no opportunity left for me to remedy it.

On the very day of our victory over the Imperialists, the French garrison, who were holding Ulm, surrendered that city to General Tungen, upon which he sent a small detachment of his troops to reinforce those who had just been beaten at Ingolstadt, and marched with the rest of his flying column to join the King of the Romans who was laying siege at Landau. The Imperialists, thus reinforced, believed themselves in a condition to undertake some new enterprise, and pitched their camp in the plain of Ratisbon. We were still in the neighbourhood of Ingolstadt when we learned that they had occupied this position, with the evident design of besieging some town or ravaging the country, and seeing that there was no time to be lost, we at once marched to give them battle should we come up with them.

In a few days' time we reached the plain on which they were encamped, but we found that they were much more upon their guard than had been the case at Ingolstadt. They had already provided for their retreat by garrisoning the woods in their rear with infantry, and after having well reconnoitred them, we came to the conclusion that it would be imprudent to attack them in the position they had taken up. Their cavalry and the rest of their infantry were in order of battle close to the woods, and in the best fettle in the world, because they believed themselves absolutely safe from our attack.

However, the determination they showed in holding to their position only made us think of how to oust them and cut up their rearguard, which we could not have done had they retired at our first approach. We quickly had fascines made, and requisitioned labourers who in a short time constructed a battery for the six field-guns that we had with us. This battery was placed half-way between us and them, within point-blank range. We constructed it with the express purpose of bringing on an attack on their part to interfere with our labourers, but they thought it better to think of their retreat when they saw the cannon being brought into position. Their troops began their march before even our cannon could get a shot at them, keeping close to the woods under cover of their infantry stationed therein, who conformed with the movement of the main body of their army.

When we saw that the Imperialists were retreating, we set our army in motion to keep them in observation without, however, getting within range of the woods, and we marched thus until the time came when they were obliged to leave their cover and enter the open country. They then quickened their pace, but we followed them up close and fell upon and entirely defeated their rearguard, killing fifteen hundred men and taking some prisoners. We camped in this plain until we had collected information as to the future intentions of the enemy. We learned that they made three long marches in succession; had at last halted near Oberkirchen, because of its excellent position as a camping-ground, and were apparently of a mind to establish themselves there in order to cause uneasiness among the population. At this news we again resumed our march with a determined intention of coming into close quarters with them, but they once more avoided an engagement, for as soon as they heard of our approach they hastily struck their camp, and betook themselves over the frontier.

Here we have an example of the condition and training of the Bavarian troops, by which they proved their courage and pluck to the Imperialists; whereas all the rest of Europe had been convinced that, since the field of Hochstett, not a single Bavarian soldier was in existence.

Whilst we pursued the Imperialists and ultimately cleared Bavaria of their presence, the State Council at Munich, unknown to the General Officers of the army, obtained from the Electress permission to send a deputation to Vienna to treat with His Imperial Majesty. This craven Council had represented to the princess that her subjects had suffered extremely and were no longer in a state to furnish the men necessary for the war, and that the state of things was such that nothing better could be done than to implore the clemency of the Emperor, at the very moment when our troops appeared to be victorious. That if Her Highness insisted on maintaining her regency, she would be acting in opposition to her country's welfare, for such action was impossible since the Battle of Hochstett; she would alienate the whole of the Germanic Body, who would make a final effort to invade her States, when it would be too late to think of entering upon a compromise. They not only feared for the loss of her States, but also lest she herself and her family should fall into the hands of the enemy, and it was impossible for them to reflect upon the possibility of such a sad result without the most heartfelt grief

They besought the princess to recall to her memory the efforts she had herself made to induce the Elector to enter upon some compromise, and to recollect the reasons she had then put forward, to lend a compassionate ear to the cry of the people who begged her to save them from the terrors of a war which could have no result but the inevitable destruction and total ruin of the whole State.

She was reminded yet again that the pay had been due to the troops since August 1st; it was impossible to pay them, and the longer peace was deferred, arrears would go on accumulating without any expectation of relief This was already causing desertion, recruits were necessary to keep the regiments up to their war strength, and through the lack of men and money the country would find itself in a very short time completely at the end of its resources. Thus, therefore, the most prudent course to take would be to make a treaty of peace at once, instead of waiting till the last extremity.

This carefully studied "Remonstrance" was initiated by the members composing the Council of State to serve their own ends. They represented the measures necessary for carrying on the war as difficult and impracticable because they were not in favour of it, and as they had the control of the finance in their hands, they found plenty of pretexts to prove the impossibility of supplying the needs of the troops and the cost of the campaign. They had, besides, no qualms in bringing to the notice of the emperor, whom they regarded already as their suzerain, the regard that they had for his interests, in order to secure his protection and rewards. It is natural to suppose that this was not entirely owing to affection only, but that fear played its part with them as well; however this might have been, the result was the same.

The Council of State had an agent in the household of the Electress in the person of the Jesuit Father Schumacher, her confessor, who attuned his pious advice with the arguments of *Messieurs* the Councillors, so that at last she determined to sue secretly for peace.

It was, however, impossible to carry on all these intrigues without their coming to the ears of our general officers, who had sent a deputation to Munich to apply for the payment of the troops. This deputation addressed itself to the council, and others responsible for such pay-merits, without obtaining any satisfactory reply; the more they persisted, the less definite was the answer they received, and obliged to go into detail on the point, they divined from these vague replies that the Electress would be obliged to make peace in order to save herself from such troublesome questions. In fact, they were informed that payment was out of the question; the Treasury was exhausted, and it was quite impossible to levy more taxes on the people.

They were told, therefore, to return to the troops, calm their feelings, and that when the State was in a position to make this payment, notice would be given. This answer opened the eyes of the deputation, and the more they considered the matter, the more sure were they that the council expected soon to be relieved from the pressure brought to bear on it by the army.

Our deputation returned much dissatisfied with the result of their journey. They informed us of their discovery, which surprised us the more as we had relied upon the fame of our victories to pave the way for a favourable reception of our demands, instead of which, far from giving us credit for all our successes, we were merely looked upon as importunate beggars.

The fidelity of the army was in no way shaken; they had a sincere desire to protect Bavaria, and all those under arms were determined to suffer anything rather than abandon the interests of a Prince who was the idol of his subjects. We went further, for our intentions did not confine themselves to the preservation of Bavaria, as we wished to push our conquests into the enemy's country, and only asked for bread and recruits.

We called together a Council of War, composed of the general officers and commanding officers of each regiment, to discuss this subject, and after having exhaustively considered all its aspects, present and future, we drew up a petition by which we made it evident that it would still be more profitable to continue the war than to make peace. We showed that any such treaty that the Electress could make on the present occasion would always be disadvantageous to her, for the Court of Vienna, which had the right to act despotically with regard to all the different members of the Empire, would never think itself obliged to abide religiously by its conditions if it found it more convenient to break them; that this arrangement between the two sovereigns would prove but a yoke under which the head must be bowed at the pleasure of the House of Austria, and that the question of consideration for the population of Bavaria was nothing but a pretext for handing it over completely to the enemy, in order that they should be in better state to furnish the subsidies that the emperor would certainly impose upon them; that it would be known, when too late, that Bavaria could keep up a much larger army, if only the State revenues were honestly dealt with.

That if any real compassion existed for the people it should be shown by every possible effort being made to prevent their falling into the hands of their greatest enemies, the Austrians, for if they became thus subject of the Court of Vienna, they would be treated as a nation which sooner or later must be restored to the control of its original ruler; thus, taxes and impositions would be showered upon them, to make as much as possible out of them in the meantime, and the difference would then be only too manifest between those imposed by their enemies and those necessary for the maintenance of an army which would be working for their independence.

If, however, all these arguments counted for nothing, and it was deemed impossible to compel the populace itself to find the cost of the war, there were yet other means at hand to provide for this, namely, to requisition the immense quantity of plate that existed in the abbeys, cloisters, convents, and parishes, receipts being given for it, and then coin it into money. Moreover, besides all this plate, there was in the churches an enormous number of bells, some of which could also be coined; so that however little the people could give on their own part, these two sources would prove more than sufficient, not only for the sustenance of the troops actually in the field, but for a considerable augmentation of their number. There still also remained the resources of the country in crops and cattle, which were so abundant that they furnished many of the neighbouring provinces with their annual supplies.

Besides this, the troops would be quite contented with six months' pay in the year, provided that they could reckon upon an honest payment of the balance due to them when matters permitted, and were not only ready to defend the State faithfully, but even to invade the enemy's territory.

In the case of the provinces of Linz and Salzburg with their open frontiers, contributions and requisitions could be made therein to add to the State Treasury, in fact, the Electress might rest assured that this action alone would oblige the Emperor to make such an important diversion of his army that France, with her inexhaustible resources, would profit thereby to send us help, as she had done in the preceding year, the only means of bringing the Elector back to his State.

Our petition was duly presented to the Electress and the Council of State, but, very far from being listened to, only served as a pretext to give the princess bad impressions of the army. The council accused us of wishing to sacrifice the country to our interests. We feared, according to them, that if peace was made we should lose our employment, whilst on the other hand, in the confusion of war, we should seize the government and inflict exactions upon the prince's subjects. They decided that peace was the best policy to pursue, and that we must not be listened to. Moreover, things had already gone too far with the emperor at the time we presented our petition; the preliminaries were settled between the two parties, and it was therefore determined to continue the negotiations, and we were not even vouchsafed a reply.

Whilst these matters were being arranged between the emperor and the Electress, the Imperial troops got into movement and appeared in the plain of Straubing. We were some distance away from this district, and acting on information received as to the above, our generals set our army in motion with the intention of attacking them and preventing them laying siege to this town, which we believed to be their design. The council at Munich learning this, and suspecting our intention, which at any other time they would have deemed most praiseworthy, sent the Sieur Neyzinguer, a member of the council, who brought us an order from the Electress by which we were forbidden in the future to commit any act of hostility against the Emperor's troops, and commanded to retire and pitch our camp in a certain locality, where we were to remain until further orders.

We were then convinced of the little attention that had been paid to our petition, and that the treaty had been concluded according to the wishes of the cowardly council, who wished to put itself under the protection of the Court of Vienna. We had many a conference amongst ourselves, and having examined the question from every point, it seemed only too certain that the Electress had been induced by the council to look upon our petition and its sound arguments as contrary to her own interests and the tranquillity of her State. Would that their reasons had been better than ours! but future events unfortunately proved the contrary.

After impartial reflection on all that passed with regard to this matter, it will be found to be absolutely certain that the propositions of the military party were sincere and pure, and that those of the ministers were influenced by fear and interest. The people were quite ready to take up arms for their own defence, and more than sixty thousand willing men could have been found to hand, who would have given the Imperialists plenty to do. If the council had only possessed a proper feeling, Bavaria could have stood by her own right, and would in all probability have escaped falling under the yoke of a foreign power. Notwithstanding the peace, she was for ten years treated as cruelly as if she was suffering from a regular invasion, sword in hand, and her princes were robbed of their freedom.

The prime movers of the council now made a secret agreement by which the Electress was to hand over to His Imperial Majesty the towns of Landsberg, Mitlitmen, Ingolstadt, Straubing, Scharting, Braunau, and Landshut, the principal fortified places in Bavaria, and to disband all her own troops, who were to retire to wherever they wished in the Empire, provided they did not leave it. Out of these she reserved the right to choose one battalion to act as her bodyguard. She was to be content with the possession of the town and bailiwick of Munich only, to serve for her maintenance and mark of sovereignty, and all the rest of Bavaria was handed over to His Imperial Majesty, to do with as his choice and will might direct—as if, in fact, it was one of his own States.

According to this treaty, the Electress was not to be disturbed in her occupation of the town and bailiwick under any pretext whatever, and no attempt was made to pay the troops their arrears of pay. The ministers were somewhat embarrassed by this last point, which they had concealed from the Electress and the emperor, and made up their minds not to pay the army, which was to be disbanded at the earliest possible date. They thought, with truth, that so long as it remained concentrated, it might claim its rights as soon as there was no longer hope or chance left for it; consequently they arranged means of breaking it up. Quarters were detailed for each regiment, so distant from each other that the Bavarian army no longer existed as such. In this distribution of the forces, my battalion of grenadiers was ordered to the town of Ingolstadt, together with the three battalions of the regiment of Liselbourg, the whole being under the command of the major-general of that name, to whom no special orders were given as to his future action, and nothing was said as to the treaty between the emperor and the Electress.

The council, fearing discontent among the troops, wished to keep this matter hidden until the moment arrived when the Imperialists should take over the various fortified towns; then, availing themselves of the princess's authority, the necessary order was to be issued to each commandant with all the emphasis necessary to bring about strict obedience. The gist of this order was that the troops should lay down their arms in the towns they were occupying, and after having received the Imperial garrisons they should be disbanded, and depart as private individuals, each one as he found convenient. The "Honourable" members of the council hoped, by sending us these orders only at the actual moment of the surrender, to rob us of any time for reflection; but notwithstanding their precaution, we discovered their designs in time for our garrison to confer together as to what should be done in the case, and to make them render the justice due to us.

The contents of this treaty, which excited the curiosity of the whole world, gradually became common property, and it was with downright grief that I learned that there was no mention therein respecting the French grenadiers—an ominous omission that gave us no grounds for a favourable view as to our ultimate fate. Some asserted that we should all be shot to rid the country of a nuisance, whilst others thought we should not even have that honour accorded us, but were convinced that all the grenadiers would be hanged in the wood of Ingolstadt as deserters from the Empire; in fact, of all those who discussed our fate, there was not one who did not condemn us to death: the only question to their minds seemed to be the particular form this would take. It is true that there were many things which might be laid to the account of the battalion—firstly, it was entirely French; secondly, these Frenchmen were, in fact, deserters from the Imperial service; thirdly, they had been guilty of excessive plundering.

But supposing this regiment was treated like the Bavarians, with the permission to disband and disperse, it would have been no better off, for it was impossible for them to traverse Germany in order to reach France without being massacred by the peasants. We were looked upon as enemies by the whole of the Germanic League, and we thus found ourselves in the midst of the Empire at the mercy of an infuriated populace, and without a chance of succour or aid of any kind. I was responsible for these unfortunate soldiery, whose minds had been charitably filled by indiscreet people with vivid pictures of the misery threatening them; in fact, so dismal was the lot foretold for the French grenadiers that one really felt that they were beyond hope.

M. de Liselbourg, a perfectly straightforward man, was deeply sensible of the injustice about to be perpetrated without the knowledge of the Electress on troops who had served with so great a zeal, and was by no means averse to assisting them to right their case before surrendering to the Imperialists such a town as Ingolstadt, which, owing to its fortifications, magazines, and arsenal, was the most important fortress in the Bavarian States. He being unwilling to act entirely upon his own responsibility, consulted his lieutenant-colonel, M. de Florimont (later major-general), and me. We, the senior officers of this garrison, agreed unanimously that without being unfaithful to the interests of the Electress, we could and should, before surrendering the place, insist upon proper arrangements being made for our troops, and that we should hold out until this was granted. Also, that in the event of our having to withstand a siege we should then be acting as against the emperor and the Bavarian Ministry only, since the princess could not possibly intend to inflict on the troops an injustice of which she knew nothing.

To be on the safe side, we also settled that we should prepare a petition to present to her, which should explain our reason for not surrendering Ingolstadt. After we had decided upon the course we should take, we informed the rest of the officers of our garrison, who were delighted to find us so disposed to devote ourselves to the general welfare, and each one declared his intention of shedding the last drop of his blood rather than surrender the town before satisfaction had been afforded us.

When I saw that all the officers were of this mind, I thought the time had come to bring forward a design I had already thought out, but which I had not hitherto dared to make public; it had to do with my French grenadiers. I pointed out to our principal officers that, without in any way prejudicing their interests, I should propose that a fresh treaty should be made on our behalf, on the supposition that we had been forgotten, as was reported to be the case, in that made by the Electress. I reminded them of the service my battalion would render them if it became necessary for us to stand a siege by the Imperialists, which in itself should make them see the expediency of doing what they could for us. It was then agreed that no arrangement should be entered upon which did not include our grenadiers, and this clause was embodied in the petition that we had ready to send to Madame the Electress when we thought it necessary.

At last the day on which the Imperialists were to enter Ingolstadt, November nth, was announced to us on the previous evening in an order from the Electress. This stated that we were to evacuate and hand over the place to the Imperialist garrison, after having handed the keys to Maréchal d'Herberfeld, the Imperial general, and returned the arms to the Arsenal; that this was the wish of Her Highness, to violate which would be to incur her displeasure, and who, having judged it necessary to disband a portion of her troops for the welfare of the State, thanked the garrison of Ingolstadt for its services, and directed that it should betake itself wherever it desired.

There was not a word in this order as to the payment of the troops, and no reference to my grenadiers; the officers of the garrison having had it read to them were cut to the heart to find this injustice carried through to the bitter end. They were so irritated that the resolution they had taken not to deliver up the place was strengthened; nevertheless, in order to acquaint the Electress with the fact that in taking this line of action our intentions were in no way intended as rebellion to her wishes, we at once sent off an express envoy to present her with our petition.

This contained the detailed reasons which obliged us to refuse entry to the Imperialists, and we at once took all necessary precautions to prevent our being surprised.

Maréchal d'Herberfeld did not fail to appear next morning about ten o'clock with a body of cavalry and infantry, which he left in an open plain near the town. He then advanced with several officers and a deputy from the council in Munich to call our attention to the order and the intentions of the two powers. We had been careful to occupy the lines as far as the outlying fortifications, and to man the ramparts and covered-way with our infantry.

As soon as he appeared MM. de Liselbourg, Florimont, and I advanced to the farthest point in our lines to meet and enter into explanations with the general, who appeared to be most surprised to find us maintaining an attitude so contrary to that which his orders had led him to expect. He was annoyed at the idea of retracing his steps, and together with the deputy from the council, began to point out to us the rashness of the step we were taking.

He told us that the question of default of the pay was not one upon which evasion of the treaties and orders of His Imperial Majesty and the Electress could be founded, and that our refusal to obey constituted open rebellion which we wished to cover under a poor pretext, and finally advised us to think this over before he retired, as he feared lest our conduct should cost us too dearly. When we saw the high and mighty view that he took of the matter, we told him that for our part we could only counsel him to retire, and that quickly, lest it cost him dearer than us, for he had no time to lose in which to withdraw his troops out of the range of our cannon. This he did without further parley.

Our refusal to surrender Ingolstadt made a great stir at the Courts of Vienna and Munich, complaint was made to the Electress of the non-observance of the treaty, and she was requested to give orders of a more stringent nature to compel us to obey. The council itself was extremely irritated at our boldness, and sent us a new order under the name and authority of the Electress in which there was no mention whatever made of the issues raised by us in our last petition, but declared that if we did not obey as soon as we should have received it, our action would be looked upon as mutiny, and punished as such.

This new order caused us little astonishment; we were convinced that the council alone were responsible for these threats, and certainly not the Electress, to whom it was a matter of little or no importance whether the town fell into the hands of the Imperialists now or later.

The mischief being done, our conduct could not make things worse; we knew, besides, that Her Highness would in no way benefit from the arrears of pay refused to us, but that it was the ministers or the Viennese Court who would profit thereby. Having thus duly considered every phase of this matter, we stood firm, and took extra precautions against being taken by surprise.

However, in order not to delay matters, we prepared a new petition even more circumstantial than the first, by which it was clearly proved that there was nothing in our action contrary to the interests of the Electress: it only effected the emperor, or at the most the States which had been ceded to him.

Also, that in simple equity we should be paid, for if it was not done now out of the revenue of the abandoned country, the Elector would find himself one day in the unfortunate position of being pledged to satisfy us, simply because he had not forced the Imperialists to do so when it was possible without prejudicing the interests of the Electress. We besought her very humbly to look upon our action in as favourable a light as possible; we had no intention of doing anything contrary to her interests or to the respect we owed her, and begged her to leave the Emperor to settle with us, as it was evident the control over the troops and fortresses was no longer in her hands.

Our petition was written in French, the princess knew no German, and being given into her own hands, had all the effect that we could reasonably expect. She declined to interfere further with the fate of Ingolstadt, and left the Court of Vienna to settle the matter as it might think fit.

We remained undisturbed and without any news until the 27th of the month, when the King of the Romans returning from the siege of Landau with Prince Eugene, visited Maréchal d'Herberfeld, who had his headquarters four leagues from Ingolstadt. The King of the Romans continued his journey to Vienna, and left to Prince Eugene the question of arranging this affair. Prince Eugene, with praiseworthy moderation, wished to know from our own lips why it was that we refused to surrender as purposed by the Electress. He therefore sent a lieutenant-colonel to us to say that he wished we would send one of our number to him, with whom he could confer as to the difficulties which gave rise to our refusal. No sooner had M. de Liselbourg assembled the officers of the garrison than it was decided that I should bear this "commission," and I was sent straightway to Prince Eugene. The prince received me with much kindness, and, with none present

The most Serene Prince Eugene of Savoy, Knight of the Order of the Golden Fleece, Privy Councellour to his Imperial Majesty, President of the Council of War, and Generalissimo of all his Forces in Italy &c.

PRINCE EUGENE

but our two selves, I had the honour of pointing out to him, in his private study, the justice that would be brought about by satisfying the demands of these troops, who had done their duty with such zeal and repute.

I informed him that the money we claimed would be of no profit either to His Imperial Majesty or to Madame the Electress, and of the fact that this sum still owing to us constituted the sole reason for our refusing to surrender. As to the exclusion of the regiment of French grenadiers from the treaty with *madame* the Electress, I pointed out that as they were not Bavarian subjects the omission had evidently occurred either accidentally or with malicious intent, and that it would only be equitable to draw up a special treaty to decide the fate and ensure the safety of the regiment.

The prince then asked me what I hoped to gain by such a treaty.

"I would ask Your Highness," said I, "that His Imperial Majesty should graciously grant the safe departure of the regiment of French grenadiers from the town of Ingolstadt with all the honours of war— that is, with drums beating, colours flying, arms and baggage, together with the servants and all Frenchmen that could be found in the town. That it should be accompanied by commissioners and a proper escort as far as the town of Strasburg by the shortest route. That the daily march should be not more than five leagues daily, resting each third day, billets should be regularly marked out for us, and that transport for the sick and the baggage should be furnished us *gratis*. That the commissioners and the escort should take entire charge and superintendence of the billeting and such like matters, so that by the regiment taking no part in this, any pretext by which the antipathy existing between the Germans and French could be aroused might be avoided; and in order to ensure that all these conditions were observed, His Imperial Majesty should send hostages to the town of Strasburg to await the arrival of the regiment."

Prince Eugene listened to me attentively, and asked me in his habitually calm manner if I had well thought out the proposals I had just made, and whether a foreign regiment, alone in the centre of the Empire, could expect all the honours I demanded, or, to put it plainly, dictate to the emperor conditions that the garrison of Ingolstadt would not obtain if it was ten thousand men strong. He gave me to understand that I must limit my demand to a passport for each of our grenadiers to enable them to leave in safety whensoever they individually wished, and that this even would only be granted as a favour, because our regiment had no claim to any conditions over and above those granted to the garrison of Ingolstadt. That although we had been forgotten in the conditions of the treaty with the Electress, he would be pleased to issue these passports upon his own responsibility, in accordance with any detail of numbers that I might furnish him with, so that each person could leave individually or, if thought best, in groups of ten, and that that, together with the pay owing to us, was all that he could grant us.

He added that he was making every effort to satisfy the garrison and to remove any excuse for delaying the evacuation of the place, and that if I accepted the advantageous proposals that he made me, we should receive the money and passports at once. I again represented to the prince that while the proposals he had so graciously made appeared to be reasonable and fair, and passports on any other occasion would be all that was required, still that they would not meet the case in which we now found ourselves. Attention had been drawn to our regiment, and the world had decided its fate and sentenced it to death. Consequently, the peasants of Swabia, accustomed to bloodshed and plunder ever since the Battle of Hochstett, would pay no respect to passports carried by unarmed Frenchmen; and the cruelty of these people had been so much increased by the bad behaviour of our grenadiers towards them that it would now be practically impossible for our people to pass through the country without being massacred on the road.

I begged His Highness to agree with my views and to believe that I had no attention whatever of laying down the law in the heart of the Empire, but that it was only our dire situation that forced me to ask for these favours; that our solitary regiment was hardly an object which could affect the glory of the emperor, and that the honour I asked for had but our safety as its end.

The prince, after having remained silent for some time, consented to my reasonings. He wished, however, before showing this to oppose other arguments, in order to see if I should firmly persist in the attitude I had taken up. He pressed me so hard that I was driven to tell him that the regiment had already acquired so great a reputation that in support of the same it would find it more glorious to perish in a bastion at Ingolstadt than to take the chance of being massacred by some miserable peasants This would not fail to happen unless he was good enough to grant the conditions I proposed to him, and I respectfully gave him to understand that this was our final decision and that of the whole of the garrison.

He understood from this interview that we were resolved to die in Ingolstadt if we did not obtain these terms. Moreover, he saw that it was not to the emperor's interest to risk his own troops to force us, or to retard in any way the occupation of the place, and he did me the honour of saying that the evidence I had put forward prevented an entire refusal of my propositions, but that he must have time for reflection, and told me to wait in his quarters for a final reply.

I left the prince in a very satisfied frame of mind, and found in his ante-chamber a numerous company of distinguished people, among others Maréchal d'Herberfeld, who complimented me on my mission. He told me that he would gladly have made us advantageous proposals himself. He had put our views before the King of the Romans; that it was upon his own advice that Prince Eugene had remained in his quarters to decide upon our differences. Whilst d'Herberfeld was talking to me. Prince Bareyter, brother-in-law of the King of Poland, joined us with an inquisitive air. I knew that these gentlemen would have given anything to know the outcome of my interview with Prince Eugene, but I affected not to be aware of this, and answered their polite remarks as vaguely as possible.

We then talked of matters regarding the details of the actions which had taken place during the campaign, and I learned that four troopers of Bareyter's regiment had had a great quarrel over the division of the spoil I had left on the banks of the Danube, when I swam that river after the action at Schelemberg, and that one of them had been killed as the result. The prince told me that by reason of this dispute my coat had been brought to him, and he had learned my name from the papers in the pockets, then, hearing that I had charge of this mission, my adventure recalled itself to his memory, and he wished to express how glad he would be to do anything for me that lay in his power. I had the honour of finding myself seated next to him that day at Prince Eugene's table, and in order to mark his good feeling towards me, he made me drink several more bumpers with him than is usual. Thus passed the first day, and on the next this prince again made me sit by him at table, and caused the same series of bumper toasts to be drunk, not that this, however, led me to exceed in this respect, as I only acknowledged those that he drank.

In the afternoon he made me propositions the nature of which surpassed anything that I could have hoped, had my duty and nationality permitted me to accept them. Maréchal d'Herberfeld joined with him in suggesting that I should enter the Emperor's service, and both promised me all their support. They tempted me by saying that they had sufficient influence at the Viennese Court to obtain me the command of a regiment of Frenchmen, such as I now commanded, should I think fit. They told me that an infantry regiment in the Emperor's service was worth at least twenty thousand crowns yearly, and if I had scruples in carrying arms against my own country, means would be found to give me employment in Hungary or with the King of Poland, and that in my peculiar situation I might well regard myself as being without a master, for, according to the treaty with the Electress, I was entirely free to act as I liked without offending against honour or propriety. They also told me my country would not give me great credit for my scruples, as one individual more or less in a kingdom was of no consequence.

The advice of these gentlemen was certainly to my own interest, and I saw as well as they did that the treaty with the Electress would save me from any imputation that might be made upon my conduct. On the other hand, I should always carry with me the regret of having accepted conditions which would have obliged me to support the advancement of my country's enemies. The regiment without doubt would have followed me, in fact, I believe it had that idea in mind, but this in itself made me quite averse to the proposition. I therefore thanked them without arguing the point, and thought it best to leave the matter open without giving a decided answer.

Prince Eugene called me into his private room the same evening. He, for some time, still opposed the propositions I had made to him, but finding me provided with fresh reasons to support those I had already put before him, he determined to grant them, with the exception of that relating to the despatch of hostages to Strasburg, or permission to take with us German servants above the age of fifteen. He said that hostages would be quite unnecessary, for he would send Imperial orders to all the provinces and principalities through which the regiment would have to pass, to see to the observance of all the articles in the treaty.

Commissioners, together with the escort detailed to accompany us, would supply everything, and I could now go back to Ingolstadt, to return again after six days, in order to give him time to obtain the signature of the treaty by His Imperial Majesty; he would then hand it to me and tell me pretty nearly the date of our departure. In the meantime he would arrange for the payment of the whole garrison; I was empowered to assure them on this point, and that everyone would be satisfied. He also added, with a laugh, that I knew what I was about in arranging capitulations, and that this one went well by the side of that of Rain. I was surrounded on my arrival at Ingolstadt by the whole of the officers of the garrison, who were impatiently waiting to hear the result of my mission. I made them my report, and it appeared to give everyone the greatest satisfaction.

Our Frenchmen, above all, were in the seventh heaven; their good fortune seemed to surpass their greatest expectations, for they found themselves covered with distinction at the very moment at which they had given themselves up for lost. On account of the course we had resolved upon, and were ready to take if necessary, there was not one who had not felt the full force of the gravity of the situation, and there were some even who were so affected by the melancholy prospect of their destruction, that they could hardly bring themselves to believe it possible that such excellent and honourable conditions would be sincerely carried out.

By this treaty I had an excellent opportunity to save Boismorel from the prosecution which might have been got up against him at Munich in the absence of his partisans. In order not to miss such a chance I despatched an officer the same day post haste to acquaint him of the news, and to tell him to pack up some things and join us (for there was no difficulty in evading his guard); in the meantime I would arrange a lodging for him.

I called upon and reported this to M. de Liselbourg, who, to please me, was good enough to agree to the course I had taken, on condition that Boismorel should never appear in public and still less at his own house, so that he should be relieved of all suspicion of connivance at his escape. Next day I saw Boismorel arrive, overjoyed to find himself at liberty and to feel that the moment had come for his return to France. As he could only appear about the town *incognito*, his sole companions besides the officers of the regiment were two French engineers, Parisians, who were in Ingolstadt before the Battle of Hochstett, and with whom he contracted such a close friendship that they never left him. So happy was he in the companionship of these gentlemen that he soon forgot his late troubles and all the services I had just rendered him; like the serpent in the fable he repaid me only with ingratitude.

CHAPTER 9

Quarrel With Boismorel

I set out from Ingolstadt to report myself to Prince Eugene on the day he had appointed for me to receive the articles of our capitulation. Boismorel, like the rest of the garrison, was perfectly aware of the object of my journey, and that there was no question of further negotiation. I found everything arranged exactly as the prince had kindly promised me. He himself handed me the articles of the treaty, assured me that the commissioners were then at work upon lists for the payment of our garrison, and that when this was complete we should receive our money. I was empowered to tell our people that they would not be asked to evacuate the place until two days after everyone had been settled with; he could not state positively the date of our departure, because it was necessary to communicate the terms of the treaty to the princes through whose territory we should have to pass, and to avoid confusion in the detail of our billets.

He said further that some time must pass before all was in order, but that if when we left Ingolstadt things were not in readiness, he had arranged that we should wait in the little town of Scheremhausen until our route and escort arrived, which, as far as he could judge, would be on or about December 15th. This over I took my leave of the Prince and returned to Ingolstadt, where I arrived rather late and prostrated with a sick headache. As on the previous occasion I found all the officers assembled at the house of M. de Liselbourg, excepting Boismorel; I forthwith made my report, gave the articles into the hands of our general, because contained therein were the promises of payment to the garrison, and then being no longer able to support my malady I went home to bed.

I had made up my mind to start for Munich early next morning, where lay all my property, to make use of the time before our departure and put in order various matters I had charge of. I got into my dressing-gown immediately on arrival at my lodgings, but passing the time with some arrangements connected with my journey was still up and about when I saw a regimental *garçon*-major[1] enter the room with a message to say that Boismorel wished to see me. I pointed out to him that it was impossible for me to go out, and as far as our business was concerned, several officers of the regiment who were at M. de Liselbourg's, and who were asked to do so, had doubtless informed him on the subject, so that there was nothing to tell him that he did not already know, and, besides, I should call on him next morning before starting for Munich.

A short time after the *garçon*-major had left another messenger arrived on the same errand. I asked him if Boismorel was alone, and as he replied that he was at supper with the two engineers, I had no doubt that he wished me to join their party, and therefore sent my thanks for the invitation with the same answer as previously; but I was wrong. Boismorel seemed to have thought that it was my duty personally to report to him my arrival and the result of my mission, not being aware that the *commandant* of the garrison was the proper person to whom such matters had to be reported. Furthermore, he did not really belong to the garrison, because he was supposed to be actually in irons, and as an officer is struck off all duty when merely under arrest, he was not in a position to demand anything from me as commanding the regiment, or even from the most junior subaltern.

Boismorel's feelings were hurt, and thus he had sent these two messengers to remind me to come and fulfil my duty; they, seeing the awkwardness of the situation, had not dared to deliver me the message as given, and had simply said that he wished to speak to me. The engineers also, equally ignorant of the rules of the service, had strengthened him in his opinion, making out that his authority had been slighted, and that I was trying to assert myself as the commanding-officer of the regiment. All this was quite enough to put him into such a furious temper that after my second reply he started off, entered my room swollen with rage, and demanded a reason for my disobedience.

I had retired to bed when I saw him enter, followed by the two messengers, who, however, discreetly remained by the door. Approaching me in a hectoring manner, he said, "Well, sir, it seems that I am to

---

1. An officer so-called in the old French service. He was selected from among the lieutenants of a regiment to assist the *aide*-majors in the general detail of duty.—James.

be obliged to come here myself to bring you to a sense of duty. Do you know that I am your colonel, and what that means?"

"Yes, sir," said I, "I know you, and if you knew yourself equally well, you would not have troubled yourself to come to my house just to pay me a compliment"

However, to enable him to get out of his mistake and recover his temper, I told him with calmness the details of the messages his people had brought, and the answers I had given; how, in the belief that he wished me to join his party, I was obliged to refuse on account of my condition, but he was so wrapped up in his own importance that he still believed I wished to ignore him, and was so full of what the engineers had put into his head, that my reasons were of no avail. Far from recollecting what he owed me, he made use of what I said to overwhelm me with such low abuse that I was ashamed to hear such words from a person of his position. It was in vain for me to point out to him that he had other means at hand for asserting what was due to him, if he believed himself to be insulted, but I said that although I was starting the next morning for Munich, my time was at his disposal, and he could have the satisfaction he wished for.

Instead of listening to this, he made threatening gesticulations with his hands, and flourished his fist in my face. Then, seeing this game had gone far enough, and in the fear that I should receive the first blow, I thought it best to be beforehand with him, and so, not having any words ready at the moment to apostrophise him with, I gave him a heavy blow with my fist full in the face, which made him stagger. He was so astonished at this that he forgot he had a sword at his side, and in another instant we had grappled with each other. When the two officers heard our struggles, they and my valet rushed in and separated us. Then Boismorel, still forgetful of his sword, threw himself upon the sentry at the top of my staircase, and endeavoured to wrest his gun from him, but the grenadier held fast, and his efforts were of no avail.

Whilst this was going on, I dashed into the next room for my arms, and the thought that I should be ready for him sooner than he liked, inspired him with such fear that he rushed down the stairs, and made off precipitately to his own house. When my anger had calmed somewhat and I was in a condition to think, I could not conceive what evil star could have led me into such an unfortunate business, for I certainly had some reason to think that the author of it would have sacrificed himself for me, in recognition of the trouble I had taken in getting him out of prison and thence to Ingolstadt. I had procured him his liberty, perhaps even saved his life, but far from remembering this, he had just put us into the unfortunate position of having to draw upon each other.

Having been struck, honour now demanded that he should wash out the affront with blood. I had no doubt, therefore, but that I should have to fight early next morning, and in order that he should have nothing to reproach me with regarding the satisfaction to which he was entitled, I put off my journey to Munich till the afternoon. I made a point even of walking in the principal square for a long time so as to show people that he could find me if he wished, but I never heard a word from him.

I then thought that he, knowing I had to go to Munich, wished to meet me outside the town, so I mounted my horse in the afternoon, and stopped on purpose to talk with an officer in the square, to give him time to catch me up on the road, but I had to continue on my journey without seeing him or anyone representing him. Arrived at Munich, I found the inhabitants in a state of consternation, all gaiety had vanished, and this town, which had been so brilliant last winter, full of society and the affairs of the French Army, was plunged in gloom.

About eight days after my arrival a lackey belonging to a lady of rank came to say that his mistress hoped I would call upon her with reference to a matter of importance. I was not acquainted with the lady in question, and could not imagine what this important business could be; however, I made my call. What was my surprise when on entering the room I found therein my fair one of Straubing with her mother. They threw themselves on my neck one after the other, with such studied eagerness that one could have sworn that they, especially my amiable princess, were animated with the most violent affection. Our *adieux* at Landshut were nothing in comparison with the tearful tenderness she feigned to show at this moment, and she played her part in the comedy with such effect, what with the prostration of her feelings and languor, that anyone would have thought she loved me to madness.

She mingled reproaches with excuses for what had occurred when I went to see her in the country; she complained of my sudden departure without even thinking it worthwhile to inquire for her; and then said that it was the surprise of our meeting that had been the cause of her not showing me all the attention she could have wished. She really had been overcome almost to the extent of fainting, but

MAP OF BAVARIA

that did not prevent the delight she had felt, though at the time she was incapable of showing it. She had recovered by the next day only to find I had gone, when despair took the place of joy, but learning that I was at Munich for a time she had come there expressly to see me and reproach me for my indifference. For a young lady of her rank to take such an important step was the greatest proof she could give me of the attachment and esteem in which she held me, and that I ought to take this explanation at its proper value and effect a perfect reconciliation between us.

Although she understood that I was about to return to France without keeping faith with the love that I had so often sworn to her, she felt that I was too good-hearted a man to wish to leave her without the accomplishment of that she had so hoped of me, and she had, therefore, made up her mind to sink all differences between us, and to follow me wherever I judged fit to go. The journey to France would be no obstacle to her; she would undertake it with pleasure, and, lastly, it would be impossible to live without me.

After very few words of reply I bowed and retired. I could not conceive how people of their position could play such different roles in so short a period of time, and found it extraordinary that this young lady's affection should have resuscitated just at the moment that I was leaving the country. I well recollected the manner with which she had received me when I found her in company with her imbecile countryman, and I could scarcely think, after being so off-hand with me, that she could really imagine that her tricks could have any effect upon my feelings. The more I thought over the matter, the more grew the dislike I now felt for her, so I concluded that some unforeseen marriage had robbed her of her lover, or perhaps even death, and that as a last resource she had played these wiles so as to get me to take her to France where her adventures would be unknown.

A few days later I left Munich, after having asked my orders and taken my leave of the Electress, who did not appear to be annoyed with what had happened at Ingolstadt; on the contrary, she treated the liberty I had taken with all the kindness in the world. I learned that the garrison at Ingolstadt had been paid all that was due to it, the Imperialists had entered the place, and that our regiment was quartered in the little town of Scheremhausen, waiting for the escort to conduct them according to the treaty.

I joined the regiment without delay, and no sooner had I set foot in my billet than M. de Florimond, the two engineers, and several other officers who were passing to France by favour of my treaty, came to tell me that in my absence they had arranged with Boismorel that we should not settle the difference between us until the last day's march before entering France, because it had been intimated that the Imperialists were going to put off the time of our departure in order to see how the matter would end. They reckoned, it seemed, that the event would be productive of some pretext to disturb the regiment and so cause its desertion in a body. It was, therefore, necessary in the interests of the king and the many honest folk who hoped to travel under the protection of the battalion, that we should observe a truce until we were on the frontier; then, without prejudicing anyone, we could wipe out our difference. Boismorel, at their request, had consented to this arrangement, and they hoped that I would not oppose it.

I told these gentlemen that there was no evidence whatever that the Imperialists had such designs concerning us, or still less that they were in the least aware of what had passed between Boismorel and me, but that, as they thought proper that there should be several days truce between us, I had nothing to say against it. Besides, it lay with Boismorel to demand satisfaction from me, and he was at liberty to keep silence as long as he thought fit, though by putting the affair off there was always the fear that he would raise fresh difficulties by reason of his passionate temper. They told me that they had thought as I did, but they had provided for this, and hoped to keep him in check.

The warning turned out to be only too true, for Maréchal d'Herberfeld, now commanding this province since Prince Eugene had left for Vienna, annoyed at the rebuff he had received from us at Ingolstadt, thought to revenge himself by altering the date of our departure so as to bring about desertion in the regiment. The 15th and 16th of the month had already gone by without our hearing a word on the subject—a silence that gave rise to considerable consternation, and I was again called upon to go and interview Maréchal d'Herberfeld.

The general availed himself of excuses as to the way he had been prevented from giving us this information, and raised withal several further difficulties, which I set to work to clear up. In the course of our conversation I convinced him that some evil-minded person must have set the rumour going as to a difference existing between me and Boismorel, and that there was nothing in it I also pointed out that our long detention in the country was neither to the emperor's interest or that of the inhabitants of Scheremhausen, as our grenadiers were a heavy tax upon the district that they were quartered in, and that they would be quite delighted to stay any length of time. In fact, I told him so many things of the sort that he finally determined to fix Christmas Eve as the day of our departure, assured me that the commissioners and escort would be at the gates of the town that day to conduct us, and, moreover, that a very honest and peaceable set of men had been chosen for this work, with whom we should be perfectly satisfied.

I left quite contented with the result of my mission, and brought veritable relief to the minds of our people when I produced such good news.

But Boismorel had not yet quieted down; his evil passions caused him to imagine means of revenge without risking his life, and in such a way that no one could make a personal accusation against him for failing to keep to the arrangement he had made. To accomplish this, he availed himself of the disposition and temper of his lieutenant, who might have been called his double. He was a young gentleman from Champagne, full of fire and energy; neither well educated nor experienced, easily taken in, and incapable of seeing the inwardness or truth of any proposition made to him. Boismorel persuaded him that I intended to do him a harm; that he knew as a fact that I premeditated cashiering him when he arrived in France on account of his friendship for himself, and that as he was in fear lest he should thus become a victim to my jealousy, he advised him to avenge himself upon me before I had time to do anything of the kind. This young officer was so struck with Boismorel's advice that he incautiously let fall countless threatening remarks against me. The Chevalier de la Bastide, who was extremely attached to me, found out all this, and fearing some sudden outbreak, reported the details to me when I returned from my interview with General d'Herberfeld.

I was therefore on my guard when on the same day I accidentally met the lieutenant in one of the streets. It struck me that here was a chance of disabusing his mind by explaining matters to him, and stopped him for this purpose; but I found him so prejudiced against me that without further ceremony he showered abuse upon me in such a high voice, and a manner so entirely wanting in due respect, that I drew my sword and hit him with the flat of the blade to show my resentment at his words. I then stepped back to give him time to defend himself; but a number of people who were attracted by his voice came up, separated us, and saw us to our respective quarters.

Boismorel was overjoyed when he learned that the affair had

turned out in a way that made withdrawal impossible before matters were brought to the usual climax, and that the lieutenant must demand satisfaction from me, since no official objection, on the score of his being but a subaltern, could now be put forward. He hoped that this active and robust youth would relieve him of the danger he would incur in fighting me, and he spent the rest of the day doing his best to excite all the fury and rancour that lay in his nature. He advised him to arm himself with a thick stick in order to hit me before I had time to draw my sword, should he be able to surprise me, so as to wash out the insult of the blow I had given him with the flat of my blade, and with this object sent him next morning to prowl round my quarters.

I was in the act of dressing when I noticed him from my window parading the square, stick in hand, so in order not to delay the satisfaction he intended to derive from me, I finished my toilet as quickly as possible, and sallied out to look for him without troubling much about his stick. I could not see him in the square, so took the direction of Boismorel's lodgings, where I thought it likely he would be, and saw him in the street talking to the colonel through the window. As soon as I was sure that both had seen me, I made my way towards a gate of the town to gain space for our battle, and avoid the possible contingency of our being separated as had happened on the evening before. The lieutenant followed on my heels, and seeing me pass through the gate got it into his head that I had taken this road with the intention of avoiding him. This idea increased his courage to the extent that he quickened his pace, shouting, "Stop, stop! you are not going to escape from me."

I was on the bridge over the ditch of the town when his voice rang harshly in my ears; hurt by the unworthy insinuation conveyed by this threat, I turned, sword in hand, and in two bounds was upon him. He had barely time to draw his own, and discard the stick, which he had now no chance of using in the way he had planned. The tactics I confronted him with were so contrary to his expectations that they contributed much to his disadvantage; however, he did his best to defend himself, but was confused, lost his head, and was quite unprepared. I soon saw that I could easily finish off my man, and had, happily for him, plenty of time to reflect that if I killed him the fact of his death would, doubtless, be made the cause of some awkward trouble. Hence I only wounded him twice in the arm and disarmed him. I gave him his life that I had in my power, although I was well aware that I should not have met with the same fate if I had been at his mercy, for Boismorel had commended me too warmly to his care.

Several officers who had their suspicions of this affair, and whom curiosity had brought to the spot, heard me reprimand him for his evil intentions, and for being capable of following such advice without realising that he who gave it simply wished to sacrifice him for his own revengeful purpose. I made him see how mistrustful he should be of such pernicious gossip, and that he should profit by the experience he had just undergone to avoid mixing himself up with other people's quarrels. In point of fact he appreciated this, and did all he could to bring himself back again to my good opinion of him, the which I granted him with pleasure. Boismorel, who awaited with extreme anxiety the outcome of our combat, was aghast when he learned the advantage I had gained over his friend and the lecture I had administered to him after our encounter, and for the time being let the matter rest.

The day of our departure, as arranged with Maréchal d'Herberfeld, came at last; the escort and commissioners joined us at Scheremhausen, and we took the road to France on the 23rd of December. There were no troops left in Bavaria, but those belonging to His Imperial Majesty and the battalion left at the disposal of the Electress. All the Bavarians had been disbanded according to the treaty, and many who knew not where to go joined the emperor's service. Care was taken to send these men to Hungary or Italy, lest they should be seized with a desire to rejoin their sovereign.

It was not given to the Electress to see the good faith of the treaty kept for any length of time. To her sorrow she saw the Court of Vienna, under various frivolous pretexts, send a *commandant* to Munich to see that nothing occurred there contrary to the interests of the emperor, and Her Highness now saw from several indications that nothing but unhappiness was promised for the future. She wished to safeguard her family, so she asked for a passport for Rome. The Court of Vienna, taking this opportunity to complete its designs, granted the passport for the person of the Electress only, and sent her five children to Gratz, so that there should be no motive for unrest in the Bavarian States.

The considerable revenue of the country contributed effectually to the cost of the war, and only proved too clearly how well it could have held out, as we had declared. If the worst had come to the worst, it could but have suffered loss of army and country. As it was, the Elector's subjects were a prey to the subsidies laid upon them by the

Court of Vienna, which amounted annually to at least thirty millions of French money.

Such was the end of the Bavarian War, with the details of which very few people in Europe have made themselves impartially acquainted. I could not well have added to or left out any of the incidents thereof without weakening the truth, and if I had but as much elegance as impartiality, I know that my memoirs would be more presentable than they actually are.

We now found ourselves fairly on our road with the commissaries and a hundred and fifty *cuirassiers* as escort under the command of a captain, a man of mark in the Empire. He arranged the details of our billets, halts, marches, and transport with all the exactitude that we could have wished for, and brought about so good a feeling between the *cuirassiers* and our grenadiers that it appeared as if both were serving under the same flag. Thus our journey was as comfortable and peaceful as possible; the officers messed together day after day, and these pleasant moments inspired them with the idea of trying to bring about a reconciliation between Boismorel and me.

They believed that they had discovered a plausible excuse to this end in giving a different aspect to our affair, and persuaded themselves that it was a simple misunderstanding of no consequence, and what had passed in the privacy of my chamber was no evidence that there was deliberate intention on either of our parts to give offence; that we had always been friends up to the time of this trifling occurrence, and that there was no reason for enmity in so small a matter. Moreover, as no one could possibly have the right to criticise us on this point, we ought to suppress our feelings, and make it up as good friends should.

The first proposals as to this arrangement were made to Boismorel, as they naturally supposed that if he agreed to them there would be no further obstacle to our reconciliation. He it was who had been struck. I was in the position of owing him satisfaction, so that if he was content, I ought to be likewise. Any scruples that Boismorel may have had were soon got over, for he was by no means sorry that means were being devised to enable him to avoid the risk incurred in the meeting which he ought to have demanded from me. He swallowed his own disgrace, persuaded himself that these gentlemen were right in their premises, and gladly accepted their propositions.

After assuring themselves of Boismorel, they came on at once to interview me; but I could hardly believe that his consent was really genuine or that there might not have been some misunderstanding in the report they made me. It appeared, however, that the matter was beyond question, and instead of having to give satisfaction, sword in hand, to Boismorel, I was to be let off with the embrace of amity. This arrangement was followed by much conviviality, which continued until our arrival at Strasburg on January 8th, 1705.

Maréchal de Marsin, who was in command there, received us in the most gracious manner possible, and covered us with congratulations on our good fortune in being able to preserve the regiment by means of an honourable treaty, in spite of such adverse circumstances. He told us that he had orders to send us to Mons, in Flanders, by a route that he would point out, but that he wished us to rest eight days in Strasburg, so that he might have the pleasure of entertaining us. He kept the Imperialists who had accompanied us for a similar purpose, showed them all the hospitality that lay in his power for three days, and on their departure directed two waggons full of choice wine to join their train, one of champagne and the other of Burgundy, as a present to the officers, who went on their way rejoicing.

During our stay at Strasburg I noticed that the Chevalier de la Bastide, who ought to have appeared more contented than anyone, was, on the contrary, extremely gloomy and prepossessed. I had the greatest affection for him; he was a companion of the most kindly nature and brave in action, and as he was much attached to me and I had rendered him some service, I was interested through him in the result of my work.

Such was our friendship that we were accustomed to hide nothing from, and ask anything of, each other. Moved by the expression of his countenance, I asked him to tell me the source of his melancholy, if it was but a manner of affecting to hide his joy at finding himself back in France, or whether something unfortunate had occurred to him which he had not dared to tell me of. I assured him that if the latter was the case, I was absolutely desirous that he should declare it to me, and that it appeared to me very strange that he should have waited for me to ask him about it.

When he saw that I insisted upon this, he tendered several reasons to put me off; I pressed him again on the score of our friendship, and with friendly threats extracted from him that the cause was of such a nature that he would prefer it concealed for all time; but he trusted that notwithstanding the obligations he owed me already, I would not cease my interest in him when I learned the facts of the case; and he begged me to continue a protection which he was now more than ever in need of.

"I am not," he said, "what I told you I was when I presented myself to you on the first occasion; I assumed a name and a standing to which I had no right. We were in a foreign country, where I believed that by calling myself a person of quality I would the sooner get employment. As a matter of fact, had you known that I had never been in the service and who I really was, you would have thought you were doing me a great favour even by enlisting me as a private carabineer. You have been the means of my obtaining an important post, one that I could fill in a foreign land, but now that I am at home it will be no longer possible for me to keep up my disguise. A hundred times have I thought over the course I should take. I would take arms in the service of the emperor were it not for the grief I should cause you when you came to learn of my desertion. How much rather would I take my chance and follow you than commit an act that would cause you pain, but the confidence I have in your protection and friendship lead me to hope that you will not abandon me.

"I was born," continued he, "at Villeneuve d'Agenois. My name is Galand, my family is not a noble one, but is *bourgeois*, and the oldest in the town. My father died and left me but a small sum, though this did not prevent my mother planning to see me married as soon as possible on account of my being the only son. This done, I found myself entirely without the means to keep up my household, so set to work in a small business on credit given me by some merchants of Bordeaux, who supplied me with some merchandise. I then opened a shop, but my want of experience and liking for cards soon exhausted my means, and nothing remained to liquidate my account with the merchants. Default spelled imprisonment, and being quite unable to meet my liabilities, I was obliged to desert my wife and children and fly abroad to save myself

"One of my neighbours, named Roux, found himself in the same case. We agreed to go off together to seek our fortunes, and we were happy enough to meet you. He, bolder than I should have been, took the title of count, and persuaded me to take that of Chevalier. Judge now of my sad case. I foresee that as soon as we join the army I shall meet many of my neighbours now serving, who will be much astonished at the name of Bastide and my rank as captain of grenadiers. They will guess that I have only reached my position by means of a borrowed name and rank, my promotion will excite their jealousy, and they will not fail to inform the world of a history in which the term bankrupt will not be spared. My creditors, who will without doubt duly receive the information, will crowd upon me either in person or through their agents, and aid in making public my real status in life; all this is inevitable.

"If I had reached the post I hold by regular grades, merit would overcome the fact of my origin, but that a bankrupt should all at once become a captain of grenadiers is inconceivable. My adventure will come to the knowledge of Maréchal d'Arcko, who will be gravely astonished that I should have taken him in with an assumed name.

"These reflections drive me to despair, and I see but one single remedy for my troubles that you can possibly procure for me, but this would be asking too much of you after the story I have just told you, which probably has aroused your utmost indignation. I well see that there is nothing whatever left for me to do but to rejoin the Imperial escort, and throw myself into their ranks."

"Not at all," said I to him; "I have sufficient experience to see that your misfortune is due rather to your bankruptcy than bad faith. Ever since I have known you, you have shown yourself to be an honest man, and I make no more of your having deceived me than that I have deceived the Elector in procuring for you your company in the grenadiers. No one could have held the post better than you in the interests of the prince. Your comrade died in action, which will always be to the honour of his memory, and I have no regrets whatever in having introduced two such fellows as you. Simply tell me the means by which you think I could extricate you from your difficulties, and if they are in any way possible, I will spare nothing to carry them out, and prove to you that when once I have given my friendship it is forever."

The poor boy, with tears in his eyes, threw himself upon my neck, saying that as I was so kind, it would necessitate my accompanying him to his own part of the country, and leaving the regiment to move on to Mons without us. To turn this journey to account, he would write and describe to his wife and relations the plight he was in, together with his intention of satisfying his creditors and relieving his family, for which his affection had never lapsed.

He added that if I rendered him that service, many officers now on leave at Villeneuve, his creditors and neighbours, seeing that I was fully conversant with all his affairs and interested therein, would be silent with regard to this news, which they would have otherwise attempted to connect with the regiment; they would become gradually accustomed to his presence, and would perceive nothing strange in his conduct. Even supposing that someone did speak against him, my presence in his neighbourhood would suffice as a reference or witness in his favour, and with all his creditors satisfied, as he hoped would be the case on his arrival, he trusted that they would not show any bad feeling towards him.

Bastide told me this with such feeling that I was truly affected by his troubles, and did not hesitate a moment in telling him to write home at once, and that I was quite ready to accompany him.

I then informed Boismorel that I intended to profit by the remainder of the winter season, and go into the country to put various matters in order, taking Bastide with me.

He was charmed to find himself relieved of the presence of two individuals who stood in the way of his ambition to be the sole head of the regiment, and to pose as its saviour. He even flattered himself that I intended to retire altogether, and gave the regiment to understand this. I however wrote to Maréchal d'Arcko, who was with the Elector at Brussels, and reported to him fully all that had passed in the regiment, my proposed tour, my return to Mons before the opening of the campaign, and then set off with Bastide.

Our journey was without incident, and we arrived at Villeneuve very near the date named to his relations. So determined were they to give me a good reception that they assembled their friends, etc., to the extent that they could hardly have made more preparations in the case of the advent of an ambassador than they did for me. The nobility and principal inhabitants heaped attentions upon me. Nothing could have been more gracious than the manners of these gentlemen; every day there were fresh entertainments, sumptuous repasts followed by dances and balls, and I spent the carnival in the most agreeable fashion. Nevertheless, all this pleasure-making did not prevent our arranging the affairs of Bastide, otherwise Galand, which took such a favourable turn that all his creditors declared themselves quite contented.

I gave him such a high character that no one considered his sudden change in position in the least strange, and he was regarded as a man who really deserved still better fortune. A number of officers, who were then on leave in the country, became accustomed to recognise him and his rank in the regiment, and our journey fully realised its intentions.

Bastide's affairs established, my presence became no longer necessary, so I left Villeneuve the second week of Lent to pass a few days in Bordeaux, to fill in the time before my return to Flanders. Besides the convenience of passing Lent there, the desire to see my own friends again was the real object of my journey; as regards the lawsuit I had left there, it had passed from my memory so completely that I never thought of it for one single moment.

But my adversaries had by no means forgotten it: they had profited by my absence and my so-called flight to obtain a judgment in their favour. They had been awarded costs to a considerable amount, and I had been notified to pay the same within four months, failing which they had power to imprison me. As soon as they heard that I was in the district, they had no doubt whatever but that I should go to Bordeaux before returning to the army, so they determined to have me arrested at any cost.

To this end they arranged with a sheriff's officer named Lalande, a one-eyed, bold, and enterprising man—a person who would not pay any regard even to a parliamentary bigwig if it was a question of gaining money. They informed him of all my habitual movements about the town, and the inn at which I usually lodged, so that he could at once find me when I arrived. This worthy, who took care to get daily information regarding me, at last found out that I was in the town, and prepared all his batteries for action. Although he had no reason to believe that I expected anything of this, he nevertheless did not picture the affair to himself as easy of execution; he had been told that I was not the most docile of men, and had insisted on an advance of thirty *pistoles* as against the expense he would have to incur to ensure my capture. He enlisted six men whom he believed to be the most suitable for his purpose, and they arranged the details between them so that there should be no chance of missing me. They decided upon following me until I should pass in front of the prison gate, correctly reckoning that I must sooner or later take this road, if it was only to go to the Fair of the Bourse (which is close by and which opened on March 1st).

Again, they found means to get the lackey I had engaged on my arrival in Bordeaux to join their band, and with all these preparations they had every confidence that they would be able to carry out their purpose. For four days they tracked me down without finding an opportunity to seize me. At last one Sunday about sundown, when I found myself in the Rue des Argentiers, which leads to the gate of the court, followed by two porters (for luckily the chair I had with me was only for show), the archers saw me take the road they had counted so much on, and waited until I was exactly opposite the door of the court to attack me. Then I suddenly felt myself seized from behind, from shoulders to feet, to the cry "Prisoner in the King's name!"

I fully believed at the moment that this was a practical joke on the part of some of my friends, but seeing a strange face in front of me with a most villainous expression, the possessor of which seized the hilt of my sword to snatch it from me, I realised that this was no pleasantry. There was not much time to make up my mind; it was necessary to plan and defend myself at one and the same instant, and now I saw quite clearly that this was some manoeuvre on the part of my old enemies. The efforts that this band made to secure me were of the most violent and prompt nature. Some set to work to seize me by the legs, others got me by the shoulders, and others again round the waist, whilst Lalande did his best to disarm me.

It was lucky for me that I happened to be endowed with some considerable strength, for, without boasting, I have never found the man who could resist me when roused; and as my passion grew my power redoubled itself. It served me marvellously in my violent struggles to shake off these seven great ruffians, who threw themselves upon me with all desperation. Lalande it was who tore at the hilt of my sword to wrest it from me, whilst the others grasped me tightly, in order to prevent me defending myself; but happily the sheath being firmly fixed by its hook to the belt, the blade was drawn out bare.

As soon as I saw it glitter, I instantly struggled furiously, threw myself forward, and caught it a foot from the point. To seize and break it with a turn of my wrist was the result of one movement, so that I found myself master of at least the point. Finding myself thus armed with a dagger, which he who had seized my sword was unaware of, I renewed my efforts, which gave my arms sufficient liberty to stab right and left two of my assailants in the breast, which instantly put them out of action. A third, who had me by the shoulders, received another before the four others had time to notice how it all came about. Lalande, who saw his band wavering, flew at my neck in order to rally them, shouting desperately, "Help in the name of the King! Help in the name of Justice!"

But he had scarcely time to get a hold when I drove his head back with my left hand, the better to plunge my spike into his stomach, and felled him like a log at my feet without having had the chance of stabbing him. Then as I let him alone in order to keep myself on the defensive, he was picked up; and I did not fail this time to deliver my point, for I stabbed him in the breast, and almost in the same action, snatched his sword from him without his noticing it. He merely placed his hand upon his wound, and precipitately retired in fear lest I should renew my attack. No sooner had I relieved Lalande of his sword than I caught sight of a fifth man, who, with some courage still left in him, had just bared his blade. I immediately advanced upon him to treat him to a sword cut, when this worthless wretch, perceiving me ready to attack him, howled as if he had already received his death blow, and fled through the crowd, upsetting several women whom he found in his path.

As soon as he had thus saved himself, I noticed a calm come over the scene, and it seemed as if I had no one else from whom to fear any injury, but not wishing to rely too much upon appearances, I turned about on all sides in order to ascertain if there were not more combatants about; and I then saw two men, who kept behind me as if they wished to keep out of my sight. They were the remnant of this pleasing band, who, seeing themselves abandoned by their leader and comrades, neither dared attack me or to break through the crowd, lest in their efforts to force a passage, they might make me aware of their presence, and thus be caught before they were able to escape. Besides, it was not so easy for them to get through, for, owing to the great crowd that had packed themselves together, there was no semblance of a gap anywhere. What was really surprising was that amongst so many people not one was found with sufficient generosity of feeling to come to my assistance. My two porters even took to their heels at the very beginning of the affair.

The archers shouted so effectively, "Help for the King! Help on the part of Justice!" without my uttering a syllable, that they all credited me with being guilty, and none cared to come forward in my defence.

Recognising the two bailiffs by their pale and anxious faces, I approached them, and such was their fear that they stood quite immovable. However, I reassured them by telling them that they had nothing to be afraid of, that I despised them too much to do them the honour of killing them, but that it was my express desire that they would before leaving the ground find me my hat, peruke, and the hilt of my sword, without which I should certainly withdraw the mercy I was extending them.

These two wretches tremblingly searched for my property, and luckily found it on the field of battle, and with the profoundest submission, assisted to replace the peruke upon my head. I took the opportunity, whilst they were so humbly rendering me their service, to reprimand them in a loud tone of voice, so that everyone could hear me distinctly.

With a repentant air they explained that Lalande had engaged them without giving them any details, that he kept all the papers, and that they had believed it to be only a question of debt. I let them go, and so overpowered with fear were they, that no sooner had they got eight or ten paces off than they took to their heels in dread lest I should change my mind. Then a murmuring arose among the spectators, who showed regret at not having come to my assistance, perhaps because there was now no longer any necessity.

This business was quickly reported all over the town. My friends thronged to offer their services and inquired of me as to the details of my offence, so that they could take measures to ensure my safety. I told them that I was myself ignorant of how the matter arose; one of the bailiffs had certainly said that he believed it was a question of debts, but this, however, could not be the case, as I had never borrowed a farthing from anyone, and from this reply they came to the conclusion that the matter was more serious than it appeared to be on the surface. They pressed me to retire to some place of safety, but I assured them so strongly that no harm could possibly come to me that Messieurs Leglise and Grenier, parliamentary councillors, took me to call upon M. l'Albessard, Advocate-General, now President at Mortier, and begged him to send an order to the sheriff's officer to deliver him up the papers, so that my case could be examined and further consequences avoided. He was kind enough to lend himself to the affair in the most obliging way in the world; he impounded the papers, and in a very short time I settled the costs that had been obtained against me, and the matter was closed.

I was very much touched by the attention paid me by the advocate-general, and the gracious manner in which he rendered me this service, which was by no means his last. I owe him the perfection of gratitude, and I shall not forget it as long as I live. To be insensible to a service rendered with such promptitude and good feeling is characteristic of ungrateful natures.

The archers took no proceedings against me as to their wounds; perhaps they believed it would be useless so to do against a soldier who did not belong to the town, and who was consequently in a better position to avenge himself on them in the future; besides, as the little rebuffs that they had sustained were all in their way of business, they probably had no right to ask any recompense from the authors of their misfortune. However that may be, I heard nothing further from them except in form of apologies when they knew of my later return to Bordeaux.

I had scarcely settled this affair than I received letters from Mons, by which I was informed that Boismorel had entered the town at the head of the regiment in the manner of a triumph, as if he himself had carried his soldiery safely through all the dangers they had undergone; these airs availed him nothing, as care had been taken to give the Elector full particulars of what had passed between him and the Marquis de Massey, and his escape contrary to the orders of the Electress. Copies of the inquiry which had been instituted against him had been forwarded by the princess to his Electoral Highness, and two days after his arrival he was again imprisoned. Nevertheless, by the influence of the Duke of Orleans he had been enabled to extricate himself from this unfortunate position at the cost of being cashiered from the king's service.

I learned further that in deference to his illustrious protector he had had the luck to be taken back as *aide-de-camp* to the Elector with his rank as colonel; that the difference we had had between us had been much noised abroad, particularly at the house of the Duchess de Crouy, which was a daily meeting-place for all the *élite* of the town. He, having wished to take part in these gatherings, was, however, given to understand that he would get but a bad reception, as he bore the stain of having been struck without having exacted the proper satisfaction. In order to clear himself he had published an outrageous story by which he attempted to prove that I had absconded to avoid a duel, and would certainly never reappear. In fact, so successfully had he played his part that I was now the guilty one in the opinion of the whole garrison, and these libels obliged me to demand satisfaction of him.

This letter filled my inmost soul with vexation; despair seized me when I thought of so many good people so prejudiced against me, and that on my rejoining the garrison I should be regarded with contempt. I regretted having gone so far out of my way on account of Bastide as to accompany him to the country; I ought to have led the regiment to Mons, where my presence would have prevented all these slanders, or at least if an attempt had been made to utter them I would have been in a position to put a stop to them before any impression had been made. I longed to be in Mons to avenge upon so knavish a trick, and after receiving this letter made no long stay at Bordeaux.

The question of my marriage which was in the course of being arranged had been occupying my mind, but the time was too critical to think about this now. I put the matter off till a quieter period, as I wished to wait until I could first obtain a truce to the untoward events which poured in succession upon me.

Just about this time I received a letter from Maréchal d'Arcko, who informed me from Brussels that Maréchal de Villeroi, by the king's direction, had asked the Elector for the regiment of grenadiers, and His Highness had been pleased to mark his preference for it by keeping it in his service, and had arranged to present him with a regiment of hussars in its place. Nevertheless, the Elector, cut off from his dominions and at the end of his resources, found it impossible to maintain the regiment, he had decided therefore to form it into a single company, under my command, and to employ the officers according to their seniority.

The regiment of the Electoral Prince having been organised, this company was to march at its head; I was to be in sole command of the French grenadiers; besides which His Highness gave me the rank of lieutenant-colonel in the regiment itself. By this arrangement I entered the service of the Elector of Bavaria with the consent of the king. I thus found myself more at liberty to demand satisfaction from Boismorel, as the Elector readily gave his assent to necessary duels, however premeditated. His Highness had already found it very strange that Boismorel and I, who were under his orders and of established position in his service, could have set such bad examples by allowing our difference to pass in silence.

I left Bordeaux for Mons (after having told Bastide to join me there), and called whilst passing through Paris upon the Marquis de Ricous, whom I found reduced to despair at the reverse of his fortunes brought upon him by the Battle of Hochstett. He had been in some sort discredited ever since, and this weighed upon him to such an extent that his health was shattered and he died shortly afterwards. I felt the deepest grief at the loss of one who had given me so many practical proofs of his friendship. I arrived at Mons three hours after midday, and having entered the town by a side road, dismounted at a secluded inn so that my arrival should be unknown to anyone. As soon as I had settled down in my room I sent to ask one of the senior captains in the Electoral Prince's regiment, named Grondeur, to come and speak to me. This officer was one of those fellows who never have any hesitation in drawing their swords, he even made rather a business of it, so that I thought I could not apply to anyone better able to point out to me the most appropriate spot on which to settle the quarrel between Boismorel and myself, and to carry my challenge for me. I was sure that in case of a difficulty he would know how to make things easy.

Grondeur appeared without keeping me waiting, and being informed of my intentions said he quite understood what had to be done; that he could show me a quiet spot absolutely suited to the purpose, and that he would put himself at my service with the greatest pleasure. He added that if Boismorel accepted the challenge, of which he had no doubt, he would act as our guide; that there could not be a better opportunity of settling this affair once and for all, as no one in the garrison was aware of my arrival, and he would therefore go at once and find Boismorel, who he was sure would be of the same opinion. "You wish apparently as challenger," said he, "to leave him the choice of weapons?"

"Certainly," I replied. "I accept in advance any conditions that you may make so long as Boismorel appears on the ground."

Grondeur set out to find Boismorel, who evinced extreme surprise on learning that I was in the town and that I intended remaining *incognito* until I had obtained the satisfaction I demanded of him. He had so fully persuaded himself that I had quite left the service that, in his astonishment, he hardly knew how to answer Grondeur. At last, after having remained some time in perplexity, he replied that the king had forbidden duelling, but he was in the habit of strolling in the streets, and if I required anything of him I had only to attack him on our meeting, when he would defend himself Grondeur did his best to explain matters to him, but he stuck to his point, and the only answer I could get was this regulation of the king's, to which Boismorel intended religiously to adhere.

Nevertheless I again sent Grondeur, and begged him to make Boismorel understand that the pretext he had devised to avoid fighting could only lead to his dishonour; that he knew as well as I did that we were responsible to the Elector for our actions; that he himself, now an outlaw from France, had no one to rely upon but this prince, who was sure to have a bad opinion of two people of our standing if we did not follow the customs prescribed by honour. Also that we were too much in view of his court and troops to evade this duel, and that for a long time past he had owed it to himself to have forestalled me in my challenge. He, however, was not disturbed by these arguments, and I was obliged to leave two days later to report myself to Maréchal d'Arcko at Brussels, without having had the chance of coming across Boismorel. The only hope left me was that of meeting him on the field, when I reckoned that he would have no excuse left him for evading the satisfaction that I demanded of him.

CHAPTER 10

The Campaigns of 1705 and 1706

In 1705 the army in Flanders was commanded by Maréchal de Villeroi.

The conquests of France now reached as far as the confines of Holland, and resulted in her possession of a chain of fortresses which covered an immense extent of country.

Besides these lines which served to defend the Spanish Low Countries, we had also fortified positions, constructed with all possible care, which formed a second line of defence against any designs that the enemy might entertain on the territory of the two Crowns. Since the beginning of the war neither side had as yet made any attempt to carry on a campaign in Flanders itself; Italy and Germany had hitherto attracted the particular attention of all the powers concerned.

France, however, fearing a further development of the successes gained by the Allies on the Rhine, sought to create a diversion by raising dissension amongst the Dutch. To this end we had prepared a larger army than any we had had in the previous campaigns, and as soon as Maréchal de Villeroi had mobilised it, he left our lines and invested the little town of Huy. The Elector of Bavaria, who was then at Brussels, was not long in joining him; and Boismorel, in his capacity of *aide-de-camp*, was obliged to follow His Highness, which gave me the hope that he would be no longer able to avoid granting me that which he had refused at Mons. I saw him arrive, and immediately made up my mind to let him know my intentions the first thing next morning.

To carry my challenge to him I enlisted the services of the Sieur Hoguan, an Irishman by nationality, a lieutenant-colonel in the Electoral Guards, and a man of courage, now a lieutenant-general of the king's army in Portugal. He straightway went off to find Boismorel, resolved to make the latter arrange the hour and weapons. I had purposely taken Hoguan to a coppice in which was a little clearing used as a saw-pit, a most suitable place for our affair, so that he could acquaint Boismorel of the spot at once in case he accepted.

Hoguan was successful in his mission, settled that we should meet at six in the evening of the same day at the place agreed upon, and that we should fight with swords. He who happened to arrive first on the ground was to wait until seven o'clock and whistle or call, so as to make his arrival known. Finally, there were to be two witnesses to the fight, who were merely to act as umpires, following the Bavarian custom in prearranged duels, and the Sieurs Hoguan and Nicolini were so appointed.

The hour arrived, and all four of us appeared at the place appointed as the field of battle, Hoguan accompanying Boismorel while I brought Nicolini.

The others arrived a second or so before us, and set to work to call out at the very moment that I appeared before Boismorel. As I was annoyed at his being beforehand with me, I drew out my watch to point out to him that it was not my fault, for six o'clock had not then struck.

I perceived whilst paying him this attention that he was not over-pleased at my self-possession, and that he was suffering much from the want of that characteristic himself. He wore a troubled look, which marked the agitation passing within him; but I did not keep him long in suspense, for as soon as I had replaced my watch I drew my sword, and we set to with fury. We had some grounds to fear each other; Boismorel was the most apt and skilful man in France in the use of arms, and I was about his match, although bred in a part of the country which, owing to our bringing-up and the rude air, makes for clumsiness.

However, having left home very young I had since breathed a purer air, or perhaps nature had worked somewhat in my favour, so Boismorel was aware that he had quite as much to fear of me as I of him. We had each made many thrusts, and tried all the ruses we knew without scoring a hit on either side, though once I thought I had noticed a slight resistance to the point of my sword; but there was nothing to show this in my adversary's expression, and our combat became fiercer and fiercer until we came to close quarters. Then each did his best to trip up his opponent, but so skilful were we both in this art that we found ourselves forced to grapple with each other arm to arm.

I proved myself here the stronger, and at the second attempt I grassed my man, and presented the point of my sword to the pit of his stomach to force him to give up his arms and cry for mercy; but our two seconds separated us, telling me that as I had his life in my hands, I had ended the affair more gloriously than if I killed him outright, and they allowed Boismorel to keep his sword. Nevertheless, a private misgiving at thus leaving my enemy in possession of his arms after his defeat caused me to watch his movements, and well for me that I did so, for as soon as he was on his legs again he suddenly lunged out at me with his sword to the full extent of his arm, with such violence that, although I parried the thrust, the blade pierced my coat and waistcoat just over the navel, and passed between my skin and shirt. Our friends were greatly surprised to see me obliged to defend my life against a man who owed me his own. They were distressed beyond measure at their carelessness, but they could do nothing further as the next instant we were fighting so furiously that it would have been more dangerous to attempt to separate us than to allow us to continue the combat.

Once more, then, we desperately thrust at each other with victory still in the balance; again I felt a slight resistance to the point of my sword as if it had hit something, but I did not see my enemy wince, and our set-to continuing without the slightest relaxation, we once more came to close quarters. As soon as I had gripped Boismorel, I threw him to the ground, face uppermost, at my first effort, and I could then have taken his life without offending honour, because after the deed he had just committed he had rendered himself unworthy of the slightest mercy. I could not help feeling that, given a hundred less creditable opportunities of taking mine, he would not have shown me mercy in any one of them. However this may have been, when I found myself the victor, my resentment faded, and I found myself relenting.

By way of precaution I presented the point of my sword to our witnesses, to show them that they were not to interfere this time until I had disarmed him, when all at once Boismorel began to cry out in a half-stifled voice that he was dead. We at once turned to him, and he was so pale that we had no doubt that he was dying. Our first thought was to tend his soul and body, and to this end our seconds hurriedly set out, the one for a chaplain, the other for a surgeon, whilst I re-mained at his side. I had no need to request him to make a formal surrender of his sword, as he had dropped it out of sheer helplessness; my only fear was lest he should die in my arms before the return of our friends, and wishing, should this happen, that he should do so in a proper state of mind, I raised him into a sitting posture by propping him up against me, and exhorted him to die a good Christian. He with difficulty forgave me being the cause of his death, but, finally, affected by the remarks that his case inspired me to make, he commended his soul to God, admitted that he had brought all upon himself, and that he deserved his fate.

As soon as I believed that I had given a better turn to his thoughts, I asked him if he did not wish to make any arrangements regarding his family or others, and told him that he had only to commission me, and I would carry out his directions exactly as he might order me. He hardly answered this question, only saying that he would be dead before help arrived, though he begged me urgently to take the portrait of the cook, which he wore as a relic next his heart, and place it in her hands on the first opportunity. Our interview was finished by the arrival of our friends, who with all diligence had brought with them the surgeon-major of my grenadiers, a most skilful man, who, after inspecting three wounds that Boismorel had sustained in his body, and which he had not felt during the heat of the fight, told us that he hoped to save him. His first action with regard to these injuries was to well suck them—the most sovereign remedy to apply to all wounds caused by iron.

Whilst this was going on, I noticed the Chevalier de la Bastide, who had arrived with my valet and three horses, which he had taken care to bring with him in case of accident. Bastide, who saw blood upon my coat (which I had hitherto been unaware of), made sure that I was wounded, and insisted upon examining me.

I assured him that I felt nothing and was in no way hurt, but he would not be denied; indeed, I really thought he would strip me naked to search me; so I set to work to look myself, and then, wishing to use my left hand, found thereon a swelling, back and front, the size of a nut. It had been pierced right through, and the swelling was caused by the accumulation of blood without its hurting me, as by good luck no tendon had been injured. I judged that I must have received it when rushing into close quarters. I sucked my wound myself, and, without plasters or much pain, shortly afterwards found it had healed.

Suction and bandaging seemed to relieve Boismorel, and he was able to mount one of my horses, which was led by my valet M. Hoguan and the surgeon-major then accompanied him to his quarters, which were in a large abbey, where the Elector and Maréchal de Villeroi were lodged. He was so well known that his mishap would soon be published abroad among the headquarter staff, so I thought it best to be on the safe side and keep out of harm's way. I and Bastide betook ourselves to two captains of the Nivernais regiment, the Chevalier de Montelemberg and la Pairière de Villeneuve d'Agenois, the former of whom is now brigadier in the king's army. I slept the night with them, and next morning early requested the hospitality of Baron de Bourlemont at his *château*, two leagues distant, pending news of Boismorel's condition, and so as to be in a position to ensure my safety in case of his death. I there heard that his wounds were going on as well as could be expected, and twelve days later the surgeon-major called to assure me that his skill was no longer needed. I ordered him to go and report on my account to Maréchal d'Arcko, who would willingly speak to the Elector, who in turn would doubtless send a messenger to tell me to present myself at his court as if I had never absented myself.

I soon found myself in attendance on the *maréchal* to thank him for all his kindness. He told me without any affectation that he was glad of my success, after which I presented myself before the Elector, in whose eyes I could read approval of my action. The courtiers followed suit in showering congratulations upon me; but the more these courtly personages complimented me, the greater was the chagrin of Boismorel, to whom all this was duly reported.

His annoyance was such that he could never bring himself to be reconciled with me again, and service with the Elector having become distasteful to him, he joined that of the King of Spain, thanks to the influence of the Duke of Orleans.

After this matter was over I had just time to join in the assault of an outwork belonging to the fortress of Huy, called the Red Fort, and commanded the grenadiers told off to carry it by storm. This assault was of a different character to that which usually obtained in such cases, because it was necessary to employ escalading, and I lost many men who were thrown from the tops of the ladders. The lieutenant who had fought with me at Scheremhausen was amongst them; the poor lad was shot while climbing the very ladder on which I was myself, and the ball entered the top of his breast and passed through his entrails.

One could not believe his recovery possible, but the care taken of him and the strength of his constitution pulled him through, so that his cure was regarded as a species of miracle. He was rewarded by promotion to captain, and I received as my share many honied speeches

DUTCH CARICATURE OF PRINCE LOUIS OF BADEN

from the court officials. The outwork carried, the town capitulated the next day, June 10th.

After the reduction of the town of Huy the army lay siege to that of Liège by surrounding the place without opening any trenches before the citadel, which is one of the largest existing. Liège is a very large mercantile town, situated on the river Meuse, and almost entirely undefended.

The enemy, whose design was to continue their conquests in the Alsace country, suffered the capture of this town without changing their plan of campaign. Milord Marlborough was on the Moselle with a considerable force, where he awaited the arrival of Prince Louis of Baden with the Imperial army. He then intended to force the frontier at Traerbeck,[1] and drive back our army, which was strongly entrenched in the neighbourhood. France, afraid lest these two allies should invade the Electorate of Treves and the Comté de Chigni, or even German Lorraine, which is hard by the Metz district, desired rather to draw them in the direction of Flanders, where the country was covered by a chain of fortified towns suitable to ward off reverses, an advantage wanting to us on the Moselle. This was why we pressed the attack upon Liège, so as to force the Dutch to recall Marlborough, which was eventually done.

This general, seeing no sign of Prince Louis of Baden, did not give a thought to his non-arrival, though he could not have been ignorant of the allegations made against this Prince. The belief was so general as to the latter's understanding with France that a print had been published in Holland representing him asleep upon a sack of *louis d'or*, as an allusion to the sums reported to have been given him by France to keep him inactive. Marlborough was pleased to find an opportunity, such as in the relief of Liège, to leave a country in which his army was beginning to find it difficult to subsist. We had just begun the trenches before the citadel when we heard that he was on the march towards us, and thereby fulfilling exactly the intentions of France.

Our generals now decided that it was unnecessary for us to continue the siege; it was abandoned at the enemy's approach, and we took cover behind our lines, near a village called Meerdorp, to observe his movements. These lines, constructed at our leisure, were cannon-proof, with wide parapets and extremely deep ditches, but they covered so great an extent of ground that our army was unable to occupy them throughout

---

1. Probably the frontier village of Traubach.

In order to obviate this defect a detachment of considerable strength, under the orders of a lieutenant-general of the king's army, was posted on the left of our position, a measure which appeared to secure us against surprise. However, Marlborough, whose army was superior to ours in number, formed a plan to attack us. The precautions we had taken rendered the enterprise a difficult one; our lines had all the posts and sentries necessary to preserve communication, patrolling was kept up regularly every night, the main army was at hand ready to reinforce the detached force, and the suspicion of danger was so slight that it was calculated that we should be able to keep the enemy fully occupied there the greater part of the campaign. But, notwithstanding all this, they found a means of entering our lines without any great effort and almost no loss.

Milord Marlborough struck his camp on the night of July 8th, marched his army in several columns, so that no one was able to divine his intentions, and appeared at break of day in front of the force under the lieutenant-general posted on our left flank. Our patrols by this time had returned to camp, which was wrapt in slumber; consequently when he arrived in sight of our lines he could see that we were making no movement or attempt to defend them. He then ordered his infantry to advance, who immediately rushed two of the gates and broke down a length of parapet to allow his cavalry to enter before the lieutenant-general's detachment had the chance of opposing them, or even to warn the army to come to its help.

So sudden was this action that the enemy were actually able to form up in our own lines before our people had left their camp, although immediately the news was brought to Maréchal de Villeroi he had had the alarm beaten and marched to oppose them; but it was too late; the enemy had secured the position, and it would have been extremely rash to have attacked them, as the flanking detachment, which was of considerable strength in itself, was now in full retreat. We then occupied the camp at Lierre, a small town near Antwerp, and remained there whilst the enemy recaptured Huy.

Then, anxious for the town of Louvain, we marched to take up a position covering it, and encamped along the little river Oberichen, which runs through it. Shortly after pitching our camp, we saw the enemy make their appearance, and post themselves nearly opposite to us. Only the river separated us, and we were so much in view of each other that neither army could make the slightest movement by daylight without the knowledge of the other.

Our position was additionally advantageous, inasmuch as we not only protected the town of Louvain, but many other places as well, because we commanded the passage of the river. The enemy, realising the necessity of crossing it in order to throw themselves on Brussels, or any other place, with the object of obliging us to retire, resolved to attempt the passage by a surprise similar to that which they had already made upon our lines, but experience had now taught us to be more vigilant. Posts of observation were placed above and below the army with sentries connecting the various points; and to see that everyone did his duty, general officers were daily told off to go the rounds by day and night. It is by no means easy to effect the passage of a river by surprise in the face of such precautions; pontoons have to be constructed, and such work could not be carried out in view of our sentries without being perceived.

However, the enemy, resolved on making the attempt, chose a very dark night to move up the river a league beyond our right flank. Before them marched a train of copper pontoons, with their platforms and joists for bridging purposes; they brought up batteries of cannon to protect the operation, and got everything ready for the passage of the river at break of day; but if night hid their movements from our eyes it could not prevent us using our ears. Notwithstanding the fact that they created but the minimum of noise, yet the calm of the night rendered the smallest sounds perceptible to the ear, and our sentries becoming aware of something unusual, warned their officers, who, listening in their turn, were convinced that the enemy were on the move.

Ever since we had been at this river, the generals of the day had visited our outposts with extreme exactitude every night. As is well known, "officers of the day" are officers told off for duty day by day, consisting of a lieutenant-general, a major-general, a brigadier, a colonel, a lieutenant-colonel, and a major, whose duty is to parade the guards in front of the camp, supervise their distribution, attend at the relief of the outposts, and be ready to march with the inlying picquets of the army in case of need. On this occasion I was acting in the capacity of officer of the day, and making a tour of the posts on our right conjointly with the lieutenant-general and the brigadier; the other officers on duty were visiting the left, when we received a report from those at the point opposite, where the enemy were launching their pontoons, as to a noise they had heard, and their suspicions as to the reason thereof.

As soon as we had assembled each placed his ear to the ground, so as to hear better, and we were convinced we could detect the sound of planks being placed in position. The lieutenant-general despatched his *aide-de-camp* to warn the Elector and Maréhal de Villeroi, and as the noise soon got more distinct, he sent me with further information. I arrived at M. de Villeroi's quarters as day broke, and found him mounting his horse; after having made my report, he ordered me to accompany him to the Elector, whom we found mounted in front of the camp. He was gazing through his glass at the enemy's camp to try and distinguish their movements, and whether they had struck it, when an officer arrived from the garrison of Louvain who confirmed the report of their march.

Maréchal de Villeroi had not wasted a moment in getting the army into movement. It was already in column of route when he came up, and on the march to the point where the enemy were constructing their bridge. This smartness prevented us being surprised a second time, saved the town of Brussels, and perhaps some other places as well.

I was still with the Elector and the *maréchal* when the enemy, who by this time had finished their bridges, opened an artillery fire upon two of our picquets who were annoying them. As soon as I heard the first shot I asked permission of the Elector to rejoin my own men, and together with M. de Gassion, lieutenant-general in the king's army, who was also with the prince, galloped off to the head of the column to rejoin the regiment. The enemy, however, had begun to cross the river by the time the head of our column had arrived on the high ground commanding their bridges, and although it was some distance from this point to the river, they were nevertheless surprised to see us so ready to oppose them, as they thought us to be still in the arms of sleep, so they hurried into battle formation in a little plain between the heights and the stream as fast as they could push their men across.

But neither did we lose any time; the leading brigades were ordered to descend, and the main column in rear, which followed in quick time, being at hand, the whole were formed to engage the enemy in front and on the flank, whilst our batteries were brought into action, to open a direct fire upon the exits from their bridges. We were then directed to advance and attack them before a greater number were able to effect the passage. But Marlborough, seeing his efforts checkmated, recalled his troops, who repassed their bridges and retired with a loss of more than a thousand men. They encamped upon the heights on their side, and we did the like on ours, whilst we watched each other with the greatest care.

Our regiment was one of those ordered to attack the enemy's flank. We marched on the extreme left of our column, and in order to arrive at striking distance we had to traverse some fields along the river-bank, so open and exposed to the fire from their batteries that we lost five captains, eight lieutenants, and eighty soldiers before we were able to gain the shelter of a large hedge, studded with thorn trees. The reason why their battery did so much damage was that each cannon was loaded with three shots at a time, a new invention on the part of someone unknown to me, which has not remained in practice, as it shortened the range so much. Our regiment was one of the first victims of this experiment, and suffered considerably, but the others hardly lost a man. However, it appeared to some of us at the time that we received a recompense in the form of a miracle vouchsafed to us by the Almighty at the very place where we had been so maltreated: a miracle which, though it appeared astonishing enough to excite the admiration of the universe, turned out to be but the effect of imagination, as I will now show.

On our way to the attack we passed through a deserted village just before entering the open fields. There a young drummer, who had amused himself by foraging among the rubbish left in the street, found a crucifix stuck on cardboard, which he carried off with him. After we had run the gauntlet of the fields and found ourselves in tranquillity behind the hedge, he leaned against an old thorn tree, and either thoughtlessly or on purpose inserted this bit of cardboard into a deep crevice of the trunk, thinking nothing more about it. After the action our regiment was the only one ordered to encamp in the very field where we had been so hotly saluted, the hedge in question forming the front of our camp, and it chanced that one of our men, looking for wood to boil his kettle and finding nothing dryer and more suitable for the purpose than the old trees therein, set to work upon the very one containing the crucifix, and soon split off a supply of chips with his hatchet. This caused the crucifix to jump apparently from the heart of the trunk, as the hacking with the axe had destroyed any traces of a crack.

The soldier was so amazed to see this image emerge from the middle of a tree-trunk that he had not the slightest doubt but that it was a manifestation from the Divine Power which should lead to his salvation, and regarded himself as the chosen agent of a miracle, and forthwith gave vent to his excitement in loud shouts of joy. Other soldiers nearby who ran up to him were so struck by the story he told that they also proclaimed the miracle as loudly as he, and finally the chaplain of the regiment hurriedly appearing on the scene, was as convinced as the rest of the miraculous nature of the occurrence. The more the matter was gone into the more extraordinary did it appear—a crucifix bedded in a tree-trunk, scatheless, and without a sign of any point of entry!! In the end it was settled by the chaplain that the tree should be regarded with veneration as the matrix which had contained a precious relic for an untold number of years, and that in order to do due honour to both, he would daily celebrate the Holy Mass before it. To this end an altar was immediately constructed against the tree, with a small roof to protect it in case of bad weather, the crucifix was fastened to the altar, and the little chapel was adorned in every possible manner.

The soldier never left his crucifix; during the celebration of Mass he took charge of the altar in the sincere belief that he had been selected by the Almighty to make this miracle known, and he composed his features rather after the fashion of those directors of seminaries who are looked upon as the Elect. The whole day long he remained glued to the tree with a serious look on his countenance, distributing relics to the good souls who came to beseech favours from "Saint Crucifix." These relics consisted of little bits of the tree, which he reverently cut off and passed over the surface of the crucifix with much ceremony, while the devotees remained on their knees at the foot of the altar, then, having wrapped the holy chips in paper, he handed them to the recipients. In return for these each suppliant, according to his means, placed offerings on a plate which lay on the altar, and these were duly shared every evening between the chaplain and the soldier.

This miraculous image produced an immense sensation throughout the army and the neighbouring country, and its wonders augmented day by day. Sometimes it was a lame man, who, having been carried before the tree, had instantly found himself able to walk without his crutches; then the deaf, dumb, and blind, who had heard, spoken, and seen—in fact, all who were infirm received relief according to their faith. There was always a continuous crowd in attendance; the Elector even, and the Maréchal de Villeroi, who were passing our regiment one day, had the curiosity to pay it a visit, and placed a handsome offering in the plate. A fortune might have been made out of this devotion, and would really have come to pass, had not the true origin of the miracle come to light, for the indiscretion of the drummer put an end to the business.

The drummer, who recollected having slipped the crucifix into the thorn tree, confessed the fact to the chaplain with all its attendant details. The devout priest, who was drawing a solid income, thanks to the faith of the populace, exhorted him to be careful lest he should do anything to interfere with the good works which were being done, and warned him that he would be guilty before God if he did not keep silence. He gave him to understand that a pious intention was always acceptable as a means for procuring the salvation of souls, promised to give him a portion of the offerings, and, as a matter of fact, did give him something to hold his tongue. But when our drummer found himself so far interested in the matter, he examined the sum of the receipts more closely, and discovered that the chaplain and the soldier kept the lion's share to themselves, giving him apparently only a dole.

He therefore went straight to M. de Mercy, the colonel of the regiment, with whom I was at the time, and reported to him the whole of the mystery. The chaplain was summoned and confronted with the drummer, and a beginning was made by reproaching him with the abuses he had permitted with regard to his image, and his avarice in taking remuneration for the little bits of wood that he gave out as relics. He was told that the receipt of such offerings, the sad result of the credulity of an ignorant and rude people, only went to prove him to be a greedy grasper, and his companion as well. It might have been thought that this would have somewhat disconcerted his reverence, but he kept his countenance, and replied with an air of assurance that he had only followed the example of many famous divines who had perhaps less foundation to work on than that supplied by this crucifix, and that as to the custom of making offerings, the prayers that accompanied them were not the less acceptable to the Almighty, to whom it mattered but little as to the form they took, so long as the souls were led along the road to salvation.

"Very well," said M. de Mercy, "if such is the case the image must be left in the country here, for as we shall be but a short time in this place, and you cannot cart about with us the tree which has brought forth the image and the relics, I shall send it to the Capuchins of Louvain;" which he forthwith did, but the good Fathers received the present and its story with much indifference, and since then nothing whatever has been heard of it.

The two armies remained encamped for some time yet in their respective positions until the enemy marched three leagues up the river, when we did likewise and halted opposite to them, still separated by the stream.

By this time we were not far from Brussels, which lay on our right, and it was believed that the enemy intended to make a dash for this place, but in this case they would have to traverse the forest of Waterloo which was of vast extent; after several attempts, which ended in nothing but the shifting of their camp to no more than a league distant, the campaign came to an end.

France was very lucky in thus being able to stay the enemy's advance both on the Rhine and the Moselle, and the king marked his satisfaction by the present of a hundred thousand crowns, which he made to Maréchal de Villeroi. This General certainly rendered all the plans of the Allies abortive; their only success was a little one in Alsace, to wit, the capture of Haguenau, an almost defenceless town.

The last campaign had been so favourable to France that she became convinced the wheel of Fortune was turning in her favour, and that she should therefore take the opportunity to strike terror in the hearts of her enemies.

To bring this about a battle in Flanders would be necessary; she had in reserve, should a reverse occur, a number of fortified towns which would be a means of defence for the frontier by checking the enemy's advance and giving us time to replace our losses, and in case of success Holland and the German frontier lay open to us. By invading Holland, France could mine the resources of the enemy, for they drew therefrom their chief supplies of money and all kinds of munitions of war.

Thus we began the campaign of 1706 in Flanders. Great preparations were made, and to realise our project we mobilised about the beginning of May one of the finest armies ever seen, which took up a position overlooking the Plain of Ramillies, its left resting on the wood of Waterloo, with the right in the plain itself. The enemy recalled detachments they had in the Cleves and Limburg districts and the garrisons of several of their towns to reinforce their army in every possible way to resist us, or to attack us themselves if they saw a favourable opportunity of so doing.

With these intentions the enemy appeared in the Plain of Ramillies, but owing to its vast extent, instead of posting themselves exactly opposite us, they took up a position at the end of the plain, the left of their army resting on a marsh near a village named Tavier, whilst in front of their right they had a series of very deep ravines, which rendered them unassailable at this point. The ground bordering on these ravines, although dry to all appearance, was none the less impracticable, and in this position they awaited our attack.

France was burning for the fight, her plan of campaign was decided upon, and it would never have done to have missed the first available opportunity; that which now presented itself was believed to be a favourable one, so our generals set to work to reconnoitre the plain.

The marsh which protected the enemy's left served to cover our right flank as we advanced—but the ravines on, and in front of, their right were not perceived by us, or the fact that they would prevent our attacking them there.

It was believed that neither side would have any advantage over the other in the combat; acting upon this opinion, it was decided to take the initiative and attack the enemy at once.

It was on May 23rd, the Day of Pentecost, that this action took place, as fatal to France and Spain alike as was the Battle of Hochstett (Blenheim), and although the number who perished on the field was not excessive, the losses it brought in its train later on were almost as considerable.

It appeared as if ill-fortune pursued the House of Bavaria with a greater persistence than in the case of any of the other Powers.

It had been arranged that if Bavaria was lost the Elector should obtain as compensation the Burgundian Circle or the Spanish Low Countries, and now the Battle of Ramillies snatched this Crown from him as Hochstett had robbed him of Bavaria.

So vast was the plain at Ramillies that we were able to march our army on as broad a front as we desired, and the result was a magnificent spectacle. The army began its march at six o'clock in the morning, formed into two large columns, the front of each consisting of a battalion; the artillery formed a third, which marched between the two infantry columns. The cavalry squadrons in battle formation occupied an equal extent of ground, and there being nothing to impede the view, the whole force was seen in such a fine array that it would be impossible to view a grander sight.

The army had but just entered on the campaign, weather and fatigue had hardly yet had time to dim its brilliancy, and it was inspired with a courage born of confidence. The late Marquis de Goudrin, with whom I had the honour to ride during the march, remarked to me that France had surpassed herself in the quality of these troops; he

PLAN OF THE BATTLE OF RAMILLIES

believed that the enemy had no chance whatever of breaking them in the coming conflict; if defeated now, we could never again hope to withstand them.

When the leading battalions of our columns arrived near the marsh on our right their direction was changed a quarter left, followed by those in rear, with the immediate result that the army found itself in battle array two lines in depth parallel to the position of the enemy, who were now within range of our artillery. It was then noticed that they were moving troops from their right to their left; but it was impossible to divine their intentions, though the sequel showed that as the safety of their right was ensured by the ravines which divided us from them, they sent the bulk of their forces to their left to make more certain of crushing our right, which they feared on account of the presence there of the king's household troops, the Maison du Roi. We, on our part, so far relied upon the valour of our troops who occupied this wing that we actually denuded it to reinforce elsewhere.

Could we have foreseen the ravines which prevented our left from closing with the enemy's right, we should have made different dispositions, and otherwise employed the troops sent there, who proved to be of no use whatever in the battle.

There was yet another point to which no attention had been paid, but which had an important bearing on the result, and that was the village of Tavier, which lay beyond the marsh, nearly equidistant from the enemy and ourselves. Although in order to occupy it, it was necessary for either side to cross the marsh, it was yet essential to both to seize it before the beginning of the action. The cavalry were formed on the extreme flanks of both armies on the edge of the marsh, which was but a pistol-shot in breadth and only practicable for infantry; hence, whichever infantry occupied the village, they could line its edge, open a destructive fire, and destroy the cavalry without any risk whatever. The enemy, who were the first to appreciate this fact, sent fourteen battalions across the marsh to seize it, and then our generals realised the result this would have on the course of the battle, and resolved to drive them out before the action began.

This village was the scene of the opening of the engagement, and the fighting there was almost as murderous as the rest of the battle put together. The following dragoon regiments were told off for this: the King's, d'Aubigni, de Notât, and two others whose names I have forgotten; all were ordered to dismount, and were joined by the infantry regiment Greder-Suisse, the whole making five regiments of dragoons and three battalions, and finally our Bavarian brigade was added. In the order given to each it was omitted to show the details of the troops forming the detachment, or to appoint a rendezvous on our side of the marsh, so as to prevent one or another attempting anything before the rest were assembled. The units were at some distance from each other in the first instance, and being uninformed as to whom they were to work with, each took their own line to reach the village, ignorant even as to whether there was a likelihood of its being defended. Our brigade formed part of the right wing of the first infantry line, not far from the centre, and consequently some distance from the marsh when we began our advance on the village.

As soon as the respective armies began to cannonade and bombard each other, I had ordered flourishes to be played upon our *hautboys*, to entertain us the while, but the booming of the guns that went on all round so startled our musicians that they disappeared like a flash before anyone noticed it, and transported the melodious sounds of their instruments to some quarter where the harmonies were not quite so discordant. However, we set out, and passed along the right of our line to reach the marsh without knowing if any other troops had preceded us, or if others were to follow us; we thought, in fact, that we only were told off for the expedition, and preserved in our march all the order possible to maintain among troops anxious to win renown before the eyes of an army. The enemy's cannon, however, did some damage to our brigade, because in passing the length of the line we found ourselves exposed to several batteries, which had already opened fire upon our battalions.

I noticed, when passing the Maison du Roi, that there were large intervals between the squadrons, and that their formation was disproportionately extended. This made me think that the principal attack was not to be made here; that there was some other and more dangerous point that had had to be provided for; and that reliance had been placed upon the Maison du Roi, all picked men, at this point. When these gentlemen saw us pass the head of their squadrons they evidently thought that we were coming to support their right on the marsh, and by the graceful applause with which they greeted my grenadiers, this seemed to give them some pleasure; they recalled the action of Schelemberg, and made known to us how much they counted on our valour in the coming engagement; but they soon found that they could hardly reckon upon us, as we continued our march and crossed the swamp.

Our brigade was commanded by a colonel in the service of the Elector of Cologne, and consisted of his regiment and our own. M. de Mercy, our own colonel, should have commanded it, but he had been sent to Italy before the opening of the campaign with orders from the king and the Elector to raise the Royal Bavarian regiment, which was intended for the Chevalier of Bavaria, the present count. The colonel rode at the head of our brigade, when we were on the point of entering the marsh; he had it sounded, and doubtful as to the possibility of crossing on horseback, tried it first alone. He thought he had found a convenient way, so hazarded the passage, but found himself bogged in the middle with his horse upon him, and he would never have got out had it not been for the enemy's assistance, who promptly carried him off a prisoner. I then found myself in command of the brigade, and we crossed fairly easily on foot, though in some parts were over knee-deep in water.

Scarcely had my troops got over when the dragoons and Swiss, who had preceded us, came tumbling down upon my battalions in full flight, just at the time when I was re-forming my men after their crossing; they brought such alarm and confusion in their train, that my own fellows turned about and fled along with them. It appeared that they had attacked the village without waiting for us, and had been repulsed with much loss by the fourteen battalions the enemy had there, which were well posted, and outnumbered them by two to one. The Swiss perished almost to a man, and it is not surprising that a small body of troops attacking others more than double their strength in an advantageous position should have been vigorously repulsed and driven back in disorder. M. d'Aubigni was killed, and his lieutenant-colonel and many others wounded.

The runaways threw themselves amongst my men, and carried them off with them, and I was never more surprised in my life to find myself left standing alone with a few officers and the colours. I was immediately filled with rage and grief; I cried out in German and French like one possessed; I shouted every epithet I could think of to my grenadiers; I seized the colonel's colour, planted it by me, and by the loudness of my cries I at last attracted the attention of some few of them. The officers who had stood by me rushed after the fugitives, also shouting and pointing out the colonel's colour, which I still kept in my hands, and at last they checked the stampede. I gradually rallied my French grenadiers and several companies of the Cologne regiment, making in all four small battalions, very much shaken with the manoeuvres they had just gone through. I got them into fighting formation under cover of a little rise in the ground which concealed them from the enemy occupying the village, and when they were in order, and a bit reassured, I ordered them to advance for the purpose of reconnoitring the ground and the situation generally. Having reached the summit of this rising ground, I discovered that the fourteen battalions had left the village, apparently with the intention of working round the flank of the Maison du Roi, and then charging them across the marsh.

When, however, my leading files appeared over the rising ground, our opponents stopped dead, as if they thought that we were a fresh reinforcement just brought up to renew the attack, at least, so I thought; and in order not to disabuse them of this idea, I manoeuvred my people so as to increase this impression, always showing a firm front in my position to make them keep their distance. My wish was to make it appear as if we had a strong force of infantry hidden behind the rise, ready either to fall upon them in case they advanced, or to advance upon them when our dispositions were completed. During this manoeuvre I noticed that my troops were becoming unsteady at the aspect of so many opponents, and the fact that I was making no preparations for a retirement; moreover, they were uncertain whether I should not even have the rashness to hurl them against a force so obviously superior to our own; and I heard a soldier behind me exclaim with an oath that it would all end in a butchery.

The probable result that such an assertion might have produced rekindled the anger that still possessed me, so that I myself, swearing like a grenadier, demanded in stentorian tones where the scoundrel was who confessed to such a fear, declaring that I was the only proper person to act as his butcher, and finally did all I knew to find him. But not being successful in this search, I continued my impassioned address, crying out that he and his like ought to know that at any time an occasion might arise when it would be our duty to sacrifice ourselves, such things were in the nature of our business, and that at any rate the example set by the gallant men who led them ought to be quite sufficient for the miserable cowards who showed such a fear for their skins. At last the temper into which I had worked myself had the effect I desired, and my troops appeared to be much more reassured.

It is absolutely certain that a commanding officer cannot exhibit too much firmness in such perilous situations, for upon him all eyes are fixed, and it is usually by his example that the cowardice or courage of his men is decided. The position I held was of real importance, for although it was out of my power to attack the enemy in Tavier, yet I detained them in that village, from which they did not dare to emerge, and thus protected the right flank of the Maison du Roi from their assaults, in itself an important service. It is true that in the end the Allies did destroy them without employing these fourteen battalions, but even then my post afforded signal assistance, as the opportunity was given me of saving the lives of many brave men belonging to the musketeers and *gendarmes* of the guard who would otherwise have perished during the fight, as I shall now explain.

The enemy and their fourteen battalions perceiving us thus manoeuvring on the little rise, and being ignorant of our real strength, first halted, and then proceeded to retire into the village under the impression that we were going to assault their position, and from thence kept up a continual fire upon us. But as we were nearly out of range, and under the partial protection of the rising ground, this hardly troubled us, so I forbade my men to return the fire, as my intention was only to keep them amused, and so render their further efforts abortive. We had not been here very long before we saw the general action begin, and from the place where I was situated the lines of both armies were presented to my view almost in their entirety, so that hardly any of their movements escaped my notice.

Following on the cannonading and bombarding, which was maintained during the completion of the final dispositions, I saw the cavalry of the enemy's left wing march to attack the Maison du Roi, followed by their infantry in slow time, and I was able to distinguish to perfection the great number of squadrons they had detailed for this assault. The enemy advanced in four dense lines like solid walls, while we had but three lines, the third of which was composed of several squadrons of dragoons with plenty of gaps between them. As I have already said, we had not reconnoitred the ravines which separated our left from their right; they were found impracticable, and, consequently, no important action took, place thereabouts.

The Allies, who knew the ground well, had concentrated the bulk of their forces to attack our right, which consisted of the Maison du Roi, in whom we had placed, perhaps, too much faith. That they were the pick of the French Army cannot be denied, but they were crushed by force of numbers. The enemy's infantry, which connected with their cavalry and extended as far as the centre of their line of battle, had been reinforced in a similar manner, so that their right flank was much denuded of troops, and remained almost immobile. Besides this, the precaution had been taken to post a corps in reserve some distance in rear to ensure the destruction of our right flank, and in this array the enemy confidently made sure of victory before even the action had actually begun.

I now saw the enemy's cavalry advance upon our people, at first at rather a slow pace, and then, when they thought they had gained the proper distance, they broke into a trot to gain impetus for their charge. At the same moment the Maison du Roi decided to meet them, for at such a moment those who await the shock find themselves at a disadvantage. But what a contrast was shown in the *mêlée* that resulted! The enemy, profiting by their superiority in numbers, surged through the gaps between our squadrons and fell upon their rear, whilst their four lines attacked in front. Naturally, our right was soon crushed. I noticed numbers of riderless horses make their escape, and in a short time the rout became general. The enemy took our lines in flank, rode them down, and completely routed them; each thought only of its retreat. Hardly any but the Maison du Roi were roughly handled on the battlefield, but brigade after brigade broke during its retreat; the enemy made numerous prisoners, and by their pursuit drove them so precipitately and in such different directions, that for more than two months after the action it was quite impossible to mobilise the army on a campaigning footing.

I said above that an opportunity was given me to save the lives of a number of brave men on this occasion, and this is how it came about. During the onset made upon the Maison du Roi, a number of musketeers, light horse, and *gendarmes*, who had come out unscathed, attempted to re-form and rejoin their standards, but they found their road barred behind them. Whilst they hesitated as to the route they should take, they were noticed by the reserve corps of the Allies, from which several squadrons were forthwith detached to bring them between two fires. These gentlemen, finding themselves in this fix and having no other way open to them but the marsh, threw themselves into it without knowing whether it was practicable or not. They had got no further than fifty paces before they found their horses engulfed in the mud, without a possibility of extricating them, whilst they themselves, caught by their spurs, hampered by their boots, and entangled in their stirrups, were many of them under their chargers.

Happily for them the direction they had taken lay exactly opposite my position. Had this not been so, they would have fallen an easy prey to the squadrons pursuing them, and obliged to choose between musket and pistol bullet at the edge of the marsh, with the result that probably not one would have escaped. As long as I live I shall carry with me a feeling of perfect satisfaction that this opportunity of relieving the distress of such brave men fell to my lot. Seeing their plight, I felt the danger they were exposed to and the necessity of helping them promptly, so I paid no more attention to the fourteen battalions which yet remained in and about the village, but at once made a change of front with my troops, a quarter left, to line the border of the marsh on my left flank. Immediately the enemy's squadrons appeared on the further edge, with the intention of shooting down the fugitives, I ordered a volley to be fired by the whole of my line, which threw them into disorder.

A singular feature connected with this volley was the astonishment of the enemy, who were under the impression that my battalions, dressed as they were in blue and red, belonged to their side and that we had fired upon them by mistake. They set to work to signal to us to stop, but as I continued to ply them with bullets, they recognised their error, turned about and took up a position out of range, after losing many men and horses; in fact, those squadrons who believed they had our own people safe in the marsh, found there instead an almost complete defeat as their portion.

However, I saw that the remains of their squadrons had taken up a position still sufficiently within range of the marsh to enable them to knock over our bogged people with stray shots; I therefore sent a captain and a hundred grenadiers to line their side of the marsh and keep down the enemy's fire. M. de Quemin, captain of the French grenadiers, an intrepid and well-conducted man, now colonel of the Bourbon Regiment, volunteered for this duty. He posted himself on the other side, and repeatedly opened fire upon these squadrons so adroitly that not only were they obliged to retire, but others also which had arrived to reinforce them. We were now at liberty to extricate unmolested such of the Maison du Roi who were still in difficulties, though many had disentangled themselves, thanks to the opportunity we had afforded them by driving back the enemy, at whose hands they assuredly would have perished.

I ordered the horses to be extricated, which was done after many efforts on the part of my grenadiers, and returned to their owners, excepting some whose masters had not judged it convenient to wait until they were dragged out of the swamp. A few days afterwards application was made for these, and I handed them over with scrupulous exactitude. Many of these gentlemen told me their names, and assured me of their extreme gratitude, but these have escaped my memory, except one which is too well known for that to occur, namely, the Marquis de Liancourt, son of the Duke de la Roche-Guion, then a lieutenant in the *gendarmes* of the Guard, and lieutenant-general of the king's army. A corporal of my grenadiers had the good fortune to ride with him, after his extrication from the morass, as far as the town of Namur. In recompense for this service, M. de Liancourt got him a commission as a lieutenant on the retired list, with a pension for the rest of his days. He did not live long to enjoy this, as he died two years later at Strasburg from the effects of a fall.

I also indirectly learned that two of my Bordeaux neighbours were in this business—one being the Marquis de Lansac, who died last autumn, and the other was M. de Grenier.

When this affair was over I looked to see what the enemy's fourteen battalions were about, but I found they had abandoned the village and rejoined their main army, which was now in full pursuit of ours. Even the squadrons which had followed the musketeers up to the marsh had disappeared, and the field of battle was deserted. However, I remained in position with my force till six o'clock in the evening, in case of any further opportunity occurring in which I could prove to be of use; but as both armies by that hour were now far afield and everything was peaceful in our quarter, I determined to march to Namur, two or three leagues distant.

Night had fallen by the time I arrived at the gates. M. de Saillant d'Estain, governor of the town and a lieutenant-general of the king's army, was notified, and came himself to ascertain the number of troops that demanded entrance at such an hour. As he was not unaware of the fatal catastrophe that had befallen us, he was delighted to find that fortune had been kind enough to send him a reinforcement, because under the circumstances he had but a feeble garrison for a town such as Namur, which, by the loss of the battle, had become one of the most exposed upon the frontier. After having told me that unfortunately for him he had no direct command over our troops, he begged me to remain a few days, so as to give him time to communicate with the Elector and Maréchal de Villeroi, who had retired to Mons, and he would then ask for an order to keep us, in the event of the army being unable to resume the campaign, as was but too probable. This was granted him, and I remained in this town until we were needed in the field, the enemy meantime making no attempt to besiege us.

In order to give our various units the opportunity of reorganising themselves, the regiments were distributed in the frontier towns, with the result that their garrisons were reinforced and ready in event of their being besieged. The success that the Allies had just gained over us proved of the greatest importance to them, for the campaign was but beginning, and the season of the year enabled them to fling themselves on many a town, one after the other, and without the slightest fear of being disturbed, besides leaving them free to make their own dispositions and to collect the necessary munitions. Notwithstanding Maréchal de Villeroi's misfortune, it would have been more in accordance with the king's wish if this general had remained in command of the army in Flanders, but he begged His Majesty to dispense with his services, and obtained permission to retire to the court.

The enemy resumed operations by laying siege to Louvain, a very extensive town without any good fortifications. A new palisaded covered-way had certainly been constructed, together with some earthen outworks, but the whole was of but little consequence, and what resistance was offered was due to its garrison alone.

Antwerp was taken, followed by Malines and Brussels, and the capture of these towns resulted in the formation of a new rampart for the United Provinces of Holland, in which the enemy established their principal magazines to enable them to extend their conquests further afield. Shortly afterwards they possessed themselves of Ghent, Bruges, and Ostend, and all these towns were snatched from us before the first week in July.

The taxes imposed by the Allies over this extent of country greatly strengthened their financial position and gave them the means to carry on the war, whilst ours were correspondingly reduced. After the capture of the above places, they began the siege of the town of Menin, about three leagues from Lille. Although this is but a small place, it is one of the strongest in the kingdom; its fortifications are constructed after the most perfect fashion, and the late M. de Vauban, who designed them, paid so much attention to their construction that it is maintained that Menin and the citadel of Lille are the most celebrated of his works. The enemy, therefore, took greater pre- cautions in making their attack upon this place than they had in the case of the other towns, notwithstanding which, it held out for quite three weeks, and did not surrender until August 3rd. It was said that this siege cost the Allies nearly eight thousand men.

The troops composing the French Army having now had time to reorganise in the various towns to which they had been detailed, it was decided to call them out and reform the army as before, and the Duke de Vendôme was summoned from Italy to take over the command. He set out thence on August 3rd, leaving matters there in a satisfactory condition; in fact, it seemed as if the Duke of Savoy would soon have cause to repent having left the side of France, for he had been deprived of one portion of his State already, and was now in a fair way to lose the rest. The Duke de Vendôme then came to our aid in the Low Countries; he assembled the army, and encamped it between Lille and Armentières, thus covering Lille, Ypres, and Gravelines at the same time.

These were three towns of importance, and had become much exposed to attack after the capture of Menin, which took place a few days before our army re-entered upon the campaign. The advantageous position of our camp brought about a change in the enemy's tactics, and they fell back and turned aside to besiege the little town of Dendermonde, which capitulated on September 5th, and thence continuing their march to Ath, took that town also on October 2nd. Both armies now distributed themselves over the country for foraging purposes, and finally retired into their winter quarters.

Such were the melancholy results which followed on the Battle of Ramillies.

CHAPTER 11

The Campaigns of 1707-09

Of all the campaigns in this war, that of 1707 was the least eventful as far as the army in Flanders was concerned. The Duke de Vendôme began operations on May 21st around the little town of Binche, which was made the general headquarters of the army, and after several counter-marches occupied the famous camp at Gembloux, a league and a half beyond Namur. The enemy concentrated at a point two short leagues from us in a very well-chosen position; and these two powerful armies remained in observation of each other without moving until August 14th, when Milord Marlborough struck his camp with a view to surprising our lines at Xaintrom, near Mons. The Duke de Vendôme, forewarned of his intention, broke up his own camp the same day, and moved off to forestall him. For three days the two armies marched on parallel lines, so that from time to time their columns were in full view of each other. A fight was quite expected on the second day of our march, on account of a defile that we had to pass on our road.

We had struck our camp at two o'clock in the morning, owing to the proximity of the enemy and the difficulty of effecting the passage in full daylight in their presence. General Tilly with ten thousand cavalry had reconnoitred our position the evening before, and would undoubtedly have attacked our rearguard had he had a chance, but we escaped this owing to the darkness. As it was, the whole of our army had not passed by daybreak, though as a matter of fact the number left was but insignificant. A nasty little stream with difficult banks constituted our defile, which M. de Vendôme had lined with dismounted dragoons to cover the retirement of our rearguard in the case of an attack by General Tilly. The few that still remained to cross were supported by our dragoons, who checkmated the attempts of the enemy to interfere with them. Our army marched about a league further on after passing this defile, in order to reach the plain of Roeulx, where a halt was made to reassemble the various regiments which had become dispersed, and to bring order into our line of march. The Allies, who were moving on our right, were separated from us by several woods, and seeing us forming up on the plain, and not knowing our motive, took up a battle formation in case of accidents.

The Duke de Vendôme noticing this, thought they intended to attack us, so ranged his men likewise, who meantime discharged their pieces preparatory to recharging them, in case they had got damp. I was at this moment walking with Quemin in front of the line when we were much startled by the fire thus brought to bear upon us, for they were all firing in our direction; I believe that I never had a better chance of being killed than on this occasion; a battle even would have been no more dangerous. By no possibility could we obtain cover where we were, so we came to the conclusion that we had best run straight for our line; the nearer we got to it, the safer we should be, inasmuch as they were firing in the air.

After the two armies had remained some time in mutual observation of each other, they both recognised their mistakes, and resumed their march. Ours did a very long one indeed that day, and no camp was marked out or tents pitched. Each regiment spent the night under a constant downpour of rain, on the spot where it found itself in the order of march, so as to be the sooner ready to resume the advance next day and attain our lines. Success attended our efforts, and the manoeuvres carried out by M. de Vendôme gave the enemy no opportunity of attacking us or even making an attempt to seize any town, for he was ever on the alert, and forestalled them everywhere.

It is true that our army had had to forego the luxury of a baggage column for some time, and lacked every comfort, but our country's safety was ensured thereby. We saw the campaign come to an end whilst we were occupying our camp, which covered the town of Lille. It was universally believed that the enemy intended to attack it after their failure to surprise our lines at Xaintrom. But our general in the end succeeded in rendering all the enemy's designs abortive.

Prince Louis of Baden died in the early part of this year. The enemy remained on the defensive in Alsace, where M. de Villars, who was in command of the king's army, attacked their lines at Stoloffen, behind which they were strongly entrenched. He succeeded in forcing them on May 23rd without sustaining any great loss, and so complete was his victory that he captured all their artillery and baggage. He then advanced by Oeting, through the pass of that name in the Black Mountains, as far as Pforzheim, which is on the other side, laying all the country and that of Durlach under forced contributions right up to the territory of the Franconian Circle.

The advantages to us brought by these successes were very considerable, and it seemed as if fortune had ceased to be offended with us, as we had now secured our position in Flanders, besides making these conquests in Alsace. The Allies, however, recouped themselves in Italy, where they secured complete submission to the emperor, and they desired to extend their conquests further by crossing the Alps and striking a blow at one of the principal towns in France. To this end the Duke of Savoy crossed the river Var on July 11th, with the assistance of the enemy's fleet, which had approached Antibes on its way to invest Toulon. The eyes of all Europe were fixed upon this enterprise. The enemy opened their trenches, and although the siege of the town did not make very rapid progress, they managed after several attempts to seize the height of St. Catherine.

They placed their batteries thereon and began the bombardment; but Maréchal de Tessé, the governor, made a sortie with a body of his garrison, attacked and drove them from their position, and killed or made prisoners nearly two thousand men. They determined, however, still to carry on the siege, and continued the bombardment, but after many unsuccessful efforts they found themselves forced to retire precipitately, and repassed the Var September 1st. The defence of this town, which is the most celebrated French port on the Mediterranean coast, was regarded as an important victory; and it is quite certain that if the enemy had succeeded, a great portion of country would have been laid open to attack.

This campaign was still more fortunate for us in Spain. The King's affairs so much improved in that quarter that on April 25th the Duke of Berwick secured a complete victory over the enemy's forces, which were commanded by Milord Galway. The Plain of Almanza was the scene of this action; both sides fought most stubbornly, but the enemy were entirely defeated, and lost nearly eight thousand men killed on the field of battle, without counting a still larger number of prisoners. The Duke of Orleans arrived next day, took over command of the forces belonging to the two Crowns, and laid siege to Valencia, which surrendered on May 8th. After this success the prince marched direct upon Saragossa, and besieged and took it on the 25th of the same month. The Marquis de Bay, who commanded a detached column, also laid siege to the town of Ciudad Rodrigo, where the besieged offered some resistance as they bore the brunt of an assault upon their town, but they lost nearly three thousand men killed and the two thousand that remained were made prisoners of war.

M. de Bay carried this town by assault on October 4th, and on November 12th the Duke of Orleans captured the Castle of Lerida, which held out for eleven days against a regular siege. The town itself was taken by storm, but the Prince of Darmstadt, who was in command there, withdrew to the castle, and was only induced to leave it by granting him terms. Thus events within the kingdom were all favourable to the two Crowns, and the campaign everywhere had a fortunate ending, as far as we were concerned.

The town of Naples was the only one to fall under the emperor's rule, and this was inevitable, because the Duke of Escalona, who commanded there in virtue of his position as viceroy, found himself destitute of troops when the Imperialists appeared to attack it. He was obliged to abandon the town and retire to Gaieta, where he held out for a long time, but was at last betrayed by a Catalan regiment, which delivered the town into the hands of the enemy. General Thaun, who commanded the latter, having the viceroy in his power, threw him into prison after exposing him to the insults of the populace in the public square of the town, to which he had had him purposely conducted.

After the very considerable losses sustained by the two Crowns during the campaign of 1706, it might have seemed that they had more to fear for the result of that of 1707. Fortune, however, decided otherwise. I say, fortune, because, taking a natural view of the situation, the two Crowns had everything to hope from the campaign of 1706, but they lost everything, whilst in that of 1707, when they had every reason to fear still greater loss, they lost nothing; on the contrary, they won success both in Spain and Alsace.

Such is the fortune of war. Circumstances which appear to us to be the foundation of our future success often prove to be but instruments leading to our ruin.

THE CAMPAIGN OF 1708

The preparation we made for the campaign of 1708 gave the Allies reason to believe that we had important designs upon Germany. Maréchal de Villars, by forcing the lines of Stoloffen, had opened up a line of advance for us into the enemy's country by the easiest pass to be found in the Black Mountains, and, moreover, it could easily be imagined that should the Elector of Bavaria appear at this point the people of his States would rise in his favour and bring about a revolution which could be duly taken advantage of. It was, therefore, decided that the Elector and the Duke of Berwick, who had been recalled from Spain, should command our army in Alsace, and that Maréchal de Villars should go to the Cevennes, to quell the revolt there and keep it from spreading. To this end all the Bavarian regiments then in Flanders were ordered to set out at the beginning of May, and to concentrate in Alsace.

The Elector also left and went to Strasburg, leaving his baggage to follow with his troops. The cares of escort duty to the treasure and baggage fell upon my shoulders, for which purpose I had six hundred grenadiers with four squadrons of cavalry, and I started three days ahead of the troops, so as not to be hampered regarding billets for men and waggons. The number of waggons necessary for the transport of the prince's baggage and that of all the officers of his staff was very great, and they gave me so much trouble to supervise that I became an expert waggoner by the end of this journey. At every bad place on the road it always fell to me to give the necessary orders to extricate the waggons and arrange that the teams should help one another, without which all would have been in dire confusion. This march was a most troublesome and wearisome one to me.

On our arrival at Pfalzburg I received a message from the Elector to remain in that town with his baggage until further orders. These were brought me by the Chevalier de Broglio, a lieutenant-general in the king's army. The units were, therefore, ordered to camp in the outskirts of the town, where we remained for eight days, until the Elector himself arrived on his way back from Strasburg. All intention of attacking Germany had been given up, as it had been discovered that the Allies had a great scheme in hand for an invasion of Flanders with superior forces.

The Imperial army withdrawn from Italy by Prince Eugene was on its way to join that of Milord Marlborough in Flanders and had already crossed the Rhine. France did not consider it wise to lay her frontier open to attack whilst she was looking for a by no means certain result in Germany, and in consequence an order was issued to the army in Alsace to send a portion thereof to Flanders and keep the remainder to hold the enemy in check. In the meantime the whole army was placed in motion to observe the march of Prince Eugene along the Moselle, as a precaution against anything in the nature of a surprise, in event of his crossing that river and directing his march upon Flanders.

The division above referred to was to take the road by the Comté de Chigny under the Duke of Berwick in order to join the Duke de Vendôme, whilst the other was to retrace its steps along the banks of the Sarre as far as the Rhine. The two opposing armies in Alsace kept alongside of each other after the passage of the Rhine in German Lorraine, with the river Sarre between them, and after having both remained some days on the Moselle, Prince Eugene crossed it on his way to join Milord Marlborough, whereupon the Duke of Berwick marched with his reinforcements for our army in Flanders. The remainder of our force on the Moselle moved up the Sarre and occupied the camp of Landkandel near Landau, to keep in check the few Imperialists that remained in that part of the country.

The Duke of Burgundy, together with the Duke of Berry, now arrived to place themselves at the head of the army of Flanders during this campaign, in joint command with the Duke de Vendôme. They arrived about May 20th, but neither our German reinforcements nor those of the Allies were on the ground until towards the end of June, when the two formidable and well-ordered armies took the field. Ours was led by the first Princes of France, the Duke de Vendôme and the Duke of Berwick, whilst the enemy had their two most famous generals, Prince Eugene and Milord Marlborough at their head. Before the junction was effected, however, we took by surprise the towns of Ghent and Bruges.

M. de Faille, a leader of the Walloon troops, who had been grand *baillie* of the first-named place when the enemy took it, entered the town, in company with ten other officers in his confidence, disguised as peasants. With the connivance of the *burghers* they managed to introduce a detachment of our troops by a gate which they at once seized and thereby secured the town. The little garrison, which was in the fort, seeing the town thus taken, capitulated and left the same day, according to the terms of their surrender. The Count de la Mothe with a body of troops approached Bruges on the same day, and this town, which found itself at the time quite unprepared, capitulated on the same conditions as the fort of Ghent.

It was not long after we had taken these two towns that we learned of the junction effected by the Allies at their camp at Anderlecht, their immediate march on Assche whence they seized upon Lessines, and finally their passage of the Dendre without any opposition. During the time that the enemy was making these movements, our army was occupying a camp near Oudenarde, not in a particularly advantageous position, and it was decided to improve this state of things by means of certain entrenchments. The alignments of these were hardly traced out when the enemy, who resolved to attack us before this improvement could be effected, marched upon us forthwith and appeared in front of our army on July 11th. As the time of day was somewhat advanced, it was possible, had it been wished, to have avoided giving battle, and that this should have been done was quite the opinion of the Duke de Vendôme. As it was, one hardly knows how the battle began, but it did so about four hours after midday and lasted until night, being resumed more than once.[1]

Our army did not quit the field till two o'clock in the morning and then directed its march upon Ghent. We lost some excellent troops , far more than the enemy. The Duke de Vendôme, who had wished all along to avoid this engagement, was annoyed without measure at its unhappy result, and went to the extent of lamenting it in such terms that a grave misunderstanding arose between him and the Duke of Burgundy, by which the Allies duly profited. This unfortunate business was followed by a bold attempt on the part of the Allies, namely, the siege of Lille. Immediately this town was seen to be threatened steps were taken to enable it to offer a vigorous defence, so as to gain time to organise measures for its relief if such were possible, and by attacking the enemy's convoys to compel them to raise the siege.

To this end a considerable force of our best troops was sent to form the garrison under the command of Maréchal de Boufflers; this, however, in no way deterred the enemy, who invested the town on August 22nd. The Duke de Vendôme advised that they should be attacked immediately on their arrival, but it was not considered fit to carry out this advice. The enemy, taking advantage of the interval, dug lines of circumvallation, which were so well constructed that they placed themselves quite out of harm's way. It became necessary then to rely upon what resistance Maréchal de Boufflers could offer, and to

---

1. Oudenarde. "The prince who represented the lost cause of the Stuart family fought at Oudenarde on the side of the French. The representative of the dethroned and exiled dynasty was in one army—the representative of the house now appointed for succession to the rule of England was in the other."—*The Reign of Queen Anne*, Justin McCarthy.

Plan of the Battle of Oudenarde

watch for an opportunity of attacking their convoys, which often had to come a great distance on account of the length of time occupied by the siege.

As a matter of fact, favourable opportunities did arise for us to prevent the safe arrival of some of these. If perchance they had been properly attacked and their escorts beaten off, we might well have caused the Allies to suspend their operations if not to raise the siege.

The Chevalier de Broglio, a lieutenant-general in the king's army, attacked and entirely destroyed one. He seized some thousands of pounds weight of powder loaded on barges on the Escaut (Schelde); these he set fire to, and the result was such a terrific explosion that a village some distance even from the river was completely wrecked. The capture of this convoy much retarded the besiegers, and if only the next one we attacked had met with the same fate, there is no doubt whatever that the enemy would have found themselves unable to go on with the siege, as there was a want of every kind of munition of war in their camp. This second convoy, which came from the sea-coast towns, was composed of an immense number of waggons escorted by twelve thousand men, and was attacked by twenty thousand of our people, commanded by one of our senior lieutenant-generals.[2]

Our troops, who ought to have had detachments detailed for the express purpose of attacking the waggons and cutting the traces whilst the main body attacked the escort, entirely devoted themselves to a combat in the moorlands of Vignandal (Wynendael), and allowed the waggons of the convoy itself to pursue their way in all haste. Owing to this inattention to details we did not profit by our superiority in numbers, whilst the enemy on the other hand, who knew too well how to take every advantage of the ground by posting themselves in the woods, always warded off our people, and eventually obliged them to retire with some loss.

This failure prompted us to think of another way of annoying the enemy, which, though it was very well planned, ultimately came to nothing; it was to invest and lay siege to the town of Brussels. It was hoped that this enterprise would oblige the Allies to make a considerable diversion of their strength should they decide to try and relieve the town, whilst, if we captured it meantime, it would serve to counterbalance the loss of Lille. It was also believed that the presence of the Elector of Bavaria would much assist in bringing about its sur-

---

2. Count de la Mothe, who commanded a force of thirty-six battalions and sixty-two squadrons.—*Hist. Memoirs Marquis de Feuquieres*, 1735.

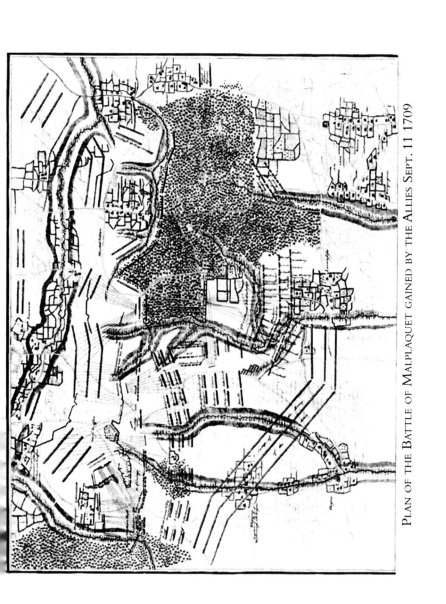

PLAN OF THE BATTLE OF MALPLAQUET GAINED BY THE ALLIES SEPT. 11 1709

render, as this prince was extremely beloved by the inhabitants. The Elector, therefore, with a comparatively small force went thither and opened the trenches. In order to protect him in his operations before the town, the precaution was taken to post a considerable detachment under one of our senior lieutenant-generals upon the banks of the Escaut, over which the enemy would necessarily have to pass if they decided to march to the relief of Brussels.

This lieutenant-general took care to entrench himself along the river, and there was every reason to hope that, provided the enemy persisted in the siege of Lille, they would lose Brussels; or that, if they attempted to go to the relief of the latter, they would have to risk an important action on the Escaut to force a passage, which would oblige them to employ so very many troops that their force before Lille would be considerably weakened. It was further arranged that as the Elector's force was not sufficiently strong to provide for its own safety in case of the Allies being able to send a relieving force to Brussels, he should be kept fully informed of all that went on, so that he should not find himself surprised in his own camp. The prince, having made all his arrangements, carried on the siege with such vigour that he soon overpowered most of the outworks, and was in hopes of attacking the main fortifications in a few days time.

The enemy, who were quite aware of his valour and skill, determined to attempt the passage of the Escaut with a force which, although a considerable one, did not prevent their continuing the siege of Lille. They preferred rather to risk the loss of Brussels than to abandon this enterprise, the more so that they were already masters of the town itself, and were almost certain of a similar result to their labours with regard to the fortress. They therefore took their chance of success with this detachment, with the result that misfortune, which followed us everywhere, willed that their troops should effect the crossing in the face of our people, notwithstanding all our precautions, and without meeting any resistance to speak of. They continued their march upon Brussels undisturbed, and no information was sent to the Elector, who believed himself to be in perfect safety.

It was not until they actually appeared before his eyes that he became aware of his dangerous position, and having no troops available to withstand their advance, he found himself forced to make a precipitate retreat and to abandon all his artillery and wounded. His rear-guard even was roughly handled, and thus the Allies both relieved Brussels and continued their siege to Lille. The enemy's passage of the Escaut, made so easily in the face of our troops, caused nearly as much sensation as our failure to capture the last convoy, and gave rise to these words with reference to him who defended the bank of this river:—

This motto's on his cutlass spied:
'Whatever else—no homicide.'

(*Il est mis sur son coutelas*
'Homicide point ne seras.')

The enemy were henceforth unmolested, and at last this famous fortress fell into their hands on December 8th, after having held out for three and a half months. They also took the town and citadel of Ghent, which surrendered on the thirtieth of the same month.

THE CAMPAIGN OF 1709

The campaign of 1709 opened very late in the season, and such was the extreme cold at the beginning of the year that since 1608 the like had not been known in Europe. It is reported that in the year 1608 the cold was so great in France, Germany, and the northern countries that the very largest rivers were frozen over so that carriages and carts were enabled to cross them on the ice; but it is not said that the corn, all the vines, fruit trees, and many other kinds also perished by reason of the severity of the cold, as actually happened this year. It became necessary to plough up the already sown fields and re-sow them to provide subsistence, which, withal, did not prevent a famine in the kingdom. Our army suffered much from its effects towards the end of the campaign, and it would have been better had the latter be-gun earlier, on account of the forage supply. As time had to be given to allow the new crops to grow, it was nearly mid- June before the armies took the field.

The enemy concentrated all their forces in Flanders. Their two ar-mies, under Milord Marlborough and Prince Eugene, were so strong that, notwithstanding all the efforts made by France, she was unable to concentrate sufficient troops to meet them in the open field. We had, therefore, to act on the defensive and to select such camps and entrenched positions as would protect and cover our country as much as possible. The Duke de Vendôme, discontented with what had oc-curred in the course of the preceding campaign, had retired, and re-course was had to Maréchal de Villars, who took over the command of the army of Flanders at the beginning of the year. The king could not have shown a greater sense of his appreciation of the worth of this general in relying upon him alone to ward off the evils which threatened France and to remedy, if he could, those which had already occurred. His Majesty was not mistaken in his choice.

When our army had assembled, we occupied a camp in a fairly advantageous position near the canal of Douai. It rested on some marshes between this canal and the village of Combrin. Entrenchments were dug, and we found ourselves so far safe from attack. The enemy made feints upon various towns; but being aware of the fact that we had withdrawn part of our infantry from the garrison of Tournai, they determined to attack this town, proceeded to invest it, and after having constructed strong lines of circumvallation, opened their trenches during the night of July 7-8th.

The fortress of Tournai is one of the strongest and most regularly laid out in the kingdom. M. de Maigrigni, the famous engineer, had devoted all his knowledge to the construction of this citadel just as M. de Vauban had in like manner done at Lille. The enemy, who were perfectly aware of all the advantages it possessed, took every precaution necessary for such an enterprise. They divided their operations into three principal points of attack, bombarded the town without ceasing, and as any idea of relief was out of the question, M. de Surville, a lieutenant-general in the king's army who commanded there, was obliged to make terms regarding the town, and withdrew into the fortress itself on July 31st.

The fortress was forthwith attacked with even more energy and resource than had been the case with the town. The glacis was countermined with numberless branches, which led from the counter-scarps under the earth and well to the front connected with pits and mines, which had been constructed to blow up the besiegers when they attempted to make their lodgements, but the enemy, to prevent such accidents, never advanced their approaches without first probing the ground, and themselves dug shafts here and there by means of which they ferreted out the mines and rendered them useless. What was most unfortunate for the besieged was the lack of food in the fortress, for in the case of such a want anything else becomes useless.

It has been pointed out that this might have been provided against during the siege of the town by obliging the inhabitants to give up the corn they had stored in their warehouses, but whether these were not inspected, or whether it was believed that the supplies were already sufficient, the fact remains that want of food contributed in no small degree to the reduction of the fortress, which called for a parley on August 30th. The enemy at first declined the conditions proposed by M. de Surville for the surrender, and recommenced their operations. However, having thought the matter over, they, three days later, accepted the very conditions they had just refused, and the fortress was handed over to them.

After the Allies had got possession of Tournai they bethought them of another enterprise, which was of no less importance than that they had just succeeded in, to wit, the siege of Mons. Their preparations were complete, and without losing a moment. Prince Eugene marched with the leading portion of his army to invest the town, leaving the rest to follow. Maréchal de Villars, seeing that the enemy were determined to seize this town, resolved to take up an advantageous position, such as would interfere with their designs. He broke up his camp on September 7th, and directed his march along the woods of Sart and Jean-Sart to a little place called Malplaquet, within easy reach of Mons, so that the enemy; had to engage him before beginning their siege. Owing to this march, a piece of work fell to my share as unexpected as it was fatiguing.

Nothing had been said to me as to the order of our march, and I had gone peaceably to bed; but I had hardly got there when I received an order to report myself at midnight at the centre of the first line to take over the command of six hundred men detailed as escort for the baggage of the army. I was obliged to pack my own things as quickly as possible, and betake myself to the point named where I was given instructions for this embarrassing commission, which I carried out by taking a different route to that of the rest of the army. Escort duty over waggons in the presence of the enemy is a troublesome affair.

In addition to the confusion that usually reigns amongst them, care has to be taken to protect them from visits on the part of the enemy, which means continuous watching with fears of surprises; in such cases an officer's loss of reputation has often depended upon a momentary negligence. Two nights and a day did I spend in this agreeable exercise, and on the evening of the second day, after having left the baggage train in a place of safety, I rejoined the army, which had just encamped in the plain of Mons, near the woods of Sart and Jean-Sart.

Our position was a peculiar one but advantageous withal. On our front lay these two woods, separate the one from the other, forming a kind of broad avenue, wide enough for twenty battalions to pass formed up side by side, which gave upon the plain we were occupying. Maréchal de Villars ordered the infantry to occupy the end of this avenue and the edges of the woods, so as to create a sort of blind alley and to prevent entrance to the plain. The cavalry remained in the plain, the Household troops in the centre, in rear of the infantry posted across the alley, and the rest on the right and left of our line in rear of the woods. The enemy could only attack us by advancing up this avenue, and we thought this was going to take place on the day of our arrival, for we saw a body of cavalry appear at its entrance. It turned out to be Prince Eugene, who merely wished to reconnoitre our position, so as to avail himself of every precaution in readiness for making his attack when the rest of his army joined him from Tournai.

As soon as we realised that we were not going to be attacked that day, the whole of our infantry set to work to entrench themselves in the best way possible, reckoning that the crisis would come on the morrow; those out in the open opposite the end of the avenue constructed cannon-proof parapets with gaps here and there to facilitate an advance in case of need, whilst those on the borders of the woods did likewise, so that in a short time our position was well fortified. The only infantry that were without any cover at all from the enemy's artillery was the Bavarian Brigade, which was in reserve in rear of the Garde Française, who held a portion of the parapet, whilst in the rear of us again were the Maison du Roi, who were equally exposed.

The Allies, not being in a position to attack us formally on the day of our arrival or on the following day, placed batteries of artillery which opened fire on every point, but specially on the Household cavalry, and as we were posted exactly in front of these, many shots intended for them constantly carried off someone in our brigade. On the afternoon of September 10th, the enemy began to construct a battery about halfway up the avenue, and during that night armed it with thirty cannon of large calibre to breach the entrenchments in the wood on our left, on which they intended to make their main attack. Thus we awaited them, lying that night in battle formation, whilst our patrols and those of the enemy kept up a constant fire whenever they came across each other.

Next morning at break of day the battery of thirty cannon opened fire, and by its continuous volleys succeeded in breaching the entrenchments in the wood on our left, and the head of the enemy's infantry column made its appearance. They came on at a slow pace, and by seven o'clock had arrived in line with the battery threatening our centre. As soon as this dense column appeared in the avenue, fourteen guns were promptly brought up in front of our brigade almost in line with the regiment of Garde Française. The fire of this battery was terrific, and hardly a shot missed its mark. I could not help noticing the officer in command, who although he seemed elderly was nevertheless so active that in giving his orders there was no cessation of action anywhere, the cannon shot continued to pour forth without a break, plunged into the enemy's infantry and carried off whole ranks at a time, but a gap was no sooner created than it was immediately filled again, and they even continued their advance upon us without giving us any idea of the actual point determined on for their attack. At last the column, leaving the great battery on its left, changed its direction a quarter right and threw itself precipitately into the wood on our left, making an assault upon that portion which had been breached.

It sustained the full fire of our infantry entrenched therein, and notwithstanding the great number killed on the spot, it continued the attack and penetrated into the wood, a success which it owed as much to being drunk with brandy as to martial ardour. If all our regiments had behaved equally well the enemy's infantry would have been entirely destroyed in this fight, and would never have been able to force their way over our entrenchments, but some of our best dressed troops did not think proper to hold their ground, doubtless not so much that they were afraid of being killed as the fear of the embarrassment they might cause the State by the difficulty that would be created later on in having to replace them!! They therefore made off to a safer quarter, leaving the position open to the enemy, and they actually during their retirement, having come across the horses of the dragoons of Notât, who had been dismounted to come to their support, mounted thereon to take the better care of them while the dragoons themselves looked after the fighting business for them.

Although the enemy had forced their way into the wood, this success did not involve their winning the battle, and if our cowards had only rejoined the brigades that they left still fighting, it would have been quite possible to have repulsed them. The nature of this wood-fighting gave no particular advantage to either side, but their only notion was to keep themselves intact to shine at the reviews to which they are such an ornament. The fighting which now went on in the woods was extremely stubborn and murderous, and victory hung in the balance.

Our generals perceived that there was a lack of infantry in the wood on our left, owing to these regiments having abandoned their position; so to supply this need the Irish Brigade, which had hitherto lined the entrenchments at the end of the avenue abutting on the wood, was ordered to move into it, and we, to our great content, were directed to take its place. I say to our great content, because since the enemy's great battery had ceased firing upon the wood it had directed its attention to us and the Maison du Roi, and we had had to stand and see ourselves knocked over without any possibility of returning the compliment.

By the time the Irish Brigade had got well into the wood it was considered to be hardly sufficient as a reinforcement by itself, and an order came for us to follow it, although there was no one else left to fill our place which would be left open to the enemy. They would not fail to seize it, as they could then attack the Maison du Roi with a great chance of success by simply lining the outside of our entrenchments, a manoeuvre quite possible for them to carry out. When the first order was brought to the brigade-major, who reported it to me, I refused to obey it, and pointed out the absolute necessity that existed for our maintaining the position we were holding; but a lieutenant-general then arrived on the scene, and ordered us a second time to march off, so sharply that all our remonstrances were useless. We abandoned our post and marched into the wood to join in the fusillade with the others. What I have just related here will be found to agree with the criticisms that have been made on the affair of Malplaquet.

It is admitted that, had the Bavarian Brigade not left its position to enter the wood, we should not have been obliged to leave the field of battle in the hands of the enemy, and as none of the critics were aware whether it took this action on its own initiative or not, M. de Villars a year later called an inquiry as to why we had abandoned such an important point in the line. We deputed M. de Quemin to represent us, who assured him in the name of the whole of the corps of the remonstrances we had taken the liberty to make at the time to the lieutenant-general who had given us the order; he also gave him his name, and added with perfect truth that we should never have left our position had not the latter emphatically ordered us to do so in the name of the king.

Whilst events were passing thus on the left, the wooded country on our right was also attacked by a column of the enemy's infantry, which had followed the advance of the first. The woods there were neither as thick nor as high as those on the left, but as the ground was much more cut up by hedges, it was on this account the more advantageous to our troops. Our right withstood the enemy's attack with admirable firmness, disputing every foot of the ground in the same manner as on our left. From the Regiment of Navarre, which happened at that time to be composed of very short men, nearly in rags, who held our extreme right, and who behaved none the less marvellously well, to the Regiment of Alsace, which extended thence to the centre held by the Garde Française, everything went always in our favour.

It was now midday, and our right and left still held their own, with no decided advantage either to the enemy or ourselves. The tangled nature of the ground intersected by woods on which the principal fighting took place had this advantage about it, that it was impossible to spread a panic; each brigade fought, as it were, independently, without being in the least aware of its neighbours' movements. As far as those who occupied the centre were concerned, it would have been a pity to have exposed them; everything went on well without them, and a victory even might have resulted had not the enemy thought of feeling their way towards the entrenchments that our brigade had just left. They had noticed that neither smoke nor fire came from them, and then their hussars, by cantering around, approached little by little until they at last discovered that we had no one left in occupation. Then, profiting by the chance thus given them, they caused their infantry to advance, who in turn protected the passage of many squadrons through the intervals in the parapet; these formed up at the mouth of the plain to charge the Maison du Roi, who had previously retired somewhat to avoid the infantry fire.

When these battalions advanced to seize our entrenchments the fine infantry holding our centre, who so far had not suffered from a single hostile shot, had every opportunity of deploying to cover the gap made by our empty entrenchments, but then they would have run still more risk of spoiling their beautiful uniforms, their most noticeable characteristic, and they therefore retired to try and find a quieter spot where they would be safe from any such rough handling. The result was that the cavalry were at liberty to pass through all the intervals in the entrenchments, and having reformed in the plain beyond, they moved straight upon the Maison du Roi, who like- wise advanced to give them battle.

The Scotch Guards of the Queen of England, most excellent troops, led the charge, which was a most violent one; and then the two sides, after the confusion of the first shock, disentangled themselves. They came on a second time to the charge, just as we learned that Maréchal de Villars had been dangerously wounded and incapacitated by a bullet through the knee. M. de Boufflers, who had joined the army the evening before simply, as he told Maréchal de Villars, as a volunteer, now sent us an order to beat a retreat. It was after one o'clock in the afternoon when this order reached us, and we were still holding our own as well as ever in our wood, where the enemy had lost very heavily without scoring any further advantage than that of sharing its occupation with us.

Had Maréchal de Villars not been wounded, it is quite certain that we should never have given up the fight, for the enemy's cavalry, which had entered the plain and then become engaged with the Household troops, could have easily been repulsed, as we had all our cavalry posted right and left, who up to then had not had an opportunity of even letting off a pistol. It would have been perfectly feasible to make them converge upon the centre, and so wipe out those of the enemy, the more so as our infantry had lost next to no ground, and were by no means so broken as to be likely to lose their grip of what they held. In short, although the enemy ultimately found themselves at liberty to undertake the siege of Mons, they owe it entirely to him who happened to wound Maréchal de Villars. As far as the battle itself is concerned, it would be impossible for them, if they impartially considered the matter, to say with truth that they really gained anything by their victory.

When we began our retreat, none of our infantry brigades were at all broken, always excepting the two famous regiments who held the centre of our line, and whose behaviour in quitting the field I have already remarked upon. Our cavalry were in excellent trim. The Maison du Roi and the *gendarmerie* alone had been engaged, and were not much disordered thereby. Our march was as undisturbed as if there were no enemy in the country. Our right retired on Quesnoy and our left on Valenciennes. It is true that as soon as our line of retreat was determined upon, and our columns began their retirement, the enemy sent out a number of squadrons to keep us under observation, but they neither dared approach our rearguard nor even make a pretence of attacking us, and there is no doubt whatever that they were filled with astonishment at seeing us thus quit the field of battle. There was no doubt, at any rate, as to Maréchal de Villars being no longer at our head.

We marched for all the world as if we were merely changing our camping-ground, without any hurry or confusion. I was with the

MARÉCHAL DE VILLARS

left wing which retired by the road to Valenciennes, which for three leagues passed through a fine open country, where we met with neither stream or defile which could afford an opportunity for the enemy's squadrons to attack our rearguard. A little further on we did reach a village, where we were obliged to cross over a fairly wide stream, which checked us for a while, but the enemy also halted, and there was some reason to fear they might attack the tail of our column during its passage. To meet this case, infantry were required, as our rearguard consisted solely of cavalry.

As it was, the whole of our infantry had already crossed, and were continuing their march, with the exception of our regiment and my French grenadiers, who held the honourable post of rear-guard to the whole of the infantry. As I crossed the stream, the cavalry who followed me had noticed the necessity of infantry support to cover the passage, without which our rear-most squadrons would have been destroyed. I met with the Chevalier de Rosel, lieutenant-general in the king's army, who was asking for infantry, which by this time was a considerable distance off; for as soon as each regiment had passed over it marched away, without waiting for the next, with the result that they were at least a quarter of a league distant the one from the other.

Seeing that the Bavarian regiment was the only one to hand, and which he regarded in the light of a foreign corps to which he dared not give a command, I begged him to give us whatever orders he thought fit, and he forthwith gave me his instructions. I then recrossed the brook, and posted my men in the gardens round the village, by which means I covered the cavalry rear-guard and prevented the enemy approaching. I might say that when I took up my position I asked the Chevalier de Rosel to wait for me, so that my infantry could retire in company with the cavalry, which he had the politeness to do, for there were yet two more leagues to march before reaching Valenciennes, over open country in which my men would have been much exposed if the enemy had followed us up, but they did not even dare to cross the stream.

M, de Boufflers took over the command of the army in the absence of Maréchal de Villars. He directed us to pitch our camps next day, the right wing near Quesnoy and the left at Valenciennes; we were thus in a secure position between these two towns, especially after we had constructed a strong line of well-flanked entrenchments along our front. The enemy, who had lost nearly twenty thousand men in the battle, hardly so much as dreamed of following us up; their only desire was to be allowed to carry on their siege of Mons undisturbed, and as we were yet quite in a position to interfere with their enterprise, they were reassured when they found we were hard at work piling earth in front of us. Sometime after we had settled down in our encampment, Maréchal de Boufflers held a general inspection of the whole army, which he found in a most satisfactory state, and in a condition to give battle at the first moment he judged necessary. It was said that this was the king's own intention, and that orders had already been prepared for the same.

A friend of mine at Versailles, who believed he was in a position to know what was going on, informed me of this, which he vouched for strongly as being correct, and even told me the date when the operations were to begin; but the famine which raged in our army put a stop to the preparations. All the corn magazines were empty; the hard frost had prevented their replenishment, and as it was imperative that provision should be made of at least a four days' supply of bread before beginning an advance, the project became impossible. M. Dangeat, Intendant of Maubeuge, who controlled these stores, when threatened with being hanged at the gate of the town if he did not find some means of providing some bread for these four days, declared that he was ready for the hanging; thus it was want of bread alone that prevented us engaging in a second battle. The enemy must have had some hint of all this, for they put off the siege of Mons, and only began their trenches on the night of 25th-26th of September.

The want of bread in our army now became serious, and we lived from hand to mouth, that is to say, the rations were distributed singly, and very often only half a ration was given out in the morning and the other in the evening, because the supply was so short in the magazines. Baking operations were confined to the meagre arrivals of flour from the surrounding provinces, and half the constituents of the bread served out consisted of bran. The rigours of the season began to tell upon us, and the result of occupying the same camp for so long a period created such a scarcity of forage in the country round that the horses which had escaped the Battle of Malplaquet actually perished of hunger at their picket ropes. The teams of the commissariat waggons also died off one after the other, and yet no move was made to take up winter quarters until all the horses in the army were ruined. Our garrison at Mons, after some resistance, made terms and surrendered on October 21st, and a little later both armies withdrew from the field. I had the honour of being promoted to the rank of colonel at the end of this campaign.

CHAPTER 12

The Allies Increase Their Efforts

The Allies, determined to increase their conquests in Flanders, strengthened their forces more and more, and spared nothing to further the seizure of our best provinces. The Dutch, above all, regarded the war carried on in their country as a benefit by which they ought to profit later on, the conquests being in their favour, and with such designs in mind these gentry regretted neither the expense nor the provision of munitions of all kinds that they were put to. So great was their enthusiasm that when the emperor, who was the moving spirit of the war, found himself unable to bear the burden of its cost, as he had engaged himself to do in his treaty with them, they supplied the deficiencies as long as they lasted without a murmur, in the hope of making a greater profit than the archduke himself, for whom their sacrifices were made.

With these objects in view their preparations were hurried on, and their army opened the campaign at such an early date that the siege of Douai was begun on April 14th. France was not yet ready, and almost the whole of her troops were still in winter quarters when she learnt that the enemy had taken the field; in fact, before the regiments which were in the Comté de Chigny and the Metz districts had arrived in Flanders, Douai was invested. Moreover, even when our army was fully mobilised it was still too inferior in strength to that of the enemy to make any head against them. The loss of Douai caused us much inquietude, as the necessity of reinforcing the garrisons of the many towns open to the Allies' attack further enfeebled our army, and finally compelled us to remain strictly on the defensive and content ourselves with merely keeping the enemy under observation for the remainder of the campaign.

The Court of France found itself further embarrassed by this unfortunate condition of its affairs, for the strongholds threatened by the enemy lay contiguous to the royal provinces; the inhabitants took alarm, and fear which exaggerated the actual peril inspired many to say that the king himself would soon fail to find safety even in Versailles. France, to counteract the evil which threatened her, made a proposal of peace to the Allies, and sent plenipotentiaries for this purpose to Gertruidemberg, but the gentlemen who represented the Dutch States acted their part with so much arrogance that it was impossible to come to an understanding with them. It was even said that their replies included insulting references to the king. However this may have been, it is certain that they were of such an extraordinary nature that the plenipotentiaries of France were obliged to withdraw on July 25th.

Douai made a better defence than Tournai or Mons. This town was an important one to us; it covered all Artois, had magnificent arsenals, and was the headquarters of the Artillery School. Although munitions of war were not wanting, it was obliged to capitulate on July 3rd. The capture of this place contributed not a little to increase the pride of the Dutch States and to expedite the departure of our deputies from Gertruidemberg. The enemy now laid siege to Bethune, which was not over-strongly fortified, notwithstanding which, its defence was maintained from July 27th to August 29th. After Bethune was taken, Ayre and Saint Venant were invested, the trenches being opened before the first during the night of the 12th-13th September, and a little later in the case of Saint Venant, which surrendered on October 2nd, the town of Ayre capitulated on the 10th. In short, the Allies took Bethune, Ayre, and Saint Venant, after which both armies retired to their winter quarters.

The capture of these four towns inspired the Allies with fresh courage, and they were convinced that France was reduced to the last extremity. It is true that she was exhausted financially, and was obliged in paying the troops to have recourse to paper money (*Billets d'ustençiles*). The officers lost three-quarters of their pay in their exchange of this for actual money, and this did not tend to improve discipline, but it was the only way then to meet this state of affairs. England had profited nothing from the conquests wrung from us on *terra firma*, which gave the king reason to hope that there would be less difficulty in detaching this country from the alliance against him, and he therefore set to work to make secret proposals to this end. William III. had died in the year 1702, soon after he had made his treaty with the emperor, and the English Parliament, on his death, had called Anne Princess of Denmark to the throne, the sister of the late Princess of Orange.

This princess had no interests in this war other than those regarding her new kingdom; the motives which induced King William to ally himself with the Emperor had no weight with the queen; thus there was no great difficulty in entering into negotiations with her. These were accordingly begun, at first very secretly, but were as time went on openly declared.

The Campaign of 1711

The Allies did not open the campaign in Flanders with that energy which had distinguished them in the preceding years. The Queen of England had begun to listen to the proposals made her by France, and Milord Marlborough interested himself less in the conquests that were being planned. The Emperor Joseph died on April 17th, and left the Empire to his brother the archduke.

It was hardly in the interests of England, or any of the other Powers of Europe, to see the Empire and the Spanish dominion under the rule of one and the same prince. However, the archduke, since his ascent to the Imperial throne, showed no signs of relaxing his hold on the kingdom of Spain, and wished rather that the further conquest of Flanders should be prosecuted with vigour. The Dutch demanded nothing better for themselves, because they would profit thereby, and therefore set-to to beg Milord Marlborough to begin the siege of Bouchain. Notwithstanding the limits set him by Queen Anne, he consented to this; the town was invested, the trenches opened about the beginning of August, and it surrendered to him on the 18th of the same month.

The conquests of the Allies were limited in this campaign to the taking of this town; it was even said that Milord Marlborough had gone too far, and they took the pretext of his having exceeded the orders of the English Court to accuse him of receiving bribes. He was severely handled on this point, and the annoyance caused him much mental distress. M. de Villars for his part took the fort of Alleures.

The death of the Emperor Joseph decided the position of Philippe V., for the departure of the archduke from Spain for Vienna was taken to be an abandonment by him of the kingdom.

France, perceiving that the emperor's election would determine a section of the Grand Alliance to listen to terms of peace, sought means to introduce the case of the Elector of Bavaria as a vital point in the negotiations on this subject, in order to demand the restitution of his territories. This was provided for by the cession by the King of Spain of the sovereignty of the Circle of Burgundy, of which the countships of Brabant and Chigny yet remained intact. These provinces which, it was reckoned, would have to be given up on the declaration of a general peace, in order to form the new buffer-state demanded by the Dutch, gave the Elector the power to send his representatives to the general *Diets* to demand the restitution of Bavaria. It was to the interest of the Dutch, in order to form their desired barrier, that this exchange should be effected.

This prince therefore set out to take possession of Namur as representing Brabant, and Luxembourg, Chigny, and after his installation, at which I had the honour to be present, His Highness took up his residence in Namur, and caused money to be coined there with his own die.

The Elector of Bavaria, who brought pleasure in his train wherever he might find himself, soon made Namur one of the pleasantest retreats in Europe. The inhabitants who, before the arrival of this prince, were distinguished by their rather outlandish manners and customs, became civilised and sociable beings. They manifested by their rejoicings the delight they felt at having the Elector as their sovereign. Amongst the *fêtes* that they organised was a combat between sailors on the river Sambre, when there was not much stream.

Several boats rushed at each other impelled by their rowers, each carrying champions planted upon the decks with lances at rest, who jousted to see which was best man. They carried small baskets on their stomachs to receive the blows which they encountered during their charge, which were delivered with force enough to upset an adversary and topple him over into the water. Such was their skill, however, that their lances would break with the shock without either combatant losing his footing; others would overthrow two opponents at a blow, making divers of them, but as these people are perfect swimmers, they were soon at the surface and shouting to be allowed to begin again.

Following on this came the game of the eel. Across the river was stretched a cord at the middle of which was attached an eel, which the competitors endeavoured to seize whilst passing at full speed standing upon the edge of their boats, and who, reaching forward to make their grasp, oftener than not found themselves in the water. There were prizes given for all these games and judges appointed for their distribution. They did not limit themselves to the water combats and the eel game, for I saw men who had placed themselves face downwards on a pivot high up in the air with arms and legs extended, and who maintained their equilibrium so perfectly that they could whirl themselves round with the speed of a windmill.

But the play with which they wound up these games was the best, to my mind, to wit, a battle on the Grande Place of the town, which was produced in an altogether original manner. It represented a quarrel which formerly existed between the inhabitants of a suburb (now included within the walls) and the town itself. In the old days, each side, wearing a distinguishing uniform, assembled in equal strength in the town square to wipe out their differences, and fought the matter out sword in hand, as gunpowder had not been invented at that time. The party which drove the other to the extreme limit of the square was held to have proved their point by victory, under the control of properly appointed judges, who decided also as to the fairness of the blows.

To commemorate this battle the inhabitants divided into two parties, one of which called themselves Meylans, the other Aures. They were formed into companies and were drilled in the art of walking on stilts, on which they maintained as solid a footing as if they had been on their own feet. They had their officers and drummers, as in the regular army; the Aures carried blue and white plumes and cockades, and the Meylans red and white. Officers were not appointed by favour. To become a captain it was necessary to have vanquished five competitors; and it would be a good thing for many States if they enforced the same regulations, things would go much better then.

The height of these stilts was an advantage from the spectator's point of view of the play, which might be described as a combat between two giant forces. At the time appointed each side arrives at opposite ends of the square, where they form up in battle array with the utmost precision. The most famous fighters are distributed along each line to receive the brunt of the shocks and the most violent attacks, and bodies in reserve are placed ready to support the points that may show signs of weakness in the course of the action. These two little armies then solemnly advance against one another with well-dressed and locked-up ranks, until they arrive near the place marked out for the combat, which is exactly half-way across the square.

Then their march quickens its pace, the two sides close with each other, and the fight begins in earnest. The elbows of the combatants are their only weapons, for their hands are engaged with the butts of their stilts, which reach up to their thighs, so that their elbows stick out like the handles of a pot, and they work these with such rapidity to upset their adversaries that they look for all the world like *teetotums*. They are so adroit in this exercise that they can use one shoulder instantaneously after another, and can stoop and recover themselves in a second. The blows given and taken are extremely brisk, and one must have a robust constitution to enlist in these troops. When one side has been so often floored that it can no longer offer any resistance, the other occupies the ground of the defeated ones, forms up in battle array, and shouts victory. Then the vanquished retire stunned and confused, and dare not put in an appearance during the subsequent *fête* held by the victors, which lasts about three days.

When the two sides advance to the attack their fathers, mothers, sisters, wives, or near relations follow in their steps, and during the action encourage them in the liveliest terms. They keep close behind them to support them lest they kill themselves by falling upon the stone pavement, to give them refreshment to reanimate their strength, and to help them remount their stilts and make them return to the charge. There is something very comic to see these women following up the giants, trembling, gesticulating, and screaming, all at the same time, to animate their husbands or relations. The cry one hears oftenest is, "*A chasse! A chasse!*" which is addressed to those who have been upset, and is intended to encourage them to be quick in remounting their stilts to rejoin the fray.

I was a witness of this famous battle, and so was the Elector with his whole court It went on for nearly three hours before one side had made much impression on the other, for as soon as the one gained any ground so soon did the other regain it, and the reserves which came to the rescue restored the balance of affairs over and over again. However, the combatants were upset with greater ease towards the end of the conflict than had been the case at the beginning. One saw these *colossi* one moment prostrated by their falls, then reappearing as if mother earth had given new birth to them. This spectacle was altogether most amusing, the bull fights, contests between various animals, and other shows of this kind were nothing in comparison; it was a true picture of war.

All these struggles and upsets at last reduced most of the combatants to a state of inanition, and many after their falls found themselves with broken legs and arms, others were breathless; in fact, there was hardly one of them left who was not completely blown. However, one of the two parties had to win, which presently occurred; the Meylands finally drove the Aures beyond the boundaries marked for victory, and the air was rent with cries of joy, amid which the losers retired more dead than alive.

THE CAMPAIGN OF 1712

The change which manifested itself in the armies of the Allies sufficiently showed the intentions of Queen Anne. Milord Marlborough was no longer in command of the English forces. He had been recalled to London to meet the accusations that had been made against him, and the Duke of Ormonde had been put in his place. The latter had secret orders to undertake nothing of his own initiative or in co-operation with the Allies, and to attend no Council of War without fresh orders from the queen. The strength even of the body of troops that he had with him on a war footing was less than had been the case in the preceding campaigns, for it consisted of no more than fourteen thousand men. The Court at Vienna, which was quite aware of the English designs, acted as though nothing was happening, and arranged with the Dutch States to make a last effort to overpower the rest of our strongholds on the frontiers of Picardy, and to carry out their original plan of reducing France to impotence.

To this end the Dutch had amassed prodigious stores of food and munitions of war, which were gathered into various magazines near at hand to the points of conquest they had in view. For the transport of these munitions the rivers Escaut[1] and Scarpe were available, up which they towed enormous barges, while the abbey at Marchiennes, the Quatre-Clochers, the little town of Saint Amand, and the Abbey of Anzim were detailed for the magazines themselves. These munitions consisted of quantities of cannon, bombs, mortars, bullets, powder and ball, flour, rice, husked barley, cheese, butter, beer, wine, and brandy. Never had better preparations been made to ensure a successful result; all these magazines and barge convoys were protected by the towns of Douai, Bouchain, and the Abbey of Denain on the Escaut, which had been doubly entrenched.

These preparations completed, Prince Eugene and the Dutch had several conferences with the Duke of Ormonde, in order to come to a decision as to the siege of Valenciennes. This was a considerable undertaking, for we had provided this town with a good garrison, commanded by the Prince de Tringry, son of the late Duke of Lux-

---

1. The Scheldte.

emburg.

This general was noted for his personal courage as well as his capacity, thus it was necessary for the enemy to take every precaution. It was also obligatory in this case that the various chiefs of the Allied army should be consenting parties in this enterprise, but the Duke of Ormonde finally withdrew from the affair, with the result that the siege of Quesnoy was decided upon instead; this did not require such great preparations, as the town was small and unable to hold a large garrison. They intended, after capturing this town, to leave Valenciennes on their flank and throw themselves on Landreci, Guise, and Bapaume. By this they would enclose Valenciennes and even Cambrai within captured territory, and make it impossible for these two towns to collect provisions or receive any help. The plans were well conceived; there was reason to fear that if the enemy succeeded in their design Valenciennes would suffer much for want of food, and affairs as they were then gave us no great promise of hope.

The enemy began their siege of Quesnoy and opened their trenches about the middle of June. The English, for their part, did not separate themselves from the allied army, but allowed the siege to progress without participating in the work. Meanwhile Maréchal de Villars occupied the camp of Noyelle, on the heights near the town of Cambrai. On this town rested the left of his army, whilst his right extended along the river Escaut, which covered his front. It was a good position, but he was unable to prevent the enemy from making a heavy attack upon Quesnoy, which surrendered on July 4th, after no great resistance and on very poor terms. Prince Eugene remained some days longer encamped near this town before determining upon a further advance.

Queen Anne, who up to this time had shown all consideration for the Allies, now saw that they took their own way without any thought or desire for her help, and made no further mystery of the treaty which she had just concluded with the king. She sent a courier to the Duke of Ormonde with an order to separate himself from the Allied army and to move his troops to the seaports preparatory to returning to England. Shortly afterwards this suspension of arms between France and England was notified to our army. The very day that the Duke of Ormonde departed, which was July 18th, Prince Eugene invested Landreci with forty battalions and sixty squadrons, following himself the next day with the rest of his army, which he posted with its left near the town, having a large stream called the Escaillon on his front.

Whilst carrying on the siege of Quesnoy his supplies had reached him by the high road of Mons; but the siege of Landreci took him so much further afield that he found his convoys were no longer safe from attack, owing to the neighbourhood of Valenciennes and Cambrai. He then looked for a safer road. He drew from the magazines he had on the Scarpe, and made a depot at the Abbey of Denain, where he had a bridge over the Escaut, and from there supplied his army. To ensure the safety of these convoys the enemy had fortified the abbey with a double line of entrenchments, and had constructed a road, equally strongly entrenched, leading thence to the river Scarpe, on which plied the great transport barges. This line of communication was so convenient to them that they could never be in want of supplies for the siege of Landreci, and it moreover ensured their communications for a further advance later on. Such being the state of affairs, they thought lightly of the English retirement, and with an army so superior in numbers to ours, they confidently resolved to make the most of their opportunity.

Maréchal de Villars, seeing the enemy on the march for Landreci, broke up our camp, and ascending the Escaut, we crossed it between Le Catelet and the Abbey of Vauselle, where we halted on July 19th. We parted with our baggage trains the next day, which were sent on to Le Catelet, when we encamped at Château-Cambresis, with the little river Selle in front of us. This camp was not far from that of the enemy, and was sufficiently well placed to cause them some uneasiness; but M. de Villars wished to get still nearer. He reconnoitred all the country between the Selle and the Sambre which ran through Landreci, and after having made his plans, marched us over the Selle in eight columns, and by three o'clock in the afternoon of 22nd July our right was on the banks of the Sambre near the wood of Ribaucourt, with the left close to Château-Cambresis.

Thick woods lay between our army and the circumvallation of the enemy, upon which they were then hard at work. For this reason we could see no sign of activity on their part, and we thought that they were merely taking their time to reconnoitre us; but Maréchal de Villars had no real intention of keeping us where we were. We stayed there during the 23rd, when twelve hundred workmen were mustered and set to work to make roads along the banks of the Sambre in the direction of Guise, although this was not the route our general had in his mind to take us.

To deceive the enemy still more, he sent some dragoons under the orders of M. de Coigny, who at fall of night took this road along the Sambre with measured tread, and so as to lead our opponents to believe that the whole of our army was on the march, they were accompanied by reliable men, extended at intervals, who shouted out in the darkness the names of our regiments, and drummers were posted here and there along the line who every now and then gave a few taps with their sticks as if to recall scattered soldiery. By this manoeuvre Prince Eugene was deceived into thinking that M. de Villars was availing himself of the darkness of night to advance against him, and watched for our advent (on a road we never took) until break of day.

M. de Villars, delighted to find that Prince Eugene had been misled by his feint, broke up his camp and repassed the Selle over the same bridges that we had crossed two days before. We had no baggage train to hinder us, but marched in the dark, knowing neither our destination nor the intentions of the general. This information was denied us, lest spies should report this nocturnal change of position; and our army was preceded in its march by an advanced guard of hussars under M. d'Albergoti, who scoured the country to prevent the slightest warning of our movement transpiring. Our advanced guard constructed bridges over the Escaut near the little village of Neuville, and our army made a magnificent march, for by eight o'clock next morning, July 24th, it had completed six long leagues.

A halt of only half an hour's duration was then made in some very flat country, and when the march was resumed over the bridges at Neuville we found ourselves in a wide open plain and in sight of the entrenchments of Denain. I only realised the design of our general when we came in view of these entrenchments and when the head of the column halted in order to wait until the rest of the infantry had crossed the bridges. In the meantime, however, arrangements were made to invest these entrenchments to a certain degree, and as the enemy's cannon were firing point-blank at us, the leading brigades were ordered to lie down to avoid the shot as much as possible. The intention had been to attack at the moment of our arrival, but M. d'Artagnan, who was directing the formation of the Brigade of Champagne to this end, thought it wiser to wait until almost the whole of our infantry had debouched upon the plain.

Prince Eugene, who had spent the night in observation of the supposed march conducted by M. de Coigny, was much astonished when it was reported to him at five o'clock in the morning that our army was well on its way in a direction quite opposite to that which he was watching, and that no information was forthcoming as to our intentions. He therefore directed his steps towards the high ground bordering the little river Selle, whence he sighted our column, and following up our advance, arrived at the Abbey of Denain at ten o'clock in the morning, still in ignorance of the object of our march. He remained in the entrenchments until we had crossed the bridges at Neuville, and our troops had taken up their positions in preparation for the attack.

The prince had up to then believed that M. de Villars made this manoeuvre with the object of finding some way of throwing provisions into Valenciennes, and made a remark to this effect to the Duke of Albemarle, the general of the Dutch troops, who was in command of these entrenchments. With this impression on his mind he thought Marchiennes might perhaps be endangered, and did not dream of an attack upon Denain until midday, when he saw our troops taking up their positions. It was clear to him then that he had been taken in by M. de Villars, whereupon he at once took seventeen squadrons of cavalry that were in the abbey and told the Duke of Albemarle to hold out to the utmost, while he himself recrossed the Escaut and took up a position on the high ground, from which he had a good view of whatever might happen.

He was not in a position to give any help to Denain, for his army was too far distant, and what was really wanted were troops ready to enter the place at once before our attack took place. The entrenchments were of too great an extent for the number expected to defend them, a small army would hardly have been sufficient, and the enemy had but eighteen battalions, although it is true that besides the lines of circumvallation which extended much beyond the little village that formed the abbey proper, there was yet another entrenchment into which, if necessary, this force could retire and hold out in an extreme case.

In the orders for the assault the front ranks of our troops were directed to sling their muskets and use their swords, so as to have greater freedom in scaling the parapets. Those in rear followed with bayonets fixed and took no fascines. We doubled rapidly forward to the ditch and scrambled in, with each other's aid, without meeting with much resistance or anything in the nature of a repulse, and although this was not effected without some loss, one does not wait to count the cost when one's attention is taken up with what is going on in front. When the enemy saw that we had penetrated their lines at more than one point, their courage failed them, and they retired with precipitation to their second line which covered the head of the village. Here we had to make fresh dispositions to attack them, and as they still felt themselves in a parlous state, they took this opportunity to retire along the river Escaut which runs under the abbey, in order to cross the bridge and join the seventeen squadrons with Prince Eugene.

Unfortunately for them it turned out that their baggage train, in its attempt to retire over the river during the attack, had blocked the bridge with a number o waggons and carriages; it collapsed and let them down into the river, an event quite unknown to the eighteen battalions which were effecting their retreat on this point. They had abandoned their second line of entrenchments in order to gain time to cross the bridge and destroy it after their passage, and Prince Eugene, who had foreseen that they would be ultimately forced to retire, was waiting to support them with his seventeen squadrons. But they had scarcely left their position before we entered it close on their heels, and finding no one to oppose us, we continued our advance to below the little village where the fields run down to the river.

Our troops then caught sight of the backs of the enemy, who were hurriedly retreating in the direction of the bridge, and at once opened fire upon them, which, notwithstanding the extreme range, spread such terror in their ranks that they broke into a run, and finding the bridge gone the rear ranks, in the dread of our fire, hustled those in front and forced them into the river, where they were drowned. The Escaut is a narrow river with steep banks which hold up the water, which is as deep at the edge as in the middle. In a moment they were engulfed in its stream, and all that were left of the eighteen battalions were two or three thousand men, who were cut off and made prisoners.

Among the drowned were four of their generals, who might have escaped had not the soldiers and officers, who threw themselves into the river at the same time, hung on to their chargers and dragged them under, when all perished together. These were Count Dohna, Lieutenant-General and Governor of Mons, the Count of Nassau, a Prince of Anhalt, and M. d'Herebertong. Among the more fortunate were the Duke of Albemarle, commander-in-chief, and nephew of Count Dohna, the Prince of Holstein Sickinga, the Prince of Nassau-Siegen, Count Corneille de Nassau, Baron d'Albert, the Counts of Lippe and Hohenzollern, and M. Zobel, all of whom were general officers and were made prisoners with many colonels and officers of inferior rank.

Plan battle Denain

Prince Eugene, who had seen us penetrate the entrenchments of Denain, brought his squadrons down to the riverbank to cover the retreat of the Duke of Albemarle, He had seen the troops marching in the direction of the bridge, but had not noticed them cross over. He could not divine what had stopped their progress, and in his uncertainty kept his cavalry in battle formation near the river for a considerable time. At last the enemy's squadrons, annoyed by five pieces of cannon that we brought to bear upon them, seeing no sign or appearance of any of their people, took their departure.

Our regiment remained halted and ready for action in the captured entrenchments, while M. de Villars was arranging further attacks and the cannonade on the cavalry was going on. M. de Quemin, noticing that we were doing nothing for the moment, remarked that if I saw fit he would fill up the time by ascertaining the number of men who had fallen during the attack. I willingly gave my assent, and told him that I should be very glad to hear his report At that moment an excellent Bavarian, who, though no longer a youth, was lieutenant in the company which belonged to me in my capacity of colonel, asked permission to accompany him, which I granted with pleasure, and off they both went They found no lack of material for their reckoning, and were adding a victim to their list when they heard him give a groan. A grenadier of the regiment of Guienne, who was loitering around to see if any of the bodies had escaped spoliation, aimed his gun at him, saying, with an oath, that he would put the poor devil out of his misery. Happily M. de Quemin was at hand to push aside the gun, saying, "Let this poor creature die if he must die."

The man took aim a second time, and finally M. de Quemin was obliged to drive him off the scene altogether. My lieutenant, who understood but little French, suggested to M. de Quemin that perhaps the dying man might understand German and that he would question him. As a matter of fact, the wounded man answered in that language; so the kind fellow, finding him to belong to his own nation, set to work to ask him questions. He asked him what part of the country he came from, and was told Bavaria. "Bavaria!" growled my old lieutenant.

"Would you serve against your prince? You ought to be shot. But what part of Bavaria do you come from?"

The other said he belonged to the neighbourhood of Ingolstadt.

"Who is your father, and what are your relations?" resumed the lieutenant.

"My mother," said he, "is dead, and I am the only son of an officer in the Elector's troops, who shortly after he had lost her put me to school at the Ingolstadt College. He was at the Battle of Hochstett, where he was apparently killed, for since then I never heard more of him. My relations then seized upon his goods, and left me entirely in want. When I grew bigger I knew not what was to become of me, so I, together with two of my companions, enlisted under the first officer we met."

The lieutenant was so strangely affected by this recital, without quite knowing the reason why, that the tears ran down his cheeks, and he was hardly able to utter a word. However, he pulled himself together and said, "What is your name?"

"My name is Oudesch" was the answer he received.

"Oh, unhappy creature! "cried he. "You are my son, and yet I should have watched your death without making the slightest effort to avert it had it not been for M. de Quemin. To think that you got yourself into such a position that either of us might have slain the other had the opportunity arisen, and yet now Heaven has brought us here to save your life."

This unfortunate youth—in the saddest state possible for man to be in—now experienced the happiness of finding again the father he had so long thought of as dead and gone. He was transported with joy, to which he gave the fullest expression in the cry of "Oh, my father!" and he threw himself at his parent's feet, kissing them with such ardour that one had all the difficulty in the world to drag him off. M. de Quemin came back at once to tell me of his adventure and to get soldiers to carry in the wounded man. He was as naked as when he came into the world, but the surgeon-major treated his wound, which healed shortly afterwards, and at the present time this young man is actually holding a commission in the regiment.

Immediately after the entrenchments were stormed and taken, Maréchal de Villars detached a force of forty-four battalions and several squadrons to invest Mortaigne, Saint Amand, Marchiennes, and Anzin, which on its way wiped out several small parties of the enemy holding fortified posts on their lines of communication. The large Dutch barges on the river Scarpe were also captured; not one escaped, and by the morning of July 23rd Mortaigne, Anzin, and Saint Amand had surrendered and their garrisons were made prisoners of war. Marchiennes alone, which had a garrison of six good battalions of six hundred men each and three squadrons under M. de Beroque, showed any desire to see the cannon fired, but in the end shared the same fate. The enemy's magazines in the above four towns were inspected on the 30th of the same month, together with all the captured barges. It is extraordinary to think how M. de Villars could have arranged matters with so much exactitude that the enemy had no opportunity of even throwing the supplies overboard or burning or sinking the barges; at any rate, all these magazines were of the greatest use in the sieges undertaken by us later on.

A hundred and twenty-five beautiful pieces of cannon, quite new, were found therein over and above the munitions of war and food, and it was reckoned that these captures were worth more than twenty millions. This affair, which cost us no more than six hundred men, was one of the most important and happy successes that France could have hoped to gain, under the circumstances in which she then found herself. It abruptly checked the enemy's movements at the moment when they were on the point of invading the kingdom itself, and it obliged them to retrace their steps and to think seriously of the protection of their own towns and country. One can imagine the extremity that affairs had come to, seeing that Landreci, the last town left to cover Picardy, was besieged by a powerful army, and was powerless to make a long resistance.

The Allies, by the capture of this town, would have been able to lay all the neighbouring provinces under contribution. As it was, they did not wait for this to give us an example of what they would have done under such circumstances, for they sent out a detachment, which, after having overrun part of Picardy, entered first Champagne and then the Metz country, and enforced requisitions in all the districts through which they passed. They halted just outside the town of Metz, burned the country houses of all those who could not produce money to ransom them, and traversed German Lorraine along the river Sarre without meeting with any opposition.

If it was possible to carry out such a bold expedition before Landreci was captured, what would they not have done later? We should have been obliged to concentrate all our efforts to defend the passage over the rivers Oise and Marne if we had not wished to leave the country open to these exactions; and then, notwithstanding the suspension of hostilities between France and England, the emperor and the Dutch could have dictated their own terms, even supposing they cared to listen to us at all.

The victory of Denain and its resultant successes obliged the Allies to listen more attentively to the proposals of peace which were made them in the following winter; they saw clearly that fortune was deserting them for us, and that later on they might find themselves in a less advantageous position to make terms. The losses they had sustained, and the changes brought about by them, were so great that their army was weakened by twenty-one battalions and three squadrons, without counting the troops with which they were obliged to garrison the towns we were now about to besiege. We, for our part, found in their own supplies the means for carrying on the war, we recalled our troops which held the various towns that we had hitherto feared might be attacked, and Prince de Tingry alone, who rejoined the army after the action, brought in eighteen battalions.

Our army encamped on the field of battle until August 6th, in order to decide upon our next operations, and to watch the movements of Prince Eugene. During this stay an order was issued that all soldiers who knew how to swim, and cared to dive for the bodies of their drowned adversaries, would receive thirty *sols* for each corpse, besides what spoil they might find on the same. An immense ditch of great depth and width was dug, into which the bodies withdrawn from the water, excepting those of the four generals which were carried away by Count Dohna's nephew, were thrown, a note of their numbers being taken. The reason of this was the fear lest these bodies might block up the locks at Valenciennes, on the Escaut, and their subsequent putrefaction bring about an epidemic in the town.

It was several days before we saw our baggage again, and the officers had experienced some discomfort owing to its absence; amongst them myself, who, before I got my own, was honoured by being assigned one of the most difficult and uncomfortable pieces of work possible to carry out. I was ordered to take twelve hundred men and march to Saint Quentin, a town some distance from the army, whence I was to fetch and convoy fourteen thousand sacks of flour to the magazines of Valenciennes, which were nearly exhausted. I had several days on the road before me, and lacked my cooking apparatus and other conveniences, the want of which caused me much annoyance. I had also during my long march to collect the great number of carts and waggons necessary for the transport of all this flour, exposed withal to the enemy's attacks, for they still lay before Landreci.

They were beginning to feel the want of bread, so that they would have found my convoy very useful to them had it fallen into their hands. I was so sure that I could not execute my order if they became

MAP OF BELGIUM

aware of my movements that I took the liberty of expressing my senti-ments on the subject, and they were found to justify proper precau-tions being taken.

Maréchal de Villars directed M. de Coigny, who was in command of a detached corps of observation, to cover my convoy, so that no ac-cident might happen. This precaution turned out to be of the greatest use, for the enemy took the field and did all that lay in their power to cut me off, but M. de Coigny checkmated their designs, and I suc-cessfully completed my journey. However, I did meet at one point a party of the allied forces, which had found a way through and made an attack without either pushing it home, or leaving a certain wood that they lined. They alarmed my convoy, and I actually lost three men; but these were my only casualties, and I brought my flour into Valen-ciennes, where it was greatly needed.

Prince Eugene well knew that, as Maréchal de Villars was in pos-session of Denain and all the Allies' supplies, his situation had become critical, and that owing to want of provisions he would not be able to continue the siege of Landreci; he nevertheless wished to see what could be done by drawing supplies from Brussels and Mons. With this object in view he altered the position of his lines, and placed the right of his army near Quesnoy, with the left on Landreci. But the Allies were not prepared for the necessity in which he now found himself, and could send him nothing; in fact, bread became so scarce in his army that four days after the action ammunition loaves fetched a crown each. He was then obliged to send back to Quesnoy the large siege guns destined for Landreci, withdraw his troops in the direction of Mons in order to feed them, and confine himself to the observations of Maréchal de Villars' intentions, which soon after became evident. On August 2nd Messieurs d'Albergoti and de Broglio had marched with the troops which had taken Marchiennes, Pontarche, and finally had blockaded Douai. M. de Villars sent them a reinforcement of six Swiss battalions, and on the sixth of the month he marched with his whole force to undertake the siege.

Our lines of circumvallation around the town were constructed with great care, and were sufficiently strong to resist any attack the enemy might make. One section ran along the banks of the Scarpe, another across a marsh, while a third was on *terra firma*. The trenches were begun during the night of the 13th-14th without much loss, the works progressed, and a very heavy fire was opened upon the town.

When the Allies saw that Maréchal de Villars was completely committed to this siege, they quitted their position at Mons and encamped in view of our entrenchments. Prince Eugene, after having made a reconnaissance, ordered each of his battalions to make a great number of fascines and gabions, which were stacked at the head of the regiments along the front of his army, to be used in filling up our trenches and the marshes. We had little reason to doubt, on hearing of these preparations, that we were going to be attacked, but had not much fear of the result, as our entrenchments were strong, and our army strengthened, while the enemy were in the opposite case.

It was said that Prince Eugene had really determined to attack us, that the surprise of the entrenchments at Denain had gone to his heart, and that he would have risked very much to wreak his revenge, but that the Dutch, who were meditating proposals of peace for the coming winter, opposed so bold an enterprise. Prince Eugene thus found himself reduced to the necessity of acting on the defensive for the rest of the campaign; he remained within his camp until just before the fall of the town, and on the eve of this event he struck his tents, and then set light to the piles of fascines and gabions which lay along the entire front of his army. As the night was a very dark one, this long extended line of fire looked like the "Northern Lights," and produced a magnificent spectacle.

Nothing out of the way occurred during the siege of Douai. The garrison was not large and gave us little trouble, but the fogs which rose every evening over the marsh, in which we had been working, brought with them miasma, which produced many diseases among our army, the least among them being obstinate fevers which gave much trouble in their curing. The majority of our officers fell sick, and for the first time in my life I found myself no more exempt than the rest of us. However, I paid little or no attention to it. It was simply a tertian fever, which did not prevent my doing my tour of duty in the trenches.

One day when I was there with M. d'Albergoti, who was in command, he expressed his intention of visiting our trenches and reconnoitring an outwork, which he wished to carry by assault. He had the kindness to put off his inspection until the shivering fit which had seized me had passed off, so that I might accompany him; he believed in my knowledge of fortification, and his good opinion of me nearly cost me dearly. He had taken up his position at a little opening in our trench, which exposed him down to the waist, to examine some sacks of earth which the enemy had laid along the tops of the palisades of their covered-way, when he was noticed, and directions given to fire upon him.

On such occasions one does not remain too long in a place like this, so he withdrew quickly to allow me to make my observations, but hardly had I taken his place than I was hit by a bullet, which, luckily for me, only passed through my hat and along the side of my head. I merely sustained a contusion, which instantly developed into a swelling the size of an egg. A trifle more to the right, and my fever would have given me no more trouble. I was not yet acquainted with the proper remedies, and had some trouble to get myself to try any; however, my friends persuaded me to listen to them, and I consented to take some medicine, but I chose my time so badly that less than a quarter of an hour after I had swallowed it the order came to break up the camp; the town and its citadel had capitulated, and our army was ordered off to begin the siege of Quesnoy.

The surgeon had imprudently given me this dose the very day that the fever was accustomed to appear, with the result that, after having marched a league, I was seized with a shivering fit, which upset me so completely that I thought the last day of my life had come; however, as soon as it had passed off I went on with my duty, fever and all, as if I had nothing the matter with me. I had relied a little too much upon my strong constitution. As it was, many officers fell victims to this disease, among others Comté de Villars, brother to the *maréchal*, who died on August 20th.

After the surrender of Douai on September 10th we set-to upon the siege of Quesnoy. The trenches and works made by the enemy when they took this place from us in the preceding June still existed, although the breach had been freshly repaired, which made its capture the easier for us. Our garrison on the above occasion had been accused of surrendering before the breach was practicable, and thus giving up the place before full necessity had arisen, and the same complaint was even made against the commanding officer himself, one of our lieutenant-generals, upon which the king ordered him to be sent to the Bastille. It is said that he justified himself, and that there was more bad luck than fault attaching to his particular conduct. His services had always hitherto been met with approbation, and his advancement was owing more to them than to his birth or family.

This town only held out for a few days, and we found therein the siege guns destined for the siege of Landreci, which the enemy left there when they broke up their camp.

Before the capture of Quesnoy, M. de Villars despatched a force to invest Bouchain, and in the siege that followed nothing novel happened. Quesnoy surrendered October 6th, and Bouchain October 2 1st. The enemy never moved during either of these sieges, and the season being now advanced, each side retired to their winter quarters.

The fever which I had caught before Douai nearly ruined my health. I had neglected to take proper remedies for it, and little by little it took such a hold on my system that when I was marching my regiment to Luxemburg, where we were to be quartered, I found myself obliged to stop at Méziéres in Champagne. I was told that there was a prisoner in the citadel, placed there by the king's order, who was one of the most skilful physicians in the kingdom, so I begged the Commandant to be so good as to have him sent to me. He immediately bled and purged me, and then gave me to follow an opiate compounded of cinchona bark, confection of alkermes, hyacinth, eyes of the crayfish, prepared red coral, syrup of absinthe, and *centaurée*.

This medicine, in truth, drove the fever out from me in four days, but whether I then gave way too much to my appetite, or that it was not quite wholly efficacious, I had a relapse three weeks later, and was about as ill as I had ever been before. I discarded my doctor, and the town major, who had been in the same condition as I was, sent me a man who had cured him by means of a different opiate. He told me that had I not already been bled and purged, it would have been necessary to have begun operations by so doing, but as I had been, he gave me his opiate at once. I took it in bolus form, made in bread to conceal its flavour, and I was obliged to take three pills as big as filberts every four hours.

Two hours after each dose I had something to eat, or else soup, according to my fancy. I continued to observe this treatment, night and day, every four hours, until I had taken all he gave me; if I had left greater intervals between the doses, the effect would have been far less prompt. The effect of this opiate was so excellent that I derived complete relief from the day on which I began to take it; up to then I had been consumed by a fire within me, but all at once this fire was extinguished, and I enjoyed a perfect ease.

I finally so far recovered my health that in a little while I found myself able to ride, and took the post to rejoin my regiment. Before taking leave of my saviour, I wished at all cost to obtain the receipt of his remedy, and arranged matters so well that he gave it to me in the most obliging manner in the world. I have thus since been able to render the greatest services to various persons given up by their doctors, by making them take it as a last resource. Even many doctors to whom I have given the recipe have found it most useful; some certainly thought the remedy too heating, though it always had the effect of reducing the fever. The latest trial I made of it was upon my coachman, who was attacked by pleurisy. Though he has not a very strong constitution, he was bled twelve times within a period of a few days; he took sudorifics and cordial drinks; poultices were applied to his side, and as no improvement manifested itself, the last rites of religion were administered to him, and nothing remained but to wait for him to breathe his last breath.

In such an extremity it was thought that no harm could be done in making him swallow some of the large pills of my opiate. He no sooner took them than he found relief, and as the first dose did not entirely root out his malady, he was given a second, which completely restored him, with the result that shortly afterwards he was able to drive my carriage again. I consider I should be rendering a service to those who may read these memoirs by inserting here the composition of this opiate, as perhaps the occasion may arise when they might find it of use, but it is important to observe the proportions of the ingredients as I have here noted them.

Opiate Febrifuge.

Quinquina	one ounce.
Tartre martial	half an ounce.
Theriaque, fine	two drachms.
Sel de Centaurée	two drachms.
Extrait de Geniévre.	
Syrup d'absinthe	two ounces.[1]

---

1. *Quinquina* = cinchona bark; *tartre martial* =*ferrum tartaratum*; *theriaque* = a pharmacopoeic preparation consisting of fifty-six ingredients: among these it contains opium in the proportion about one grain to one drachm; *extrait de Geniévre* = extract of juniper; *sel de centaurée* (centaury) is produced by incinerating the plant "*centaurée*;" the final product consists of potassium carbonate. The last ingredient explains itself, and is very old.
The whole is mixed in a mortar, with the exception of the syrup of absinthe, which is to be gradually added to the rest during the mixing. This is the opiate, the manner of taking which I have already stated above.

CHAPTER 13

Return to Munich

By reason of the conferences held in the winter at Utrecht by the powers interested in the war, the campaign of 1713 opened rather late in the season. The success enjoyed by France during the preceding campaign had restored her position and induced the Dutch to listen to the very propositions which they had rejected on a former occasion, and the suspension of arms with England and Portugal finally forced them to agree to a general peace. Each power sent its representatives to Utrecht, and bit by bit articles were agreed upon to regulate the balance of power. Spain was made to pay the bill for all the rest; she was despoiled of the kingdoms of Naples and Sicily, as well as the Milanese and its appertaining provinces, some island or other in the Mediterranean and Spanish Flanders, otherwise the Circle of Burgundy, almost all of which was now in the hands of the House of Austria.

The treaty was signed on April 11th by France, Spain, England, Holland, Portugal, Brandenburg, Bavaria, and Savoy, and two more kings appeared in Europe, to wit, the Elector of Brandenburg, who was now recognised as the King of Prussia, and the Duke of Savoy as King of Sicily, and later King of Sardinia. The Court of Vienna, notwithstanding these favourable conditions, did not find the treaty meet its views, refused to sign it, and the Plenipotentiary of the Emperor, Count Zinkendorf, departed from Utrecht in a great dudgeon on April 15th.

The emperor had made up his mind to continue the war, in order to exact better conditions touching certain points that concerned him in particular, so that if, after all, he was obliged to accept peace, it should not be said afterwards that lesser powers had restricted his demands. The greater part of our troops were in Flanders, and some time elapsed before they were able to present themselves in Alsace; but while the emperor was making his preparations to support his pretensions, the other powers were occupied in carrying out the articles of the Treaty of Utrecht.

The French and Bavarian garrisons left Namur and Luxemburg on May 27th, and handed them over to the Dutch, and on the 31st Nieuport was given up to the English. The Dutch also had Ypres and Charleroi given up to them in the beginning of June, whilst they evacuated the towns of Aire and Lille in favour of French garrisons. But these peaceful arrangements had no effect whatever in inducing the Court of Vienna to accept the treaty; it preferred rather to rely upon war to improve its position, and to this end collected all its forces to oppose those which France was concentrating to protect the Rhine frontier.

The first success we gained over the emperor was the capture by M. Dillon on June 24th of the town and fort of Kaiserslautern, the garrison of which were made prisoners of war. The same day Maréchal de Bezons, who had brought the army from Flanders to Alsace, invested Landau, where the enemy, seeing us about to lay siege to this town, abandoned Mannheim on account of the proximity of our army. The trenches were begun before Landau two days later. Maréchal de Villars joined the army at about this date, and took up his quarters at the house of the Messieurs Paris, in the town of Spires, until the arrival of his baggage train. Landau had a good garrison commanded by Prince Alexander of Wurtemberg, a thoroughly well-informed and very brave man, who took every possible opportunity of delaying our approaches, and carried out a magnificent defence of several outlying works beyond the main fortifications. He made a grand sortie, prepared during the night of July 3rd–4th, and fell upon our working parties the following morning, whom he drove in together with our covering troops.

Lieutenant-General M. de Biron, who was on duty in the trenches on this occasion, rallied our men and drove back the garrison in their turn, but this action cost him the loss of an arm. At last, though the garrison was so hemmed in that it became an impossibility for them to renew their sorties, they did not abate in the least their resistance at any of the points we attacked, and this would have been even more creditable had they not carried it to extremes. They put off the question of capitulation till too late, and M. de Villars obliged them to surrender as prisoners of war on August 20th.

After the capture of this place and a short rest, our army began its march and crossed the Rhine, on September 12th, at Offenburg, to join forces with the Count of Bourg. He had placed himself at the head of the body of troops with which he had driven back M. de Vaubonne, who then defended some lines constructed by the Imperialists to cover the town of Freiburg and the Breisgau. Our army arrived before Freiburg on September 22nd, and by the end of the month the trenches were begun.

This town belonged to the emperor himself, inasmuch as it was a fief of the House of Austria; it was fortified with great regularity, and its works were extremely well arranged. It is situated at the foot of a mountain upon which lie two forts, one above the other, which communicate with the town. The mountain on which lay these forts is commanded by its neighbours, but is separated therefrom by rocks and such inaccessible ravines that it is impossible to carry on breaching operations in the usual fashion. The provision of cover for the approaches presented equal difficulty, and the only way of supplying the place of trenches was by means of sacks of earth or bales of wool, which entailed much trouble and danger.

The town itself was easier to attack; nevertheless, when beginning the trenches before it, we began others in front of one of the forts, opposite a little half-moon work, which, owing to the contour of the ground, was named *Escargot* (*i.e.* snail), and was the only point by which access could be gained to the covered-way between the forts. The trenches before the town were far distant from those before the forts, thus two separate commands were created under two separate major-generals. The town was of a good size and its garrison a strong one, so to counteract any sorties the latter might make, we strengthened the flanks of our works with several good redoubts. Our parallels were of wide extent and of some distance the one from the other, and zigzag ditches were dug to maintain communication between them.

Nevertheless, we could not thoroughly batter the curtain and the faces of the polygon without first capturing the covered-way, on account of the manner in which the works of this town were sunk, and covered by their glacis. Moreover, there was another obstacle in the form of a half-moon work which covered the curtain, and the besieged had also constructed another small one of earth covering the main fortifications, all of which had the effect of somewhat retarding our works. The season was advancing, and there was the weather to be reckoned with; this town lay at the foot of the Black Mountains, and the effect of a single fall of snow would have given us the greatest trouble in continuing the siege.

It was not only the question of capturing the town, for there were the forts to be considered, which would require a siege to themselves, as the trenches we had opened before the Escargot turned out to be insufficient for the purpose. Under these circumstances M. de Villars did not think it wise to lose time in reaching the covered-way, foot by foot, by sapping work, and he made up his mind to risk an assault, though at the time we were yet seventy *toises* distant (fathoms). He ordered forty-seven companies of grenadiers and ten of dragoons, supported by the battalions already in the trenches, for this duty on the night of November 2nd.

Before the grenadiers and dragoons could begin the actual assault they had to march seventy *toises* across the open, for this was the distance between our works and the palisades of the covered-way, and, finally, effect a lodgement along the palisades, to get cover from the fire of the main fortifications. Time is necessary for such an operation and moments are worth much; during all this manoeuvre they would be under fire from the palisades of the covered-way itself, as well as from two bastions and one half-moon, which defended this area. As it turned out, before even reaching their goal in the midst of so many dangers, our people were obliged to remain nearly an hour exposed to point-blank cannon and musketry fire, bombs, and grenades, the results of which were so terrible as to defy description.

What again added to the furious and murderous character of this action was the fact that we had pitched upon the identical night for our attack that the besieged had themselves selected to make a sortie upon us, with the result that they had doubled their force defending the covered-way an hour before the moment when our people began their advance; and we thus had to contend with twice as many as we were prepared for. Although this rendered the fight more bloody, and at times even doubtful in its outcome, we at last carried the covered-way and effected a lodgement therein, and though it is true that we lost a number of men, no particular attention was paid to this.

The forty-seven companies of grenadiers were almost entirely cut to pieces, one captain only remained alive. He belonged to the regiment of Toulouse, and he escaped simply because he had the good fortune to be ordered to throw himself and party into a little earthen lunette abandoned by the enemy when they saw our troops rushing the covered-way.

By a piece of luck I saved the life of M. de Quemin, captain of our own grenadiers. I happened to be standing at the door of my quarters just at the moment when the brigade-major was passing on his way back from headquarters. He stopped to chat with me, and told me of the dispositions made for the attack that evening, that Quemin's company was among the forty-seven detailed for this work, and that he was on the way to hand over the orders to the adjutants of the different regiments affected, so that the grenadier officers might be warned in time for them to take up their posts in the trenches at four o'clock in the afternoon. I was much interested in all relating to Quemin; he was always quartered with me, and we were quite inseparable, so I took a glance at the orders for the grenadier companies which had preceded this one, and found that instead of my regiment coming on duty that day in the trenches, it was the turn of that of Boutler and not Quemin's.

I reprimanded the brigade-major for not keeping a better roster, and obliged him to go back to the major-general of the army to get the order corrected. I said nothing about this to Quemin until I felt that the major would have had time to get the change made, as he would certainly have insisted on marching to glory at any cost. After dinner I remarked to him that the issue of an order particularly affecting the grenadiers was expected that day, and, therefore, that it might be as well for him to prepare to march, as he would possibly be called upon to form one of the party; but about an hour later the major came to tell me that he had seen to the change being made, and that the grenadier company of the regiment of Saillant was to take the place of that of mine.

Next morning, as soon as daylight appeared, I and Quemin went round the trenches, and the first captain we found dead there was he of Saillant. He had been killed immediately on leaving the trench, and had never had time to get as far as the covered-way. A truce was declared that morning, from nine o'clock to one in the afternoon, for the purpose of collecting the dead. Numbers of unarmed soldiers came out from the town, who took away those belonging to them to their own side of the covered-way, there to bury them, whilst we did the same with our own. While this was going on many of the officers belonging to the garrison came up and talked to us and inquired for their relations and friends in our army.

When I was in the trenches I saw two brothers, people of quality, who were gentlefolk of Tresigny, one of whom was a captain in the garrison, the other a captain in our Bavarian troops. They stayed with me until the drums began to roll as a warning for each side to resume their places, and then it was a case of goodbye to fraternity. Almost the whole of the inhabitants, as well as the garrison, profited by this opportunity to get upon the ramparts, whence they had the melancholy satisfaction of a view of the dead, and could, moreover, examine the plan of our works, the disposition of our artillery, and our lines of attack.

After capturing the covered-way, we proceeded, by sapping work, to construct works to cover us from the fire of the bastions, which outflanked us on both sides, and a battery of twelve large guns, which had but to fire across the width of the ditch to batter in the breach. We also made along the edge of the ditch, which was full of water, a number of galleries by which fascines and hurdles could be passed along and thrown in, together with sacks of earth, to fill it up, and thus form a ramp by which to mount to the assault, when the breach should be ready for this. Just as all was completed, Baron d'Arsch, the governor, who had already been summoned to surrender, withdrew with the pick of his troops to the forts; but he was too late. It cost the inhabitants an immense sum to ransom themselves from pillage, and the governor was obliged to receive the women and wounded, whom he had left in the town at the mercy of Maréchal de Villars. The state of affairs was such that our general found that he could not afford to relieve him of this responsibility.

The capture of the town did not further matters much with regard to our attack on the two forts. We certainly had a large battery, which had been firing for some time past upon that of St. Pierre, but its position on the mountain side, separated as it was from its target by a vast chasm and the consequently long range, greatly minimised its effect. By means of sacks of earth and wool, approaches had been pushed forward up to the covered-way of "the Snail" Fort, but even if this was taken it would not mean much. The capture of these forts was rendered still more difficult by the existence of a road communicating from one to the other, by which reinforcements could be moved at will; we had a sad proof of this in an attack made by a major-general, without the knowledge of M. de Villars, before the town surrendered.

The attempt was a risky one; but this officer, thinking he had thoroughly mastered the means by which the work could be carried, took advantage of the opportunity when he came on duty in the trenches to try and obtain glory for himself, and give the *maréchal* an agreeable surprise. .He therefore made his attack at daybreak, and with merely the troops at hand in the trenches soon forced his way in and drove out the enemy. Our people worked hard to effect a lodgement and get under cover, but just when they thought they had effected this, the enemy sprung a mine beneath them, which sent our works flying into the air, and at the same moment considerable reinforcements were sent down the communicating passage, who fell upon those who had escaped the explosion, and chased them right back to our trenches. The result was that our labours were even less advanced than before this event.

The regiment of Mortemar, which occupied the trenches at the time and made the attack, suffered considerably, and M. de Mortemar received a ball in his face. The difficulties that presented themselves in the reduction of these forts seemed almost insurmountable. To make a breach appeared to be as impossible as the operation of mining, and our only hope was in starving out the garrisons; but M. de Villars thought out a way which was worth all the batteries and the most ingenious approaches put together, and which forced the governor to capitulate.

Freiburg is a place of importance to the emperor, inasmuch as it is not only well fortified, but by its situation covers the whole province of Breisgau, and it was nearly certain that by the treaty of peace which was then being negotiated this town would be secured to him as being part of his own private property. For this reason M. de Villars caused loaded mines to be laid under the foundations of the town defences in order to blow them up simultaneously, and so dismantle them as to render it as harmless as an open village. When all was ready he informed M. d'Arsch that he must at once surrender the forts; failing this, or should the siege be abandoned owing to the severity of the weather, he would not hesitate to blow up all the fortifications of the town; at the same time, if he judged it more to the interests of his Imperial master that the town should be sacrificed for the sake of these forts, which would then be useless, he was welcome to stay where he was, but the destruction that would take place would then be put down as the result of his obstinacy.

He added that he could give him but a very short time to think this over. The governor was much surprised at the line taken by Maréchal de Villars, and he asked for time in order to write to Prince Eugene. The general forwarded the despatch by courier to the Viennese Court, which, taking into consideration the great expense that it would be put to to rebuild the threatened fortifications, ordered the surrender of the forts. Their garrisons marched out about the middle of November, and the war came to an end with the capture of this town.

My duelling experiences had not yet ended. I found myself drawn into one during this siege rather by my enthusiasm for the king's service than anything else. One day when I was in our trenches the besieged did their very best to flood us out. There was a kind of dyke within the town for the purpose of holding up the water of a large stream which ran through it, and they opened the locks in this, with the result that the water actually ran into one of our parallels on the left of our attack. We had two battalions present at this point commanded by a colonel, who was seized with such a panic at the sight of the water that, without thinking of the result, he retired his men as fast as the water crept in, until he had quite deserted his post and reached the extreme limit of the trench.

I was then with my grenadiers where the sapping was going on, but hearing what had happened, I ran to the scene, where I found but little water, and no current which could make what there was there rise to any serious extent. I was extremely surprised to find that all that were left of the two battalions were a captain and two lieutenants, who told me of the panic and its result. I asked them if their men showed no signs of returning, or at any rate if reconnoitring patrols were not being sent out, and when the only reply I got was that they were all huddled up at the end of the trench without making any effort to ascertain the real state of affairs, I felt my anger with their commanding officer rise so strongly within me that I went off at once to where he was. In my excitement I expressed myself very strongly upon the manoeuvre which he had just executed without first reporting the case to the general officer commanding. I ordered the captains to march the regiment back again, adding that I regretted to find their reputations lowered by the panic of their commandant.

The colonel, seeing himself dishonoured by my taking the command out of his hands, and by the words which I had used in reference to him, made up his mind to get satisfaction from me, as the affair had immediately caused some stir in the trenches. The general officer on duty must have learned somewhat of the matter, for when I was standing by him at the time the colonel came up to speak to me, he saw him before I did, and remarked that my friend was on his way to join us, and that apparently he had something private to say to me, upon which he quietly retired and left us to ourselves. Sure enough, the colonel, on approaching me, declared that I had insulted him, and that he wished to have satisfaction; upon which I replied that he had dishonoured himself by his conduct, but that I was quite ready to give him any satisfaction he liked if he thought this would restore his reputation.

During this conversation we had gradually moved from the neighbourhood of the trenches, and found ourselves among some brushwood, where we drew our swords without fear of being seen by anyone. Besides, should anyone have seen us, there was nothing extraordinary in the sight of two men fighting at a time when one witnessed a death every moment, without paying it any particular attention. We kept up the fight for some time, and at last came to close quarters, when I threw my adversary to the ground, and made him give up his sword without either one of us having received the slightest scratch.

When we were on our legs again, the colonel did all he could to persuade me to restore him his sword, but the danger I had previously run in my affair with Boismorel was too fresh in my mind to allow me to accede to this. I put it under my coat and told him to follow me, and when we were quite near to the general officer's quarters, I sent my prisoner on to him to beg him to join us alone. The general did this without being noticed by anyone, and I handed him the sword, which he then passed on to my late opponent. My object in taking this precaution was simply that he might be acquainted with the fact of our having fought out our quarrel.

As soon as the forts had capitulated the troops were distributed to their winter quarters. The interview between Maréchal de Villars and Prince Eugene to confer as to the means of bringing about a cessation of hostilities is talked about even at the present time. The generals met at Rastadt and drew up the conditions of peace between the two belligerent Powers, which were signed at last at Baden on March 6th, 1714, and on the 18th, M. de Villars received at the hands of the late Duke de Berry the Collar of the Golden Fleece.

The war was now entirely over, and the only thought was of the reduction and alterations of the establishment of the king's troops. Peace was proclaimed, but in more than one part of the kingdom there was no show of rejoicings on its account. The exhausted state of the nation, and the little likelihood of any rapid recovery of the affairs of the kingdom, held out as dark a prospect in peace as in war.

It was four years since I had seen anything of my family; the different duties that had fallen to me had given me no opportunity of getting home during the winters, so I naturally thought that I should now be able to visit my relations, who much felt my absence, but I could not obtain any leave. The necessity of my presence during the winter in several of the towns in the neighbourhood of Luxemburg was pointed out to me, on account of my rank as brigadier in the army with which I had just been honoured.

It was known that in the agreement made with the emperor, Bavaria was to be given back to the Elector, and that therefore his troops would sooner or later return to his provinces, but the date upon which they would have to begin their march for this purpose was so uncertain that the commanding officers dared not absent themselves, so I had to stay in and about Trèves and Luxemburg until December 14th, 1714. The emperor had by that time evacuated the towns in Bavaria, and left the country as arranged by the Treaty of Rastadt; we then at last began our homeward march, and arrived there in the midst of bitterly cold weather. We found the people worn out by the subsidies they had been obliged to pay during ten years of the emperor's rule, but notwithstanding this, so great was their joy at the sight of their rightful prince, that there was nothing they would not do to show it.

The Imperial garrison was still in Ingolstadt when we arrived to take the town over, and more than fifteen days passed before they could complete some conditions which they were yet bound to fulfil. Whilst this was being done, the emperor's troops lived in the town, and our infantry were billeted among the peasants in the neighbourhood. These poor people had all my sympathy. Bread is always served out to the troops, but one knows full well that under these circumstances the soldier is not satisfied with his ordinary ration and pay, so I issued an order to those in my command forbidding any exactions from the householders with whom they lodged. The better to assure myself that this order would be obeyed, I called the mayors of the villages together, and told them that the soldiers were getting their pay and bread regularly, that I did not expect them to make any exactions, but that if they had done so or attempted to do so, the case had only to be reported to me, and I would put it right, because the Elector in returning to his country had no intention whatever of placing any such burden upon his people, who had already suffered so much in his absence.

"And as for our share in this business, *monsieur*," said these excellent people, "it shall not be said that our master's soldiers returned to their country, and were not entertained by us. We assure you that for whatever period they may be in our parishes, in whatever state of poverty we may have been left by the Imperialists, we shall do our very best to cheer our soldiers as well as ourselves. We have a good master, who will leave us to enjoy in peace and quietness the little left to us, and it is in his hands only whether or no we are soon at rest again."

As a matter of fact, whatever debts the Elector may have contracted during the war, he none the less procured relief for his people by abolishing the subsidies imposed upon them by the Imperialists, besides all other taxes, except that of the poll-tax on its old footing. They thus enjoyed an ease undisturbed by any changes in their financial arrangements, or in their coin, which maintained its currency, while the revenues of the Prince were collected first-hand, and went direct into the State Treasury.

All the fortified towns in Bavaria were evacuated by the Imperialists and handed over to the Elector's troops by February 25th, 1715, in exact conformity with the Treaty just ratified between the emperor and the King of France, and finally the Electoral Household, which for eleven years had lived dispersed, began to reassemble. The Elector himself set out from France, the Electress from Venice, and the Princes from the town of Gratz in Silesia. Before the departure of the latter, the emperor had bestowed the Collar of the Order of the Golden Fleece upon the Electoral Prince.

Their respective journeys were so arranged that every member of this illustrious family arrived in the Château of Lichtenberg, the prince's country residence, on the same day and at the same hour. The interval of eleven years which had passed by since their separation had so altered the princes that from children they had developed into men, and the Elector and Electress would never have recognised them had they not been forewarned. Their meeting was most touching, everyone was moved to tears, and hastened to express their joy and congratulations. But this was nothing to what happened when the electoral family left Lichtenberg and made its entry into Munich. The inhabitants raised triumphal arches of surprising magnificence, the whole of the *burghers* appeared richly dressed and under arms; and the illuminations, fireworks, and all forms of homage paid to their liege lord went on without ceasing for many days. Never was there such unmixed joy as that now experienced by this sovereign and his subjects.

As soon as I saw that everything was settling down, the soldiery idle in their quarters, and that my presence was no longer absolutely necessary, I asked permission of His Electoral Highness for leave to visit my own country. I took the liberty of pointing out to him the length of time I had been parted from my family and private affairs, in order to carry out my duty, and that I was probably the only officer who had spent over five years without an opportunity of seeing wife or children, or of arranging his family matters; in fine, that this had been so prejudicial to me that I begged His Highness to grant me leave to remain at home until recalled by my duty to his service.

The Elector was kind enough to appreciate my reasons, and gave me permission to remain at home as long as the peace should last, or until he sent me the order to return. I left Bavaria on June 15th, 1715, and betook myself to Bordeaux to look into my affairs. Here I remained for two years in ignorance of all appertaining to war, troops, regiment, and almost even of Bavaria itself. Most of my acquaintances who saw me thus inactive and unemployed, believed that I had quite left the service. As I did not see fit to enlighten them, they puzzled their brains as to why I absented myself for so long from my regiment, being under the impression that I was on the same footing as the officers in the French service, who when taking long leave have still to report themselves on certain occasions. I had no reason for correcting their impressions, but lived quietly and allowed them to give free vent to their imaginings as to my Bavarian business.

There was gossip in the country at this time with regard to the war between the Turks and the emperor. So few people were interested in such a distant matter that no one gave it any particular attention, and I perhaps less than anyone else, for, as I said before, I really hardly cared to talk of wars and rumours of wars. Nevertheless, this war was a fact, and the Elector of Bavaria, who was contemplating the marriage of the Electoral Prince with the second archduchess, daughter of the late Emperor Joseph, was delighted to find therein an opportunity for meeting the wishes of the reigning emperor. He therefore offered a body of six thousand of his troops to serve as auxiliaries in the army which was being sent off to Hungary, which offer His Imperial Majesty gladly accepted. So secretly was this negotiation conducted, that the news only gave our officers just time for them to prepare to march with the regiments told off to assist the emperor, and the period given them to get their carriages and baggage in order to fit them for such a distant campaign was a very short one indeed.

It could never have been supposed, taking into consideration the short time available and the distance of my present home, that I should be chosen to accompany these troops, but such was the intention of the Elector. Although certain persons, who would have been delighted to see themselves in my place, and who at all events were quite as capable of filling it, pointed out to the prince the impossibility of my accomplishing the four hundred leagues in time, he decided absolutely that I should be written to, and directed M. de Quemin, who was then lieutenant- colonel, to do this.

The difficulty of arriving in Bavaria in time to go on to Hungary was not the only one, for I had to surmount another born of chance. I saw myself upon the brink of being deprived of the post destined for me, and of seeing His Electoral Highness' good opinion of me changed for one of contempt and disgust, all owing to no fault of mine. This might all have come to pass thanks to my wife, who by her inept designs to prevent my departure tried to intercept the letter that Quemin had written me. She had heard the news before me, and this is how chance came to her assistance.

Serving with our Bavarian troops was an old lieutenant-colonel, a native of Bordeaux, who was then acting as captain in one of the regiments detailed for Hungary. Dubon, such was the captain's name, had a sister living then in Bordeaux (now at Bergerac), and, when he learnt at Munich that the order for my instant return was to be sent to me, wrote to her in the fullness of his joy of going himself to the war, and despatched it by the same courier that Quemin had employed in my case. He told her that I was destined to command the contingent, and would receive my instructions on the same day that she got her own letter. At the same time he asked her to call upon me as soon as possible, and express to me the pleasure he felt at the prospect of serving with me. This young lady did not fail to call immediately after receiving her brother's letter.

It so happened that the distributor of letters, who had received them on Saturday evening, did not deliver them at their respective destinations till Sunday afternoon. At the moment he brought mine he met my lackey at the door, just going out after his dinner, to whom he gave them, and this youth, who was on his way to join some comrades in a walk, stuffed them into his pocket and went on his way. I left the house soon after to join in a game of *ombre* with some neighbouring ladies, and it was during my absence that Dubon's sister called with her letter. Finding me away from home, she showed it to my wife, who, horrified at the mere idea of a war with the Turks, resolved to prevent the news reaching my ears; to this end she seized the let-

305

ter from the young lady, and begged and prayed her to speak of it to no one, but to return home as quietly as possible, for she feared that if I returned and found her there that my curiosity would be aroused thereby, and she finally made her promise the strictest secrecy in the matter.

She also called together all the servants in the house, and asked them all if any letter had been brought to me, but in her agitation she failed to note the absence of my lackey, who was then enjoying his walk. Having so far ascertained that no letter had arrived, she proceeded to give them notice that if the letter-carrier should bring any for me, or anyone else, she should be quietly warned and the letters handed secretly to her, and then, having taken all these precautions, she resumed her composure. As I did not return until rather late, she had plenty of time to consider the matter, but soon another trouble arose in her mind and gave her further agitation. It struck her that possibly I might have received my own letter at the time I left the house, and in order to clear up this point in her mind made much study of my physiognomy on my return, but, finding nothing disquieting there, was once more reassured.

But she was so much affected by the matter that she still wished to probe it in every direction she could think of, and for this purpose began to chat with me on current events, saying that whilst sitting by the window that afternoon, she had overheard two people who had stopped in the street below talking about the war against the Turks, and that one of them said that the Elector of Bavaria was sending troops. This she repeated several times without making any particular impression upon me; so, seeing this, she went on to say that Dubon had written to his sister, and that he was hoping for orders to go. I ingenuously replied that probably Dubon had invented the news himself over a bottle of wine with a boon companion, because if it was really true, I should certainly have heard of it, whereupon I changed the subject of our conversation.

My obviously sincere speech completely reassured my wife, and tranquillity reigned supreme in her mind, though it was not long before this was broken. We were supping a little later on, in company with one of my wife's young lady friends, when the subject of our talk fell upon letters, and then my lackey, who was present, remembered the one he had for me, which he routed out from his pocket and handed to me. I was astonished beyond measure at hearing my wife give a loud scream and seeing her grasp the lackey's arm in her attempt to snatch the letter from him, but I had it fast already, and as I did not know what to think of this exhibition of alarm, stood quickly aside and tore it open, when I read these words:

> Start by the post immediately on receipt of this, and use your utmost endeavour to report yourself here as soon as possible. You are given the command of our battalions in Hungary, which are to leave Ingolstadt on June 10th, and I trust that you have yet sufficient time to get there. I have been ordered by the Elector to inform you of these his wishes. Many people are intriguing to get the command in place of you, but I hope that your diligence will render their efforts useless, and in the meantime I am going to get your baggage train in order.

I received this letter on May 27th, 1717. The time at my disposal was short enough as it was, but travelling by post obliged me to go through Paris and Strasbourg, which added a detour of near a hundred leagues to my journey, happily, however, the days were drawing out now. Being absolutely determined to act in accordance with the Elector's wishes, the tears and remonstrances of my wife had no effect upon me whatever, and at a very early hour next morning I began my journey on a post horse. I stayed nearly an entire day in Paris, for the purpose of seeing a friend of mine and of obtaining a special order from M. de Torçy for the supply of post horses, and notwithstanding this, arrived in Munich at four o'clock in the afternoon of June 5th. I at once repaired to the palace to report myself to His Highness, as well as to thank him for all his kind thought of me. He received me most graciously, and did me the honour to say many kind things concerning my diligence, besides others concerning our Hungarian expedition with which he was sending his sons, the Prince Electoral and Prince Ferdinand.

CHAPTER 14

The Campaign of 1717 Against the Turks

This war against the Turks brought forth an immense amount of emulation among the young princes and noblemen in Europe, so that almost all the royal families sent their representatives, who came flocking in to serve as volunteers in the army. The presence of so many distinguished personages gave rise to a constant stream of wonderful stories of deeds of valour which those around them took every opportunity of publishing among their friends. Although these heroes, for the most part, could hardly have been called masters of the art of war, or their deeds anything but those of the most ordinary nature, the most usual occurrences were written up as extraordinary feats, and justice and truth were not always strictly observed.

They were so much surprised at their first view of the Turks, that they were convinced that the war against this nation was something far greater and more important than any that had been waged amongst Christians. Each one of these courtiers wrote from his own point of view, assigning courage and boldness even to those who had but played the part of spectators to the tragedy, in which others were the real actors. Perhaps what I shall report in these memoirs will hardly be as amusing as these histories, as I shall not quote any astonishing deed of this nature; I have laid down a law for myself to speak of things as they actually happened, and, therefore, I omit numberless unimportant details which have no special significance, and do not approach in importance many events which I have omitted in my account of the wars of France.

In the meantime, I will now continue my journey to Hungary, Our little Bavarian army embarked on the Danube at Ingolstadt on the precise date as foreshadowed by Quemin, all my affairs were in order, and my departure caused me no more trouble than would have been the case if I had never left Bavaria. Boats and rafts had been constructed for the transport of the troops, horses, and waggons, with so much care and diligence, that every convenience possible was found on board them. So great was the number that a very considerable fleet was the result, which took up a large space, and the sight of all these vessels was so entrancing that the inhabitants poured from the towns and villages far and wide to see us pass on our way. We stopped for several days at Vilshofen, a little town on the extreme frontier of Bavaria, in order to give time for the completion of some details before entering Austria.

We then resumed our journey as far as Vienna, where we arrived on June 24th, and camped on the banks of the Danube near one of the outskirts of the town, in which the officers of higher rank were quartered. We were now, from the time of our arrival, under the orders of the emperor, and therefore begged him to inspect us. Our condition justified the request, for never were our people smarter or in better form than they were then. The Elector's Mounted Grenadiers and a regiment of dragoons (which was presented to the emperor) which bore the title of Prince Ferdinand of Bavaria accompanied the infantry, and we should have been very sorry not to have appeared in our glory before His Imperial Majesty and the Court. He appeared to be very pleased with our request, and arranged that our review should be held on the following morning at ten o'clock, in front of his pleasure residence, La Favorite, about a quarter of a league from the town.

I had already had the honour of being presented to His Imperial Majesty and of kissing his hand on the very day of our arrival. The same honour was granted me by the empress-dowager his mother, the empress-dowager his sister-in-law, his wife the reigning empress, the two archduchesses his sisters, the two archduchesses his nieces, and the Princess Wolfenbüttel his mother-in-law, whereby I felt much honoured, for such an excess of affability is by no means usual in this court. I was also present while this illustrious family took their supper, and received every possible politeness from the great personages of the court.

When we paraded next morning in front of the La Favorite Palace, the emperor and all his court took their stand at the windows, from which they could see the whole of our army from flank to flank, and we finally marched past and made a very brave show. An astonishingly large crowd lined our route from the camp to La Favorite; all the inhabitants of Vienna seemed consumed with curiosity to see the Bavarians, whose reputation for valour stood very high with them. Our troops seemed to have a more foreign appearance in this Imperial capital than they had borne in France, and they therefore attracted the more attention; and, in truth, excited a deal of curiosity by reason of their uniforms and stature, as they were picked men. The emperor was more than satisfied, and his good opinion was more than justified by the event.

On the morning after our review we continued our march, and halted for an entire day at Pressburg. This town is situated on the banks of the Danube, in a very beautiful plain, and surrounded with vineyards which add immensely to its charms. The houses are substantially built, the streets well arranged, the inhabitants of a pleasing temperament, and almost all Roman Catholics, under their own bishop. I saw in this town a most extraordinary freak of nature, to wit, two young girls about sixteen or seventeen years of age who were joined together from their waists downwards; otherwise the rest of their forms was as distinct and separate as in the case of any other person. These twins lived in a convent, where they were maintained by the bishop, who had placed them there. He had done this to prevent their mother, who was quite indigent, from taking them round to exhibit their deformities, and because he feared that such a sight was sufficient to bring about a similar accident in the case of any woman with child.

A permit was necessary from the bishop for admission to see them, and this was granted to me and my companions. They had a sweet expression, and were quite pretty, one especially; and without thinking much about it, I gave the prettier one the little present of money that I had ready for the purpose, at which the other appeared to become quite jealous. She complained of the way her sister was made the recipient of all such attentions, but at that moment the other placed my present in her hand, and appeased her with words of consolation. The life and health of the one affected the other; it was impossible that one should experience any inconvenience without the other suffering to a like degree. I devoted some thought to the case of these girls, entering into the details that nature has subjected us all to in life—illnesses, etc.; and it remained on my mind for many days. I since learned from the *Gazette* that they died not long afterwards, one having survived the other but for a few days.

We also made a halt at Buda-Pesth, which consists of two towns separated by the Danube. It is a matter of at least three hundred good leagues from Buda to Belgrade, a fact that the geographers have never accurately marked on their maps. Here we repaired the boats and barges which formed our convoy, and which had somewhat suffered on the voyage, and finally we disembarked at Peterwardein on July nth to continue our journey by road, as the Danube hereabouts bends its course too much to make the water route worth while travelling by.

On the 12th we camped near a little ruined town called Carlowitz, where but a few remains only of its houses were left standing, and where the emperor concluded the last truce made between him and the Turks. We had a very long day's work the next day in going from Carlowitz to a little place called Szlankamen, which lay on the Danube. It was impossible to find a single spot on this road where water could be obtained; the winding of the Danube on its way to Szlankamen took it far away from our land road, and as it was absolutely necessary to have water at our camping-ground, it became necessary to regain the river in the one day. To accomplish this we left Carlowitz at two a.m., and all our men were provided with water before starting; but unhappily for us, it turned out to be one of the hottest days possible. The wind blew from the south, but it was hardly perceptible; the air was so oppressive that it affected the respiration of those even who could keep quiet and still, and a thousand times more so that of the soldiers on the march.

Our road lay along the edge of a plain entirely devoid of trees or shade, and to add to our trouble, there were cliffs on our flank which reflected a heat more scorching even than the vertical rays of the sun. Our men, who early in the day had drunk their last drop of water, now began to feel the torments of thirst; they became so exhausted that they could hardly put one foot before the other. Nevertheless, by extreme efforts they managed to complete eight hours of marching. But Szlankamen was yet two leagues distant when their strength entirely failed them, and a halt became absolutely necessary, exposed as we were to the stifling effect of the heat. A slight haze and a few stormy clouds now appeared, but as no breeze accompanied them, we obtained no relief in the state of collapse to which we were reduced. The rest resulting from the halt, far from easing our burden, rendered the condition of the men worse even than before, for they felt the heaviness and inability to breathe more than ever.

After remaining thus for three good hours, the question of resuming our march became imperative; but as soon as the men, erstwhile so robust, had fallen into their places, they appeared to have lost the use of their arms and legs; the most part fell flat down where they stood, others, after the greatest exertions, struggled forward a few paces, and finally the whole column again came to a standstill. Many were seized with convulsions as if in a fit. Such a sight was never seen, and I really thought that our infantry was doomed. We had sent on officers to Szlankamen to send back some barrels of water; but this would not have effected much relief; when suddenly some small clouds began to appear, the atmosphere darkened, and thunder made itself heard.

A frightful storm now burst over us. It was so severe that it carried away part of the bridges that Prince Eugene had built over the Danube and the Save, and sank a number of boats full of munitions of war. Even waggons drawn by oxen and horses were precipitated into the Danube and altogether carried away. This was followed by a steady downpour of rain, which restored our soldiers to life; they felt refreshed thereby, and one saw them gradually begin to revive like persons who had just returned from another world. Nevertheless, even when they were once more under way, they still bore a stupefied air, and did not finally recover themselves for several days. Five were left dead on the ground, and three others, who had to be carried into Szlankamen, died that night, and it was common belief that had not the heat been followed by the sudden fall of rain, all our infantry would have perished.

We had two more days' march before arriving at Belgrade from Szlankamen, so I went on ahead of the column to report the arrival of our troops to Prince Eugene, and to receive his orders as to our encampment. The prince received me in the most gracious way possible; he recognised me at once, and the same evening chatted with me regarding the capitulation of Ingolstadt, which I had arranged with him in the year 1704, while for many days later the subject of our conversations was a recapitulation of all the events that had happened before the date of the Peace of Rastadt. He referred to the mistake we had committed at the action of Malplaquet in abandoning part of our entrenchments in order to go to the rescue of the Irish Brigade in the woods, upon which I told him of the objection I had raised to the order given us, the severe comment of Maréchal de Villars upon this manoeuvre, and the explanation that we had subsequently given him. I continued that the man who wounded M. de Villars really won the battle, as our retreat and subsequent loss of Mons was only owing to the absence of our general. He also said that he had noticed at the time when his hussars had reported to him that the Bavarians had left their position to enter the wood that several battalions, mostly in blue uniforms, occupying a large portion of the entrenchments, took to flight immediately his infantry closed with them. We did not allow the matter to rest there, for in the course of the campaign the prince put before me many of his ideas and remarks of this character.

As I happened to have been in most of the actions he referred to, I was enabled to supply him with many details, so that these conversations gave pleasure to him as well as information to me regarding many points that none could tell me better than he. Having ascertained in the course of our talk that I understood the art of fortification, he gave me the order to visit and report upon the entrenchments he had made to ensure the safety of his camps, and to devote my attention to them generally.

Our troops planted their camp colours on July 16th, and were posted in the first line of the Emperor's army, which was surrounded by circumvallations, as a defence against the Turks should they attempt the relief of Belgrade, and lines of contravallation to keep off the garrison, which was a very numerous one. A corps of Ottoman troops had been pursued by Prince Eugene at the beginning of the campaign, and had retired across the Danube to escape the clutches of the Imperial army. It then threw itself into Belgrade, under its Seraskier Pasha, and so raised the garrison of this town to more than thirty thousand strong.

The town of Belgrade is situated in the angle formed by the confluence of the rivers Danube and Save. The Danube runs west to east, the Save south to north. One flank of our lines rested on the Danube, the other on the Save, thus enclosing the town with lines of contravallation, and presenting a front to the open country with those of circumvallation; our army lay between these two lines, at each end of which were bridges over both rivers, the Danube on our right, the Save on our left, with *têtes-du-pont* in the form of strong redoubts. Besides these there were advanced posts occupied by troops strongly entrenched, which protected the approaches to these bridges, our foraging parties and convoys, that on the Save, near a little place called Semlin, and that on the Danube was constructed on an island called Donauwitz.

Thus we surrounded Belgrade on the land side. Besides this we had nine well-armed frigates stationed on the Danube, above and below the town, not only to protect our transport shipping from attack by the Turkish *caiques*[1] and galleys, a great number of which were lying in the port of the town, but also to prevent the enemy maintaining any communication by means of the river. These frigates, by forming a barrier across the river, not only protected our bridges, but also prevented any attempt by the Turks to ascend it from certain posts which they occupied below Belgrade; and they formed a line like a well-armed wall that the *caiques* dared not approach, except perhaps by keeping close to the banks.

Several other frigates were placed to support a post near Orsova below Belgrade; moreover the Turks were not alone in possessing *caiques*, for we had several, well armed, for the purpose of fighting theirs. Thus no precaution was omitted for the investment of this town. The Turks, however, had managed to maintain their hold upon an island in the Danube, between the town and that of Donauwitz, which was rather an inconvenience to the bridges. Here they had entrenched two thousand men, but no great difficulty existed in attacking them, nor could they easily obtain aid from the garrison.

These people had plenty of opportunities in their favour had they known how to profit by them, but then they would have had to understand war as it is waged in Europe; they were in no real need of help, for their garrison was strong enough to keep us easily at arm's length, and even perhaps to force us to give up our enterprise. The advantageous arrangement of their fortifications should have enabled them to torment us with sorties, for the approaches to the town were easy to defend on account of two large suburbs, called *palankas*, which dominated the enceinte, one lying on the bank of the Danube, the other on that of the Save, and they had only to construct good entrenchments in front of these two suburbs and support them with the numerous garrison at their disposal. With these and all the galleys now lying in the port, the river-side portion of the town could be rendered safe from attack.

Thus the landward side only was the important one to defend, and that was not a difficult matter, after certain entrenchments and advanced works had been constructed, which would necessarily have to be forced before the attack could be made on the body of the place, all of which would have cost us much time and untold loss.

Belgrade lies in an amphitheatre, and consists of an upper and lower town. The upper town which faces the land side is fortified with a number of works without any method or regularity, having been con-

---

1. Turkish rowing boats.

structed as the necessity arose on the occasion of the various attacks the town has been subjected to in times past.

Otherwise these fortifications are very well built, with good dry ditches and counterscarps and strongly palisaded covered-ways, besides which their power of defence is increased owing to the cross-fire from one to the other, thanks to the irregularity of their position. The lower town is also well provided for, notwithstanding the absence of any elaborate fortifications, as the upper town commands it, and the number of galleys and *caiques* it gives cover to is sufficient to cause great difficulty in approaching it. Moreover, it is so thoroughly commanded by the upper town that, if it were taken, there would still be plenty of work to do to effect a proper lodgement therein, and carry out an attack upon the entrenchments that could be made dividing the two towns.

Independent of such entrenchments as could be made by the Turks in front of their Palankas, and on the ground covering the upper town, they could have yet made others across the Save opposite the lower town and its *palanka*, with a bridge to communicate therewith. They should have placed a body of troops there, which would then have occupied the very ground across the Save, which we ultimately made use of in our attack on the lower town and part of the upper, and which turned out to be the only possible way of effecting a breach. If this ground had been rendered defensive, their town would have been protected from our first approaches, or at all events we should have found ourselves obliged to force such entrenchments before anything else could be undertaken, and this would have entailed a regular siege, which would have delayed us enormously.

This entrenchment on the other side of the Save would have been of additional advantage to them, as it would have facilitated their sorties in the direction of Semlin, and interrupted our communications over our bridge on the Save, used by our convoys and foraging parties. But owing to want of experience they did not profit by their opportunities, for they left the ground open to us; there we opened our first trench and planted some good batteries, the cannon of which swept the lower town across the Save with shot and shell, and ultimately brought about the reduction of the place. They had had, moreover, plenty of time and people to put the defences of Belgrade into the state I have spoken of before we had made our own dispositions.

The corps of troops that Prince Eugene had driven before him when he crossed the rivers entered the town on June 18th; provisions

PLAN OF THE BATTLE OF BELGRADE

and munitions of war were not wanting to them, for they had abundance of both, besides artillery; one hundred cannon were counted on the ramparts and about eighty on the *caiques*, so that they had nothing to do but to make full use of all these advantages. They had certainly dug an entrenchment before the upper town; but it was not only badly designed, but was also limited in size, being only just sufficient to encamp within it the troops they were unable to find room for in the town itself. Another and still less important one in front of the *palanka* on the Save side was exposed to the fire from our batteries in the trenches along that river, a state of things that would never have arisen had they occupied that section of the field I remarked upon above.

Our Bavarians now found themselves fighting with the Imperialists, who gave us the heartiest welcome that could be imagined. All the troubles and differences that had existed between us for nearly twelve years were now forgotten, and the sole aim of each one of us was to celebrate the joy and satisfaction we all felt at our reconciliation. Our troops were an important addition to the Imperialist forces; they had a great opinion of us, and their generals showed this by entertaining our officers of higher rank for several days in succession. Our two princes were given important posts in the army, not only on account of their birth, the most ancient in the world, but because of their troops, the most important of the Allies present. The Electoral Prince had his own regiment, which I had the honour to be colonel of, and Prince Ferdinand his dragoons, which bore his name. The latter also held the rank of major-general of the Empire, and both these princes, who ranked in all respects as high-born volunteers, were distinguished above all those who were granted leave to hold this position.

The garrison of Belgrade awaited the advent of the Ottoman army of relief with as much anxiety as if it was in no wise able to defend itself This army appeared to be a formidable one, for according to rumour it should have consisted of at least three hundred thousand men, and the besieged seemed to rely so much upon it that they never dreamed of making a proper use of all the resources they had at their own disposal. Perhaps it was just as well for us that the infidels were thus so sure of our certain destruction by the host that the Turkish Emperor was sending to them; for had they believed in the necessity of defending themselves without any prospect of succour, they would soon have found a way to profit by their position, if only by means of persistent sorties, which would have been most inconvenient for us.

This they did not abstain from altogether, but it was nothing in comparison with what they could have effected, considering the possibilities they enjoyed. One attempt only could be reckoned as a true sortie, which, owing to our over-weening confidence, we drew upon ourselves, and which did us much harm. The efforts they made at the beginning of the siege, when we were at work on the lines of contravallation, had but little effect, as our works were confined to the town or land side. They merely pushed some troops into the outskirts and gardens in no particular formation, who did not come sufficiently in touch with us to produce any serious fighting. The only result was the exchange of a few shots with next to no loss on either side; and their manoeuvres in no way prevented us from continuing our work.

They acted in a similar manner on the Danube, armed twenty to thirty galleys and *caiques* and attacked some of our ships, but when they neared the latter they slackened their pace and contented themselves with loud cries and plenty of noise, and finally, after much powder had been burnt, retired without gaining any advantage whatsoever. After several other such skirmishes the garrison made a really important sortie, which, owing to our carelessness or the contempt their conduct had produced in our minds, led to a bad result as far as we were concerned. It was directed upon the trenches we had begun beyond the river Save.

As soon as we appreciated the fact that the Turks did not intend to occupy that part of the ground, and found that the width of the river would not prove an obstacle in battering the lower town, we designed a winding trench which would give us a covered-way to a point opposite it where we could plant our batteries. The place selected was a most advantageous one; all the town which lay on the gentle slope of the amphitheatre was disclosed to us; thus to bombard it was easy, as well as to pick out the magazines for our target. At the same time one flank of the upper town defences was exposed to our fire, though at rather greater range. It was therefore resolved to make our principal attack in this direction, although the only way of reaching the positions destined for our batteries was along a narrow tongue of dry land which ran along the river-side. This strip was enclosed by large impassable marshes which occupied a part of the very fine plain to which it led.

The post of Semlin was upon the high ground above the plain and marshes, and was apparently quite near enough to the part where we placed our batteries to give them protection, notwithstanding it was separated therefrom by the marshes. As a matter of fact, communication between them was impossible except by going a long way round to avoid the marshes, or by way of the tongue of land. This was an important consideration in the case of an attack upon our works, for we were thus unable to send any prompt help either from our army or from the post at Semlin, and it therefore would have been absolutely necessary to have a considerable body of troops on the spot to cover our working parties, at all events, at the beginning of the operations; but that was just what we lacked.

However, ground was broken on July 16th, and by the end of the first day a very long trench was dug without any interruption on the enemy's part. M. de Marçilly, major-general in the emperor's service, a Frenchman who had left his country by reason of some affair of honour, had the conduct of these works, with about two thousand infantry to support his working parties, and about three hundred cavalry, who were posted where the strip of dry land gave upon the plain. The Turks contented themselves the first day with watching us from the higher ground of *palanka*, which was just opposite our works, the river being between us, from which they could count us man by man; and they decided to drive us back the next day if we did not add to our strength at this point.

No one thought of reinforcing our post the following day, necessary as it really was, for as the work developed a greater number of infantry were required to occupy it, but M. de Marçilly was again sent to continue the operation with the same number of troops as before. The Turks did not fail to observe this fact, and knowing exactly not only the number of our men, but also their position, prepared to attack them. To this end they threw across a corps of infantry by means of their *caiques*, part of which were landed well below where our works were, and out of sight of our people. The rest, with some cannon, were then rowed up the river until they arrived opposite us, where they took up a position ready to support the attack in case of need.

When all was prepared they suddenly rushed at us sword in hand, in no formation whatever, uttering the most frightful yells, and then threw themselves upon our people, whom they completely surrounded, front and flanks, with the result that all, excepting some few who happened to be more in rear and who took to their heels in time, were slain and decapitated, including poor M. de Marçilly. The little cavalry detachment was ready at the first alarm, but had hardly moved a pace in advance when a cannon ball from one of the *caiques* carried away their colonel. He was the only son of M. Heyster, a marshal in the Imperial service, who was serving with the army. The lieutenant-colonel, however, led them on, but the Turks, who never stay long upon one spot, and who carry out their designs with great promptitude when once they have taken them in hand, had made off, laden with the heads of our people. According to their custom, a *ducat* is given for every Christian head brought in by their soldiery, which profit tends to animate them in the fight. Thus they cleared our trenches and regained their *caiques* before our cavalry had a chance to interfere with them.

This was the only important action that this strong garrison engaged in from the time it was shut up in the town till the occasion on which they finally left it. This mishap interrupted our operations but for a short time; troops and workmen were sent there the very same day, but much more care was taken, and the Turks did not dare to put in an appearance again. As we gradually approached the position in front of the lower town the ground widened out more and more, and we strengthened our works with some large redoubts, proof against the cannon of the upper town which commanded us, and kept us under a perpetual fire. We continued our works as far as the junction of the Save with the Danube, so that our frigates and armed *caiques*, which were lying on the latter river, were enabled to co-operate with us in case of need.

When we had thus ensured the safety of our position and constructed our batteries, we dragged up twenty-six large pieces of cannon and fifteen mortars which opened fire on July 22nd. Our particular object was to dismount the enemy's cannon, which much annoyed us, and to raze their parapets and defences, so that the town was subjected to a constant bombardment. Four other pieces of cannon were brought up the next day to effect a breach in the lower town, which opened fire with similar vigour, and the bombardment was kept up until the 28th of the month. The advanced parties of the Ottoman army of relief now began to appear, and we somewhat relaxed our attacks in order to observe their movements. Report still told of a strength of three hundred thousand men, and this made us take all precautions against an assault upon our entrenchments, for we had no reason to doubt that they would attack us as soon as ever they had concentrated their forces, according to their usual custom.

The Turks in all preceding wars against the Empire had always given battle on the first opportunity, or at all events, if they foresaw a minimum of difficulty attending it, and then, if they lost the day, they immediately retired and made off to their own homes. If victory declared itself in their favour they would then make an extremely rapid advance, not employing themselves as is the custom in Europe in discussing camping-grounds and strategy, for they believed that the only way to make war upon the Christians was to strike a blow as rapidly as possible.

It was a relief to think that their enormous armies are not composed of regular disciplined troops, for had this been so, Christianity would have been in the greatest danger, as it is, the *janissaries* from a regular infantry point of view, and the *spahis* as cavalry, form but a small proportion of their whole body. The rest of their troops are a mob collected from the populations of the vast territories of the *grand seigneur*, which the viceroys or governors of the various provinces, who are called *seraskiers*, *pashas*, or in the case of Tartary, *kams*, are required to gather together on the order being given them, and to maintain them during the campaign, which is usually quite a short one. Each of these viceroys or governors furnishes a contingent in proportion to the extent of territory under his rule, and marches it off to join the army at the time and place notified in the order sent him; thus the Ottoman Court is saved all trouble concerning mounting, arming, clothing, or pay.

As one can easily imagine, these troops are ignorant of all discipline, and are neither armed nor trained sufficiently well to make a stand against a regular force. Their only chance of success lies in superiority of their numbers or some chance accident, in which case the Turks prove themselves more dangerous than other opponents; they are so active and charge with such impetuosity, though without order, that it becomes impossible for an army which once shows its back to them to save itself by flight, or in any other way. They are most expert in the use of the sabre, those they have being usually of very excellent quality, and such is their skill in its use that, should their opponents give way before them, they produce an incredible carnage in the shortest possible time. Their other arms vary according to the nations composing their army; some carry muskets like the *janissaries*—in the case of the people called Arnauts they are long in the barrel, and carry far; others throw javelins with great adroitness; some are armed with bows and arrows, whilst some again use "couples," which are a species of lance or half-pike.

The mounted men are armed with short muskets, as well as their sabres, but none carry pistols. There is no uniformity whatever in their clothing. The *janissaries* and most of the Turks wear large heavy turbans, long robes, and very wide breeches fastened round the ankle. Others have them very tight on the leg below the knee, a coat half-way down the body, and very scanty turbans indeed. Some have but a jacket only reaching to the belt of the breeches, the sleeves of which are tight fitting and so short that their arms are bare to the elbow; their breeches also stopping short at the knee, their legs and arms bare, and with the little red cap on their heads, these look for all the world like galley slaves. Others, again, are clad in rags and tatters, with a rather scanty mantle only reaching half-way to the ground, which they twist about them according to the weather.

Their faces and complexions are as varied as their clothes. The Turks of Europe and part of Asia are fine, well-built men, good-looking, and as often fair as dark. The Tartars are small and ugly with sallow complexions, and inhabit the northern territories of the *grand seigneur*, whilst the Arnauts are swarthy, with little hair or beard. Regarding those who inhabit the southern regions—from Erzeroum, and on a line drawn through Aleppo, Babylon, Jerusalem, Bussora, Medina, Mecca, Arabia, generally on to Egypt as far as Barca and Algeria, and all the other tributary countries of the Empire—I can only say that their complexions are of a more or less olive nature according to the climate of their country.

In fine, the army that was threatening us was composed of a collection of human beings as different one from the other as there were varieties in their arms and clothing, and one might say that all the nations were represented from the Arctic to the Antarctic Circles. These troops for the most part were divided into separate small companies; each company has its own little standard, and the officers and soldiers composing it camp together under the same tent, like a short tower with a pointed roof, held up by a large mast-like pole. The *pasha* usually pitches his tent in the midst of the troops belonging to him; and thus a Turkish camp becomes an assemblage of groups of tents of all sizes according to the numbers of individuals collected by each governor. These tents and flags are of all colours, so that at a distance their camp has quite the appearance of a gigantic flower-bed full of every kind of blossom.

The tent of the grand *vizier*, who is also *generalissimo* of the army, is pitched in a place apart from the rest, and owing to the different rooms it contains, is of vast extent. It is elaborately decorated with golden and silk embroidery of varied design, and its beautiful appearance is only equalled by its great value. It comprises a very fine entrance-porch, a magnificent reception apartment of fine proportions, and a little court most artistically rendered, at the end of which the *vizier's* own tent is erected. This in itself contains various chambers and cabinets, and has behind it another court, round which the principal officers of the household have their lodgings, and, finally, further in the rear is a spacious square wherein are situated the kitchen and servants' quarters. The whole is of the most effective workmanship, enhanced by the many coloured materials used in its construction. Numberless waggons are needed to move this vast palace, and it takes five hundred men to pitch it.

Each of these nations are fed in a different fashion. That of the Tartars, perhaps, has the merit of at least being the most convenient in form, the only provisions carried by their soldiery being cheeses made of mares' milk. As soon as these cheeses are made they are buried in the ground and kept there for six months, when they become as hard as a stone. When required for use the Tartars scrape a little into a pannikin of water, stir it up with their finger, and swallow the mixture, which is as white as milk and constitutes their only nourishment. If we could all exist on such food, what a deal of trouble would be spared the world in general! I must now return, however, to the history of the siege, from which I have digressed to relate these details, which, I think, are worthy of notice.

On the approach of this formidable army of Turks many cannon were brought up to furnish the parapets of our entrenchments, platforms were constructed for them, and in one place and another we had seventy pieces in position. We made *banquettes* along the whole extent of the parapets, so that our troops could fire over them, and garnished the banks of the ditches of our entrenchments with *chevaux-de-frise*. Finally, several small advanced works were taken in hand in the direction of the Turkish camp to flank our entrenchments, and a great many scythe-blades and spikes were placed along the top of the parapets to hinder an escalade.

All this work was completed as quickly as possible, the idea being that as soon as the Turks arrived they would reconnoitre our entrenchments, and that the very next thing would be that we should find them swarming to the assault. Our thoughts might have been rather gloomy had we reflected upon the host of *infidels* now about to attack us in front as well as their troops garrisoning the town, who could assail our rear at the same moment. The whole strength of our army was but ninety thousand men, supposing every man to be present, but we had to deduct those garrisoning far-off posts that we had captured, the troops on board the ships, and those occupying the trenches. To add to our trouble, dysentery had incapacitated many of our people, so that when the Turkish army made its appearance we had not fifty thousand men with which to oppose it.

Withal, we were in such a position that we found ourselves obliged to risk an action against an incredible number of opponents without any possible chance of avoiding it. Shut in as we were between two lines of entrenchments, we could not disentangle ourselves by means of a retreat, and meeting them in the open would have been still more dangerous.

Several of the Turkish advanced parties made their appearance on July 28th, and were followed by others during the next day, who took up a position on the high ground before our camp, but beyond the range of our cannon. Soon afterwards a great number of their mounted men rode towards our entrenchments, apparently to reconnoitre, and to familiarise themselves gradually with them; they even came within gunshot, caracolling all the while, but never for long on the same spot, and made signs as if defying us to come out and exchange shots with them. They let their horses go at such a speed that we could hardly believe it possible that they could check them, even right up to the brink of our ditches; but so skilful was their horsemanship that they stopped dead there, and in an instant after had turned, and were dashing round back to the rear again.

As they wheeled round they discharged their muskets at us, holding them in one hand, and shouting in a loud voice, "*Allah! Allah!*" This exhibition of riding, and the challenges thrown at us, so excited some of our subalterns, cadets, and volunteers of a lower grade who had followed the army with the idea of getting employment therein, that they left the entrenchments on foot, and posted themselves in groups in order to open fire upon these caracollers. Both sides acted as though they were playing a game, without doing each other much harm, and we spectators enjoyed the play as much as they did.

The enemy's army continued to increase during July 30th and 31st, and finally encamped, full in our view, along the surrounding heights, on which the multitude of parti-coloured tents made a charming picture. As fast as the *infidels* arrived, the number of caracollers in front of our entrenchments increased, and the country around was also full of scattered men, doing nothing apparently except trying to find something to make the time pass. These were apparently officers, for their turbans and robes were much cleaner than was usual among their soldiers, and they were mounted upon excellent horses.

For the first few days our army was kept in fighting formation in rear of the parapets, in readiness for the attack that we were convinced was going to take place on the enemy's arrival, and as soon as one of these caracollers appeared on the scene our people opened fire, and both parties amused themselves in this way from morning to night. Cannon also were fired at them, and as these braggarts were constantly appearing, and were relieved by others, there was a continual rattle going on which helped the performance of the comedy, but had no other importance.

The Ottoman troops were all encamped by August 1st. Their camp was very long and deep, and formed a complete half-circle around our lines of circumvallation, so that our army was entirely invested. The Turks had scarcely settled themselves down before they began to construct a long and deep parallel between them and us, to protect their camp, and to strengthen this they added to the central portion facing our camp an immense oval entrenchment, with a good high parapet and a number of embrasures for cannon. This oval fortification was on as light eminence which commanded us and served them as a citadel, while the line of entrenchments upon which it was placed, and which extended right and left of it so as to shut us in, had smaller fortifications at each end, but nothing comparable to the central one, which they made their principal depot for their magazines and stores.

The reason why the Turks paid so much attention to all these precautions was that a rumour of the same nature was current among them as obtained with us; we had believed that they would attack us immediately on their arrival, and they believed that Prince Eugene would leave his entrenchments, and attack them as soon as they came in sight. They had indeed intended to attack first, but after reconnoitring our lines, they found them too strong to carry by assault, and as they did not wish to run the risk of any failure, they took the precaution of making this fortified parallel to deprive us of the chance of rushing them, in case we decided to attempt it. By this they not only neutralised our fortifications, but shut us up within them, and reckoned upon being able to blow us into the air by means of mining operations, for they finally resolved upon making approaches with trench and sap in regular siege fashion.

These measures were by no means badly planned, and were doubtless the outcome of wise counsel, and it is certain that had these people shown as much skill in the art of fighting as they did in the arrangement of their works, they would have utterly destroyed our army, and not a man would have escaped to tell the tale. All Europe knew of our trying situation, thanks to the news sent home, which represented our case to be even worse than it was, and we were looked upon as doomed men.

The greatest interest was taken as to what means Prince Eugene might employ to extricate us; much discussion arose both for and against the boldness of his tactics, and the issue was awaited with impatience. Prince Eugene alone remained unmoved by all this: it was not the first time that he had waged war against the *infidels*; he knew their limitations, and that the opportunity for him to strike his blow would assuredly come in time. He was waiting to see whether the enemy would not first commit themselves to some line of action more detrimental to their cause than that he had himself already planned, when he would take advantage of the situation to attack them.

As soon as the general saw the barrier the Turks had raised, he realised that they did not dare storm our entrenchments, and that they had some entirely different manoeuvre in their mind; and having no longer any fear on this point, he determined to make the best use of the time at his disposal. To this end he resumed the siege of the lower town, under the very eyes of this formidable army, with as much energy as he had shown before its arrival. He caused the trenches to be reoccupied and furnished in every way which would hasten on the work; the battering of the proposed breach was carried on with all possible vigour, and the shells caused terrible havoc. He even went further, and ordered trenches to be opened before the upper town, which had not been begun before the arrival of the Turkish Army, in order to occupy the attention of the garrison, and still further to complete their investment.

In connection with this we attacked a small fort which lay in a marsh, and took it by storm on August 4th. We then attacked the post on the island opposite the town, which consisted of a star-shaped entrenchment held by two thousand men. General Merçy, who had been detailed to command this expedition, had a fit of apoplexy at the very moment it started, but as he recovered himself in a short time, the movement was continued, and he was at the head of his troops when they carried this post by assault at practically their first attempt. The Turks defending it abandoned their position the moment we closed with them, in order to seek the safety of their boats, which were moored along the bank in case of need, and took refuge in the town.

This island had protected a number of boats used by them in maintaining the command of their part of the river. It was also useful to them as a point from which they could threaten our bridge over the Danube below it, by launching fire-boats full of combustibles and fitted with grappling hooks to hang on to it, and set it on fire, which, however, they never succeeded in doing.

Since the arrival of their army these attempts had become more frequent; they thought it would keep us so occupied that we should never dare to attack their island fort, and, on the other hand, that they would be able to clear the river, destroy our bridge, and open up a free communication between it and Belgrade. The *infidels* therefore were quite taken by surprise when they saw us advancing to attack the island on August 11th, at a moment, too, when they thought themselves safe from any such thing. We only had three thousand infantry and three hundred and fifty cavalry, owing to our deficiency of transport, to attack two thousand Turks well entrenched. They ought to have made a fine defence, but they deserted their post to save themselves in the town; and more than five hundred of their men were killed or drowned before they ever reached their boats.

The garrison, by our capture of the Star Fort, now found themselves entirely confined to the limits of the town wall. They dared not show themselves outside, nor even on the river-bank, which was too exposed to our fire. We also took the native suburb, or *palanka*, which lay on the banks of the Save close up to the lower town, where we were at work on the breach, thus giving us a direct road to the point where the assault was to be made; and we seized an eminence, crowned by a mosque, near the upper town on which we had already broken ground, which enabled us to make better progress with our trenches and advance our approaches.

But the progress we had made against the face of the lower town by means of our trenches, and the mortar and cannon batteries that we had in position across the Save, was far more considerable, for being now able to destroy any of the buildings at will, we had gradually ruined almost all the magazines the enemy had in that quarter. I had the good fortune to send one of the largest of these flying into the air on the day on which I was on duty in the trenches, when I held command there as major-general in the emperor's service, the rank of my predecessors in this duty. This magazine was really a laboratory full of sulphur, pitch, loaded grenades, match, shells, and all sorts of explosives. It was impossible to check the conflagration which took place during the entire day: the sulphur and pitch gave it renewed force, whilst masses of loaded grenades and shells added their explosions to the continual din.

I had this command on August 4th, and before taking it over I went to receive my orders from Prince Eugene. The prince was good enough to tell me that his mind was quite at ease now that my turn of duty had fallen upon this particular day, for the Turks had placed two large pieces of cannon near a certain tower in the upper town, which had silenced five of our batteries already, and no means of remedying this state of things had yet been found. These two cannon were so completely masked that our gunners could find no mark to aim at, and it thus became absolutely necessary to construct another battery to bear specially upon that flank of the tower near which they lay; and as I understood better than anyone else how this could be carried out, he hoped that I could arrange this whilst I was in the trenches.

This order gave me extreme pleasure, and on arriving at the trenches I saw too well the truth of his statement; I found there one of our batteries in the greatest disorder, the cannon of which had been dismounted by our own gunners to save them from actual destruction by the two large pieces in the town. These men came up to me to point out the devastation that had taken place, and the further dangers that awaited them if something was not done, and asked that a number of workmen should be sent to heighten the parapets of their battery and to strengthen them against the fire of these cannon.

Then the engineers arrived on the scene, asking for an equal number of workmen to raise *epaulments* and deepen their trenches and saps so as to give the approaches that lay between the Danube and Save more cover, and according to what each one asked for I should have needed double the number at my disposition to satisfy all their demands. I was not unaware of the fact that the gentlemen of the artillery are not always in agreement with their brethren in the engineers as to the employment of the working parties, and that they get hold of them on their respective accounts whenever they can if they have any works in hand. To avoid this, I told them that I was responsible for the affair and would see that a just division should be made of the labour at our disposal, which would content everyone, and that all they need do was to second my efforts; meanwhile I should go round and look into the whole matter.

I began by making a reconnaissance of the neighbouring ground, and finding a place which entirely commanded the flank of the tower which had caused us so much damage, I traced out there a battery for ten cannon, and set as many workmen to work upon it as were necessary to finish it. I then inspected the work which the engineers had in hand, and after having calculated the number of workmen that they required, I told them off to their duties, and even then found I had some left over. I gave my personal attention the whole night through to our new battery, so that by break of day it was ready to open fire, and shortly afterwards the enemy's two great cannon, which had annoyed us so much, were dismounted before they could make any effective reply.

I at once reported this to Prince Eugene, and informed him that all was quiet again in this quarter. The prince came himself, about ten o'clock in the morning, accompanied by all the distinguished volunteers in the army, to inspect the construction and effect of our new battery. He was most content with what he saw, and with the gracious air which always accompanied his praise, made me most complimentary remarks in the hearing of our Bavarian princes, who were delighted to hear such praise given to an officer belonging to their troops in the presence of such a gallant company. These young princes, owing to the chances of the last war, had never before seen an army in the field, and were so full of enthusiasm that they took a personal part in every operation, whenever or wherever it took place. Their only wish was to see their troops distinguish themselves above all the others.

Besides, it was not surprising to see such noble sentiments evinced by the offspring of Roman emperors of the House of Otho, who had had the power to nominate the Pope himself, whenever the See became vacant. How could they, descendants from such heroes and at the head of the most important body of auxiliaries in the army, possibly have an ignoble ambition? This desire for distinction took such a strong hold upon them both that whenever any notable action occurred between the Turks and the officers of the army, other than those belonging to their own troops, they would lament over their own lack of a similar opportunity.

I had already noticed on several occasions how greatly this feeling had affected the Electoral Prince. On one day in particular, when I had the honour of dining with him, mention was made of a captain in the regiment of Hesse Cassel, who had withstood an assault on the redoubt which formed the *tête-du-pont* of our bridge over the Save on

July 14th. A hurricane had broken and carried away the bridges, and the Turks, profiting by this, attacked the redoubt with a considerable force. They advanced with much energy and confidence, as they were aware that there was no possibility of aid reaching it, and had actually forced their way into the redoubt, but this officer, with his sixty men only, made such a surprising resistance that he repulsed and slew a great number of them.

Those present at table did not fail to do full justice to his bravery, and as they were recounting the details of the action, I watched the prince's face. He seemed mortified, and could not refrain from saying that the action would have appeared a much finer one to him had the captain belonged to his own troops, and that he would have given anything if that had been the case. I at once took the liberty of remarking that had his troops had the good fortune to fight in times past under His Highness's eyes, he would remember many an action having taken place far more noteworthy than that under discussion, and that he need have no doubt as to their valour and reputation, their sole desire being an opportunity to prove this, and that, according to all appearances, the campaign was not likely to come to a finish before His Highness would be satisfied on this point.

I argued justly, for never was a prince more thoroughly pleased than he was during the general action in which he could see his troops acting alone, detached from the rest of the Imperial infantry, deciding the day in favour of the Empire by means of incredible valour, which was published abroad, and applauded by the emperor and the whole of Europe.

Our batteries were quite safe from attack, since the Turkish guns had been dismounted, and they continued the work of creating a large and wide breach in the wall of the lower town next to the native suburb. Our shells for ever ravaged the town, and no house or mosque of any size was allowed to escape destruction. Almost all the magazines had by now been destroyed, excepting the powder magazine, which contained an infinite number of barrels, and which the besieged had taken every imaginable precaution to protect from injury. But it often happens that, in cases deserving such extreme care and attention, the grave fault of omission is committed, and this happened to the besieged in the removal of the powder from the magazine, which was quite bomb-proof owing to the depth of the subterranean chambers in the form of which it was constructed.

It happened one day that a leaky barrel caused the formation of a train of powder leading from the interior of the magazine to the last door outside, without its being noticed by those rolling it along, and this communicated with the powder inside as if it had been laid on purpose. One of our shells, which then chanced to fall just outside the entrance, set light to several barrels standing there, which in their turn lighted the train, and thereby the magazine, which flew skywards with such a terrific explosion that it even created a panic in the enemy's camp outside.

I was at the time in my tent, together with several officers, and so great was the shock that we all thought an earthquake had taken place. This occurrence completed the destruction of the lower town, which now presented the appearance of a mass of broken stone and piles of debris of all kinds. All who happened to be in this quarter were buried under the ruins of the houses, and it is said that more than four thousand persons perished by this single catastrophe. The Turkish array, scared by the great detonation, and unable to realise its cause, left their camp and opened fire with the whole of their artillery, to let the besieged know that they were under arms and ready to fight, for they had an idea that the noise they had just heard was a signal of some kind made by them. They advanced right up to our lines, and great numbers of their caracollers rode along our entrenchments making absurd demonstrations with loud shouts of "*Allah! Allah!*" but finding no sign of movement amongst us, they returned to their camp again. This terrible occurrence happened on August 14th, two days before the battle.

Whilst our attack on the Lower town was being so vigorously pressed, our trenches in front of the Upper town were also being pushed forward, so much so, that all was in readiness to begin breaching operations to bear there, but the same facilities did not exist for this as in the case of the trenches across the Save. The cordon of works with cannon which annoyed us even in our camp, had to be destroyed first, during which operation, on August 6th, a sad accident befell Count d'Estrades, lieutenant-general in the king's army, and mayor of Bordeaux.

Prince Eugene was on that day making an inspection of the trenches then opened before the town, with the princes and noble volunteers following in his train according to their custom, and whilst he was observing the progress made in the new works, a cannon ball from the town broke the leg of Count d'Estrades. This nobleman had accompanied Prince de Dombes to Hungary, and was riding with the staff of Prince Eugene. The same cannon ball carried away the heel of one of Prince de Dombes' pages, who was as close to him as Count d'Estrades himself, but notwithstanding the danger he had gone through this young prince showed not the slightest trace of emotion. The count's leg was amputated and possibly recovery might have ensued, had not his excitement, on the eve of the battle, brought on an attack of fever, when his wound took a turn for the worse, and he died two days later.

CHAPTER 15

Return to Belgrade and End of War

The siege of Belgrade was carried on under the eyes of the Otto-man army with as much order and regularity as if the latter had not been present, but at the same time we did not fail to take every pre-caution to prevent any sudden surprise. Our troops were continually on duty on the ramparts, to observe the movements and works of the Turks, for the knowledge of their capricious and impulsive method of attack, when in an instant they are just as likely to rush upon one with an army corps as with the smallest of detachments, obliged us to hold ourselves ready from one moment to another.

Their tactics, however, turned out to be altogether different to what we had expected, for it seemed that the grand *vizier* was afraid to do anything precipitately, in case he should suffer similar misfor-tunes to those of his predecessor. He had amongst his army certain renegades, skilled in the art of war, who gave him advice to which he acceded; they knew well the resistance we were able to make behind our fortified and carefully constructed entrenchments, and they coun-selled him to run no risks in attempting to turn us out on the spot. They pointed out to him that it would be necessary to open trenches, and to attack us exactly as would be done in the case of regular siege operations, and when he had sapped his way to our trenches he should construct a series of mines to blow up the entire camp at once, and should then, when all was consequently in confusion, dash forward to the attack, and victory would not fail him.

The idea in this scheme of thus neutralising our parapets was quite excellent in principle, as the affair would then turn upon a ques-tion of numbers, in which they were so superior, and what between those in their army and those in the town we should have been quite overwhelmed. It would also have been in their power to keep a large corps in reserve within their oval entrenchment, either to give support in case of need or to cover their retreat if they were not successful. The method of attack was sure, and would have succeeded had not the position we found ourselves in, owing to their works, obliged us to leave our lines and attack them ourselves. The following describes how they set to work.

When they had completed the long parallel which invested us from flank to flank, and well garnished it with artillery, they began, under its protection, to construct a number of sap ways from their oval redoubt in the direction of our camp. As soon as they had dug their way a short distance, they made fresh and spacious parallels, which served them as points for assembly, and to cover their further operations; thus they approached, protected from our fire, and without fear of sorties. So extended were their works that it became possible for them to produce a force therefrom with a front consisting of twenty thousand men, besides which their workmanship was marvellous. We watched their progress from our ramparts day after day, and kept up a continual fire, but this did not incommode them much, as they kept themselves well buried in their trenches. Little by little they neared our ditches, and we began to find that we ran more risk in showing our heads above the parapets in order to fire upon them than they did. Never before, in all probability, has a besieging army ever been seen in such a case, besieged in its turn, and by the same methods.

In fact the conditions were more favourable to those investing us than to us who were besieging the town. They hardly lost a man during the progress of their works, had no need of cannon or shells for breaching our ramparts, and had no complicated advanced work or covered-way to deal with; consequently their arrival at our ditch was an assured affair. For our part, the nearer they approached us the greater was the danger that we ran, because when once their trenches had arrived to within gunshot of our entrenchments, the fire that they kept up to cover their workmen prevented our people showing their heads, or even arms, to return the compliment, or, at all events, without exposing themselves to a considerable degree, because the nearer they approached the higher our soldiers were obliged to raise themselves in order to fire down upon them.

The Turks had, moreover, taken care to place nearly two hundred pieces of cannon along the length of their grand parallel wherever there was a rise in the ground, or in their entrenchments which communicated with it, and all this artillery produced a cross-fire which annoyed us terribly. Their cannon balls fell in showers throughout our camp, and striking the ground, which owing to the heat was extremely hard, rebounded into the air time after time, finally falling as if from the sky, and owing to their erratic course, fell into many a place hitherto supposed to be sheltered from them, but which now turned out to be as exposed as any other.

Each regiment worked hard in the position it held to place itself under cover from this cannonade, which began at break of day and did not finish until dark; heavy *epaulements* were raised opposite the enemy's batteries, but the balls, striking the earth often as not, bounded over them, and caused us much loss. We were almost all of us exposed to this danger, for it was impossible to say which place in the camp was the safest, and it practically became a question of chance. I had had a place dug out for me as a shelter wherein I was dining one day with some officers as guests, and when dinner was cleared away we left the table and sat down in some chairs close by.

A cannon ball, which had already ricocheted several times, landed right in the middle of the table, and then flew on its way beyond without hurting any one of us. Another struck the ground in the midst of five of my servants, and continued its course among my horses picketed nearby, but did no harm whatever. But there were others which passed close by me and left their traces, as in the case of a corporal who had his head taken off by one at the very moment that he was speaking to me. On that same day an officer who was riding past from headquarters stopped for a moment to speak to me, when a cannon ball carried away the quarters of his horse without its rider coming to any harm whatever. Another ball rolled between me and four other officers, who were out walking together one evening, without touching one of us. Three soldiers also were struck down together by a single ball, just as I was about to move them to another part of the parapet.

The greatest risk I ran was at a place where our infantry were lining the first *banquette* of the parapet, but I was lucky enough to catch sight of the ball ricocheting towards me; during its passage it entered and upset several soldiers' tents, the fall of which caught my eye, so that I had just time to throw myself on one side, but an unhappy soldier standing close by me received it full in his chest. Another day when I was below, on the second *banquette*, two soldiers were sitting side by side on the one above with their backs against the parapet, their heads showing perhaps an inch and a half above it, when a ball tore away the earth just at this point and the tops of their two skulls, and then passed exactly over my head, covering my coat with the brains of these two unfortunates. To record all the accidents of this nature would be impossible, but I wished to note those from which chance had saved me, and, after all, I was no more exposed to them than anyone else.

At nightfall the crashing of the bursting shells took the place of cannon shot; they threw them at us at all possible angles, and at no fixed spot, so that it was a pure chance where any one of them fell. Prince Eugene's quarters were not exempt from them, for one of his cooks had a leg blown off, and it was deemed wiser therefore to move them further to the rear, and to a less exposed position. Almost all the regiments struck their tents and took shelter behind their parapets, to which they had added *epaulements* to gain more cover; but there was a likelihood that this game could last too long, for ever since August 3rd, up to the day of the battle, our time was entirely occupied in seeking shelter from the rain of shells and cannon balls.

The fatigue of this, added to the intense heat and poisonous atmosphere, weakened our army more and more. The Turks were quite aware of this, as from time to time they received among them one or another of our Christians, who deserted in order to deny their own faith, and who at the same time informed them of the ravages in our ranks caused by dysentery and the terrible fire of their artillery. They reported that our camp was nothing better than a hospital, and that when the Turks had taken it, they would have to throw the whole into the river to avoid infection.

Although we had two hundred pieces of cannon in our entrenchments, which kept up a fire almost all the day long, their effect was almost nil. Our batteries were not on an equal footing with those of the enemy, for their camp was beyond the range of our cannon, and ours was too near their batteries to escape annoyance. The total number of cannon in position on both sides, including those of the town, in our trenches, and on the ships and galleys, amounted to nine hundred pieces, and their incessant fire would have been a pleasure to witness had it not been for the danger which accompanied it. All these batteries formed a circle around us, and it might have been said that they were purposely arranged thus to celebrate some rejoicings, so great was the order shown in the succession of their volleys.

For fourteen days did we suffer the fearful whistling of the cannon balls, but this was only a prelude to some greater event which the near approach of the *infidel's* trenches seemed to portend. We had so far no notion of their real intentions, and the strength and excellent condition of our own entrenchments rendered our minds quite easy should they attempt an assault.

The approaches and trenches by means of which they had worked up to us had given rise to the belief that their design was to cover themselves from an artillery fire, and thus gain a position close to our ditch, which done, some fine morning at break of day we should find the whole of their infantry swarming out therefrom to the attack. In this expectation our infantry had never left our ramparts since these trenches had appeared near us. It never entered our heads that they intended pushing them up to our ditch, thence to undermine our parapets in order to blow us into the air, when their entire army would be ready to fall upon us, sword in hand, and take us by surprise in the confusion that would inevitably occur.

Prince Eugene inspected, at least once a day, the entire circuit of our entrenchments, and watched the Turkish works for any indication showing an opportunity of which he might take advantage. I admired the patience of the general on these occasions, when he was accompanied by all the princely volunteers and the distinguished people in their train. Whenever he stopped to make an observation, these illustrious volunteers, in their ardour and curiosity, pushed themselves forward to get into the best place from which they could see what had attracted the general's attention, without noticing that they crowded past him and blocked his view; whilst he, for his part, waited patiently until they had satisfied their curiosity before he moved forward to look into the matter. This inspection took place daily from August 3rd to 16th, with no further casualties than those occurring to Count d'Estrades and Prince de Dombes' page.

Prince Eugene, seeing that the Turks had closed in upon us until they were only the distance of a pistol-shot from the brink of our ditch, and that our soldiers could not show their heads above the parapets on account of the fire from the trenches, now judged it time to take in hand the danger that was threatening us. It was no longer a question of relying upon our entrenchments, as their tactics would render them not only useless to us, but even a hindrance. The evil was urgent, and would have been past remedy had we delayed any longer the expedient of leaving our lines to give them battle, because there would have been hardly distance enough left between our ditches and their trenches for us to get into fighting formation.

The prince made his usual inspection on August 15th, and having seen the urgency of our case stopped at ten o'clock in the morning at the section held by our Bavarian troops, which was just opposite the centre of the *infidels'* works, their strongest point. Count Thaun, lieutenant-general in the emperor's army, had dug a trench in the earth close under our *banquette*, roofed it with his tent, and had taken up his abode therein. Prince Eugene entered this, and as the day was that of the Feast of the Virgin, had Mass celebrated, after which he entered into conversation with some of the generals and tested the opinion of each of them.

At that moment I happened to be on the *banquette* behind this tent in ignorance of what was going on, when one of these general officers left it, came up to me, casually remarked that the Turks had now got very close to us, and then went on to ask me what I should do if I was in command. I said at once that I should have made a sortie and fallen upon them two days ago, and that the case seemed to me to be very pressing indeed. He left me a moment later and re-entered the tent, the occupants of which remained therein for some time longer, by which I then saw that something important was being discussed, and that I had been questioned purposely. When he came out again he came up close to me, and whispered in my ear, "You will have your wish!"

That afternoon Prince Eugene summoned all the senior general officers of his army to his own quarters, where he held a Council of War. It was decided that our army should the next night leave camp by its various exits in order to take up our line of battle by daybreak. Orders were drawn up regarding the details to be observed in the attack, and were sent in writing to all commanding officers. I received mine between six and seven o'clock that evening, according to which all our troops were to begin to pass through four of the exits leading towards the enemy's flanks at midnight precisely, that is to say, by the two on the right and the two on the left of our line, with the least possible noise.

Each brigade was told off to the particular gate it had to leave by, that furthest on our right being assigned to the cavalry of our right wing, the infantry of the latter leaving by the next in order, which was nearer the siege works of the Turks. Similar orders were given to both wings, and with respect to the two exits on our left. After passing the gates the infantry were directed to turn and defile up the ditch, those on the right of our camp to their left, and those on the left to their right, so that these two columns might meet and form up opposite the

338

centre of the Turks, taking up their fighting order between our ditches and their trenches.

It was of vital importance that our infantry should be in position before daybreak, because it would have been quite impossible to have accomplished this defile in sight of the enemy, as their proximity and our exposed flank would have led at once to a passage of arms; therefore success could only be secured under cover of darkness. It was also noted in these orders that there was no reason to suppose that the *infidels* expected a sortie on our part, and that we should not be observed by them, provided that no manoeuvre was attempted which would discover our march; moreover, that we could hardly mistake our way, as we had the edge of our ditch as a guide, which was not to be left under any consideration; and, further, that when our two columns had effected their junction and taken up their battle formation, they were to remain halted and in their places until daybreak, in order that the attack might be made with greater precision.

The cavalry was ordered when the infantry was in position along the entire front of Turkish trenches to proceed well beyond the enemy's flanks, so that when the infantry attack was delivered at daybreak it should make a simultaneous onslaught and carry disorder among the unsuspecting Turks. There was to be no drawing of rein or slackening of fire, the movement was to be ever forwards in the direction of their great oval entrenchment, which it was absolutely necessary that we should carry by assault; for in this only lay our salvation, and as soon as we had captured it we were to see to the holding of it, rather than to be led far afield in a pursuit, as therein lay the key to victory.

One noted in these orders that the fighting position of our Bavarian infantry was still the same as on the ramparts, namely, exactly opposite the centre of the Turkish works, the point at which the *infidels* were sure to offer their greatest resistance. No thought had been given as to which quarter the moon happened to be in; if it had been up our army would have been utterly lost, but it happily set before midnight. The sortie that we were about to make was absolutely a case of conquer or die on our part, for if we had got the worst of it we had no chance whatever of withdrawing. The Turks are so marvellously quick and agile in their sabre charges, that if we showed the slightest sign of giving way before them, our destruction was assured.

We had already cautioned our troops against being scared by the yells they make in battle, and gave them to understand that the Turks only had recourse to this method of frightening their enemies because they themselves realised their own want of courage. We also warned them to reserve their fire, because as soon as our enemy saw that we had discharged our muskets they would avail themselves of their greater skill in the use of the sabre to throw themselves upon us, and we should be cut down before we had had time to reload.

On the other hand, it was necessary to maintain a steady unwavering advance upon them, with bayonets fixed, without regarding their terrifying cries, and finally that all depended on our composed and collected bearing. We further impressed upon them that the slightest slip on our part would not escape their notice, and that steadiness and an unswerving advance were essential to our success.

All our commanding officers realised the importance of the work in hand. We were about to attack a formidable army, fifty thousand men of which (for the most part *janissaries*) were occupying the trenches in front of us. These troops were supported by the whole of the remainder of their force, which could easily be moved in a very short time to the point of attack, while, should they be driven back, they had their great parallel with its fortified oval redoubt to retire on, which a small body of troops could hold against an entire army. To surmount this formidable array of obstacles we had but a force weakened by furnishing the various detached posts we had to occupy, the fatigues it had gone through, and the ravages caused by dysentery.

In fact, all we could muster for the sortie, counting cavalry as well as infantry, only amounted to between thirty-five and forty thousand men, leaving five thousand in our entrenchments to oppose the garrison of Belgrade, should it attempt to attack our rear during the night. This garrison alone, almost equal in strength to our army, could have penetrated our lines of contravallation in a moment, for the five thousand men we left in camp to defend them were in no way sufficient either to occupy them or to make anything of a stand against thirty thousand. It might have been taken for granted that the garrison would turn out at the first signal from their army, and having soon captured our camp, would proceed to attack our rear.

We should never have been able to withstand both these attacks without falling into confusion, even if we had time to offer any defence at all, for the surprise would have been too great, and owing to the encouragement mutually afforded by the enemy's two armies, not a Christian would have been left between them to tell the tale of our defeat. The *infidels*, who are accustomed to travel vast distances when they have won a victory, would then have overrun all the Empire, and the safety of Italy even could not have been guaranteed.

This, then, was the state of affairs when we found ourselves staking all on one cast. We fell into our places behind our entrenchments before dark, to obviate confusion as much as possible, the leading regiments close up to the gates, with the remainder in rear according to their places in the column, and as soon as all were covered we ordered our men to sit down to wait till the time came for moving out. This was a most excellent arrangement, for if we had postponed the parade any later, we should hardly have been able to have carried it out, so dark did it become when the moon set. In the dark it is necessary to tread on the heels of the men in front to follow correctly.

I lay down on a little straw at the head of my men whilst we were waiting to move out, and, as no one made the slightest noise, fell asleep for a moment or two; but the sleep that comes over one on such occasions, whatever the storytellers may say, is never a very tranquil one. I had already taken the precaution of seeing that my canteens were well filled with provisions, including plenty of wine, which were then packed upon a horse so that they might follow me. I have always taken care to do this, finding it to be of the greatest use on all occasions of the sort, but perhaps never more so than on this day, for after the battle everyone suffered from hunger, and still more from thirst, and many officers of rank who had not shown the same forethought were much relieved to find that I had wherewithal to minister to their needs.

At last the hour named arrived, and the four columns began to move, but we did not find the order of our march to be as easy as we had imagined, for it so happened that the cavalry column, which took a wide sweep outwards so as not to impede our infantry, who were making for the edge of our ditch, found its passage barred by a ravine which ran up towards our entrenchments. It was therefore obliged to skirt the ditch where the infantry should have marched, and as this passage-way was so narrow that few could pass at a time, some were obliged to wait whilst others pushed on to be first, and the result was delay and confusion. It took so long to get past this point that daylight began to appear before we had all left the entrenchments and recovered our places in the column.

We then fully believed that there was no further hope for us, for how could we possibly move with an exposed flank along the enemy's works to take up our proper position in front of them? They were not a pistol-shot away from the edge of our ditch; the daylight increased, and there seemed to be no doubt but that they would discover our march, and then profit by the position of affairs to signal to the garrison, who would reply by making a sortie upon us. As it was, we were within a hair's breadth of our ruin when we found the hand of the Almighty extended to help us.

Scarcely had daylight begun to appear, when an extremely dense fog arose, the first we had seen since we pitched our camp. As the light increased, so did the fog; it enveloped us as in a cloud, and although it rendered us invisible to our opponents, we could see about ten paces in front of us. This divine assistance was of far greater use to us than the obscurity of night would have been, for the noise caused by our march was converted into a smothered sound, which, as they saw nothing and knew how close they were to our entrenchments, the enemy imagined must proceed from behind our parapets, whereupon they opened a terrific fire through the fog, with the result that a continual stream of missiles were rushing just over our heads.

The whistling created by this hurricane of balls and bullets was so vehement that it could not fail to cause some fear. It really seemed as if they were all passing close to our ears, for we had no idea whether they were actually aimed at us or not. The particular position that I was in was far worse than that of the men on foot, for I was on horseback, as is the usual custom among the commanding officers of foreign troops in action, and had the shots been aimed the least bit lower, I should have been the first to have caught them; as it was, my horse was so frightened at this continuous rattle that he kept his head turned away from it close to his side.

Yet that strange fate, which either lets us go scot-free or nullifies every precaution we may take decreed that one of our colonels and the lieutenant of my own company, who was marching close alongside of my horse, should fall at one of the first of the enemy's volleys, whilst I, who, humanly speaking, ran far greater risk than they did, received no hurt whatever, either then or during the battle, which lasted for six consecutive hours.

Although the fog did not last very long, the action began before it had cleared away; but this was owing to an accident. The Maréchal de Palphy, who was superintending the right wing of our cavalry, was marching it forward to gain the flank of the Turks when he met with a long trench lying across his path that they had constructed during the night, and which he had been unaware of owing to the fog. He was on the point of dashing into this when his cavalry was subjected to such a heavy fire from it that they were obliged to fall back, after losing a great number of men; he, however, continued his advance later on more in the direction of the enemy's camp. A portion of our infantry wing, which outflanked the front of these works, moved to the support of General Palphy, and the action gradually became general in the obscurity of the fog.

The Turks, owing to its density, were unable to grasp the situation, and fired away in front of them without seeing a single person to aim at. We, for our part, contented ourselves with occasional discharges from small groups, sufficient only to maintain our communication with each other, and which, delivered, as they were, right in the faces of the enemy, scared them to such a degree that they fell back in confusion to seek cover in their trenches. Whilst we took advantage of this by seizing and occupying several of their saps and trenches, the fog lifted as rapidly as if a curtain had been drawn at a window, and allowed us the sight of the finest day one could have wished for. Upon this the Turks, still in disorder, and seeing our troops advancing upon them front and flank, determined in aspect and with unbroken ranks, were seized with the fear of being surrounded, for our army had all the appearance to them of being more numerous and imposing than it really was.

Then their troubles increased, for far from attempting to restore order in their ranks, they rushed first to one trench and then to another, firing at random in a way that enabled us continually to gain ground. However, as there was a very considerable distance to cover before all these works could be cleared and their great entrenchment reached, it was highly important that they should be kept on the move. Our Bavarian infantry, being opposite the centre of this network of ditches, were exposed to a merciless fire, and owing to their position, were called upon to make the greatest efforts to force all these works in detail, and thus indeed decide the fate of the battle.

As soon as the fog had vanished, and the Turks had gained a clear view, they poured a terrific fire upon us, which killed a number of our people, but in no way checked the ardour of my men; they made use of a most varied assortment of weapons, for javelins and arrows accompanied the bullets that fell amongst us. Being mounted, I attracted their special attention, and, moreover, in my red coat, I doubtless appeared in their estimation as a person of importance, for one of their number, a man of great stature, hurled a javelin at me, which passed close by my side and buried itself in the ground. I had it brought to me, and having sheathed my sword, carried this javelin for the rest of the day. I also had the luck to notice in time a *janissary* kneeling behind a ditch in order to take a steady aim at me, owing, no doubt, to my horse and red coat. I had just time to turn my charger sufficiently to escape being hit when at the very same moment an arrow grazed my shoulder and pierced the arm of a soldier in one of our rearmost ranks.

Our situation was a trying one, as we were only able to advance by forcing and carrying by assault a succession of trenches, of which there were a great number occupying a wide extent of ground, before arriving at the great battery. This obliged us to appear in the open time after time to contend with opponents who were under cover, and who, consequently, had every advantage over us. Such was the lot of the Bavarians throughout the whole battle, which could be well compared with the experiences they underwent at Schelemberg. But what will seem to be really extraordinary is the fact that this body of infantry, occupying a central position in our line of battle, fought single-handed and unsupported except by one battalion of the regiment of Hesse Cassel, drove its way through the Turkish lines to the foot of the great battery, and then, after halting for a moment to re-form, stormed, took it, and planted the Bavarian colours in this stronghold, and finally had to wait until the unharmed and slow-moving Imperial infantry had joined them.

One would have naturally imagined that the right and left of the line would have advanced in a similar manner, and thus have supported our flanks; as a matter of fact, not having anything like such difficulties to deal with, they could easily even have got on ahead and forestalled us. However, it was not only quite the other way, but one of their generals did his best to delay us at the very beginning of our advance, and if we had obeyed him, the Turks would have had an opportunity of remedying their disorder, taking up the offensive, and defeating us.

Our Bavarian troops, before the fog disappeared, had already made a beginning by capturing several trenches, so that when it became clear they were discovered to be quite separated and well in advance of the remaining battalions.

The general officer commanding this section of our line had actually taken the precaution of covering the front of his own infantry with *chevaux-de-frise* without allowing them to leave the counter-scarp of our ditch, as if he himself dreaded an attack on the part of the Turks; and when he saw us thus detached he despatched his *aide-de-camp* with an order for us to return and rejoin him. I felt that this order must have been dictated by reasons of which we were ignorant, and that it was obligatory to obey it, so I checked my men in order to file them along a trench in this direction; but as soon as the Turks caught sight of this movement, they left their cover, and with fearful yells, prepared to charge down upon us. Seeing this, I re-formed my force in its original position to resist this attack, whereupon they at once re-entered their trenches. The general, thinking we had no intention of rejoining him, sent his *aide-de-camp* a second time to repeat the order with an earnestness which convinced me of the importance of acting upon it.

I again, therefore, began to move my men towards the point named, when the Turks at once prepared to resume their attack. I then saw that the manoeuvre which we were desired to carry out would undoubt-edly be very prejudicial to the end we had in view, and that we ought, on the contrary, to devote our energy entirely to keeping the enemy for ever on the move by constantly pressing them in what order we could. I re-formed my men a second time just as the Turks showed signs of making their sortie, and was preparing to advance when the *aide-de-camp* appeared for the third time with the same order, annoyed that it had not been already obeyed; but I no longer saw it in his light. I told him that he could inform his general that I possessed Prince Eugene's written instructions as to what I had to do, and that these were not that we were merely to hold a defensive position on the edge of our ditch behind *chevaux-de-frise*, for by this means we should never drive the enemy out of his trenches, and still less carry the great entrenchment by assault as he expressly ordered should be done.

I further told him that he could remain where he was as long as he saw fit, as we would form a *chevaux-de-frise* to protect him, and I then resumed our advance with all the eagerness in the world. This, then, explains how it was that our infantry fought unsupported, excepting by one battalion of the regiment of Hesse Cassel. Their uniforms were blue like our own; they followed our steps without flinching, and, indeed, never left us.

It took us four long hours to fight our way from trench to trench, so great were their numbers and the extent of ground they covered. Our colours waved before the eyes of the generals, and distinguished volunteers and, in fact, the whole army, alone in the midst of the smoke and storm of shot; at one moment they were swallowed up in the trenches, and the next were seen rising beyond them, always advancing and ever gaining ground from the Turks. This sight filled our princes with a great joy, though the uncertainty of the outcome might well have caused them to hesitate to show it.

We received no help from anyone in this rough work, though I ought to give a word of praise to the dragoons and *cuirassiers*, who, as soon as they saw us engaged, left the left flank and found a way across a large number of trenches, in order to form up in our rear and act in support of us. The dragoons of Wurtemburg were the first to arrive; they deployed into a solid and deep line, which in its turn was prolonged by the cuirassiers. But this reinforcement hardly eased the efforts we had to put forth to maintain our advance, as we now had to level passages for the cavalry at every trench we took by throwing the earthen parapets into the ditches to enable the horses to cross over. Although we only profited by their presence, the labour incurred thereby was a pleasure to us, and they seemed to infuse our Bavarians with a greater spirit of emulation than ever.

Although these were really very fine troops, they found themselves unable to take as active a part in the work as we did; still they were always at hand and ready to be made use of as a last resource. At last we found that we had worked our way right up to the foot of the great oval entrenchment—the key of the Turkish position—wherein all those we had been driving before us had taken refuge, supported by the whole of the rest of their army.

This fortification lay upon a slight eminence, at the foot of which it was possible to attain some degree of cover from the enemy's direct fire, and so close up were we that their cannon hardly annoyed at all. When clear of the trenches, I called a halt to examine the position and form up our men. Whilst this was going on I employed myself in reconnoitring the lateral lines of their great parallel; these I found to be strongly held, while a large plain in rear was covered by the whole of their cavalry, which was neither in rank nor in any order at all customary with regular troops. They nevertheless formed an immense line, with a front four times as long as that of our own, which could have completely surrounded our army if the Turks had had the courage to come out and fight in the open.

This horde of cavalry had a savage look about them, especially the Tartar portion, which was distinguishable from the rest by its shabby appearance. It made no movement whatever, contenting itself only with shouting from time to time, "*Allah! Allah!*" And although these piercing yells from a multitude of throats made a din too horrible for words and sufficient to reach the clouds, it had no effect upon our men, who by this time were quite accustomed to this sort of thing. I also noticed some of their principal officers riding up and down in front of their troops at full gallop, flourishing their sabres and calling upon their men to follow them, but not a man stirred; whereupon they would raise their arms to heaven to show their grief and despair at not being supported by them.

The *infidels* were so panic-stricken that they no longer appreciated their own strength, and everything appeared so desperate and terrible to their vision that they dared not approach us. It was only owing to the existence of their last lines of entrenchments that the two hundred thousand men who composed the Turkish Army now held out at all. They showed by their bearing that at our first attack they would give way as they had done from their trenches; and from that moment I reckoned upon our certain victory. However, the short time we halted came as a ray of hope to them, and they reopened a very heavy fire and renewed their cries, but happily almost all their shot passed over our heads.

At this moment an officer of the janissaries, who doubtless imagined that our ardour was burning itself out and that the entrenchments had frightened us, climbed up upon the parapet of an embrasure, flourishing a huge sabre to encourage his people; but he had but a short time to inspire them in, as I had him fired at, and he was instantly killed. He was one of the finest men that I have ever seen in my life.

Just as this occurred a lately appointed Imperialist lieutenant-general, who knew none of our officers, came up to where we were, and as he saw me at the head of our infantry and imagined I held some important post, he addressed me with the inquiry as to who was in command of the Bavarians. As I noticed that he spoke rather excitedly I did not see fit to satisfy his curiosity at once, and only replied by asking him if he had anything to report.

"What do you mean?" cried he in a passion. "How are you going to answer for all the disasters you are bringing about? By pushing on like this you are exposing the army to a total defeat!"

"It is quite open to you and the rest of the army to be as far to the front as we are," I replied; "we have paved your way so far, and if we could have reached this point surely you could do likewise, and follow a finer example than you have set."

It was now perfectly obvious to me that we could not expect to receive any further assistance, and that we should have to finish single-handed the work in hand just as we had begun it I therefore at once dismounted, and we forthwith began the assault of the great entrenchment. The Turks now immediately redoubled their yelling and howling, but nothing shook the determination of our men; they took no notice of the risks incurred, one and all furiously clambered up through a hail of shot and fire, and we finally threw ourselves into the work with such rapidity that the Turks were seized with a panic and took to flight. I ought to say, however, that, when climbing up the parapet, I caught sight of a line of Imperialist infantry approaching from our left in order to join us, and at no great distance from us, but those on our right on whom we had been ordered to retire did not put in an appearance for some time after the flight of the Turks.

As soon as we had gained the interior of this great work, we lost not a moment in turning its cannon upon the enemy; I had them served with cartridge and ball as promptly as possible, and we had no sooner begun to effect this than I saw the grand *vizier* himself, halfway between the spot where we were and his camp. He had halted with a large group of officers formed in a circle around him, as if he was holding a council of war. Here, I thought, was an opportunity for showing a piece of politeness by saluting the generals before attending to the rank, and file, so as soon as the first cannon were loaded, I had them laid and fired upon this distinguished assemblage, with the result that one ball alone diminished their number by three, who were left dead on the field.

This group was so astonished to find their own cannon opening fire upon them that each individual straightway fled at the top of his speed in the direction of their camp. Then with this fine example before their eyes, their cavalry and infantry did their best to follow it by the same road, and this scattered mob of troops made off at such a speed that they soon became completely lost to our view. I took care, however, that they should have a constant accompaniment of cannon shots to attend them in their flight, which were fired at random among them, and I have no doubt that the whistling of the balls added strength to their legs and put more life into their movements. My charger now arrived, led by the drummer to whom I had handed it over at the time of the assault, and I was riding around to superintend my soldiers in their novel work as artillerymen when an officer came up to tell me that Prince Eugene and the princely volunteers were coming our way.

I advanced to meet him, to take over any orders he might wish to give me, but the instant that he halted, the Electoral Prince pushed his way through the crowd, fell on my neck, and did me the honour to kiss me in the height of his joy with inexpressible tenderness. He almost had tears in his eyes. Prince Eugene was good enough to add much praise to the caresses of the Electoral Prince, regarding the part we had taken in the course of the action. Whilst these compliments were being showered upon us, an Imperialist general arrived on the scene so full of what we had done that he broke in upon what the Prince was saying in order to explain the success of the Bavarian troops, to whose undaunted conduct he attributed the success of the battle, adding that their colours were always to be seen leading the advance, alone and unsupported, their men never wavered once during the action, but had stuck to their work until they had crowned it by the capture of the great entrenchment.

Prince Eugene heard him out, and then replied in a quiet voice, "Well, well, sir, in what way have these men improved upon their usual behaviour?"

"Ah, sir," I cried, "how delicately can your Highness fashion a compliment! "and truly the answer he made expressed all that one could possibly have wished said.

Perhaps those who may read my memoirs, and who have not heard the Battle of Belgrade properly discussed, will think that there is too much one-sidedness in the details I have just given. I admit even that the rank that I held in the Bavarian troops might afford grounds to suspect me of this. But there are too many distinguished witnesses of this action for me to dare to tamper with the truth of the facts, in order to pander to my own vanity by doing honour to the Bavarians. Those who before me wrote on the subject had no reason to show any preferences, and I cannot prove my sincerity better than to quote word for word a passage to be found in the second volume of the book called *The Campaigns of Prince Eugene in Hungary*, to wit: —

It would be impossible to give too high praise to the Bavarian infantry; they contributed enormously to the winning of the battle, for, carried away by their warlike ardour in the heat of the action, they left the first line in which they had been posted, notwithstanding the efforts of generals commanding their wing to keep them there, and the various attempts to moderate their impetuosity; they unceasingly pressed on in advance upon the

Turks, opened up a way through them, and by putting to flight all who opposed them, gave time and opportunity to the troops following in rear to form up and get into fighting formation. Finally, when at one point after another this infantry found itself joined by other bodies of troops, it renewed its efforts, took up its advance again and drove its way through the enemy, and continued these tactics until the battle was finally won. The whole army witnessed this fine feat of arms, and *Monsieur* the Prince Electoral of Bavaria, who with the other volunteers always accompanied *Monsieur* the Prince Eugene, was so over-whelmed with joy at the sight of this that after the final shock he ran and kissed Monsieur de la Colonie, colonel of his own regiment, who had greatly distinguished himself in the fight.

Thus I have but given fuller details of facts which have been al-ready stated publicly in print, a single paragraph of which includes more praise than will be found in several of those in my memoirs put together. In my account of these deeds I have had but in view the glory of the Elector of Bavaria and his troops, and there is no ground for belief that a self-seeking spirit is involved. The public accounts have flattered me more than I should ever dare to do, and it would certainly not strike me as seemly to say that I had distinguished myself in the way reported in the book I have quoted above.

The Turks were by this time in full flight, and the whole of our army, which had now come up and joined us, took up its position beyond the great parallel in battle formation, in order to observe whether the enemy's rout was assured or not. Prince Eugene wished to have no doubt upon a point of such importance, so kept his army in readiness to fight exactly as if the enemy were in front of him, and detached several hussar and native regiments in pursuit of the *infidels* to discover how and in what order they were making their retreat.

Although the Turkish camp lay open before us, not a man left the ranks in search of loot; our troops were kept strictly in hand, as it was feared lest the excitement caused by pillaging would produce confu-sion among them. It has often happened that leave given to pillage has brought about the loss of a newborn victory when the disorder created among the plundering victors has given the conquered an opportunity of rallying and profiting by the confusion. As soon as it was reported to the general that the Turks were completely routed, and that the regiments sent in pursuit of them were fully engaged in slaying the fugitives, he ordered thirty men from each battalion and regiment of cavalry to go and collect everything that had been left in the camp; he directed that the articles they brought in, of whatever description, should be taken to each unit, in order that an equitable distribution should be made.

The troops told off for this duty grounded their arms, and were marched to the enemy's camp with as much order and regularity as if they had been entering upon some fresh manoeuvre, whilst the army itself remained under arms until their return. This was the opportunity to produce my canteens and provisions, which proved most welcome; the rest and tranquillity had aroused our hunger and thirst, and as we now had a good chance of doing things in an orderly manner, all of our officers who needed sustenance got their share, and never did repast give such great satisfaction.

The loot from the enemy's camp did not amount to much, with the exception of the grand *vizier's* tent (which was reserved for Prince Eugene) and those of the *pashas*. The battle had lasted six hours, so that they had had ample time to save the best of their possessions. They only left behind them the heaviest and most difficult things to carry off, such as provisions, coffee, camels, buffaloes, waggons, and tents. I had for my share a magnificent eagle of a very fine breed, which had belonged to the grand *vizier*; I had him sent to Bordeaux, where he died from poison. We returned to our camp in peace, Prince Eugene in the meantime sending in pursuit of the enemy yet more squadrons of light cavalry, which for three days inflicted a frightful slaughter among them.

So panic-stricken were they that the grand *vizier*, who had retired in the first instance to a town called Semendria, with the intention of rallying the debris of his army, thought his position there to be so dangerous that he suddenly left it, after setting it on fire, as he feared we might occupy it to our profit. The peasants also of the neighbouring provinces threw themselves upon the runaways and slew numbers of them, and their rout, together with their loss on the field of battle, cost them more than twenty-eight thousand men, while we, who never proceeded further afield, lost over eight thousand.

This defeat brought about the fall of Belgrade, and the garrison's sole thought now was to arrange a capitulation. Their surprise was great when they learned of the complete rout of the Ottoman army, as they had been waiting a signal from the latter to leave their lines and fall upon us. The officers of the garrison told us that they never dreamed that we were in a position to attack their entrenched army seriously, and this was why they had determined to remain inactive. After such an extraordinary miracle, therefore, they had no hesitation in submitting themselves to the dictates of fortune. The *seraskier* in command offered terms the morning after the battle, when the articles were all signed, and a gate of the town was handed over to our keeping.

Four days' grace were given to the inhabitants, so that the Mohammedan element could leave with their families for any part of the country they might choose for their habitation, and a large number of boats were placed at their disposal, for use in the transport of themselves, their goods, and chattels. These people were much to be pitied, for they left the most part of their possessions and elected to go out into the world rather than give up their religious faith, whilst the Jews, native inhabitants, and schismatic Greeks remained in the town in the enjoyment of all their goods. The governor was also obliged to hand over to us all the Christian slaves, and the deserters who had left our army and entered the town.

It is astonishing that Christians could have ever been so foolish as to give themselves up to a garrison at a moment when it was in danger of being captured, and that they should have abjured their religion in the hope of ensuring their liberty. These unhappy people were all handed over to us, and what seemed most extraordinary to me was to see among them an Italian Chevalier of the Maltese Order, who had been impious enough even to tread the cross under his feet before the *seraskier* and had had himself circumcised. I heard him accused of these abominations by two small German boys in my presence, who had been captured by the Turks in the gardens where they had been amusing themselves with eating plums. They accused him of being one of the ringleaders in this form of perversion, and to have been more vindictive against the Christians than even the Turks themselves.

All prisoners who were convicted of having so denied their religion were impaled in front of our camp, a punishment that the Turks are accustomed to inflict upon their own criminals. The Maltese *chevalier* was, however, saved from this fate, as Prince Eugene wished him to be condemned by the judges of his own Order, and to this end caused him to be sent to Malta to stand his trial there. The garrison and the Mohammedan inhabitants left the town on the 22nd. I witnessed their start, but never caught a glimpse of the face of one of their women, on account of the care they took to prevent such a thing occurring.

Even the meanest of them covered themselves up in a thick piece of linen, which, passing over from the back of their heads to the front, was tucked into their sashes, so enveloping them that nothing could be seen of them except their figures, which were upright and well formed.

As soon as the garrison had evacuated the place a hundred and fifty men were told off from each battalion to clean the town, clear away the ruins, and put the streets and houses into a condition to be rebuilt and lived in There were so many corpses under the ruins of these houses that a disgusting smell tainted the air, and it became absolutely necessary to do this. The emperor published it abroad throughout the neighbouring countries that all who wished to take up their residence in Belgrade would have a house and a piece of ground given to them, and that they would be exempt from all taxes for a series of years. The town, which was divided into parishes, the mosques serving as churches, now possesses a large population, and lies in a country which produces grain and fruit in abundance of a most excellent quality.

The Jews and natives cultivate vines, the grapes of which are extremely good, whilst the melons, which are sown broadcast in the fields, are of an exquisite flavour. The pasturages are rich, and the herds so numerous that our meat in camp never cost us more than two *sols* the pound in French money. It was the same with regard to fish, for they abound in the Danube and the Save. There is a third river opposite Szlankamen called the Theiss, and it was a common saying that one-third of it consisted of fish and two-thirds water. This country is a healthy one for all animal life, and those people who have settled there are certain to find all their wants amply filled. The climate is much the same as that of Marseilles, but the soil is richer and more fertile, while its produce is of a far better quality.

All sorts of game abound, especially partridges, quail, blackcock, woodhens, wild turkey, pheasants, without mentioning deer. Although the practice of grafting is unknown, yet their fruit is superior to that of France. We lived very well during the whole period of our stay there, and the wines of Burgundy, Champagne, Germany, Hungary, and Italy were not wanting, some being transported by the Danube, others by the Save. But notwithstanding we were in the midst of all these good things, the climate disagreed so with our health that we were much troubled with dysentery, though perhaps the immoderate consumption of fruit by our soldiers went some way to assist the spreading of this disease among them. A great number perished, and the officers were no more exempt from it than their men. Prince Eugene himself had a slight attack, but it soon passed off, though I for my part kept as well as if I had been in my native land.

The Turks abandoned two more fortified towns below Belgrade without waiting for us to attack them, and still another one, much larger and further away, called Orsova. They made a show of defending the latter, but when they saw us quite prepared to attack it they left it to its fate, as they had the two former. We seized two more towns on the river Save, Shabatz and Mehdia, and nearly all these towns were found to contain artillery and war-like stores. A column was also sent into the province of Bosnia, in which is situated the town of Zvornik, an important place on account of the territory it defends. It was occupied by the Turks, and we quite hoped that they would abandon it at our approach, as they had the other towns, but we found we were in error as to this. A detachment of inferior strength only was sent to lay siege to this town, which, besides the usual fortifications, was possessed of a separate citadel.

The Turks allowed the town to be breached, the assault took place, and our troops put all to the sword who were not able to take refuge at once in the citadel. The town being in our hands, the attack of the citadel was then undertaken, though it was already the beginning of October when the trenches were opened. The rainy season delayed matters further; our detachment was not strong enough to carry on the siege and withstand as well the relieving force expected, and having heard that the Turks had assembled a considerable body of troops on the frontier to oblige us to raise the siege, we finally retired without completing the capture of the citadel. Here our campaign came to an end, and each side retired to their winter quarters.

Our Bavarian troops were ordered to Upper Hungary, a country far distant from Belgrade, for we had twenty-seven days of marching, not counting rests, before we arrived at our destination. I had the command over two provinces in this country during that winter. The inhabitants have always been most rebellious in their conduct towards the emperor; they have waged many a war in order to withdraw themselves from the Imperial rule and set up a sovereign of their own. In the last of these Prince Ragotzi held all the most important fortified towns in the country, and had money stamped with his own device.

When the principal people learned that I was a Frenchman and the men under my command were not Imperialists, they were delighted, and looked forward to a period of greater tranquillity with us than they had enjoyed with the emperor's troops. Their hopes were not in vain; we were accustomed to make the best of our fare in winter quarters, and were quite contented with what luxuries those in authority were pleased to afford us. The country is everywhere intersected by small mountain ranges, rather bare and arid, with fairly fertile valleys of no great extent between them. There are many mines in these mountains which produce various minerals, among them gold as pure as any in the world, which is purified in the country itself at a little town called Kremnitz. The emperor had money coined there, the *ducats* of which carry the name of the town over all Germany.

This gold is much renowned, and the Jews set such store by it that at Vienna they give five *sols* over the value for each piece of money. Five leagues away is another small town called Schemnitz, where silver is worked from mines in the neighbourhood, but this is not so pure as the gold. Besides these gold and silver mines, there are others of tin, lead, copper, quicksilver, antimony, and iron, of which the most productive are the copper, in which a great trade is carried on. The chief occupation of the inhabitants is the working of these mines by means of extremely deep pits, by which they descend below the ground, where they find the veins. What they earn thereby makes up for the barrenness of their lands, and helps them to exist.

Silver is commonly found in the same mine in conjunction with copper, and a piece of ore may often be seen, silver on one side and copper on the other. There is a spring close to Kremnitz the water of which has the property of attracting particles of iron and substituting copper in its place; sheets of iron are placed therein, allowed to remain there for thirty or thirty-five days, and when they are withdrawn are found to be no longer of iron, but copper of the same nature and quality as that extracted from the mines. It is true that these sheets thus converted into copper do not leave the spring in the same solid form as when they were thrown in, for their surface becomes uneven and full of holes and lumps, like large sponges.

The water itself has a very corrosive property, and as the spring forms a brook of some length, animals drinking from it might easily be poisoned. Guardians are appointed by the emperor in order that no one should profit by a monopoly of its properties. German connoisseurs who find themselves in these parts have goblets and cups made for them out of this iron converted into copper, which they gild, and have verses in their language engraved thereon referring to the singularity of the metal, such as:—

Heyzen Warich,
Kupfer bin ich,
Gold Vedekmich.

This can hardly be translated either as regards sense or rhyme; it merely means "I have been iron, now I am copper, and I am clothed in gold." The country is by no means disagreeable; the inhabitants appear to have amiable manners; their chief language is Latin, and their schools teach no other, all their writing and conversation being carried on in this tongue. They, however, have a patois among them which they call Chalavak; but this is only spoken by the lower orders. Their houses are extremely well built and very comfortable, chiefly on account of their large halls and balconies. Rudeness of manner is far less common with them than among the Germans, and they are far more amusing and polite in society. We held a number of balls and feasts during the carnival, at which I enjoyed myself exceedingly.

The sex is beautiful, but very reserved, and the wives strictly loyal to their husbands. They are ignorant of such things as intrigues or lovers, and yet they have more liberty of action than exists among their sex in any other part of the world. The men are dressed like the hussars one sees in France and Germany, and always wear high boots, the gentry being distinguishable by their long spurs, similar to those of the period of Henry IV., which they wear with their gala costume.

The women, too, have the same sort of boots, which fit as close to their legs as stockings, and are of all colours; stockings or socks are unknown to them, while as regards their dress they wear spotless stay bodices with long and very ample petticoats, and over all a robe of Polish fashion, with elaborately embroidered buttonholes down each side. I am now referring to their usual costume; but some add long black veils wreathed round the brow, and falling at the back as low as the bottom of the skirts; and these fine transparent gauzes tend to increase the brilliancy of their complexion. The wines are very good and cheap. The hills are everywhere covered with vines, for this is the country which produces the celebrated Tokay wine so renowned throughout Europe.

Ever since the people had been deserted by Prince Ragotzi they have been under the rule of the emperor, and had always had Imperial troops quartered upon them in the winter season, who had treated them with every kind of severity. They experienced so great a difference in the peaceful and unselfish manner in which we abode amongst them, that, in recognition of this, they of their own accord made many handsome presents to our officers and soldiers. When we left their country for the next campaign these poor people manifested the greatest regret at our leaving them. They were in dread lest the Imperial regiments should come to replace us, for they had lived in the hope of our occupying their district for all time.

Whilst I was in this country I had the honour to receive, at the hands of one of the emperor's officials, a gold medal, as an Imperial recognition of the Battle of Belgrade and my rule of the province in which we were quartered. Its great weight renders it of much worth, but it is of still more value to me on account of the courteously worded inscription in the German tongue. I preserve it as a valued relic on account of the illustrious hand from whom it emanated.

We quitted our quarters in Upper Hungary to begin the campaign again on May 20th, 1718. The army once more assembled at Belgrade, but all acts of hostility ceased between us and the Turks, and the only talk was of an honest and durable peace or, rather, a renewal of the truce. According to their custom, the *infidels* will only conclude a truce with Christians, in which they avoid with care the mention of the word peace: this being a religious question among them. There were many long conferences on this subject while the campaign lasted, and at last a truce was arranged between the two powers without any occurrence taking place which could have been called war.

It was a very advantageous one for the Empire. Hitherto her frontier only extended as far as Peterwardein, and now she was given all the territories conquered by her in campaigns of 1716 and 1717, which comprised a vast extent of country in the shape of the Provinces of Bosnia, Servia, part of Wallachia, and the Banat of Temesvar. The famous stronghold, Belgrade and Temesvar, remained in her hands, and would prove to be of service not only to resist the *infidels* in case they attempted an invasion, but also as bases from which to extend her conquests in the countries they yet possessed in Europe.

Our troops were employed during this campaign in working at the restoration of the town of Belgrade and the construction of a new fort across the Save, exactly where I said the Turks ought to have entrenched themselves, and from whence we conducted our attack on the lower town. Belgrade is now protected on that side, and is altogether one of the strongest fortified towns in Europe.

All the differences between the Turks and Imperialists being brought to an end by this campaign, our Bavarian troops were sent to pass the winter in Croatia, which borders upon the northern part of Italy, and in the early spring of 1719, after receiving the formal thanks of the emperor, found themselves once more on the road to Bavaria, where, according to all appearances, peace had put an end to our campaigning.

This, then, is the history of my actions and the events from which I have gained my experience in the art of war; also that of every campaign which took place from the time I left the company of Gentlemen Cadets at Charlemont. to the Peace of Belgrade. These brought me the dignity of *Maréchal des Camps et Armées*, and the position to hope for still higher honours had the war continued.

Envoi

In the beginning of these memoirs I alluded to the fact that our family consisted of six children. Now, as I have hitherto spoken only of myself, it may very easily happen that some people, either through their carping minds or jealousy of the rank I have attained, might attribute the silence I have maintained regarding my brothers and sisters to a feeling of vanity or contempt on my part. I could, however, justify myself on this account, but, without going into great detail on a subject that could hardly interest the reader, I would say for my own satisfaction that a brother, a sister, and myself are all that are left of our family; that we have descendants, and that my other brother died a number of years since.

He was my eldest brother; he came into the world in 1670, and married at the age of seventeen. So great was his desire to enter the king's service that he left his wife three years after his marriage to take the rank of an infantry lieutenant in a free company belonging to one Château-Charles. This was the beginning of his career in the service, notwithstanding the difficulty in obtaining such a post without passing through the cadet company I have mentioned. A little later the company of Château-Charles fell into the hands of M. de Bitry, now engineer-in-chief of the Château Trompette and the government of Bordeaux, who contracted a very close friendship with my brother.

My brother did not remain long in this capacity, as he obtained the better post of Commissary of War for the province of Languedoc in the twenty-fourth year of his age. This was an important employment at that time, and it became still more so in the hands of my brother, as by virtue of it he became later on "*Ordonnateur*" to the king's army in Italy.

Unexpected troubles then fell to his lot which would take too long to recount, but it is nevertheless certain, if he had lived, that he would have filled important posts in the last war. He was well on the road to success, and had all the necessary aptitude, a far-reaching mind, a taking manner, and much experience in business affairs. Besides this, he was one of the finest-looking men in the kingdom, with a charming expression, and above all, he was an absolutely honest man. He was unfortunately killed in an action against the Imperialists in 1702, wherein his conduct did honour to his memory.

He left at his death, with his widow in Périgord, two boys and a girl of a still tender age. I saw to the education of the two boys, and gave the eldest a company in the regiment of the Electoral Prince when he was fourteen years old. I also intended to provide for the future of the daughter, and had already placed her in a convent for educational purposes, but the mother upset my plans by marrying her very young, and very indifferently, whilst I was away with the army. The widow also remarried, and she herself looked more to satisfy her own disposition thereby than to make a suitable match. She had already been the cause of serious trouble to my brother, and after his death acted in no way honourably.

With regard to my sister, she also has two children who for many years since have been in the service of the king in Spain, where they hold important posts. The eldest son was appointed in 1721 Commissary-General of Cavalry of the kingdom of Chilly, which he selected in preference to a governorship offered him in the same kingdom. He is very rich, and owes his fortune and advancement entirely to his services and attention to duty.

Besides these two children my sister had four girls, who are poorly married in Périgord. Their families are numerous and badly off, and the widow of my late brother is in the same case.

As for me, I have a son who is now councillor in the Parliament of Bordeaux, and a daughter who is still quite young.

LEONAUR

ALSO FROM LEONAUR

AVAILABLE IN SOFTCOVER OR HARDCOVER WITH DUST JACKET

IRON TIMES WITH THE GUARDS *by An O. E. (G. P. A. Fildes)*—The Experiences of an Officer of the Coldstream Guards on the Western Front During the First World War.

THE GREAT WAR IN THE MIDDLE EAST: 1 *by W. T. Massey*—The Desert Campaigns & How Jerusalem Was Won---two classic accounts in one volume.

THE GREAT WAR IN THE MIDDLE EAST: 2 *by W. T. Massey*—Allenby's Final Triumph.

SMITH-DORRIEN *by Horace Smith-Dorrien*—Isandlwhana to the Great War.

1914 *by Sir John French*—The Early Campaigns of the Great War by the British Commander.

GRENADIER *by E. R. M. Fryer*—The Recollections of an Officer of the Grenadier Guards throughout the Great War on the Western Front.

BATTLE, CAPTURE & ESCAPE *by George Pearson*—The Experiences of a Canadian Light Infantryman During the Great War.

DIGGERS AT WAR *by R. Hugh Knyvett & G. P. Cuttriss*—"Over There" With the Australians by R. Hugh Knyvett and Over the Top With the Third Australian Division by G. P. Cuttriss. Accounts of Australians During the Great War in the Middle East, at Gallipoli and on the Western Front.

HEAVY FIGHTING BEFORE US *by George Brenton Laurie*—The Letters of an Officer of the Royal Irish Rifles on the Western Front During the Great War.

THE CAMELIERS *by Oliver Hogue*—A Classic Account of the Australians of the Imperial Camel Corps During the First World War in the Middle East.

RED DUST *by Donald Black*—A Classic Account of Australian Light Horsemen in Palestine During the First World War.

THE LEAN, BROWN MEN *by Angus Buchanan*—Experiences in East Africa During the Great War with the 25th Royal Fusiliers—the Legion of Frontiersmen.

THE NIGERIAN REGIMENT IN EAST AFRICA *by W. D. Downes*—On Campaign During the Great War 1916-1918.

THE 'DIE-HARDS' IN SIBERIA *by John Ward*—With the Middlesex Regiment Against the Bolsheviks 1918-19.

LEONAUR

ALSO FROM LEONAUR
AVAILABLE IN SOFTCOVER OR HARDCOVER WITH DUST JACKET

THE ART OF WAR by Antoine Henri Jomini—Strategy & Tactics From the Age of Horse & Musket

THE MILITARY RELIGIOUS ORDERS OF THE MIDDLE AGES by F. C. Woodhouse—The Knights Templar, Hospitaller and Others.

THE BENGAL NATIVE ARMY by F. G. Cardew—An Invaluable Reference Resource.

THE 7TH (QUEEN'S OWN) HUSSARS: Volume 4—1688-1914 by C. R. B. Barrett—Uniforms, Equipment, Weapons, Traditions, the Services of Notable Officers and Men & the Appendices to All Volumes—Volume 4: 1688-1914.

THE SWORD OF THE CROWN by Eric W. Sheppard—A History of the British Army to 1914.

THE 7TH (QUEEN'S OWN) HUSSARS: Volume 3—1818-1914 by C. R. B. Barrett—On Campaign During the Canadian Rebellion, the Indian Mutiny, the Sudan, Matabeleland, Mashonaland and the Boer War Volume 3: 1818-1914.

THE CAMPAIGN OF WATERLOO by Antoine Henri Jomini—A Political & Military History from the French perspective.

THE AUXILIA OF THE ROMAN IMPERIAL ARMY by G. L. Cheeseman.

CAVALRY IN THE FRANCO-PRUSSIAN WAR by Jean Jacques Théophile Bonie & Otto August Johannes Kaehler—Actions of French Cavalry 1870 by Jean Jacques Théophile Bonie and Cavalry at Vionville & Mars-la-Tour by Otto August Johannes Kaehler.

NAPOLEON'S MEN AND METHODS by Alexander L. Kielland—The Rise and Fall of the Emperor and His Men Who Fought by His Side.

THE WOMAN IN BATTLE by Loreta Janeta Velazquez—Soldier, Spy and Secret Service Agent for the Confederancy During the American Civil War.

THE MILITARY SYSTEM OF THE ROMANS by Albert Harkness.

THE BATTLE OF ORISKANY 1777 by Ellis H. Roberts—The Conflict for the Mowhawk Valley During the American War of Independenc.

PERSONAL RECOLLECTIONS OF JOAN OF ARC by Mark Twain.

Lightning Source UK Ltd.
Milton Keynes UK
UKOW05f2240310714

236160UK00001B/53/P